ROUTLEDGE LIBRARY EDITIONS: EDUCATION AND RELIGION

Volume 1

JEWISH EDUCATION AND LEARNING

JEWISH EDUCATION AND LEARNING

Published in Honour of Dr David Patterson on the Occasion of His Seventieth Birthday

Edited by
GLENDA ABRAMSON AND TUDOR PARFITT

LONDON AND NEW YORK

First published in 1994 by Harwood Academic Publishers

This edition first published in 2019
by Routledge
2 Park Square, Milton Park, Abingdon, Oxon OX14 4RN

and by Routledge
52 Vanderbilt Avenue, New York, NY 10017

Routledge is an imprint of the Taylor & Francis Group, an informa business

© 1994 Harwood Academic Publishers GmbH

All rights reserved. No part of this book may be reprinted or reproduced or utilised in any form or by any electronic, mechanical, or other means, now known or hereafter invented, including photocopying and recording, or in any information storage or retrieval system, without permission in writing from the publishers.

Trademark notice: Product or corporate names may be trademarks or registered trademarks, and are used only for identification and explanation without intent to infringe.

British Library Cataloguing in Publication Data
A catalogue record for this book is available from the British Library

ISBN: 978-0-367-13819-6 (Set)
ISBN: 978-0-429-05630-7 (Set) (ebk)
ISBN: 978-0-367-13823-3 (Volume 1) (hbk)
ISBN: 978-0-367-13825-7 (Volume 1) (pbk)
ISBN: 978-0-429-02875-5 (Volume 1) (ebk)

Publisher's Note
The publisher has gone to great lengths to ensure the quality of this reprint but points out that some imperfections in the original copies may be apparent.

Disclaimer
The publisher has made every effort to trace copyright holders and would welcome correspondence from those they have been unable to trace.

Jewish Education and Learning

Edited by
Glenda Abramson

and
Tudor Parfitt

Published in honour of Dr David Patterson
on the occasion of his seventieth birthday

harwood academic publishers
Switzerland • Australia • Belgium • France • Germany • Great Britain
India • Japan • Malaysia • Netherlands • Russia • Singapore • USA

Copyright © 1994 by Harwood Academic Publishers GmbH, Poststrasse 22, 7000 Chur, Switzerland. All rights reserved.

Harwood Academic Publishers

Private Bag 8
Camberwell, Victoria 3124
Australia

3-14-19 Okubo
Shinjuku-ku, Tokyo 169
Japan

58, rue Lhomond
75005 Paris
France

Emmaplein 5
1075 AW Amsterdam
Netherlands

Glinkastrasse 13–15
O-1086 Berlin
Germany

820 Town Center Drive
Langhorne, Pennsylvania 19047
United States of America

Post Office Box 90
Reading, Berkshire RG1 8JL
Great Britain

Library of Congress Cataloging-in-Production Data

Jewish education and learning : published in honour of Dr. David Patterson on the occasion of his seventieth birthday / edited by Glenda Abramson and Tudor Parfitt.
    p.   cm.
Includes bibliographical references and index.
ISBN 3-7186-5324-9
1. Hebrew literature, Modern--History and criticism. 2. Jews--Education--History. 3. Judaism--Study and teaching (Higher)--History. I. Patterson, David, 1922-   . II. Abramson, Glenda. III. Parfitt, Tudor.
PJ5017.J48 1993
909'.04924'007--dc20   93-5601
                                                                          CIP

Cover Artwork : Copyright The British Library.

No part of this book may be reproduced or utilized in any form or by any means, electronic or mechanical, including photocopying and recording, or by any information storage or retrieval system, without permission in writing from the publisher. Printed in Singapore.

CONTENTS

Foreword		vii
Notes on Contributors		ix
Introduction		xv
1	Smolenskin and the Revival of Hebrew Education *Tudor Parfitt*	1
2	Bar-Ilan University—A Question of Identity *Harold Fisch*	9
3	Ancient Academic Activity and the Origin of the Pentateuch *Calum M. Carmichael*	23
4	Hebrew Language and Literature at the Hebrew Union College: Jewish Institute of Religion 1876–1930 *Ezra Spicehandler*	37
5	The *Maskil* as *Lamdan*: The Influence of Jewish Education on *Haskalah* Writing Techniques *Tova Cohen*	61
6	Notions of Yiddish *Dovid Katz*	75
7	The Teaching of Jewish Law in British Universities *Bernard S. Jackson*	93
8	Jewish Education in the Byzantine Empire in the Twelfth Century *Nicholas de Lange*	115
9	Criteria of Modernism in Early Hebrew *Haskalah* Literature *Moshe Pelli*	129
10	The Controversy between M. L. Lilienblum and the World of the *Yeshivot* as Depicted in "Mishnat Elisha Ben Avuyah" (1878) *Yehuda Friedlander*	143
11	Religious Education in Israel: A Perspective *Noah Lucas*	157
12	Jewish Attitudes to Greek Culture in the Period of the Second Temple *Martin Goodman*	167
13	The Content of Jewish Education and its Responsibility within the Jewish–Christian Encounter *Alice and Roy Eckardt*	175

14	The Berlin Hochschule für die Wissenschaft des Judentums: Marginalia–Personalities–Reminiscences *Edward Ullendorff*	195
15	Chaos in the Bible? *Tohu vavohu* *Terry Fenton*	203
16	Greek Language and Philosophy in the Early Rabbinic Academies *A. Wasserstein*	221
17	*'Aggadah* and Childhood Imagination in the Works of Mendele, Bialik and Agnon *David Aberbach*	233
18	Jewish Education in 19th Century Russia in the Eyes of Mendele Mokher Sefarim *Shmuel Werses*	243
19	The Role of Higher Education in Zionist Society *S. Ilan Troen*	261
20	Smolenskin, Ben-Yehuda, and the Jewish Education of the Future *George Mandel*	279
21	Purpose and Language in Two Seventeenth Century Paduan Hebrew Chronicles *Alan David Crown*	287
22	Moses Mendelssohn as Political Educator *Lionel Kochan*	299
23	David Patterson: A Bibliography *R. May*	307
Index		315

FOREWORD

I have known Dr Patterson since he came to Oxford many years ago, and I know of no man who combines his kindness, professional and personal integrity, common sense and administrative skills to such a degree. His success, amazing only to those who do not fully appreciate his qualities, is in itself evidence of his gifts.

He is a man with exceptional sincerity and purity of heart. All that he has done—the administration of the Oxford Centre, his relationships with the trustees and the staff, the pastoral care of the students and the judgement he has shown in selecting distinguished scholars from Israel and elsewhere to become fellows of the Centre—seems to be successful. The security of the Centre owes everything to his approach, which is at once clear, intelligent, modest and morally moving, and has helped gain the financial support of various individuals who, I believe, might have resisted a more "dynamic", more insistent or less truthful and dedicated applicant. His remarkable success in obtaining funds—at times very large ones—on which all academic institutions depend, is directly due to Dr Patterson's personality: he is anything but a professional fundraiser. It is his head and his heart which have done it all.

In addition to this work for the Centre, he has done truly original work on nineteenth-century Hebrew literature in Russia—a comparatively neglected field which provided the base without which the modern Jewish renaissance, particularly of the Hebrew language and the culture of contemporary Israel, could scarcely have developed.

In short, his combination of moral, academic and administrative qualities should be the envy of any Head of a college or institution in any country. He is a learned, charming, decent and wholly admirable human being, and so, indeed, is his wife, José, whose devoted activities in the Centre deserve great gratitude and praise.

Isaiah Berlin
Governor of the Oxford Centre
for Postgraduate Hebrew Studies

NOTES ON CONTRIBUTORS

David Aberbach is Associate Professor of Hebrew and Comparative Literature at McGill University, Montreal. His books include: *At the Handles of the Lock: Themes in the Fiction of S.J. Agnon; Bialik; Surviving Trauma: Loss, Literature and Psychoanalysis* and *Imperialism and Biblical Prophecy 750–500 BCE*. Professor Aberbach was supervised by David Patterson for his Oxford M.Litt. and D.Phil.

Calum M. Carmichael is Professor of Comparative Literature and Adjunct Professor of Law at Cornell University, New York. A Senior Associate Fellow of the Oxford Centre for Postgraduate Hebrew Studies, he has given the Sacks Lecture (1982) and the Fourth Annual Jewish Law Lecture (1992). He has been a Guggenheim Fellow, a Senior Fellow of the National Endowment for the Humanities, and the Director on three occasions of the National Endowment for the Humanities Summer Seminars for College Professors. In 1994 he will be a Robbins Fellow at the Law School, University of California, Berkeley, USA. His most recent books are *The Origins of Biblical Law* (Ithaca, 1992) and, as editor, *Studies in Comparative Legal History, Collected Works of David Daube, Volume One, Talmudic Law* (Berkeley, 1992).

Tova Cohen is a former student of David Patterson's at Oxford. She now teaches Hebrew Literature at Bar-Ilan University in Israel.

Alan David Crown holds a personal chair at the University of Sydney in the Department of Semitic Studies. He is a Senior Associate Fellow of the Oxford Centre for Postgraduate Hebrew Studies, and a council member of the Societé d'Etudes Samaritaines, Paris. His books include *The World of Israel Weissbrem* (1993), *The Samaritans* (1989) and *A Companion to Samaritan Studies* (1993).

Alice Eckhardt, L.H.D., is Professor Emeritus of the History of Religions at Lehigh University, Bethlehem, Pennsylvania and Senior Associate Fellow of the Oxford Centre for Postgraduate Hebrew Studies. Her latest book is *Burning Memory: Times of Testing and Reckoning* (Pergamon Press, 1993).

Roy Eckhardt, Ph.D., is Professor Emeritus of the History of Religions at Lehigh University, Bethlehem, Pennsylvania and Senior Associate Fellow of the Oxford Centre for Postgraduate Hebrew Studies. His most recent book is *Reclaiming the Jesus of History: Christology Today* (Fortress Press, 1992).

Terry Fenton graduated in Oriental Studies from Exeter College, Oxford. After serving as assistant Keeper of Western Asiatic antiquities at the British Museum and Lecturer in Akkadian at the University of Manchester he went to the Department of Biblical Studies at Haifa University, Israel, in 1971, and served as Head of Department in 1972–5 and 1987–90. His principal areas of research and publication are in the fields of ancient Semitic linguistics and the history of religious ideas in the ancient Near East and Israel, with particular attention to Ugaritic language and literature. He studied under David Patterson at Oxford and has been a Research Fellow of the Oxford Centre for Postgraduate Hebrew Studies.

Harold Fisch was born in Birmingham in 1923, and was educated at Sheffield and Oxford (his studies were interrupted by service in the RNVR 1942–5). In 1946–7 he was chairman of the Inter-University Jewish Federation. In 1947 he served as Appointed Lecturer in English at Leeds University, leaving there for Israel in 1957 to join the faculty of the of the newly established Bar-Ilan University as Associate Professor. He was appointed full professor in 1964, rector of the university in 1968–71 and Professor Emeritus in 1989. Harold Fisch has been active in public life in Israel and is well known around the world as a scholar and critic. He has written widely on Shakespeare, Milton and Blake, on modern Jewish authors both in Hebrew and English, on literary aspects of the Bible and has contributed to other areas of Jewish and literary scholarship. Among his books are: *Jerusalem and Albion: The Hebraic Factor in Seventeenth Century Literature* (1964), *Hamlet and the Word* (1971), *The Zionist Revolution: A New Perspective* (1978), *A Remembered Future: A Study in Literary Mythology* (1984) and *Poetry With a Purpose: Biblical Poetics and Interpretation* (1988).

Martin Goodman studied Classics at Oxford and wrote a doctorate on the history of Galilee in the early rabbinic period. After a brief spell as Kaye Junior Research Fellow at the Oxford Centre for Postgraduate Hebrew Studies, he went to Birmingham as a lecturer in ancient history, returning to the Centre in 1986 as Solon Fellow in Jewish–Christian relations in the Graeco–Roman period. Since 1991 he has been Reader in Jewish Studies at Oxford and a Fellow of Wolfson College.

Bernard S. Jackson is currently Queen Victoria Professor of Law at the University of Liverpool. He has held visiting appointments at Harvard, Jerusalem, Israel, Paris, France, and Oxford (the Speaker's Lectureship in Biblical Studies). He is the author of *Theft in Early Jewish Law* (1972), *Essays in Jewish and Comparative Legal History* (1975), *Semiotics and Legal Theory* (1985), and *Law, Fact and Narrative Coherence* (1988), editor of *The Jewish Law Annual*, and a past president of The Jewish Law Association. He held the Littman Fellowship at the Oxford Centre for Postgraduate Hebrew Studies in 1977 and has been a Senior Associate Fellow since 1984. In 1993 he served as Honorary President of the British Association for Jewish Studies.

Dovid Katz was born in Brooklyn, N.Y. in 1956, where he attended the Etz Chaim, East Midwood and Flatbush yeshivot. He was the first to major in Yiddish linguistics as an undergraduate at Columbia University where he earned his BA in 1978. His doctoral thesis at the University of London, "Explorations in the History of the Semitic Component in Yiddish" was completed in 1982. He has taught Yiddish language and literature at the Oxford Centre for Postgraduate Hebrew Studies since 1978. He initiated the University's B.A. and M.Phil options in Yiddish literature (1982), an international summer programme in Yiddish (1982), Oxford's doctoral programme in Yiddish (1984), an English language series entitled *Winter Studies in Yiddish* (1987) and a Yiddish language series, *Oksforder yidish* (1990). He is the author of several dozen papers in Yiddish linguistics, two books of Yiddish fiction and *Amended Amendments: Issues in Yiddish Stylistics* (Oxford 1993). Dr Katz is Wolf Corob Fellow in Yiddish Studies at the Oxford Centre and at St Anthony's College, Oxford.

Lionel Kochan was, until his recent retirement, Bearsted Reader in Jewish History at the University of Warwick. He has also lectured at the Sorbonne, Washington, Berlin and the University of Kiel in Germany. He was the first incumbent of the Littman Lectureship in Jewish History and Politics at the University of Oxford. Among his publications are the award-winning *The Jew and His History* (1977), *Jews, Idols and Messiahs* (1990), and *The Jewish Renaissance and Some of Its Discontents* (1992), based on the Sherman Lectures he delivered at the University of Manchester in 1991. He is at present engaged on a major study of the concept of idolatry in Jewish thought. This work was initiated during Dr Kochan's tenure of a fellowship at the Institute of Advanced Studies, Hebrew University, Jersualem.

Nicholas de Lange was a pupil of David Patterson at Leo Baeck College, London, and later at Oxford. He is currently Lecturer in Rabbinics at Cambridge. A founding editor of the *Bulletin of Judaeo–Greek Studies*, he has written extensively on Byzantine Judaism. He is currently preparing an edition of Byzantine Jewish texts from the Cairo Genizah. He has also worked on aspects of ancient and modern Judaism and Jewish–Christian relations, and has published translations from medieval and modern Hebrew.

Noah Lucas is Librarian and Fellow in Israeli Studies at the Oxford Centre for Postgraduate Hebrew Studies, Hebrew Centre Lecturer in Politics at Oxford University and Senior Associate Member, St Antony's College, Oxford. Dr Lucas is the author of *The Modern History of Israel* (1975). He graduated in Political Science from Glasgow University, and Washington University, St Louis, Missouri. Dr Lucas has taught at Southern Illinois University, The Hebrew University of Jerusalem and Glasgow University. He was Senior Lecturer in Politics at the University of Sheffield before coming to Oxford in 1988.

George Mandel has been a fellow of the Oxford Centre for Postgraduate Hebrew Studies since its inception in 1972 and is currently the David Hyman Fellow in

Modern Jewish Studies. He is a Hebrew Centre Lecturer in Oriental Studies at Oxford University, and a Research Fellow of Green College, Oxford. Dr Mandel has written on Eliezer Ben-Yehuda and on the revival of Hebrew as a spoken language in modern times.

Tudor Parfitt studied Hebrew and Arabic at Oxford where David Patterson was first his tutor and later the supervisor for his doctoral dissertation. He taught first at the University of Toronto was briefly James Parkes Fellow at the University of Southampton, during which time he was an Associate Member of the Oxford Centre for Postgraduate Hebrew Studies and, in 1974, was appointed to the School of Oriental and African Studies where he is now Reader in Hebrew and Jewish Studies, and Director of the Centre for Jewish Studies.

Moshe Pelli, Professor and Director of the Judaic Studies Program at the University of Central Florida, Orlando is the author of *Bema'avkei temurah* [Struggle for Change] (1988); *The Age of Haskalah* (1979); *Moses Mendelssohn: Bonds of Tradition* (1972); *Getting by in Hebrew* (1984); two novels (1961, 1965); eight children's books (1963–80). He was awarded the 1991 Abraham Friedman Prize for Hebrew Culture in America by the Hebrew Language and Culture Association of America, for his contribution to Hebrew culture. He was Visiting Scholar at the Oxford Centre for Postgraduate Hebrew Studies in 1984 and 1991.

Ezra Spicehandler is Professor Emeritus of Hebrew literature at the Hebrew Union College – Jewish Institute of Religion, Cincinnati, Ohio. For fourteen years, he was the director and later the Dean of its Jerusalem campus. He was the editor of the Modern Hebrew Division of *Encyclopedia Judaica* and the author of many articles in the fields of modern Hebrew literature and Judaeo-Persian studies. Among his works are, in Hebrew: *Yehoshua Heshel Schorr and Yahadut Iran*; in English *Hebrew Short Stories* and *The Modern Hebrew Poem Itself* co-edited with Stanley Burnshaw and T. Carmi. He taught as a Visiting Professor of Hebrew literature at the Hebrew University and was a Skirball Fellow at the Oxford Centre for Postgraduate Hebrew Studies (1991–2). He was a member of the Presidium of the Zionist Council and served as president of the Labor Zionist Organization of America. In 1991, he was awarded the Neuman Prize in Modern Hebrew Literature.

S. Illan Troen is the Lopin Professor of Modern History at Ben-Gurion University of the Negev, Beersheba. He is Director of the Ben-Zvi Centre for the History of Eretz Israel at Ben-Gurion University and a Visiting Fellow of the Oxford Centre for Postgraduate Hebrew Studies where he co-chairs a research seminar on Israeli history. His recent publications include as co-editor *The Suez-Sinai Crisis 1956: Retrospective and Reappraisal* (1990); *Organizing Rescue: National Jewish Solidarity in the Modern Period,* (Frank Cass, 1992); and *Zuwanderung und Eingliederung von Deutschen und Juden aus dem Gebiet der Ehemaligen Sowjetunion in Deutschland und Israel* (1993). The focus of his current research is Zionist settlement policy.

Edward Ullendorff, obtained his M.A. in Jerusalem and his Ph.D. at Oxford, before holding academic appointments at the Universities of Oxford and St Andrews. He was then Professor of Semitic Languages at the University of Manchester and was the first Professor of Ethiopian Studies at the School of Oriental and African Studies, London University, then Professor of Semitic Languages, and is now Emeritus Professor. For the past thirty years he has been a Fellow of the British Academy (Vice-President, 1980–2). In 1972 he received the International Haile Sellassie Prize for Ethiopian Studies. He has published many books and articles in the fields of Semitic languages and Ethiopian studies.

Shmuel Werses is Professor Emeritus at the Hebrew University, Jerusalem. Since 1953 he has taught modern Hebrew literature in the Department of Hebrew Literature. In 1989 he was awarded The Israel Prize for his achievements in the research of Hebrew literature. Among his many publications are the following: *Sippur ve-shoresh* (1971); *Bikoret ha-bikoret* (1982); *Bein gilui le-kisui* (1984); *Mi-Mendele 'ad Hazaz* (1987); *Megamot u-zeramim ba-sifrut ha-haskalah* (1990).

INTRODUCTION

The topic of our volume dedicated to David Patterson on the occasion of his seventieth birthday is 'the Academy' which our contributors have interpreted in various ways (one contributor chose to address the question of 'chaos' which given the circumstances in which most of us labor is not entirely inapposite). The choice of 'the Academy' seemed obvious in the light of the culminating achievement of David Patterson's long and distinguished academic career: the foundation and development of the Oxford Centre for Postgraduate Hebrew Studies which began life, as David is fond of recounting, in 1972 in one room of Oxford University's Oriental Institute. The Hebrew Centre, as it is popularly known, is 'a centre of excellence, a powerhouse of learning, a place of dignity', as David has put it. In the twenty years since its foundation in 1972 the Centre's list of academic visitors reads like a roll-call of modern Judaic scholarship and creative literature; its bibliography is extensive and its activities reflect its nature as a formidable educational institution.

The Centre has come a long way in a short time. David Patterson has expressed his hope that it will eventually help, in some measure, to replace the great centres of Jewish learning lost in Europe, and form a bridge between Israeli scholarship and the world. The Centre has become truly a major focus of Jewish learning outside Israel: it is, indeed, in every sense of the word, a Jewish Academy.

But a volume devoted to various aspects of Jewish education is a fitting tribute to David Patterson for reasons which go far beyond his creation of the Hebrew Centre. The Centre, after all, came relatively late in his career. His entire life's work has been education: first as a high school teacher in Israel, then as university teacher, first in Manchester then at Oxford and as visiting professor at Cornell, Northwestern, Hebrew Union College and Mount Holyoke. His many students, undergraduate and postgraduate, a number of whom are represented in this volume, have known his generosity of spirit, the great hospitality of his wife José, his encouragement and the warmth of his interest. And it is the recognition of these human qualities, without which any kind of education can be a sterile business, that has made the editing of this volume such a pleasure and privilege.

Glenda Abramson
Tudor Parfitt

SMOLENSKIN AND THE REVIVAL OF HEBREW EDUCATION

Tudor Parfitt

The period of the *Haskalah* witnessed a gradual transformation in the range of meaning that could be applied to the term 'Jewish education'. In the middle of the eighteenth century, in Europe as well as in Islamic lands, Jewish education concerned itself, with very few exceptions, with traditional subjects taught in a traditional way. Prior to this period, Jewish educational institutions had undergone but slight modification over a period of many centuries. But with the *Haskalah* not only did traditional institutions such as the *heder* and the *yeshivah* undergo substantial changes, at least in some parts of the Jewish world, but in addition the notion had taken root that for education to be 'Jewish' it did not necessarily have to be traditional or religious.

One of the means by which this expansion in the meaning of the term had been achieved was by a parallel expansion in the roles assigned to Hebrew. As more and more secular texts were created in Hebrew, or translated into Hebrew from European languages so the body of pedagogic material in Hebrew burgeoned. But, in addition, changes in the educational use of Hebrew were to have far-reaching consequences not only on Jewish education but also on the revival of Hebrew itself.

One of the chief figures in the process both of the revival of Hebrew and the revival of Hebrew education in the second half of the nineteenth century was Peretz Smolenskin (1842–1885). Smolenskin's attitude towards Hebrew and the revival of Hebrew[1] is associated with his views on the state and future of the Jewish people as a whole. He believed that the Jews were a nation of a very particular and specific sort bound together by the Torah and the Hebrew language, by faith and common sentiment. For Smolenskin, the Torah and the Hebrew language were the main pillars of the Jewish people — in a sense the land of the Jews. As part, then, of the principal capital of the people Hebrew had to be treasured, nurtured and guarded; its use for certain national purposes should be encouraged, its abuse guarded against, its development carefully monitored. Most of all, he argued, the chief function of Hebrew should be to express and encapsulate the spirit of the people. This latter point might have been made by any nineteenth century nationalist bent on language revival of whom there were many: the idea that the soul of the language was inextricably linked with its language was commonplace.[2] But here any major similarity between Smolenskin and European language revivers stops. Smolenskin was perfectly aware of what such language nationalists were striving for in terms of language reform and language shift but it was only in an extremely limited sense that he took their aspirations and efforts as a model.

In the first volume of his new journal *Ha-shahar*, shortly after his arrival in Vienna in 1868, Smolenskin compared the attitude of other national groups to their languages with that of the Jews to Hebrew. 'All other nations', he wrote:

> will erect for themselves monuments in stone, they will build towers, they will shed their blood like water lest the name of their people and language be erased from the face of the earth. They look forward with desperation to the day of salvation when they achieve their political independence, and if that day is far distant — that does not stop them looking forward to it.

Smolenskin's subsequent argument is a sort of *kal va-homer*: if the gentiles go to such extremes for their languages when they had land, monuments and other national trappings to concern them than how can the Jews do less whose only relic of the ruins for their political past is Hebrew? In the case of the Jews the betrayal of the language would be no less than the betrayal of the nation. In the context of what was happening to Hebrew at the time — namely its steady and much lamented erosion at least in the secular sphere[3] — Smolenskin's *cri de coeur* can well be understood. But none the less, and for quite understandable reasons, he refused, in fact, to go as far as the gentiles and adopt the radical and revolutionary positions they had in many cases espoused. His declared reason for this was clearly stated: other nations could do as they liked, they could modify or revive their languages as they wished; but the Jewish nation was special, it was utterly *sui generis* and its language practices would remain *sui generis* too. He made this point explicitly in an article in *Ha-shahar*, 'Et la'asot' (1872–3)

What applies to the Jewish people's faith and hope for the future also applies to its language; as every aspect of this people's faith is based on spirit, thought and Torah, and as its hope in its future redemption is in the realm of spirit, thought and Torah, because no-one has ever instructed the people to put this hope of redemption into practice and indeed the people would neither think nor hope of redemption brought about by their own hands, thus in the same way is its language merely in the realm of spirit, thought and Torah. Its teachers do not urge the people to transform it into a language which they would speak all day long; they would neither want this — nor indeed is it permissible; rather they think of teaching it as the language of the Torah.

Other peoples who are governed by foreign rulers, such as the people of Poland, Bohemia, Ireland and so on, struggle with all their might to restore their national sovereignty and revive their national language, and as a result they are in a state of constant war both with their rulers and the other peoples who make up the state in which they live. They can be good citizens neither to the country in which they live nor to the other national and linguistic groups. This is because they despise peace and seek war, they reject the language of the state and as a result sow discord and dissension.

Now the Jewish people, as Smolenskin went on to explain, was not cast in this mould. The Jews hoped for redemption but they would not renounce their love of their motherland on account of that hope any more than a man would give up worldly pleasures on account of the world to come. 'Thus it is with language' he continued. 'Just because a Jew studies Hebrew and understands Hebrew does not mean that on its account he will give up other languages; because in every aspect of life in the outside world he needs the language of his country and his own language serves only as a monument and support for his spirit.'

Here and further on in the article Smolenskin set his face firmly against the revolutionary linguistic activity that had been going on and was still going on in the Austrian Empire and elsewhere in Europe. Not even the most ardent and reactionary supporter of the Imperial system could have been more dismissive of the claims of other nationalists and language reformers than Smolenskin. He clearly believed that the existing situation with certain modifications would ensure that the Jews could lead a normal national life.

By explicitly stating that the Jews would not engage in revolutionary activity in the realm of language (or in any other way) he preordained that any programme for action would be of a severely limited nature. His proposals in essence were that the young should all study Hebrew for an hour every day, that Hebrew should be maintained as the religious language of the Jews, that it should be used for certain cultural purposes — but not all — and he specifically argued that books describing the style of life and history of the Jews (such as Graetz's *History*) could very usefully be written in other languages than Hebrew as a means of eradicating anti-Jewish prejudice among the gentiles. His reasons for preserving Hebrew were to maintain the Jewish faith, to guard against heresy, and finally to unite the Jewish people throughout the world by creating an element of Hebrew education common to all. The passage from 'Et la'asot' shows that with respect to language issues as well as other matters Smolenskin had solidly conservative, anti-revolutionary, pro-law-and-order views; he disapproved of attempts by other nations to rock the Hapsburg boat either politically or linguistically. In other words, within certain limits, he was in favour of preserving the linguistic *status quo* both within the Empire and within the Jewish people. All of which implies with the greatest clarity that he approved of diglossia, and disapproved of the arguments of Czech, Slovak, Hungarian and other nationalists that one language could and should serve all language functions.

If any reader of *Ha-shahar* might on the basis of this be tempted to conclude that Hebrew was, or should be, a sort of Jewish Latin performing for the Jewish people the kind of role Latin had performed and to an extent still did perform for Christian Europe Smolenskin was quick to put him right. In a footnote to 'Et la'asot' he argued that Latin was the exclusive language of priests, but within Judaism every Jew was a priest; Latin was not an inherently holy language as an original language of scripture whereas Hebrew self-evidently was; Latin was an international language, Hebrew was par excellence a national language. And at this point in his argument Smolenskin made an observation of considerable interest: 'Those' he wrote 'who know Hebrew can write anything they like in it, as a living language lacking no word or expression; and to this day Oriental Jews speak in it, as if in a living language, even those who do not understand writing, and it is only by means of Hebrew that we can know them and them us. . .'

The burden of this passage is to prove that Hebrew was a living language, not a dead one like Latin. Smolenskin was far from consistent on this point as we shall shortly see, but the other aspect of this passage which we cannot ignore is his comment on spoken Hebrew. Here, too, there is something of a contradiction with what he had written elsewhere in the article where he had maintained that 'the people' i.e. the Jews of Eastern Europe would not wish to speak Hebrew nor indeed would it be permissible from a religious point of view for them to do so. Here he says Oriental Jews speak Hebrew as a matter of course. What is Smolenskin implying here? Is he saying that Oriental Jews tend to illiteracy? Is he saying that Oriental Jews are bound by different religious laws? Or is this no more than the confusion of a tired and overworked editor? Overall it seems that his view may be tinged by a sort of Jewish 'orientalism' which perhaps draws on the old legend of Sambatyon and the stories of the lost tribes who somewhere in the world would one day be found speaking Hebrew as their normal language. Or perhaps he had some more specific and historical example in mind such as the fact recorded by a number of observers that Jews in Palestine on occasion spoke Hebrew among themselves[3]. In any event by raising the matter of spoken Hebrew at all, and by alluding to the Oriental Jews' alleged ability to speak it even if they could not read it, he placed the matter in the public arena and it would be most surprising if Ben-Yehuda for instance had never read this passage and, perhaps, subliminally or otherwise, been influenced by it.

Be that as it may, the main purpose of revealing this information was to prove that Hebrew was a live language and thereby to attack Hebrew's many detractors. This he was to do again in his famous and controversial article 'She'elat ha-yehudim she'elat ha-hayyim' (1879): 'Like the lamentations of those who mourn the Hebrew language — the beautiful, forlorn, bereaved language, abandoned by its children are the insults of those who say it is a waste of time and serves no useful purpose, its strength is meagre and it cannot express wisdom in the gates.'

And yet in this article he maintained that Hebrew was not alive but dead: 'Those that want to prove that Hebrew is a living language in every sense [which is pretty much what he had tried to do in Et la'asot] will succeed in proving nothing; for a lie does not become truth just because we want with all our heart for it to become truth.' To prove this new thesis he used an illustrative example which may have been heard with some regularity in Vienna at the time:

> The Hungarian people are not in fact the greatest, most valiant or awesome people in the world — even though every Hungarian will tell you that they are, nor will the Czech language ever become the predominant language in the Empire even if the government were to encourage it. . . similarly we will not be able to turn Hebrew into a living language — since it is dead and no longer spoken. And if we translate from all languages, from all disciplines, from *belles lettres* and from poetry and if all the translations are good (which in fact occurs but once in a hundred

times) even then the language would not be alive and our desire to do that which is impossible will make us fail even in that which is possible.

Smolenskin, warming to his argument, went on to maintain that not only was Hebrew dead but that it was better for the Jewish people that it was so: 'For we too' he wrote 'we too, the whole nation, are we a living people? Are we living the life of a living nation which survives by its sword, on its own land and according to its own laws?'

Of course it was this kind of comment that was to provoke the response of Ben-Yehuda in his famous open letter to Smolenskin (1880), although Ben-Yehuda did not berate him, as he might have done, for his apparent change of position on Hebrew's status. As we have seen, after 1881 Smolenskin changed his emphasis with respect to certain national issues, but his attitude towards Hebrew did not undergo any transformation: that is to say it was still conservative and his various pronouncement carry with them a strong whiff of disapproval of those too enthusiastically engaged in the pre-revival.

In *Ha-shahar* 11 (1883) for instance he complained:

> There has been a lot of discussion on how to 'expand' Hebrew: and for the most part people have got on with it as they liked, so that today Hebrew is (not one but) a hundred languages; here you have someone expanding its vocabulary with Talmudic words, mixing straw with wheat, while there you have another busy embellishing it with words from newer languages which in Hebrew guise are like forest sprites in human forms. . . and there you have yet a third who lavishes useless gifts upon it in the form of new words he has created for himself — demons he has given birth to which will destroy the language. And together they have contrived to destroy the appearance of the language — turning it into something repulsive.

Further on in this article he tempered his position somewhat with regard to words introduced from Semitic languages but foreign words and neologisms — 'alien corn planted in the Hebrew vineyard' he condemns as 'bastards and foundlings' and, mixing metaphors, as 'a cataract in the eye of our ancestral language'. But he encouraged the enriching of the language by culling material from traditional sources: 'We must' he wrote 'pay attention to the scriptures and draw from this sea pearls which no-one has seen before, for indeed there are many words in scripture which no-one has ever noticed and these can be gems.' And in this spirit he proposed a few new words of his own based on biblical roots: *megamat panim* for aspiration; *tenuah* for prevention; *matanah* for tolerance: none was destined for a long life.

In this 1882 article Smolenskin again stressed the life, richness and flexibility in the Hebrew language.

> I myself do not understand why people complain about the poverty of the language. I have never felt that it is poor and that we should go around collecting alms for it. In the lands of the East where they speak Hebrew they do not spend all their time in research, they use whatever word comes to mind and they can do as they wish when they speak the language — but not in writing — but as far as writing it is concerned *we* lack nothing.

He concluded then that as the Jews in 1882 had neither land nor independence and had no desire to speak Hebrew in Europe the situation that prevailed was altogether satisfactory as Hebrew was quite adequate for written purposes. 'And if ever we are fortunate enough to have a land like the Hungarian people and we need a living language we shall not have to go begging to other nations — we really have a language.'

This conclusion is not quite so up-beat and radical as it sounds. The previous article in *Ha-shahar* — to which Smolenskin was here responding — was written by 'Shoresh' (probably the pen name of S. Rubinstein). 'Shoresh' had made what was perhaps the first suggestion to set up a Hebrew language academy on the model of European language academies: he proposed that this institution should be called *Hevrat bonei hurbot sefat 'ever*. Consisting of a hundred 'tested masters of Hebrew' the academy would have as its major function the task of collecting neologisms 'and refining them as silver'. This, 'Shoresh' noted, was what the Hungarians had done and in half a century they had transformed their language from a low status language to a language which was now 'noble, its writers and poets do marvels... and why do not we do likewise?'

'Shoreshs' suggestion was a wise one. The expansion of the language as Smolenskin himself recognized was getting out of hand. At the time there were around a dozen competing Hebrew renderings for train and railway, mail and postman and a whole range of other modern concepts. A regulatory body was needed and would have speeded up the process of revival. Smolenskin rejected the idea although a few years later an unsuccessful attempt was made to found one in Jerusalem. Hebrew was to have to wait another twenty odd years before a more or less regulatory body was established.

In his own literary work Smolenskin was faithful to his ideals. He rarely used foreign words; when he did as in the case of *'bursa'* for stock exchange — he apologized — and preferred on the whole to use what were not infrequently absurdly clumsy circumlocutions. In the whole of *Kevurat Hamor* for instance there is only one foreign word: champagne. Smolenskin's attitude towards Hebrew insofar as it can be measured by his contradictory and ambiguous public pronouncements undoubtedly owes something to his background. Like so many other Russian-Jewish intellectuals who formed the background of *Hibbat Tziyyon* he was careful, responsible and perhaps not very adventurous. He was so horrified by the results of the German *Haskalah* that he was reluctant to ape the gentiles even in ways which would in fact have served his cause.

Space will not permit me to deal at greater length with Smolenskin's contribution to the revival of Hebrew. It may however be that his intellectually based argumentation for the proposition that Hebrew was the national language of the Jews (not at all self-evident at the time), his important work championing Hebrew in the educational realm, his prolific literary and publicistic output in Hebrew all contributed to the creation of what may be termed a pre-revival Hebrew *langue* which may markedly underlie the development of post-revival Hebrew. But his proprietorial attitude towards Hebrew, and his conservatism in language matters, no doubt to some extent the product of a general satisfaction with the political *status quo* of the Austrian Empire, both countered a more radical tendency best represented by Ben-Yehuda but which had other adherents in Europe. Finally, his repeated assertion that somewhere in the East Jews spoke Hebrew as a matter of course may have had some effect on the decision to use Hebrew as a language of instruction in the new Jewish schools in Palestine and hence on the revival of Hebrew as a spoken language.

Notes

1 For some meticulous and detailed work on the kind of Hebrew used by Smolenskin see David Patterson, *A Phoenix in Fetters: Studies in Nineteenth Century Hebrew Fiction,* Maryland, 1988, *passim.*
2 See T. Parfitt and M. Turcanová, 'A comparison of the work of Eliezer Ben-Yehuda and L'udovit Stur', in *Eliezer Ben-Yehuda,* Oxford, 1981, pp 40 ff
3 J.L. Gordon's famous poem *Lemi ani 'amel* exemplifies this point. See T. Parfitt, 'Ahad Ha-'am's role in the revival and development of Hebrew' in J. Kornberg, *At the Crossroads: Essays on Ahad Ha-'am.* On Smolenskin and Ahad Ha-'am, see D. Patterson, 'Ahad Ha-'am and Smolenskin', *ibid,* pp 36ff and see G. Mandel's article below, pp 281ff.

BAR-ILAN UNIVERSITY
— A QUESTION OF IDENTITY

Harold Fisch

David Ben-Gurion expressed the feelings of many in the early fifties when he opposed the plan to establish a religious university in Israel. He could go along with a college for Jewish learning—a kind of modernized *yeshivah*—and he could bring himself to recognize the need for another university. But he could not support an institution which tried to be both together—a *yeshivah* and a university. Bar-Ilan had to manage without the Prime Minister's blessing, also without that of the Minister of Education, Ben Zion Dinur, who conspicuously absented himself from the opening ceremonies[1]. In an attempt to neutralize the opposition, the founders of Bar-Ilan renounced any claim to public funding and undertook to raise the necessary budgets solely from overseas philanthropy. It was a valiant gesture but in the course of time Bar-Ilan had no option but to seek public funding like every other institution of higher learning in Israel. Modern universities, it turned out, cannot exist from private endowments and contributions—certainly not in Israel—and Israeli students are simply not able to pay the kind of fees that might cover the deficit. That is just one indication of how little the founders had foreseen the true scope and the immense difficulty of the plan they had set in motion.

Professor Dinur, as well as being Minister of Education, was of course also a professor at the Hebrew University. That institution likewise expressed its collective disapproval down to 1960. In that year it was represented for the first time at a Bar-Ilan occasion when it sent its Dean of Students to attend the degree ceremony for Bar-Ilan's second graduating class. This was a somewhat grudging recognition of a new sister-institution.

But it was a beginning. Zalman Aranne, who in 1955 had replaced Dinur as Minister of Education, showed a warmer understanding of the aims of the new university and it was under his firm guidance that the Council for Higher Education in 1969 finally granted general recognition to Bar-Ilan University as well as to its younger sister in Tel-Aviv. Until that date it often seemed to people at Bar-Ilan that the Council, dominated, as was perhaps natural, by Hebrew University representatives, was seeking to block the growth of the new University rather than to help it along.

Paradoxically, equally emphatic opposition came from the *yeshivah*-world. The university is situated only two or three kilometres from the great Lithuanian *yeshivot* which have been transplanted to Bene-Berak (though by a quirk of municipal boundary-drawing the university is actually an enclave of Ramat-Gan). Bar-Ilan, a coeducational institution with the young ladies not outwardly very different from the co-eds of any other college in the western world, a would-be Torah-institution and yet one which had a place for Jewish philosophy and the 'scientific' study of traditional texts, was anathema to the heads of the great *yeshivot*. It aroused more suspicion and consequently more hostility than a professedly secular institution would have done.

The Cecil Roth affair in 1964 was an example of this. Roth was of course an observant and traditionally-minded Jew—in fact entirely Orthodox in the Anglo-Jewish manner. On his retirement from the Readership in Jewish Studies in Oxford—a position which he had occupied with great distinction for many years—he settled in Jerusalem and at the same time took up a visiting appointment in Jewish History at Bar-Ilan at the invitation of the acting president, Joseph H. Lookstein. But Roth was not to have much pleasure from his association with Bar-Ilan. Shortly after his arrival, a number of *yeshivah* figures, including the highly influential Rabbi Zvi Yehuda Kook, head of *Yeshivat Merkaz Harav*, launched a public attack on the university for admitting so heretical a figure to teach a Jewish subject. Roth's offence was that in Chapter 1 of his *Short History of the Jewish People* he had briefly summarized some of the critical approaches to the patriarchal narratives, although without actually taking a position as to whether these are history or legend. As for Moses, whilst noting that there were critics who doubted his historicity, Roth had affirmed that 'the memory of a people...and written records of immemorial antiquity' counted for more than potsherds.[2] But to give a hearing to a teacher who could even raise such questions was to compromise Bar-Ilan's claim to be a religious institution. The resulting furore was clearly embarrassing to some members of the University's Board of Governors, especially to its Israeli chairman, Moshe Hayyim Shapira, then Minister of the Interior and a leader of the National

Religious Party. But it should be said to their credit that they did not bend to these outside pressures and made no move to terminate or otherwise interfere with Roth's appointment. As for the faculty, it issued a forthright public statement rejecting the criticism out of hand and affirming total support for Roth and his right to present his views in the Bar-Ilan setting.[3] For those of us, such as the mediaeval historian, Avrom Saltman and myself, who had known Roth in England, the notion that such a man might be disqualified from teaching on doctrinal grounds was inconceivable and even absurd. Had the University yielded on this question, I believe we would have resigned our own posts. After all, we had come to teach at a university, and whilst we were committed to the ideological aims of Bar-Ilan we were also committed to the idea of a university as a place of free inquiry. On this principle there could be no compromise.

II

Looking back on these long-forgotten struggles and animosities, it may seem that they were only a sign of that 'rivalry of scholars' which we are told 'increases wisdom'[4]. In the year 1990 the *yeshivot* no longer pay us much attention; indeed, Bar-Ilan has even developed its own *'yeshivah'* in the form of an 'Institute for Higher Torah Studies' attached to the University and providing an environment of more intensive Torah-studies in the *yeshivah*-style for those who desire it. Of that more later. As a University it claims equal status in every respect to its sister-institutions in Jerusalem, Haifa, Tel Aviv and Beer Sheba. Bar-Ilan has now grown to an immoderate size with over 10,000 students, more than 800 professors and lecturers, and extensions at Safed, Kedumim, Ashkelon, and Zemach. It has an operating budget which in 1990 exceeded $50m—some 60% of which was provided from state funds. Its former students occupy positions of eminence in all walks of public life (the present Minister of Education is himself a Bar-Ilan graduate) including professorial posts at other universities in Israel and abroad, among these being the Hebrew University of Jerusalem itself! Many of its teachers and departments have achieved high distinction and the University Press publishes some half a dozen internationally recognized journals in various specializations. Bar-Ilan obviously emphasizes Jewish Studies but it has also pioneered important developments in a surprising variety of areas: it developed Israel's first undergraduate programme in computer-science, its Natural Science faculty has patented several promising inventions in the field of cancer treatment and detection, and one of its chemists has even synthesized a cosmetic cream for preventing the ageing of the skin! Its

School of Education runs a programme directed by Professor Pnina Klein for the treatment of over a hundred children suffering from Down Syndrome. Professor Sinai Deutsch of the Law Faculty runs a much used and much valued computerized service for supplying information on Jewish law and Jewish legal sources to lawyers and law-courts. It is called 'Shema'— an acronym for *sherut mishpat ivri*.

According to all the usual criteria for measuring academic achievement, Bar-Ilan University would thus seem to be something of a success story. It may be thought that those like myself and a dozen other still-surviving senior members of the faculty appointed in the fifties by the University's first president, the late Professor Pinkhos Churgin, might take pride in this growth and congratulate themselves on the evident realization of the dreams of the founding fathers—Churgin himself and his supporters, both lay and academic, in Israel and America. This, however, would be to hide ourselves from a basic, unsolved problem. It is a problem which lies at the heart of the conception of Bar-Ilan and upon which Ben-Gurion somewhat brutally laid his finger. Is it feasible in this twentieth century of ours to set up a University which should also embody the conception of the *bet-midrash*? And I say *bet-midrash* because we are not talking about *Jüdische Wissenschaft*, that is, the 'Science of Judaism' for which there is clearly a place in modern universities and which is, in fact, a flourishing academic industry in our time; we are talking about *Torah* in the existential sense of a personal commitment, an ideology. Bar-Ilan, in theory at least, demands the heart and soul as well as the intellect. Is this any longer compatible with what Cardinal Newman called 'the idea of a university'?

It is all a little like the State of Israel itself. Securely established though it is in so many ways, its very existence remains problematical. Is it a State of Jews or is it a State of Judaism, representing the irruption of the Jewish myth into the world of the twentieth century?[5] This latter possibility, which many see as implicit in the very foundation of the State, creates profound embarrassment for friend and foe alike. Bar-Ilan embodies a miniature version of the same crisis of identity. Is it a religious university simply in the sense of a place where Orthodox Jews study and teach, or is it one which seeks to view the world from the perspectives provided by Jewish tradition? The latter possibility is exhilarating for some, deeply disturbing for others. It raises questions not only about the nature of the university in our day, but about the secular suppositions on which our whole society is based.

III

On the face of it, we might argue, there is no problem. Surely there can be nothing more Jewish than higher education! What were the academies of Sura and Pompaditha but seminaries in which scholars devoted themselves to the analysis of concepts and the interpretation of texts? And what was the famous 'vineyard' of Yavneh, but a grand lecture theatre where the students assembled in rows to hear the words of the great doctors of their time?[6] R. Judah the Prince would hold forth at Usha in much the same fashion as we imagine Abelard lecturing at Mont St. Geneviève or Notre Dame a thousand years later. And those places of scholarly resort, we should remind ourselves, constituted the beginnings of the University as we know it to-day.

The formal aims of Bar-Ilan University, as laid down by its founders thirty-five years ago, seem to assume an unproblematical symbiosis of Torah and the best that has been thought and said in the world. 'The University', they declared,

> would promote study and research in all spheres of knowledge as well as in all aspects of Judaism....[it] would maintain a lively interest in scientific and cultural developments in the world at large....As a religious institution, Bar-Ilan University regards the sacred principles of Judaism as that which gives its singularity to the Jewish People. It is a basic purpose of the university to cherish and guard these principles and to produce men of culture, research and scholarship, imbued with the knowledge of Torah, the spirit of historic Judaism, and the love of mankind.

This sounds not only high-minded but also easy. And in fact it is easy as long as these aims remain simply a banner like the biblical motto on the Oxford University coat-of-arms, and do not require implementation by university committees and Boards of Studies. But the founders saw to it that Bar-Ilan's commitment to cherish and guard the sacred principles of Judaism was built into the programme of studies in the form of a required minimum of instruction in both the Oral Law and Written Law for every student. Not only that, but as already noted, the question of Bar-Ilan's corporate identity is bound up with the identity of the State of Israel. This is the subject of a deep and continuing struggle within Israel society. All are involved in the battle for the soul of the new generation. Shall we have a religious state or a secular state? No-one can be indifferent to this question and to imagine that one can opt out of the debate is to deceive oneself.

By declaring itself to be a 'religious university' Bar-Ilan clearly situates itself in this context. It is rather like being identified as a Jew in an alien society. One can wear the badge with pride or with shame, but as Sartre has taught us, Jews cannot cast it off. It is the effect of their situation in the world, of the way other people define them. In a deep sense the Jew is defined by the anti-Semite.[7] Similarly, in the context of present-day Israel, where the lines are clearly drawn between *'dati'* and 'non-*dati'*, Bar-Ilan is defined by its very assumption of the title 'religious university'. If it does not willingly accept the identity thus implied, it will be imposed on it by others. As a result, the university finds itself obliged to seek to understand the meaning of its existence as a religious foundation. It cannot claim a kind of academic neutrality or immunity, much as many of its teachers and students might prefer this.

IV

In dealing with this fundamental issue—one which has exercised the university community continuously from the beginning—we have in practice come up with three different solutions. Though these models or solutions appear to be mutually exclusive, they are in fact applied simultaneously with different degrees of emphasis and different measures of success. The first is what one may term the 'assimilationist' model; it arises from the deep need to be like other universities, in particular like the Hebrew University of Jerusalem where, of course, many of Bar-Ilan's senior teachers were themselves trained. The Hebrew University is ideologically neutral, in accordance with the European continental tradition of *Lehrfreiheit*. The ideal is 'pure' learning and research. According to this model, scientific rigour is both aim and method; universities have no ideal beyond that. Of course to object to 'academic freedom' would be like objecting to motherhood. It was the principle invoked unanimously by the university faculty in the Cecil Roth affair. *Lehrfreiheit* in the sense of a guaranteed freedom of scientific inquiry, of non-interference by outside bodies—whether of state or church—in the affairs of the academy and its scientific pursuits is a principle which Bar-Ilan has courageously maintained since its foundation. There is no disagreement about that from within the academic community.

But *Lehrfreiheit*, as understood by Wilhelm von Humboldt and those associated with the establishment of the University of Berlin and other German universities in the 19th century, implied something more than this. The state would not interfere in the life of the academy; but by the same token the academy would not interfere with the State! It would not seek to influence the world outside its walls. No spiritual or moral message would emanate from the universities to hamper the designs of statesmen and politicians, however evil these might be.

The history of modern Germany has shown where such ideological neutrality can lead. A philosopher like Martin Heidegger can nobly pursue the highest truths of Being and at the same time become an instrument in the hands of an evil dictatorship. The academy has been made void of spiritual significance. Or to put it more correctly, the absence of ideology is itself an ideology and a sinister one at that. It presupposes that the pursuit of truth in art, literature and science can proceed without reference to other truths, those relating to 'the whole duty of man.' It is an ideology precisely opposite to the scriptural teaching that 'the beginning of wisdom is the fear of the Lord'. A consequence of *Lehrfreiheit* in this sense was that the deportees arriving at the entrance to the concentration camp at Bergen-Belsen in 1944 would on occasion encounter an SS officer capable of greeting them with quotations from Homer's *Odyssey* in faultless Greek![8] It is a sobering lesson for those who inhabit the academy in our own times.

If universities, then, do not teach us how to live and what to believe; if, in short, they do not *educate*, what is to be done, according to this model, with the obligation 'to cherish and guard the sacred tenets of Judaism'—an obligation built by the founders of Bar-Ilan into the very fabric of the university? Here is an ideological assertion if ever there was one. The answer that those I have termed 'assimilationists' will give us is that Bar-Ilan is first and foremost a university like every other university, and that its religious character is to be rolled over from the content of teaching and research to become a function rather of the students' extra-curricular activities. Also that this character will be preserved by the mere fact that a great majority of the teachers (and a rather slimmer majority of the students) are chosen from among the personally observant.[9]

Those committed to this model—and they represent an important element in the university community—find themselves involved in many contradictions, but it may well be that without the kind of pressure they exert, the university would not have attained the standards of academic excellence which it may boast of in so many fields. So that it is perhaps as well that the voice of this group is very audible in all discussions of this kind. But of course, there are other voices. American-trained professors, for instance, do not bring with them quite the same rigid notions of *Lehrfreiheit*. In the USA it is notorious that universities generally yielded to the wave of radicalism which swept over them in the 1960s and modified their policies and programmes accordingly. Such ideological orientations are matched by other forms of pressure, usually from state or federal government agencies, involving the encouraging or discouraging of certain types of research.

Universities are, in short, not completely isolated from the world around them. And then Americans are also accustomed to the idea of universities sponsored by various ethnic and denominational groups. There is Brandeis University in Massachusetts, Wesleyan University in Connecticut, Notre Dame in Indiana and a Mormon foundation, Brigham Young University, in the State of Utah. Their denominational character is not felt as being in any sense a disqualification. Of course the essential pluralism of American society and the principle of separation of Church and State tend to nullify any ideological claim or challenge which such institutions might seem to pose. Religion is a private matter and even when adopted as the official basis of a university institution, it obligates no-one, neither the teachers nor the students. In Israel, religion is not exactly a private matter in this sense.

Notwithstanding such obvious differences, American thinking has been more hospitable to the ideological orientation laid down by the founders of Bar-Ilan. Teachers with American backgrounds do not feel on the whole that any academic principle is compromised by a curriculum which expresses the religious character of the University. Or perhaps one ought to say: a curriculum which *also* expresses the religious character of the University. Because it is from the ranks of our American colleagues and friends that the second model has emerged, one which I would like to term that of 'parallel lines which never meet'. The chief proponents of this view have been influenced in particular by the example of Yeshiva University in New York. As is well known, that institution, or rather its undergraduate division, consists of two separate structural elements, the *Yeshivah* (formally known as 'The Yitzhak Elhanan Theological Seminary') and the College. Students attend both programmes—the *Yeshivah* in the morning, the College in the afternoon and evening. There is no serious attempt at integration. The success of this system cannot be gainsaid, if success is measured by the number of graduates the system produces who are at one and the same time equipped with a good, liberal arts degree qualifying them to proceed to graduate school, and equipped also with some of the basic skills of the traditional Talmud-student. Any interaction, however, between these two learning activities would be incidental, a matter to be left to the curiosity of the individual student.

Influenced by such thinking and aided by the generosity of the New York philanthropist, Mr. Ludwig Jesselson, Bar-Ilan University some ten years ago established the Institute for Advanced Torah Studies—a *yeshivah*-style programme for men—and, corresponding to it, a *midrashah* for women—both of these institutions housed in lavish accommodation in the Judaica Studies complex, but significantly set apart from the Faculty of Jewish Studies proper. The Institute For Advanced Torah Studies (or *kolel* as it is popularly referred to) has attracted some 300 students who receive special grants to enable them to pursue an intensive regime of Torah-studies (chiefly Talmud) for some twenty five hours each week—this in addition to the regular BA programme in their chosen speciality. The majority of the students have come to Bar-Ilan from other *yeshivot* mainly of the *hesder* type[10] and welcome the opportunity to carry on with their Talmud-studies in the manner to which they have become accustomed, whilst pursuing a course of instruction leading to the BA in law, economics, or computer science, or some other speciality, at the same time. The *midrashah* for women attracts a rather larger number of students—around six hundred. Thus the system works, and though it embraces only a fraction of the total student population, it has turned out to be an interesting addition to the University's range of options.

It is worth noting that this model is supported by leading members of the Faculty of Natural Science. It would seem to be easier for them to contemplate parallel programmes which do not communicate with one another because, in the nature of things, their faith and practice do not impinge, or impinge very little, on their everyday scientific pursuits. Mathematics will be the same for the observant and the unobservant Jew alike. For them a religious university can fulfill its purpose if it enables one to have the *bet-midrash* experience *in addition to* the academic experience. To this end, it is perfectly acceptable for the programme of Jewish studies to be conducted by teachers who are not academically trained. Some of the Law professors also feel at home with this arrangement: the *bet-midrash* experience provides their students with a useful grounding in Jewish law. It serves as a kind of field-study, whilst their academic programme in the Law Faculty itself supplies these students with what is missing in the *bet-midrash*, that is, a critical methodology, and a historical and comparative approach.

The difficulty arises for those working in the humanities, in particular: history, philosophy and literature, and also very obviously in some of the behavioural sciences such as psychology, sociology and anthropology. These subjects raise religious questions at every turn. How can one study Peter Berger on the place of religion in a secular society, or medieval drama, or *Crime and Punishment,* or Karl Popper on the poverty of historicism, without bringing the texts and theories concerned to the test of one's Jewish learning-experience? Or conversely, without confronting one's inherited Jewish intellectual and moral values with the challenge often posed by some powerful text or theory which seems opposed to those values? Can one deeply ponder a Shakespearean tragedy, a sermon by Donne, or a poem by Gerard Manley Hopkins without questions involving one's Jewish faith being raised? A dissociative model is clearly unsatisfactory in reference to these areas of study and many others. At the best it would lead to something akin to the late-medieval doctrine of double-truth; at the worst it could result in confusion, evasion and intellectual dishonesty.

The fact is that the founders of Bar-Ilan did not visualize a double-truth system. As noted earlier, they spoke of raising 'men of culture, research and scholarship, imbued with the knowledge of Torah'—a formula which yokes together culture, science and Torah in a notable zeugma, suggesting that the scientific training acquired would be functionally congruent with Torah. And in the original programmes of instruction devised by the founder the two types of learning-experience were in fact both provided by academically trained teachers using similar methodologies.

Pinkhos Churgin, founder and first president of the University, had been a professor at Yeshivah University but his work there had chiefly centred on the Teachers' Institute where he served as Dean for some thirty years, before launching the plan for a religious university in Israel. The Teachers' Institute differed from the *yeshivah* proper precisely in that it provided a varied programme of Jewish studies of a modern kind conducted by regular college teachers. The students attending the Teachers' Institute had chosen this option in preference to the *yeshivah*-programme in which the other undergraduates of Yeshiva University were registered. It was the model of the Teachers' Institute which Churgin had brought with him to Israel in 1955.

Armed with this precedent, Churgin and his advisers devised a system of courses in Bible, oral law (that is Midrash and the Talmuds), Jewish philosophy and history required of all students in the University and conducted as an academic programme for credit. The teachers involved in this programme were and are to this day regular professors and lecturers in the different departments of the Faculty of Jewish Studies, though they are generally chosen for their special pedagogic skills. This programme, probably the most extensive and complex of its kind anywhere in the world, provides more than two hundred courses of two hours per week designed for different classes of students and adapted to their different levels of attainment. Some are given in languages other than Hebrew for overseas students and new immigrants. This programme of required courses in Judaica occupies something like a quarter of the total classroom time of the students in all the university's faculties with the exception of Arab students, who substitute from a list of general courses, and those registered in the *kolel*. It is by any standards a vast undertaking. Students have different views on the value of this requirement but by and large all derive some benefit from it, and a significant number, especially of those who come to Bar-Ilan with secular backgrounds, have testified to its giving them a unique educational opportunity.

All this, however, does not quite add up to a recipe for a religious university. And the teachers of the Faculty of Jewish Studies are the first to warn their colleagues in all discussions on 'the religious character of the University' that the burden of this obligation, as formulated in the 'Basic Aims' cited earlier, must not be placed exclusively on the programme of required courses in Judaica. It must be a function of the university's educational activity as a whole. This brings me to the third solution which has been applied (though less directly than the others) in Bar-Ilan's attempt to express its character as a religious university. We may term this solution for semiotic convenience—the 'Oxford model'.

No-one at the founding of Bar-Ilan or since had Oxford University and its colleges in mind, but Churgin's original plan envisaged a relatively small college community (not exceeding a thousand students), in large part residential, its students and teachers handpicked by the president himself in order to ensure a uniform cultural and religious tone. And this is in fact how Bar-Ilan was conducted during the first three or four years of its existence. That is not unlike the Oxford ideal, perhaps not so much that of the Oxford of our day but of a pre-modern period when the aim was to educate gentlemen in the spirit of Christian Humanism. This religious and cultural ideal was advanced less by frontal teaching and research than by the impalpable effect of conversation—for instance, at dinner in Hall. Bar-Ilan has no 'Hall' and never thought of regular, communal dinners as a way of transmitting and sharing values; nevertheless the original conception, like that associated with the Oxford of an earlier day, was of a community gathered together and united by a common purpose.

This notion of the educational purpose of the university is not entirely forgotten even today. The founders of Bar-Ilan, had they read it, would have sympathized with the views of a latter-day Christian humanist, Sir Walter H. Moberly, then Chairman of the Universities' Grants Committee, who wrote in 1949 of the need for such a common purpose: 'Does not a university stultify itself', he asked 'if there is no coherent scheme of life for which it stands, no coherent picture of the universe which it presents?'[11] They visualized Bar-Ilan as having such a coherent scheme of life, a purpose. This purpose included academic excellence—indeed some of Bar-Ilan's most distinguished graduates were members of those first small classes—but the university aimed at something beyond academic excellence. What did Matthew Arnold term it? Sweetness and Light! And though, for Arnold, the main source of light was Hellenism, he was also well aware of the Hebrew phrase inscribed on Oxford's banner: 'God is my light and my salvation'. He would have found much in common with the founders of Bar-Ilan.

The community spirit was more difficult to maintain as Bar-Ilan grew to its present size in the great expansion of university education during the sixties and seventies. It was also difficult to maintain in a society which denied to students the ease and cultivated leisure which have normally characterized the life of an Oxford college. Israeli students after three years in the Army and with reserve duty constantly cutting into the school year, have little time for conversation and debate or indeed anything else beyond the many tutorials, lectures and examinations needed for obtaining a degree. Moreover, they will often be married and will be using whatever leisure time they have to earn money to pay fees and support their families. Some of the required courses in Jewish studies will, in these circumstances, be crammed into summer courses in order to interfere as little as possible with the major subject of their choice. There is little time for Sweetness and Light.

Nevertheless what I have termed the 'Oxford model' has never been totally lost sight of. Bar-Ilan may claim to have a certain ethos, which marks it as different. To formulate this negatively, one may note that there are few, if any, violent demonstrations, the drug phenomenon is rare, extravagant modes of dress and personal appearance are not much in evidence. Expressed more positively, the sense of a spiritual community has been cultivated over the years in various ways. There have been, for instance, the '*shabbat*-together' programmes held on campus for faculty and students. At one period immediately before the outbreak of the Lebanese War, a particularly successful series of communal *shabbatot* were organized on a departmental basis. That is to say, each department would arrange a programme for a particular *shabbat* which would focus on some religious topic of particular interest to the students of that department. The participants were housed at one of the dormitories and married students brought their wives and sometimes children as well. These were social as well as cultural events. Such meetings still continue in a modified form, arranged by the campus rabbi.

But this special ethos or special range of interests also finds more strictly academic forms of expression. Though there is no formulated university policy in this, departments often develop interests peculiarly suited to the 'religious character' of the university. The Law Faculty since its establishment has laid particular emphasis on Jewish law; in other faculties there are courses on halachic aspects of economic theory, on Jewish music, Jewish historiograhpy and of course Jewish philosophy. In fact the Bar-Ilan Press publishes *Da'at*, the only academic journal devoted exclusively to Kabbalah and Jewish philosophy. Major international conferences sponsored by Bar-Ilan's various faculty bodies have been held on such subjects as Prayer in Our Time, The Bible and Us, The Apprehension of the Divine, the Search for Jewish Identity. In this respect attention may be drawn also to the series of publications of the Kotlar Institute for Judaism and Contemporary Thought based at Bar-Ilan. These include two volumes in English, *Modern Jewish Ethics*, edited by Marvin Fox of Brandeis and *Kinship and Consent: The Jewish Political Tradition and Its Contemporary Uses*, edited by Daniel Elazar. Professor Elazar of the University's department of Political Studies, conducts an ongoing workshop on the covenant-idea and its impact—a central theme for many of those engaged in studying the 'interface' between Judaism and the modern world. Bar-Ilan is clearly a peculiarly appropriate location for the exploration of such topics.

No-one would pretend that a grand synthesis of science and religion or philosophy and religion is any longer possible, the kind of synthesis that seemed for Maimonides or for the medieval doctors at Paris or Oxford to be within reach. Bar-Ilan does not expect to issue a new *Guide to the Perplexed*. But leaving out such big words as Religion and Philosophy and concentrating instead on words like ethics, *halakhah*, biblical patterns, the covenant-idea, Bar-Ilan's teachers can claim to be doing something towards fulfilling the aims of their foundation.

What Bar-Ilan should be doing and what I think at its best it does, is to pose the right questions. The effect of juxtaposing Torah and modern thinking in different, specific areas is to generate a critical attitude to both— to our traditional sense of what Torah is and to the accepted wisdom of the schools. Both will come out a little changed as a result of such juxtaposition. In my own work on biblical poetics, by placing modern literary theories beside the situation that seems to be presupposed in certain biblical pericopes, I find myself forced to do some rethinking in both areas. Such an enterprise is sustained not by the belief in the emergence of a synthesis; it is sustained rather by the belief in the value of dialogue—a dialogue between Judaism and its sources on the one hand, and those many sources of secular enlightenment which demand the attention of scholars in the modern university. It is ultimately by the honesty and persistence of such dialogue that Bar-Ilan will be judged.

August 1990

Notes

1. For an able summary of these early dissensions see, Aryeh Ben-Yosef: 'The Beginnings of Bar-Ilan University' [in Hebrew] in *Bar Ilan: Annual of Bar-Ilan University: Studies in Judaica and the Humanities IV-V: Decennial*

Volume 1955-1965 (Ramat-Gan, 1967), pp. 11-13 (English synopsis on pp. xii-xxix). There were also powerful voices on the other side. Ludwig Lewisohn, the novelist, made a passionate plea on behalf of the new university which he felt might have a special redemptive role in the modern history of Israel. He termed the creation of the new university "an event of high and unrivalled significance." (See *The Jewish Review [London]*, 24 June, 1955). Edwin Samuel condemned the Israeli government and the Hebrew University for boycotting the opening ceremonies. 'Common courtesy alone,' he remarked, 'would require representation at an opening ceremony.' (Letter to the Editor, *Here and Now*, 20 October, 1955.) Other materials bearing on the early history of the university are to be found in *Pinkhos Churgin: Vision and Legacy*, ed. L. Bernstein and R. Yankelevitch (Bar-Ilan University Press, 1987).

2. See Roth: *A Short History of the Jewish People* (London, 1936), pp. 6-8.
3. The University's attitude is correctly acknowledged by V.D. Lipman in his biographical entry on Roth in the *Encyclopedia Judaica*; and see also Chaim Raphael, 'In Search of Cecil Roth,' *Commentary* 50, September, 1970, 75-81.
4. B.T. *Baba Batra*, 21a.
5. On the multiple identity crises (for Muslims and Christians as well as for Jews) to which this ambiguity gives rise, see, by the present author, *The Zionist Revolution: A New Perspective* (London, 1978), *passim*.
6. Cf. B.T. *Berakhot*, 63b-64a. Mishnah *Eduyot* 2:4.
7. Cf. Jean-Paul Sartre: *Anti-Semite and Jew*, trans George J. Becker (New York, 1965), pp. 67, 69, 136.
8. This was the experience of Rabbi Aaron Schuster of Amsterdam as reported to me in private conversation.
9. Whilst the university seeks out suitably qualified students from the religious school system, it has never closed its doors to non-religious applicants. The admissions policy is notably undefined on this point. Every department wants good students and intellectual promise is not confined to the graduates of the religious high schools. Complicating the situation is the strong competition of the *yeshivot*, especially the *yeshivot-hesder* (on this see note 10 below) which are often more successful than the universities in attracting the better students from the religious schools.
10. These *yeshivot*, unlike those transplanted from Lithuania, such as 'Slabodka', 'Ponivesh', 'Mir' etc., have a *hesder* (that is, an arrangement) with the Army whereby the students spend a large proportion of their time doing army service and training - usually in frontline combat units. The *hesder*, consisting of alternating periods of study and military duty, is spread over five years and, in some *yeshivot*, over six years. By the time the *hesder* student gets to the *kolel* at Bar-Ilan, he is thus likely to be about 24 years of age.
11. Walter H. Moberly: *The Crisis in the University* (London, 1949), pp. 112

ANCIENT ACADEMIC ACTIVITY AND THE ORIGIN OF THE PENTATEUCH

Calum M. Carmichael

It is not until the Book of Sirach (51:23) in the second century B.C.E. that there is explicit reference to a school in ancient Israel. For earlier times we can only infer their existence and speak loosely about scribal schools, learned elites, wisdom circles and the like. To be sure, the approach to ancient history that is rooted in a nineteenth century historiographical model of 'positivist' chronological accounting of events and institutions would be uncomfortable working with such inferences. Fortunately, the limitations of such an approach are being increasingly recognised.[1] In his recent essay, 'A Darkling Plain: Jews and Arabs in Modern Hebrew Literature' (Oxford: Yarnton Trust, 1988), p. 6, David Patterson quotes the Aramaic proverb, 'For the wise man, a hint is sufficient.' I hope that the hints I see for ancient scribal schools in biblical antiquity may be judged by him as not falling too far short of the maxim's commendation.[2]

My thesis is this. If, as I think I can demonstrate, Israelite national traditions—for example, those in the Books of Genesis and Exodus—were used for the purpose of setting out lists of ethical, legal and religious rules, the likeliest source of this kind of scribal activity is a school setting. The stories constitute the 'cases' to be judged. Ancient teacher and student bring to the case at issue their knowledge of existing law, ethics, and religion, and set down rules and principles in relation to the case.[3] Once we appreciate just how intimately linked is the legal and literary material in the Pentateuch, we can observe in a new light why the Pentateuch takes the form that it does, namely, a curious mixture of law and narrative. In what follows I illustrate the thesis in relation to the well-known story of Shechem's seduction of Dinah in Genesis 34.

The story has a curious beginning. Jacob's one and only daughter, Dinah, takes it upon herself to visit the women of the land. Curious, because she is unaccompanied, without the protection of a male of her family. Curious also in that the people she calls on are Canaanites, an ethnic group that stands for all that is offensive to Israelite sensibility. The Hivites, as they are called, represent the snare of acquiring a different religion. The historian Schürer, in accounting for the greater number of female converts to early Christianity spoke of, 'The peculiar susceptibilities of the female heart towards religious movements.'[4] He was, in the matter of early Christianity, missing the mark—in a quite dramatic way[5]—but the view is expressed in biblical material that foreign women can exert a powerful influence upon their Israelite husbands in matters of religion. The downfall of Solomon is, remarkably, and surely exaggeratedly, attributed to the wrongful religious influence of his foreign wives (1 Kgs 11:1-13).

In any event, none of these issues—Dinah's boldness in venturing forth on her own; the religious issue, in particular, female seductiveness spilling over into ideological influence—is made explicit in the story as it is recounted in Genesis 34. The author's contempt for this Canaanite group comes out in a peculiar way. He calls the head of the Canaanite group Ass, Hebrew Hamor, and his son Ass's shoulder, Shechem. The explanation for this derogatory name-calling is the well-known incident of the first recorded indulgence in over-drinking, namely, Noah's inebriation. One of his sons, Ham-Canaan, saw his father, Noah, lying naked in a drunken stupor. For reasons not at all clear, to look upon the naked father constituted an offence that merited the fate that each succeeding generation of Canaanites would be subservient to all other ethnic groups, to the Israelites, for example. The ass as the proverbial beast in the service of humankind was consequently an appropriate metaphor to express contempt for the Canaanites.[6]

I continue with the story in Genesis 34. Shechem, the son of the Ass, Hamor, seduced Jacob's daughter, Dinah. But to win over a man's daughter in such a direct way offended her family's honour. In specific terms, it is described as a humbling of her *('innah)*. Shechem, the seducer, wanted Dinah as his wife and had his father enter into negotiations with Jacob's family to attain this end. Jacob, in turn, involved his sons in deciding the matter. At stake was not just the marriage of their sister to a suitor who had to make good his informal means of winning her over. The whole issue of the family's ethnic identity was, at least from the point of view of the sons, also at stake. Curiously, Jacob, the father, whose name was to become Israel and, consequently, to be synonymous with a cultural and religious identity as distinctive as any, before or since, was much more accommodating in his attitude.

From time immemorial it has been commented upon that when two families marry one will regard itself as superior to the other. 'The mule says the horse was its father' is the way an Arabic proverb alludes to the matter. In 2 Kings 14 a thistle was foolish enough to request a marriage for his son with the daughter of a cedar. Freud, living in the pretentious social world of turn of the century Vienna, comments in more mundane terms about such matters.[7] On another level, it is also true that from time immemorial where a marriage brings together people of different cultural backgrounds similar issues of supposed superiority or inferiority arise. We might think of Persian-Greek, Roman-British, and Mexican-American marriages.[8]

In Genesis 34 the sons of Jacob stake out the high moral ground in regard to their sister's marriage to a Hivite. They think of themselves as possessing a superior sexual morality: 'Such a folly [they mean Shechem's seduction of Dinah] ought not to be done in Israel,' they assert. Circumcision for them means a distinctive cultural identity not to be compromised by admitting any male Canaanite, whose uncircumcised condition became a metaphor for their supposed religious primitiveness. There is no doubt that the attitude of these sons, two of them in particular, Simeon and Levi, became the dominant one in biblical literature. It is the viewpoint of the author of the story and is seen to transcend the pragmatic, flexible attitude of the older—and should we say wiser—Jacob.

The sons of Jacob, Simeon and Levi, pretend to go along with the attempt to forge mutually advantageous commerical and connubial arrangements between the two groups. They are involved in a ruse, however, of deadly consequences. They suggest that a merger of their two clans can proceed if the male Canaanites become circumcised like them. Circumcision might have powerful associations at the cultural and religious level, but, manifestly, if we disregard twentieth century advances in medical practice, it means much at a purely physical level. To be sure, the physical and the cultural are rarely apart. There would be no Christianity today aside from Judaism if some early influential followers among those who believed Jesus to be the Messiah had not abolished the requirement of circumcision in the matter of religious conversion. While that requirement was in place during the time of New Testament Judaism it is no surprise that women converts to the early Christian movement outnumbered men.[9]

'On the third day,' we read, 'when they were sore,' manifestly, because of the process of circumcision, Simeon and Levi fell upon all the male Hivites and slaughtered them. Shechem had offended with his impetuous act of penetrating their sister. He, in turn, with all his fellow males, pays for the misdeed in mirroring fashion. Mutilation of the male organs enables the avengers to choose their time and cut the Hivite males down completely with the sword.

Jacob is incensed at what his two sons have done. His community is few in number, the other Canaanite communities will hear of what has happened to their kinsmen, and they will seek revenge. Simeon and Levi, however, have the last word: 'Should he [Shechem] have treated Dinah as a harlot?' They have the last word on the matter on the occasion and, because their statement ends the story, their view probably represents that of the biblical author himself. If proof of this observation is needed, we might note that in the sequel to the story the threat to the Israelites' existence is removed by God who visits terror upon the surrounding Canaanite cities (Gen 35:5). By and large, the introduction of the deity into a narrative represents the view of the recorders and redactors of biblical traditions.

Jacob, on the other hand, true to his stance in the account of the incident in Genesis 34, in a farewell address to his assembled sons in Genesis 49 takes up his condemnation of Simeon and Levi's action. In an impressively wrought composition, characterised by wordplays, irony, and animal metaphors, Jacob reminds the two sons of the trouble *('akar)* they had brought upon their group (Gen 34:30): they had slain a man—he means Hamor, the representative head of the Hivites—and hamstrung *('aqar)* an ox. The latter reference, so puzzling to literal-minded interpreters, alludes to the trouble brought upon Jacob's own house, the house of the ox, because Simeon and Levi had made them vulnerable before their enemies, the other Canaanite groups. The animal comparison, the ass (Hamor), underlying the reference to 'a man' evokes the comparison of Jacob's group to the ox *(shor)*. It is a most appropriate one. Elsewhere it (or its analogue, the comparison to the wild ox, *re'em)*, describes Israel's fighting capacity.[10] To hamstring an animal — the horse, for example, during military clashes in the time of Joshua and David (Jos 11:9, 2 Sam 8:4) — is to incapacitate it for use in battle.

Jacob's comments about Simeon and Levi reveal features characteristic of his remarks about his other sons. There is the use of animal comparisons: the 'man' alludes to Hamor (Ass), the 'ox' to Jacob. There is wordplay: the term *'aqar* 'to hamstring' is inspired by the term *'akar* 'to trouble', because it picks up exactly Jacob's meaning in Gen 34:30. Jacob refers to himself but he stands for his entire house as is made clear in his final comment about 'I and my house'. There is irony. The anger that fueled Simeon and Levi's slaughter of the man (Hamor) also caused the hamstringing of the ox (Jacob). This is how, negatively, the father views the sons' deed. They, however, had viewed it in an opposite light: in slaughtering Canaanites they were doing a favour to their own group. Jacob sarcastically refers to his sons' stance when he comments, 'For in their anger they have slain a man, And through their favour *[ratzon]* they have hamstrung an ox' (Gen 49:6).

Seduction, Witchcraft, and Bestiality

I turn to the use of the story on the part of whoever (probably a scribe of the Deuteronomic school) set down certain rules about seduction, witchcraft, and bestiality in the Book of the Covenant (Exod 22:16-19). A legal historian would want to ask the following questions about these rules. Why in the collection of material in the Book of the Covenant are there but these two sex laws? Why is the rule about sorcery a female offence? How do we account for the sequence whereby a rule about seduction follows one about hire (Exod 22:14, 15); it, in turn, by one about sorcery and then by one about bestiality?

Do these rules fit the characterisation of early law codes in other societies, for example, the laws of Eshnunna or the Roman Twelve Tables, namely, where some of the most fundamental rules of law are not recorded, and those rules that are recorded seem to be introducing reforms, or settling doubts?[11] The answer would appear to be probably not. A more major question is why are all the rules in the Book of the Covenant ascribed to Moses in a historical setting that has no basis in reality for a good many of them? And why are the rules inserted into an ongoing narrative?[12]

I wish to argue that if we take stock of two salient, inter-related features of biblical narrative we find a new way of understanding biblical legal material. The first feature is that the narratives recount beginnings: the creation of the world, the origin of shame (Adam and Eve), the first murder, the first bout of drunkenness (Noah), the first fathers of the nation, the first form of enslavement of an ancestor of the nation, namely, Jacob with Laban, the first open outbreak of idolatry (the golden calf), the origin of kingship, and so on.

The second, related feature of the narratives is that they record how what happens once tends to repeat itself in a succeeding generation. There is a sense in which even the world is re-created after the flood; Lot's drunkenness is like Noah's in that members of the immediate family abuse the *paterfamilias*; Abraham's problem with his attractive wife when they are in foreign parts repeats itself for Isaac with Rebecca; Jacob's servitude under Laban is paralleled with Joseph's under Potiphar, and then with all Israel under the pharaoh. Ishmael's loss of primogeniture to Isaac, Esau's to Jacob, Reuben's to Joseph, Manasseh's to Ephraim constitutes but one pattern of similar developments over succeeding generations which, if we scan narratives from Genesis through to the accounts of the history of the kings, can be demonstrated many times over.

The first major observation to be made about the legal and ethical material in the Book of the Covenant—we can include also the decalogues in Exodus 19, 34, Deuteronomy 5, and the laws of Deuteronomy 12-26—is that, using the same body of narrative literature, the material represents a parallel to the process of redaction that has produced the collections of narratives. The rules in the Book of the Covenant focus upon a first-time occurrence of a problem in the history of Israel (beginning with Jacob/Israel). For example, Jacob's service under Laban, when he, the first Hebrew slave, served fourteen years for Laban's two daughters, prompts the rules about a Hebrew slave who comes to a master without a wife; who receives a wife from the master; and rules about the rights of daughters when a father sells them as concubines (Exod 21:2-11). The lawgiver is likewise alert to how the same problem—as we shall see, for example, in regard to sorcery—shows up in succeeding generations.

A second major observation has to do with a convention common in antiquity, especially in Near Eastern wisdom literature: the wise man or seer who sees in a way that no one else does, and who sets forth wise counsel for posterity. Moses is cast as such a type. He is the lawgiver, we are to understand, who makes judgments upon matters in his own lifetime, in the lifetime of those fathers of the nation who preceded him, and upon matters that will arise in the future life of his nation. His perspective is congruent with the one that has shaped the entire body of biblical narrative from Genesis through the history of the kingship. The convention in question probably reflects a real-life setting in wisdom circles, namely, a teacher instructing his students in law, ethics, religion, and wisdom.

At some point, biblical narratives were subjected to ethical, legal, political, and religious scrutiny and given a complex, sophisticated form. (Much of this literary effort may be attributed to the Deuteronomic writer[s].) Probably about the same time other judgments upon issues that were raised in the course of this scribal activity were set out separately, and recorded in the collections of rules in the Book of the Covenant, the Book of Deuteronomy, and the three decalogues.

The incident recorded in Genesis 34, and commented upon by Jacob in Genesis 49:5-7, is an example of a narrative that reveals a process of judgment and counter-judgment at work.[13] Jacob is negative about Simeon and Levi's solution to Dinah's problem, but it is affirmed as the right one by the recorder of the story, who is alert to the later history of the Israelites and the Canaanites. The lawgiver in Exod 22:16-19, aligning himself with the recorder's stance, sets out certain judgments on issues in the story.

Ancient scholarship and Pentateuchal origin

Seduction (Exod 22:16, 17) 16 And if a man entice a maid that is not betrothed, and lie with her, he shall surely endow her to be his wife. 17 If her father utterly refuse to give her unto him, he shall pay money according to the bride-price of virgins.

Source (Genesis 34) Dinah, Jacob's daughter, was seduced by Shechem who then sought to make her his wife. Despite negotiations about a bride price he was refused her.

It can be demonstrated that the rules that precede this rule about seduction focus on Jacob's dealings with Laban.[14] Many of these dealings centre on Jacob's payment in services, a bride-price, for his two wives, Rachel and Leah. Indeed, Laban's final concern was for the welfare of his two daughters. In particular, he wanted assurance from Jacob that he would not afflict, humble (*'innah*) them should he take wives in addition to them (Gen 31:50). The tradition that next raises the topic of marriage is in Genesis 34, the next stage in Jacob's life, and provides the subject matter, not just for this rule about marriage to an unbetrothed girl who has been seduced (and humbled, *'innah*, Gen 34:2), but for a succession of rules. In what is a typical procedure, going from an issue in one generation to a comparable one in the next, the lawgiver moves from one father's concern about the humiliation of his daughters to another's concern about the humiliation of his daughter.

The rule takes up the issue of the girl's humiliation from the tradition about Jacob's daughter, Dinah, and her seduction by Shechem, the Prince of the Hivites, who then sought to pay a bride-price and make her his wife. One reason the rule pursues the topic is that this incident is the first in the nation's history where the topic of a virgin's seduction appears. A central feature of the story is the refusal of the Israelites to give Dinah to Shechem. This, too, is the special bias in the rule, the father's refusal to give his daughter to her seducer. Such a narrow bias is always a telling sign that, if a comparable one exists in a narrative, the influence is likely to be in the direction of story to law. It is just not realistic to assume that the incident about Shechem's seduction of Dinah has been made up in order to illustrate a specific bias in some rule. As is the nature of a story, it is idiosyncratic: the seducer is a Canaanite, and spurious negotiations over a bride-price are a cover for killing him. Moses, we are to believe, takes up the topic for an Israelite society: no foreign seducer but an Israelite seducer is denied her, although the rule's formulation, it might be noted, does not in fact exclude the development in the story. In it the bride-price is negotiable. Shechem offered to pay as much as Dinah's father and brothers might ask (Gen 34:11). The rule recognises a current rate of value for a virginal girl which the seducer is required to pay should the father refuse to give him his daughter.

David Daube argues that the rule, looked at in its own terms, assumes a negotiable bride-price in the initial dealings between the father and the seducer. He speculates that the reason for the father's refusal is an economic one. The father sets the price so high that the seducer cannot or will not pay it. The father none the less collects one sum from him (the current rate) and can look forward to another sum from a future suitor.[15] While this set of circumstances may well be an example of the kind of situation to be reckoned with in such matters, it does not account for the rule's formulation, its *ratio legis*. However we might speculate about the specific reasons for the father's refusal, it might be best, in light of the rule's link with the story, to suggest that the rule's intent is to prevent within Israelite society any deception or hostility comparable to that which arose between the parties in Genesis 34. The lawgiver places a check on the dealings between the two parties because, should they break down, an end result is always in focus. An economic solution to a problem has this capacity to sidestep uniquely personal issues in a dispute.[16]

Witchcraft (Exod 22:18) Thou shalt not suffer a witch to live.

Source (Genesis 34) Dinah took it upon herself to visit the foreign Canaanite women. While among them she was seduced by a Canaanite Prince, Shechem.

For this rule, so fateful in the history of witchcraft in the western world, we are again to assume that Israelite tradition was evaluated by Moses. The first suggestion, or potential example, in this history of an Israelite woman's contamination by evil foreign influence was Dinah's presence among the Canaanite women. She it was who took herself into their midst, and who was seduced, 'treated as though she were a harlot' (Gen 34:31), by one of their distinguished males. So, on the one hand, in placing herself among Canaanite women and, on the other hand, in taking on the status of a harlot, Dinah suggests an identity that is akin to a certain kind of foreign woman met with elsewhere in biblical tradition. In it the combination of sorcery and harlotry becomes proverbial for pernicious influence upon the Israelites by foreign women, Jezebel, for example (2 Kgs 9:22). Such a proverbial view underlies the personification of Nineveh as a harlot who is expert in witchcraft (Na 3:4)

It is the seer Moses who is alert to the potential danger in the case of the first Israelite daughter, and consequently constructs the prohibition against a sorceress. The death penalty for her corresponds to the punishment of Shechem, which was determined not by his seduction as such, but by his being an uncircumcised Canaanite—with all that that represented in religious terms—who had seduced a daughter of Israel.[17] Indeed, the extreme development in the story is owing to this anti-Canaanite bias. The story itself is not explicit in its negative evaluation of Dinah's presence among the Canaanite women. What reveals its stance, however, is the subsequent notice about Jacob's instruction after the slaughter of the adult male Hivites. Jacob had to order that, because of the incorporation into his tribe of the surviving Hivite women and children, the foreign gods in the midst of all the people be put away (Gen 35:1-4). Also pertinent in revealing the narrator's stance is the further notice that God destroyed any Canaanite city in the vicinity of Jacob and the people (vs. 5). The inhabitants of these cities would, as Jacob himself had pointed out (Gen 34:40), automatically have aligned themselves with their fellow Canaanites who had been slain by Simeon and Levi.

By relating the law to the story we can explain why it is about a female offender only. This text is in fact the only one in biblical material that has the feminine form 'sorceress' *(mekashefah)*. The other texts use either the masculine form or the term 'sorceries'.[18] The common view that sorcery was especially a female interest may not be so accurate.[19]

A sure indication that later Israelite history is anticipated in these rules,[20] especially the awareness of idolatrous Canaanite influence, is to be seen in the code's epilogue. It explicitly warns about the confrontation of the Israelites with Canaanite religion and mentions, among others, the Hivites (Exod 23:23, 24).[21]

Bestiality (Exodus 22:19) Whover lies with a beast shall surely be put to death.

Source (Genesis 34; 49:5-7) Shechem, the son of the 'Ass' Hamor, lay with Dinah, the daughter of the 'Ox' Jacob/Israel.

The rule prohibits bestiality, and we would be hard pressed to know why such a practice should invite condemnation. The English writer Laurie Lee observed that 'quiet incest' flourishes where the roads run out.[22] So, too, is it with bestiality. It would be anachronistic to introduce later notions of natural and unnatural, such as we find in Philo,[23] into this particular rule. It is just not likely that what herdsmen sometimes did occasioned this prohibition. The participial form, 'Whoever lies,' can include a female offender too. She is openly cited in the prohibition in Lev 18:23 and 20:16.

It is again the way in which a narrative is used to raise topics that explains the rule's formulation. Shechem, the son *(shekhem*, shoulder) of the ass, Hamor, seduced and lay with *(shakhav* as in the rule) the daughter of the ox, Jacob, whose group is compared to the animal, the ox, precisely in reference to its troubles with the Canaanites (Gen 49:6). The figurative meaning in the story, and in Jacob's death bed comment upon it, elicits the lawgiver's prohibition: no sexual congress between a man or a woman and an 'animal'. The death penalty corresponds to Shechem's fate, and is intended to include any Canaanite male or female, who may like Shechem become involved with an Israelite 'ox,' or any Israelite male or female, who may like Dinah become involved with a Canaanite 'ass'. Such a development calls for an extreme response, precisely because of the religious attitude that motivated Simeon and Levi in Genesis 34, and is shared by the author (or redactor) of that story and the lawgiver.

The rule should not be separated from its meaning in the context of the anti-Canaanite sentiment of the story: no sexual involvement between an Israelite and a Canaanite.[24] The term *behemah*, 'beast,' typically refers to those animals owned and used by man such as the ox and ass; and should indeed be confined to these two because of the rule's inseparable link with the story.[25] In summary form, the rule might be best paraphrased as: a Canaanite, like Shechem, who lies with an Israelite 'ox,' or an Israelite, like Dinah, who lies with a Canaanite 'ass,' shall be put to death.

The difference in formulation between the two rules about the sorceress who is 'not to live,' and the rule about the person lying with a beast, who 'dying, shall die,' may be accounted for in light of their shared background. The former, as B.S. Childs rightly points out,[26] is a term for the sacred ban (Numbers 31:15; Deutermony 20:16; 1 Samuel 27:9-11), the extirpation of idolatrous agents. Dinah's contact with the Hivite women only suggested the later problem of actual idolatrous influence and the sanction against the sorceress focuses upon such later developments. Shechem, on the other hand, this 'ass,' does die for his offence against Dinah and the more concrete 'shall surely die' may echo his fate. Underlying each rule is the concern with idolatry, but in the case of Dinah, the lawgiver ranges beyond the details of the story.

If my interpretation of the prohibition against bestiality is correct, we have to assume that the lawgiver had before him the story of Shechem and Dinah. Moreover, because the laws he sets down are part of a narrative history, we should draw the somewhat obvious conclusion that each law was to be understood in relation to its relevant story. When the laws were formulated, most likely in a scribal school, they were integrally linked to the narratives. In other words, the laws were never intended to be read independently of the narratives *at this early stage* in the origin of the Pentateuch.

Notes

1. See D. Cohen, 'Greek Law: Problems and Methods,' *ZSS* 106 (1989), 81-105.
2. From another angle the maxim points to a characteristic of an outstanding teacher: in Heraclitus's phrase, 'neither telling, nor concealing, but indicating'. David Daube remarks how in Talmudic literature God is sometimes depicted conducting himself like a great teacher with a gifted pupil, 'supplying a signal but leaving room for interpretation and choice of action', *Appeasement or Resistance And Other Essays on New Testament Judaism* (Berkeley: University of California, 1987), 114; cp. *Civil Disobedience in Antiquity* (Edinburgh: University Press, 1972), 71.
3. The parallel to this Israelite educational activity is the schools tradition in Babylonia. Near Eastern law codes represent the hypothetical legal judgments of a learned elite. This academic setting explains why the codes contrast with what we know of everyday law from legal contracts and the like. For a recent discussion, see R. Westbrook, *Studies in Biblical and Cuneiform Law* (Paris: Gabalda, 1988), 4, 123; M. Malul, *The Comparative Method in Ancient Near Eastern and Biblical Legal Studies AOAT* 227 (1990), 105-07, 129, 138 n. 75, 149. Mathematical circles in ancient Babylonia proceeded similarly. Their school texts 'sometimes exhibit only very remote connections, if any, with practical questions', O. Neugebauer and A. Sachs, *Mathematical Cuneiform Texts AOS* 29 (1945), 1. For the remarkable link between Babylonian mathematics and biblical historiography, see the seminal articles by D. W. Young, 'On the Application of Numbers from Babylonian Mathematics to Biblical Life Spans and Epochs,' *ZAW* 100 (1988), 331-61, and, 'The Influence of Babylonian Algebra on Longevity Among the Antediluvians,' *ZAW* 102 (1990), 321-35.
4. See D. Daube, *Ancient Jewish Law* (Leiden: Brill, 1981), 11, translating E. Schürer, *Geschichte des Jüdischen Volkes im Zeitalter Jesu Christi*, 2d ed., pt. 2, 1886, 561: 'Am meisten erwiesen sich auch hier, wie bei jeder religiösen Bewegung, die Frauenherzen empfänglich.'
5. See note 9.
6. In passing, Noah's pronouncement on the occasion that 'Japheth shall dwell in the tents of Shem,' has its place in the history of Jewish education. In the first half of the second century A. D., Simeon ben Gamaliel II appealed to this oracle to support his position that the Torah could be written in Greek (Palestinian Megillah 71c). For the Rabbis Japheth stood for Hellas and Shem for Jewry.
7. 'Every time two families become connected by a marriage, each of them thinks itself superior to or of better birth than the other,' *Group Psychology and the Analysis of the Ego*, 3d ed., (London: International Psycho-Analytical Press, 1945), 55.
8. See D. Daube's comments in *Civil Disobedience in Antiquity* (Edinburgh: University Press, 1972), 16.
9. So D. Daube, *Ancient Jewish Law*, 3.
10. Deut 33:17; Num 23:22, 24:8; cp. Num 22:4; 1 Kgs 22:11; Amos 6:12, 13.
11. See D. Daube, 'The Self-Understood in Legal History,' *JR* 18 (1973), 126-34.

12. Increasing attention is being paid to this question. See G. C. Chirichigno, 'The Narrative Structure of Exod 19-24,' *Bib* 68 (1987), 457-79, and B. S. Jackson's forthcoming book on the *Mishpatim*, the *Speaker's Lectures* delivered in 1985-86 at Oxford.
13. A process that proved to have a long history, see M. M. Caspi, 'The Story of the Rape of Dinah: The Narrator and the Reader,' *Hebrew Studies* 26 (1985), 25-45; 'The Story of Dinah - Scripture, Reader, and Midrash,' *Beth Mikra* 94 (1982/83), 236-55 (Hebrew); R. Pummer, 'Genesis 34 in Jewish Writings of the Hellenistic and Roman Periods,' *HTR* 75 (1982), 177-88. Dinah may have been raped but there is no warrant in the text for this conclusion. The term *'innah* means to take a woman without observing the legal formalities, D. Daube *The Exodus Pattern in the Bible* (London: Faber and Faber, 1963), n. 6, 65, 66.
14. See C. M. Carmichael, *The Origins of Biblical Law* (Ithaca: Cornell University Press, 1992), 155-58.
15. See his review of L. M. Epstein, *Sex Laws and Customs in Judaism* (New York: Bloch, 1948), in *Book List of The Society for Old Testament Study*, 1950, 54.
16. No wonder psychoanalysts compare money to faeces: 'both the result of specifics dissolving into formless mass,' D. Daube, 'Money and Justiciability,' *ZSS* 96 (1979), 15. Daube further comments, 'Justice, too, could be said to be faecal, in a high degree denying the uniqueness of things...finds expression in abstract rules, to be administered indifferently, Book of Common Prayer, even-handedly, Shakespeare, ending where mystery begins, Burke.'
17. S. R. Driver raises the longstanding issue as to whether the narrative in Genesis 34 is one in which individuals really stand for tribes. He points out that, after the conquest, Israelites and Canaanites dwelt in Shechem side by side (Judges 9). In that there is almost a complete identity of expression between Genesis 33:19 and Judges 9:28, the name Shechem that signifies the place in the latter text may in Genesis 34 be really a personification of the inhabitants of the place. Consequently, we may not be dealing with the sexual seduction of Dinah by Shechem, but with the religious seduction of Israel by a Canaanite tribe, *Genesis* WC 9cd. (Methuen: London, 1913), 307-08.
18. See the listings by S. R. Driver, *Exodus* CBSC, 229-30.
19. Even the evidence from the Neo-Assyrian period (900-600 B. C.), which might suggest that the sorceress was more prominent than her male counterpart, requires much more rigorous analysis. See A. Rollin, 'Women and Witchcraft in Ancient Assyria (c. 900-600 B. C.)' in *Images of Women in Antiquity*, eds. A. Cameron and A. Kuhrt (London: Croom Helm, 1983), 34-45. Later Talmudic statements require their own analysis in terms of time and place, e.g., *Bab. San..* 67a, 'Because mostly women engage in witchcraft.'
20. The rule about cultic prostitutes in Deut 23:17, 18 covers different generations of Israelite involvement with Canaanites beginning with the incident in Genesis 34. See C. M. Carmichael, *Law and Narrative in the Bible* (Ithaca: Cornell University Press, 1985), 240-43.
21. Contrary to almost all commentators ('One of the most difficult problems arises from the complete omission in vv. 20-32 of any mention of the

preceding laws' [so B. S. Childs, *Exodus* OTL, 461]), I see a substantial link between the code's epilogue (Exod 23:20-33) and the preceding laws.
22. *Cider with Rosie* (London: Penguin, 1959), 206.
23. *De Spec. Leg.* 3. 37-50. The characterisation of the coupling in Lev 18:23 as confusion *(tevel)* may, however, come close.
24. It is probably going too far to suggest, as does U. Cassuto *(A Commentary on the Book of Exodus* [Jerusalem: Magnes 1967], 290), that the prohibition is anti-idolatrous in the sense that Canaanite culture celebrates, for example, Baal's intercourse with a heifer (in order to avoid death as a result of the devices of Mot the king of the netherworld). For the text, see J. C. L. Gibson, *Canaanite Myths and Legends*, (Edinburgh: T. and T. Clark, 1977), 72. Cassuto, followed by other commentators, avoids a plain meaning for the prohibition, that is, they do not view it as condemning bestiality as such, but in a religious context. The prohibition in Deut 22:10, about not ploughing with an ox and an ass together, also focuses upon the incident in Genesis 34 but from another angle. See C. M. Carmichael, *Law and Narrative*, 195-97, 203. Ben Sira (in the Hebrew and Syriac texts) uses this prohibition in his counsel, 'Happy the man who marries a wise woman, and does not plough with an ox and an ass together' (Sir 25:8).
25. The term is not used figuratively in the Old Testament, presumably because of its inclusive character. In the context of the rule it is intended to refer to the 'ox' and the 'ass,' and having done so the figurative meanings have then to be read.
26. *Exodus* OTL, 477.

HEBREW LANGUAGE AND LITERATURE AT THE HEBREW UNION COLLEGE — JEWISH INSTITUTE OF RELIGION 1876–1930

Ezra Spicehandler

This paper is a revised and enlarged version of an article published in 1976 which dealt with the place which modern Hebrew language and literature occupied at the Hebrew Union College—Jewish Institute of Religion (henceforth HUC-JIR) during the first century of its history.[1] In the article, I indicated that the shifting attitudes toward modern Hebrew at the HUC-JIR were the result of social and cultural changes which occurred within the Jewish world in general and the Reform movement in particular.

I

From the outset, modern Hebrew literature had served as the vehicle of the Haskalah which advocated the reformation of Jewish social, cultural and religious life in the nineteenth century so that Jews might be integrated into the modern era—objectives which were shared with the Reform movement, itself an outgrowth of the early German *Haskalah*. The conflict between the Reform movement, and the Hebrew renaissance began when the latter increasingly became the advocate of Jewish nationalism and particularly after the rise of Zionism. Like the early *maskilim*, leaders of the German Reform movement primarily viewed Hebrew as the medium by which to address coreligionists who had not yet mastered the German language. By the 1830s, however, German had become not only the vernacular of an increasing number of German Jews but their literary language as well. Consequently, it rapidly replaced Hebrew as such. The founders of German Reform, seeking to make the synagogue more attractive and its prayers more comprehensible to the social class which they addressed, introduced the German sermon and German prayers into the synagogue liturgy. Nevertheless, most Reform rabbis and laymen maintained a degree of affection for 'the holy tongue' and retained the key passages of the Siddur in their Hebrew original. Scholars like Geiger clearly expressed their doubts as to the necessity of the survival of Hebrew literature and as to the merits not only of modern Hebrew literature but even of much of medieval Hebrew poetry. Yet even he occasionally published in excellent Hebrew.[2] Hebrew was, after all, the language of the Bible and of Jewish learning. Even the non-Jewish world counted it among the classical languages and the opinion of the non-Jewish world mattered very much to modern Jews. Consequently, many Reform rabbis and scholars had a deep veneration for Hebrew, a feeling not extended to embrace the rising Jewish nationalism of either the *Hibbat Tziyyon* movement or political Zionism.

Isaac Meyer Wise, the founder of the *HUC*, was a spiritual heir of the German Reform movement. As such, he reflected this ambivalence. In pre-Zionist days, he favoured the settlement of Jews in Ottoman Palestine but later consistently opposed political Zionism and, at least after 1897, the *Hibbat Tziyyon* movement as well.[3] At the same time, he frequently expressed a deep, sympathetic interest in modern Hebrew letters. He not only subscribed to several Hebrew periodicals but supported their publication in both Europe and America and applauded the revival of Hebrew as a modern language.[4] In a paper given during the meeting of the World Congress of Religions at the Columbia exposition in 1893, he lauded the achievement of modern Hebrew journalists who

> ...rejuvenated the Hebrew to a language of modern culture with an abundant terminology for all sciences, industry and commerce so that the ancient language of the Bible is now expanded to a complete vehicle of modern society.[5]

On several occasions rabbis and professors at the *HUC* penned Hebrew paens and broadsides in Wise's honour.[6] S. B. Schwartzberg, the editor of *Ner Ma'aravi*, the sole Hebrew periodical then appearing in America, praised him for his moral and financial support:

> Dr. Wise...eagerly supports the *Ner Ma'aravi*. Four times he wrote in his journal *The American Israelite* ardent words urging our people in the United States to aid our endeavors. The sublime

words which he utters on behalf of *Ner Ma'aravi* testify that Wise loves our tongue.[7]

Psychologically, perhaps, expressions of veneration for Hebrew enabled certain anti-Zionist rabbis to share some common ground with more ethnocentric Jews and with Hebrew scholars. This philo-Hebraism, however, might have had deeper roots. I suggest that it was a subconscious manifestation of repressed ethnic feelings. Moreover, in Reform Jewish circles which were neutral toward the rising Zionist movement or were only mildly hostile to it but acknowledged its vitality and historical significance, love of Hebrew was a riskless commitment.[8]

Nevertheless, during the early years of the *HUC*, no instruction in either modern Hebrew literature or language formed part of the curriculum. Only shortly before Wise's death in 1900, were courses in Hebrew literature introduced because of the attitudes of Moses Mielziner who served as interim president of the *HUC* between 1901 and 1903 and his confidant Gotthard Deutsch. An editorial in the *HUC Journal*, the student's magazine, praises this decision:

> The course of readings in new-Hebraic literature...promises the most gratifying results. The study of modern Hebrew is essential to an American Jewish theological student. By means of it, he can enter into intellectual association with his coreligionists, and appreciate their ideals and aspirations, study their ways of life, their *Weltanschauung* and their attitudes toward Jewish questions...Students of the HUC, let us study Hebrew![9]

Caspar Levias, a committed Zionist and an active Hebraist, taught the new subject. He selected *Ha-tsofeh le-veit Yisra'el*, Isaac Erter's collection of anti-hasidic satires, which advocated radical and social reforms in Eastern Europe. The following year, Levias offered readings in Taviov's *Sifrut Yisra'el* for intermediate level students and selections from Ahad Ha-'am's *'Al parashat derakhim* for more advanced students.[10] Ahad Ha-'am's cultural Zionism appealed not only to Reform Zionists but to the leadership of the American Zionist movement.[11]

Under the leadership of Mielziner and Deutsch, neither of whom was a committed Zionist, the fierce anti-Zionism of Wise's administration was decidedly softened.[12] Addressing the *CCAR* in 1899, Mielziner declared:

> Neither you nor I belong to the so-called Zionists who dream of re-establishing a Jewish state in Palestine. However, all of us cherish and revere the memory of the land which once was the home of our ancestors, the land which is called correctly the Holy

Land, since from Zion came forth the Thora and from Jerusalem the word of God.[13]

Gotthard Deutsch[14] who served as Professor of history at the College from 1891-1921 was a competent Hebraist. An early opponent of political Zionism, he would gradually grow more sympathetic to Zionism. In 1905, Deutsch visited Palestine and lectured in Hebrew at the old auditorium of the National Library in Jerusalem on the 'Essence of Jewish History and its Philosophy'. According to the news report in Ben-Yehuda's *Hashkafah*,

> He expressed his joy and his emotions at 'the privilege of setting foot on the land of the fathers and even more on appearing at the National Library in Jerusalem and lecturing in Hebrew'. He was delighted at seeing...on the soil of Israel, people who believe and strive to add new [episodes]...to past Jewish history. He firmly believes that our hope has not yet been lost.[15]

During this voyage, he stopped at the Zionist Congress in Basle.

Deutsch cooperated with the local Zionist organization and contributed to Zionist funds. He notes that he had chaired a Zionist meeting in Cincinnati in which he expressed his hope of spending his up-coming sabbatical in Palestine and perhaps teaching there.[16] He became the faculty member called upon by most Zionist dignitaries whenever they visited Cincinnati: Shemaryahu Levine, Nahman Syrkin, Meir Berlin, Stephen Wise, Menachem Scheinkin, Nahum Sokolow and Richard Gottheil, the President of the Zionist Federation and Jacob De Haas.[17] Scheinkin solicited his assistance in selling plots of land in Palestine to Cincinnati Jews. Earlier, when Zvi Hirsch Masliansky, the noted Zionist preacher, visited Cincinnati Deutsch, with Wise's approval, invited him to address faculty and students. Masliansky spoke in Hebrew as did Deutsch who chaired the meeting.[18] In his memoirs, Masliansky describes Deutsch as 'an erudite historian, a veteran Hebraist and an expert scholar of ancient and modern Hebrew literature'. Masliansky's visit had a dramatic effect on the student body. Judah Magnes would later claim that as a result, he was converted to Zionism.

As the official historian of the *CCAR*, Deutsch reported significant anniversaries in the lives of Hebrew and Yiddish writers, among whom were Abraham Mapu, Micah Josef Lebensohn, Kalman Schulman, Jacob Steinberg, Joshua Bershadski, Gerson Rosenzweig, J. L. Peretz, Sholom Aleichem, Mendele Mokher Sefarim,[19] Ben-Avigdor and Micah Joseph Berdiczewski.[20] He published articles on Peretz and Shalom Aleichem in the *American Israelite*. He also recommended that the *CCAR* grant stipends for scholarly projects undertaken by A. M. Luncz and Judah David Eisenstein and urged the *CCAR* to underwrite the publication of one of the volumes of Eliezer ben Yehuda's dictionary.[21] Deutsch was in contact with Reuben Brainin whom he first met in Vilna at the editorial offices of *Ha-zeman* in 1905. Brainin notes that 'he spoke a peculiar Yiddish which he made up himself....He related lovingly to everyone of the literary works of the Jewish people.'[22]

During the First World War, Deutsch discontinued writing his diary in German and henceforth kept it in Hebrew.[23] He published several articles in modern Hebrew and wrote several articles on various historical topics. On many occasions, Deutsch delivered public speeches at the *HUC* in Hebrew. When in 1903, as acting President, he ordained the graduating class, he gave the charge in Hebrew.[24] From time to time, he would read some of his own class lectures in Hebrew.

By 1903, the number of Hebraists and, at least, cultural Zionists on the faculty was impressive. Of its six full time members besides Deutsch, three were committed Zionists.[25]

Henry Malter had been a member of a small circle of brilliant young Hebraists who were studying or living in Berlin at the *fin de siècle* (Micah Joseph Berdiczewski, Mordecai Ehrenpreis, Isaiah Thon and David Neumark). Malter, like Ehrenpreis and Neumark was associated with the literary activities directed by Ahad Ha-'am, then editor of *Ha-shiloah* and mentor of *Ahiasaf*, the cultural Zionist publication house that was planning to publish *Otzar ha-yahadut*, a modern Hebrew encyclopedia.[26] Throughout his life, Malter published extensively in the Hebrew periodical press, translated and updated Steinschneider's *Jüdische Literatur* into Hebrew, edited a Hebrew translation of a work by Al-Ghazali[27] and a scientific edition of *Masekhet ta'anit*.[28]

Caspar Levias, appointed in 1895, taught Bible and Aramaic. At Bialik's behest, he published his major work *Dikduk aramit bavlit* in Hebrew (New York, 1920). Levias wrote many articles in the field of Hebrew philology and conceived the idea of editing a linguistic dictionary of the Hebrew language of which only two volumes appeared.[29] For many years, Bialik tried to publish the remainder but was unable to raise the funds for the project. He also agreed to publish Levias' Hebrew medical dictionary but never succeeded in financing its publication. Bialik referred to both works in a letter to Judah Magnes as being 'two marvellous lexicons....The medical dictionary is a wonderful and large thesaurus of all the medical terms found in our literature.'[30] Levias was also a pioneer in developing modern grammatical terminology in Hebrew, although most of his innovations are now obsolete. He also left in manuscript a Hebrew translation of Jacob Qirqisani's book on Jewish sects.[31]

Judah L. Magnes (taught 1901-03) became a prominent American Zionist leader after he left *HUC* and later, the first president of the Hebrew University. His personal magnetism, youth and romantic Zionist views had a marked effect upon many students. Magnes's enthusiasm over the renaissance of Hebrew literature was typical:

> In every Jewish cultural revival, the Hebrew language has played an important part and today, when the Jewish nation is again witness of the marvel of its own renaissance, when like the old tree in the springtime, it is shooting forth new cultural blossoms, the Hebrew language is again fulfilling its mission as the national vehicle through which young Judah expresses his fears and hopes.[32]

Both Ephraim Feldman and Sigmund Mannheimer were Hebraists. Feldman (taught 1883-1910) was, according to Michael Meyer, 'a gifted teacher of philosophy'.[33] He would later support Caspar Levias in his controversy with Kaufman Kohler, in which Levias's pro-Zionism was a major issue.[34] Sigmund Mannheimer's (taught 1884-1909) sole book was *Mefales nativ*, a Hebrew reader and grammar which appeared in at least twenty-four editions beginning in 1873. He was known as the 'poet laureate' of the College and penned commemorative verses in Hebrew, German and English, many of which appeared in the *HUC Journal*.[35] Mannheimer was an avid supporter of modern Hebrew literature.

On the faculty, then, after Isaac M. Wise's death, only Moses Buttenwieser (taught 1897-1934) was an uncompromising anti-Zionist—an ideology which he shared with David Philipson and Louis Grossman, two local rabbis, who were part-time instructors. When the first *Hebrew Union College Annual* (henceforth *HUCA*) was published in 1904, it included several articles on modern Hebrew literature:[36] Meyer Lovitch wrote on Isaac Erter (pp 225-34), Nathan Gordon on Joseph Perl's *Megalleh tmirin (pp 235-42)* and Judah Magnes on Bialik (pp 177-86).

Hebraist and pro-Zionist sentiments were even stronger among the student body as reflected in the *HUC Journal,* the student magazine founded in 1896 and published monthly during the school year until 1903. Zionist and anti-Zionist sentiments were expressed with great ardour, despite the fact that students were often pressured into opposing the new movement.[37] By December 1898, its editor, William H. Fineshriber, in an apparent rebuttal of a resolution which the Union of American Hebrew Congregations passed in 1898 that 'America is our Zion',[38] wrote: 'We do not regard Washington with the same emotions with which we think of Jerusalem; the historical associations are lacking; the much despised but necessary poetry is not there....what of it if Zionism of today is not practical.[39]

In the *HUC Journal* during 1898-99, at least six articles were devoted to Zionism[40] including Caspar Levias's 'Justification of Zionism'. An entire issue in the following academic year took up the Zionist question with the participation of Isaac M. Wise, Gotthard Deutsch, Louis Grossman (opposed), Bernard Felsenthal and Richard Gottheil (in favor).[41] Undoubtedly, the Zionism of so many students upset the administration. In an editorial of February 1900, the editor confessed that there were Zionists on the editorial board of the *Journal*.

Articles on Hebrew literature often appeared within its pages. Abraham Rhine wrote about M. Z. Mane and about the *Ma'asef*.[42] He would later publish a first-rate book on J. L. Gordon, an expansion of his rabbinical thesis.[43] Rhine's introduction to this work is indicative of the growing desire of American Jews of 'Russian' origin to gain recognition as cultural equals of the Germans and to claim for themselves a place in the history of the struggle for emancipation and religious reform:

> The study of this period...will come in the nature of a revelation to the reader to whom the Hebrew language is a terra incognita. It will unfold...a tale of the struggle between the old order of things and the new, between medievalism and modernity. He will meet with men of power and of genius...whose life was a constant batle on behalf of enlightenment and civilization...a study of nineteenth century Hebrew literature cannot but tend to raise the Russian Jew in the estimation of his American brother, and bring about a clearer understanding between them.[44]

In December 1900, a special section entitled *Hebraica* was introduced in the Journal which was devoted to Hebrew literature. Max Raisin, as editor, explained its purpose:

> The intention is to acquaint my fellow students with one of the most interesting phenomena in the Jewish world, the revival of the old Hebrew language and the rise of the new Hebrew literature based on the ruins [sic] of the Biblical, Talmudic and rabbinical literature... This literature is nowadays the great link which connects hundreds of thousands of our coreligionists in Russia, Galicia, Palestine, and even America, and is the great factor which molds...their spiritual life, and inspires them with that great and lofty ideal of revival of Judaism through the regeneration of the Jewish nation. In its present form, this

literature is a combination of occidental and oriental ideas, of many of the old orthodox Jewish sentiments with those of modern progressive Judaism... Zionistic as it is in its general tendency, it is by no means an expression of one-sidedness and narrow mindedness.

Raisin also urged the reading of this literature because it contained important articles and works in the field of Judaic studies.[45] In subsequent issues, he discussed Bernfeld's biography of S. J. Rapoport, reviewed Brainin's book on Mapu and applauded Ahad Ha-'am.[46] Before emigrating to the United States and coming to the *HUC*, Raisin had been a contributor to *Ha-shiloah*, and he continued writing boks and articles in modern Hebrew mainly on American Jewish life and Reform Judaism, including his autobiographical essays in *Dappim mi-pinkaso shel Rabbi*. Raisin's was the first academic thesis ever written in modern Hebrew.[47] Other Hebrew or Yiddish writers treated in the *HUC Journal* were Mendel Silver's review of the first edition of Ahad Ha-'am's '*Al parashat derakhim*[48] and an essay on Ahad Ha-'am and Reform Judaism,[49] and Jacob Raisin's on Isaac Ha-levi Satanow in which he mentions the Hebrew writers Dolitsky, Bialik, Wessley, and J. L. Gordon.[50] Jacob Raisin would later publish *The Haskalah Movement Among Russian Jews*.[51]

It is difficult to gauge whether the majority of the *HUC's* students were Zionists but it is clear that they formed at least a large and influential minority. How to explain this spate of pro-Zionism and Hebraism so early in the history of American Reform Judaism—a movement then, officially committed to anti-Zionism? As indicated, not all Reform rabbis, professors and laymen, were anti-Zionists. Many harbored latent or subconscious sympathies for Zion or Hebrew or both. Some assumed positions of leadership in the infant Zionist movement.[52] By the *fin de siècle*, the number of younger rabbis and rabbinical students of Eastern European origin had grown from year to year. According to Max Eichorn, forty-eight percent of the student body admitted to having parents of Eastern European origin or to having been born in Eastern Europe themselves.[53] It is likely that the percentage was higher since some students were either ashamed to admit that they were not 'Germans' or, if they came from Galicia, claimed that their families were of 'Austrian' origin. Jewish ethnicism had greater appeal to Eastern Europeans than to those who stemmed from *mittel Europa*. This explains why both Wise and Kohler condemned Zionism as an importation by *Ostjuden*.[54] Eviatar Friesel has pointed out the appeal which Zionist ideology had for second generation American intellectuals and the interplay of attraction and repulsion for it among certain Reform Jews. Finally, some students unconsciously expressed their 'oedipal rebellion' against the anti-Zionist stance of *HUC's* Administration and the Reform establishment by supporting the counter-ideology.

These factors must be considered as the antithesis to the anti-Zionist thesis of classical Reform thinkers, an antithesis which would ultimately bring about first the synthesis that would result in their adoption of cultural Zionist views followed by their gradual embracing of pro-Zionist views after the *Shoah* and the establishment of Israel and ultimately by the Reform movement's officially joining the World Zionist Organization in the 1970s.

II

Nevertheless this process, at least insofar as the administration of the *HUC* was concerned, received a setback in 1903 with the election of Kaufman Kohler to its presidency. He was a stern combative personality committed to the anti-ethnicism of 'classical' Reform Judaism and moved to suppress much of this overt pro-Hebraism. In his first address to the students in the Fall of 1903, Kohler declared:

> The College should have a thoroughly American character. The students should endeavor to be imbued with the American spirit.... Neo-Hebraic Literature may be necessary for the Russian Jews who have no genuine national literature from which to derive culture and idealism. For us the English literature is a source of culture, wherefore Neo-Hebraic Literature will be abolished here.

During his tenure modern Hebrew would not be taught at the College.[55]

Kohler began his presidency (1903-1921) in an imperious mood. *HUC*, he insisted, was not a secular academy but the Rabbinical College of an ideological religious movement. Michael Meyer quite correctly entitled the chapter dealing with his tenure as 'A Theological School for Reform Judaism'. It would be Reform Judaism as Kohler viewed it: 'not by Romanticism and Ritualism or Legalism, but by the accentuation of the eternal principles of our prophetic truths can our faith be revitalized'.[56]

His 'classical' Reform ideology considered Zionism, and in his view, Hebraism, to be a retreat to Jewish separatism and a negation of 'universalist' Judaism.[57] He insisted that students and faculty attend all religious services and decreed that all student sermons must be approved by himself personally before they were delivered in the College's synagogue.[58] One wonders whether the discontinuation of the *HUC Journal* in 1904 was the result of his stern paternalism or, at least, if his attitude was a contributory cause of its demise.

Unfortunately, no minutes of faculty meetings during Kohler's first years are extant. We do know that he set about to 'reconstitute the faculty [and]...replace those individuals who either lacked scholarly qualifications or were out of sympathy with his views on Reform Judaism—or both'.[59] Often, the second reason was predominant while the first, at times, was used as the mere diplomatic device for the elimination of the more blatant pro-Zionists on the faculty.

The first to leave was Judah Leon Magnes in 1904.[60] Soon Henry Malter clashed with Kohler not only over Zionist issues but over the ideology of the Reform movement.[61] Malter published an article in the *HUC Journal* in which he propagated his Zionist views. He would later claim that Kohler banned the publication of its last part.[62] Kohler also interfered with Malter's courses of instruction. Malter resigned in December, 1906. His letter of resignation only enumerates his grievances regarding the conditions of his employment including his salary, but behind all this lurked the ideological and personal quarrel with Kohler.[63] Things again erupted when two additional Zionist professors, Max Margolis and Max Schloessinger, both appointed by Kohler, openly came into conflict with him. Margolis had been an anti-Zionist before his appointment in 1905 but converted to Zionism shortly afterwards. Schloessinger resigned in 1907 following a reprimand by the Board for insubordination after he had absented himself from teaching in order to attend a banquet in New York honoring Shemaryahu Levine despite Kohler's prohibition.

Margolis was, by far, the greater scholar. He refused to tolerate Kohler's decision that he be removed from the teaching of the *Prophets* because of his 'Zionist bias' and submitted his resignation to the Board in protest. Despite his mustering of considerable support among students, colleagues and rabbis, the board overwhelmingly upheld the president and Margolis left.[64]

The so called anti-Zionist purges became a *cause célèbre* in the American Jewish community.[65] With the exception of Michael Meyer, Reform scholars who discuss this episode insist that Zionism was not the real issue. Zionist leaders and pro-Zionist journalists, on the other hand, vehemently argue that it was.[66] Meyer correctly asserts that 'these factors played a role in the dispute: money, personalities and Zionism.'[67] The Zionists, of course, stress Kohler's anti-Zionist motives.[68] The Hebrew press reacted to these events by attacking Kohler. Ahad Ha-'am joined the fray with a short note which appeared in *Ha-shiloah*.[69] Years later David Neumark refuted these remarks after they were reissued in *'Al parashat derakhim* (Odessa, 1921), vol. IV, p. 105:

...these teachers were not driven away at all but resigned voluntarily. One of them submitted his resignation for a... reason which had no connection to the Zionist question.[70] He could have remained at his post even after... his resignation had he so desired. Two teachers[71] indeed [resigned] because they were unable to work together with the president who was an anti-Zionist, but they, too, were not compelled to resign.[72]

While Kohler emerged victorious from this controversy, his was a pyrrhic victory. Looking for replacements, he found it difficult to find scholars who were not tainted by the 'Zionist Hebraist heresy'; except for Julian Morgenstern whom he chose to fill Margolis's seat in Bible, a scholar who was both of German parentage and a committed non-Zionist. Other candidates were either neutral but understanding of the Zionist programme, or Zionists like David Neumark whom he named as Professor of Jewish Philosophy in 1907.

Neumark was a prominent Hebrew writer, a co-worker with Ahad Ha-'am in their Berlin days and a devoted cultural Zionist. Another well recognized appointee to the chair of Talmud and Rabbinics, was Jacob Lauterbach (in 1910) who, though not explicitly a Zionist, was certainly a sympathizer. The three Americans whom Kohler appointed toward the close of his presidency could likewise, hardly be classified as anti-Zionists.[73]

The Zionist-Hebraist problem also led to contention with the student body. When in 1914, its literary society invited Professor Horace Kallen, a Zionist intellectual, to address them, Kohler rescinded the invitation accusing Kallen of having dismissed the concept of 'the mission of Israel' as 'barbarous and egoistical' and declaring that 'he did not adhere to any religion'. A number of students signed a letter which was sent to Kallen apologizing for Kohler's discourtesy; they were immediately disciplined. Pressures exerted by Reform Zionists led to a ruling by the Board of Governors which, while it confirmed the president's right to control programs at the HUC's synagogue, insisted that he may not prohibit lectures held elsewhere on the campus provided they were religious in tone.[74] Earlier, James Heller, the son of Max Heller, a prominent Zionist rabbi, had also been denied the right to deliver an impassioned Zionist sermon at the synagogue. The ban was now rescinded.[75]

Kohler, who had been subject to increased criticism for his inflexibility, began sharing his authority with his faculty toward the end of his presidency. His censorship of student activities eased. In June 1915, the *HUC Monthly*, a new student publication, was launched in which Hebraist and pro-Zionist articles were frequently published. Its first editor was Abba Hillel Silver, already a recognized Zionist youth leader, who would become a major figure in American Zionism.

Volume II of the *HUC Monthly* is typical of its editorial policy. In addition to James Heller's controversial Zionist sermon, it included another such sermon by Jacob Meyer,[76] a report of a debate on Zionism between Nathan Isaacs and Julian Morgenstern of the faculty (pp 211 ff) and a pro-Zionist article by Harry Richmond.[77]

Much space was devoted in the *Monthly* to modern Hebrew literature and, to a lesser degree, to Yiddish literature. During his student years, S. Felix Mendelsohn frequently contributed articles on major Hebrew and Yiddish authors: Mendele Mokher Sefarim on the occasion of his eighteenth birthday, Shalom Aleichem, Ahad Ha-'am and Moses Leib Libenblum. Essays appear on Simeon Frug, Bialik, Judah Leib Novakhovich, Abraham Mapu, David Pinski, Jacob Gordon, Alter Druyanov, Scholem Asch, Mordecai Zeev Feierberg, Saul Tchernichowsky, and Hayyim Brody. Translations from Yiddish and Hebrew poetry were done by Sheldon Blank, Abraham Fried, Marshall Taxay and Samuel Baron.

General articles on Hebrew literature are fewer. Jacob Marcus favourably reviewed Abraham Waldstein's *Evolution of Modern Hebrew Literature*; Israel Harburg discussed 'The Struggle for Reform as Reflected in Modern Hebrew Literature'; and Gotthard Deutsch, 'America in Haskalah Literature'.

The process of Zionization and Hebraization of the student body was of course a product of the changing Jewish world. The First World War had shattered the naive optimism which had dominated both German and American Reform Judaism. The horror of the war, the undermining of Eastern European Jewish life during and following it, the Russian revolution, the rise of anti-Semitism in Europe and its growth in the United States in the 1920s and 1930s—all shattered the hopes that mankind would soon attain the messianic age. Zionism's pessimistic appraisal of the Jewish condition was reinforced by its promise of Jewish renewal and the audacity of its project for national rebirth. Moreover, the fact that by 1930, the majority of students was now of Eastern European origin with a strong sense of Jewish ethnic identity accelerated the trend toward Zionism. According to Max Eichorn, by 1930 almost ninety percent of the student body were native born, fifty-six percent of Eastern European parentage, sixty percent considered themselves to be pro-Zionist and only nine percent, anti-Zionist. The *HUC Monthly* clearly reflected this trend.[78]

In April 1918, H. G. Enelow asserted that 'to maintain that Reform had sought to destroy the sense of brotherhood in Israel is to utter an absurdity'.[79] Typical of the change of mood was the program which Max Raisin suggested for the solution of the Crisis of Reform Judaism:

> It must be a Reform... in the traditional Jewish spirit... not the least of which [is] the Hebrew language, Jewish religious melodies, reverence for Zion as the source of the Jews' supreme moral achievement and the doctrine that the Jews today, as they have always been, are still one people, by racial [sic] and nationalistic [ties] no less than by religion.[80]

Less strident but equally reflective of the new mood, Jacob Marcus criticized Claude Montefiore's 'separatist' attitude toward other Jews. 'American Jewry, on the whole, has never attempted to reject the racial [sic] one-ness of the Jew.'[81] Harry E. Wessel explained his Zionist commitment. Jewish studies led him to conclude that 'all that was considered worthy... is grounded on the assumption of a Jewish nationalism'[82]. While this view was rejected by 'some Jews who lived in Germany... in another part of Europe Jews were serving the spirit of their dormant nationality... I saw new signs of life... Zionism had struck the spark of my enthusiasm... I was no longer an indifferent observer of Jewish life in the past but I shared that life.'[83]

Recalling earlier days at the College, Wessel remarked:

> Zionism at the time was taboo... [In] the College pulpit, a non-religious Zionist was prevented... from addressing the student body[84] and permanent exponents of [anti-Zionism] were being invited to address the students and combat their recalcitrant attitude... Many of the strongest... and independent thinkers among the students were avowed Zionists. Since the *CCAR* has taken a middle position which is a willingness to assist in rebuilding Palestine, these facts have no great present significance but a few years ago the force was sufficient to secure firmly my attachment to a struggling cause.[85]

He concluded by quoting a prominent anti-Zionist rabbi who had asked: 'Are there any students at the *HUC* who are not Zionists?'

By 1924, a Hebrew title was appended to the masthead of the *Monthly: Yarhon talmidei beit ha-midrash le-rabanim be-sinsinati*. In 1927, a student curriculum committee recommended the introduction of a course in 'current Jewish problems and modern Jewish literature in English, Hebrew and Yiddish'.[86] Another editorial entitled 'Judah Magnes and the Hebrew University', while voicing misgivings about 'practical Zionism' affirmed: 'there is no greater question that manifold returns can come from our support of a Hebrew culture nurtured at the Hebrew University.'[87] Another urged the adoption of the *Ivrit be-'ivrit* method in Hebrew instruction.[88]

The Zionist ideology which from the beginning had the greatest appeal for the Reform rabbinical student was quite naturally Ahad Ha-'am's cultural Zionism. David Neumark, more than any member of the faculty represented this brand of Zionism. On the occasion of his fiftieth birthday, he was described in the June issue of 1918 as

> ... Both a Reform Jew and a Jewish nationalist... Just as his Reform ideas are different in degree and in kind from the accepted ideas of most of the Reform leaders of our day, so his conception of Jewish nationalism is different and... superior to that of the rabid chauvinists among the younger Zionists... Most of his utterances are given in a vehicle not largely understood by the mass of our people and the outside world... in Hebrew.[8 9]

The author quoted Neumark's reservations about political Zionism. Zionism is 'only a means to a greater end, the preservation of the Jewish soul and Jewish racial [sic] integrity'. Neumark had criticized political Zionism's lack of historical perspective and its commercialism; 'it is ready to buy Palestine for money, and sell our past for a stretch of territory.'[90]

In a quasi-prophetic editorial Jacob Weinstein discussed plans for the formation of the Jewish Agency in 1928, and warned of the dangers of 'philanthropic Zionism' and its new appeal to the wealthy. He attributed the newly found enthusiasm of Reform philanthropists for supporting the Zionist project to the decline of the number of indigent Jews in the United States and the emotional need which the rich have to find an outlet for their charity.[91]

> The ethics and religious philosophy of Reform waxed in liturgy and spun out in metaphysics, appeals even less to a generation which throbs but does not think. It is hardly to be wondered [that] the lay leaders... should jump at the chance of accepting Palestine... Palestine as a well organized philanthropic project may become the 'religion' of Jewry in the vicarious sense that charity was... in the immediate past. What this will do to the nationalist ideology and Kultur philosophy of Zionism should make its leaders tremble. This gift of non-Zionist money and Reform Rabbis speaking for Palestine may be like the gift of the Greek horse which caused the fall of Troy.[92]

In this new atmosphere, a Hebrew speaking society was organized in 1929 dedicated to 'the love of Hebrew culture in the original language' and named in memory of David Neumark.[93] The Hebrew announcement of its programme claims that its membership included one third of the student body and lists both Professors Cohon and Idelsohn as its sponsors. *Agudat* (then *Agudas*) *Neumark* met at Professor Cohon's home every two weeks. On 11 January 1929, David Yellin, the Palestinian scholar, addressed the society.

For several years, a Hebrew section now appeared regularly in the *Journal*, participants including Professors Henry Englander,[94] Abraham Idelsohn, the Hebrew educator and poet, H. A. Friedland, Nelson Glueck and Judah Magnes who invited *HUC* students to study at the Hebrew University. Articles by Moses Cyrus Weiler, Albert Bilgray and David Seligsohn described life in *Eretz Yisrael*.

The Hebrew supplement also contains a few Hebrew poems composed by the students. The literary quality of these contributions in both prose and poetry is rather pedestrian; they, however, reflected 'enthusiasm for the Hebrew word'. The Hebraist atmosphere at the College was depicted in an essay which appeared in the *Journal* of May, 1930.

> We notice... that Hebrew seems to be read and spoken more at the College now than in 1900, that the sentiment seems now to be more in favor of modern Hebrew, ceremonialism and Zionism, that the ideal rabbi is the Jewish scholar, and the mission of Israel idea is languishing at death's door. Hebrew... classical or modern is becoming... an important phase in the life of our students... And if the students are able to put their ideas into practice... we will undoubtedly see a development of Hebrew interest among the Jewish laity and probably a development of a real Hebrew culture, that there has been an increase of students of Eastern European parentage... and that the majority of Jews now in America are also of Eastern European origin...[95]

During Kohler's presidency, David Neumark was the faculty member who, more than any of his colleagues, personified Hebraism. Before he left Europe, he had become a distinguished Hebrew essayist.[96] As a member of a circle of young scholars studying in Berlin both at the *Hochschule für die Wissenschaft des Judentums* and Berlin University, he had attracted the attention of Reuben Brainin who persuaded him to write an essay on Friedrich Nietzsche for *Mizrah u-ma'arav*, a new journal which Brainin had founded.[97] After receiving both his doctorate and his rabbinical ordination in Berlin in 1896, he was recruited by Ahad Ha-'am to serve as a regular contributor on philosophical subjects to *Ha-shiloah*, founded that year. When Ahad Ha-'am began organizing the staff for the projected Hebrew Encyclopedia, *Otzar Ha-yahadut*, Neumark was invited to be the section editor for Jewish philosophy.

Kohler offered the post of Jewish philosophy to Neumark in 1907. In his view, except for his Zionist commitment, Neumark was eminently qualified to fill the chair. He was a graduate of the Reform Jewish seminary of Berlin, possessed an earned doctorate of philosophy and had published a serious work in German. If not a German, he was, at least, a Galician and not, in Kohler's eyes, a troublesome Russian. He was a co-worker, if not a complete disciple, of Ahad Ha-'am but unlike the latter he insisted that religion was still the primary element of the Jewish national culture. Moreover, despite his traditionalism, he was committed to a liberal interpretation of Judaism. He was, therefore, able to maintain his particular brand of cultural Zionism and yet get along with Kohler.

Neumark published works in German and English, but the greater portion of his scholarly output was in Hebrew.[98] When the *Ivriah*, the local Cincinnati Hebrew society which he helped to found celebrated the appearance of the first volume of his *Toledot ha-'ikarim be-Yisrael* (Odessa, 1913), they were able to elicit a warm letter of congratulations from Ahad Ha-'am who wrote:

> I was pleased to see... that even in the Cincinnati College... a bastion of the opponents of Hebrew nationalism, Neumark has succeeded in cultivating such students as yourselves,... devoted to our Hebrew language and culture... I have known, respected and loved Neumark ever since he was a student at the *Hochschule* in Berlin, sixteen years ago, and we have maintained a loyal and friendly relationship to this day. He was one of my chief aides at *Ha-shiloah* from its very inception... When he left for Cincinnati, I found the matter very strange... How could a man like him, a nationalist, Zionist Jew to the very strings of his heart find satisfaction in working at... an educational institution built upon entirely different premises? For many years, he published important works in philosophy and I had surmised that Neumark had limited himself to his speciality, finding satisfaction solely in his scientific work. Now, I see that I was mistaken... He did not shirk his duties as an educator and managed to inspire... some young men who were studying under him and to wake in their hearts a love for those national ideals which he had brought with him from overseas. His book... also attests that... he has not ceased laboring in the field of our national literature, although I believe that not even one of his colleagues... deems it his duty to devote some of his energy and knowledge to literature in our language.[99]

Neumark contended that if one eliminated the religious factor from the Jewish historical experience 'the very ground on which it stands would sink'.[100] As a Reform Jew, he insisted that Judaism is an historical phenomenon. Each generation defines for itself a Judaism... different from that of its predecessors and its successors.[101] The only constant which persisted in Judaism is the commitment to monotheism and ethical law. If other elements of Judaism are subject to change and refinement, they must be set within the Jewish historical framework or cease being Jewish, that is, 'the link with the past can only maintained via its national form'. A religious Judaism without its ethnic base was rootless, 'like a thought without the brain which thinks it... A living being requires both a body and a soul.'[102] Zionism's task is to cure the inner life of the nation. This can be done only by the creation of a cultural center in *Eretz Yisrael* because 'Our national *Shekhina*, cannot be maintained among us, except in *Eretz Yisrael*.' He faulted political Zionism for ignoring this religious factor 'The Zionist idea must profess a positive attitude toward the religion, if it does not, it will never bring about national redemption.'[103]

Neumark argued that cultural Zionists like Ahad Ha-'am were really unconscious Reform Jews.[104] In an interview responding to this allegation, Ahad Ha-'am rejected this view, insisting that religious reform must spring directly from committed and not assimilated Jews.[105] He also spurned the 'mission of Israel' idea as an assimilationist ruse. In another context, he argued that if rich American Reform Jews were really committed to prophetic Judaism they would concern themselves with the plight of American blacks.[106]

Neumark's synthesis of Reform Judaism with Zionism and particularly with Ahad Ha-'amism gave legitimation to the growing pro-Zionist, pro-Hebraist trend in Reform Judaism. Early Reform Zionists argued along similar lines, particularly Bernhard Felsenthal and Max Raisin. The latter, certainly, must have gleaned some of his own views from both Ahad Ha-'am and Neumark.

This tendency was later to find expression in the pro-Zionist Columbus platform which replaced the anti-Zionist Pittsburgh platform of 1887, the main architect of this new statement being Samuel S. Cohon, the devoted disciple of Neumark.

Notes

1. 'Hebrew and Hebrew Literature', *HUC-JIR at One Hundred Years* (Cincinnati, 1976), pp. 453-76. The reader is also referred to Michael Meyer's

comprehensive history of the *HUC-JIR* entitled 'A Centennial History' in the same volume, pp. 3-169. *HUC-JIR* is the composite name given to the combined institution when the *HUC*, founded 1875 merged with the *JIR*, founded in 1922.

2. See his correspondence with Joshua Heschel Schorr, *Nachgellasene Schriften* (Berlin, 1875), vol. IV, pp. 327-29. Cf. ibid., p. 286.
3. A detailed account of Wise's attitude toward Zionism and Jewish settlement in Palestine appears in James Heller, *Isaac M. Wise. His Life, Work and Thought* (New York, 1965), pp. 587-612. Until Basel (1897), Wise supported 'colonization' of Palestine. Following the Congress, he fiercely rejected Jewish nationalism, contending that Jews were only a religious community who owed their undivided allegiance to the country in which they resided. To him, a Jewish 'return' to the ancient homeland was an obsolete, romantic and impractical idea and those advocating it could endanger the status achieved by Jews in modern society.
4. James Heller, op. cit., pp. 546-54. See *American Israelite*, vols. XXXIV (1888), p. 4 (April 27, 1888); XXXVI, no. 32, p. 4 (Feb. 12, 1891), for example.
5. 'Bibliography of the Jewish Periodical Press'. The paper appears in *Judaism at the World's Parliament of Religion* (Cincinnati, 1894), pp. 405-407, published by the Union of American Hebrew Congregations. The lecture on the Jewish press was given at a special Jewish convocation held in conjunction with the Congress.
6. A few examples are to be found in the *CCAR Yearbook*, 1898, pp. 61-62, the *HUC Journal*, vol. I, no. 7 (March-April, 1891) and vol. III: 6-7 (March 1899).
7. *Tikatev Zo't Le-dor 'Aharon* (New York, 1898), pp. 20-21. Other early American Hebrew authors were hostile to Wise because of his anti-Zionism. See Jacob Kabakoff, *Halutsei ha-sifrut ha-'ivrit ba'amerikah*, pp. 12, 98, 109, 171, 199, 215, 256. Although Gershon Rosenzweig the editor of *Ha-pisgah* published a scathing satire against him, 'Zohar hadash' in *Ha-pisgah* IV:14 (27 Tammuz, 5652 = 1892), likening him to Laban (pun on Hebrew "white" i.e. Weiss in German) who hounded Jacob; in an earlier letter to Gotthard Deutsch, dated March 1, 1890, he sent his regards 'to the sage and famous Rabbi, the grey eminence of our literature, Dr. Wise' (Kabakoff, op. cit., p. 215, 256); or is the 'sweet satirist of Israel' simply exercising his craft?
8. This may explain friendly attitudes toward Hebrew of such firm anti-Zionists as Wise or David Philipson. In fact, the early American Reform rabbinate was hardly unanimous in its anti-Zionist position. While until the 1930s the majority was hostile towards Zionism, from its beginning, the Central Conference of American Rabbis (henceforth CCAR) contained a minority of prominent Zionist members. The CCAR also had many non-Zionist members. For a discussion of this division see, Evyatar Friesel, *Ha-tnu'ah ha-tziyyonit ba-artsot ha-brit* (Tel Aviv, 1970), pp. 27-30, 89-108.
9. *HUC Journal*, vol. IV, no. 4, January 1902, p. 84.
10. *HUC Catalogue*, 1901-2, pp. 30-32.
11. Friesel, op. cit., pp. 77-89.

12. See Michael Meyer, *A Centennial History*, pp. 23-24, 52. 13. *CCAR Yearbook*, vol. IX (1899), p. 62. Mielziner published a Hebrew verse eulogy on the first anniversary of the death of Isaac Meyer Wise, *HUC Monthly*, vol. V, no. 4 (March, 1901).
14. On Deutsch see: Samuel S. Cohen, *HUC Monthly*, vol. VII (1924-5), pp. 185-88; Joshua Block, 'Gotthard Deutsch', *Sefer hashanah le-yehudei Amerikah*, X (1942), pp. 456ff., Max Raisin, *Dappim mi-pinkaso shel Rabbi* (Brooklyn, N. Y., 1941), pp. 220-28; *Mi-sefer hayyai*, pp. 78, 43-54; Adolph Oko, 'Selected List of the Writings of Gotthard Deutsch', *HUC Monthly*, Vol. II, no. 8 (May 1916), p. 214.
15. *Od lo avdah tikvateinu*, clearly a direct quote from Ha-tikvah, *Hashkafah*, vol. VI, no. 69; 18 Iyyar 5665(1905), pp. 23-24.
16. Deutsch's Hebrew diary entries, March 20 and May 8, 1919.
17. In 1900. See Friesel, op. cit., p. 96. De Haas noted in his diary that except for Kohler there were actually no anti-Zionists at the College. See Friesel, ibid., and De Haas in *The Maccabean*, February 1905, p. 66. This is, of course, somewhat inaccurate.
18. Masliansky, *Zikhronotai* (New York, 1929), pp. 190. Cf. *HUC Journal*, Vol. I, no. 1, January 1896. Friesel states that Masliansky spoke at the College at the beginning of the [twentieth] century. If so, that was his second appearance. See Meyer, p. 30.
19. *CCAR Yearbook*, XXVIII (1918), p. 74.
20. Ibid., XXXII (1922), pp. 274-75.
21. Ibid., XX (1910), p. 83, XXII (1912), pp. 287-88.
22. Reuven Brainin, *Kol kitvei Brainin*, II (New York, 1936), pp. 264 ff.
23. It is in the *American Jewish Archives* of the Hebrew Union College.
24. The full text is reproduced in Meyer, op. cit., p. 256, note 26, from the Deutsch diary entry of June 28, 1903.
25. Henry Malter, Judah Magnes and Caspar Levias.
26. Not to be confused with Judah David Eisenstein's *Otzar Yisrael* which was published in the United States in 1907-13 and in which both Deutsch and Malter participated. Ahad Ha-'am's project was aborted for lack of funds.
27. *Ma'mar 'Abu Hamid Al-Ghazali bi-tshuvot u-she'elot* (Berlin, 1894).
28. *Masekhet Ta'anit min ha-talmud ha-bavli*, American Academy of Jewish Research Publications, no. 1 (New York, 1930).
29. *Otzar hokhmat ha-lashon* (Leipzig, 1914-15).
30. *Iggrot H. N. Bialik* (Tel Aviv, 1939), Vol., V, p. 114 (November 24, 1930); p. 211 (April 2, 1933); IV, p. 272 (June 20, 1929); cf. Vol. IV, p. 277; V, pp. 63, 176.
31. For further details of his life and achievement see his letters in *Ha-toren*, nos. 1-3 (Nisan-Tammuz 5683 (1923) *Ha-doar*, vol. III (1923), pp. 8-7; *Ha-'olam*, vol. XIII (1925), p. 325.
32. *HUC Annual* (1904), p. 178.
33. Op. cit., p. 61
34. Meyer, op. cit., p. 62. It is likely that Feldman supported Levias on purely personal grounds, since Kohler also sought to dismiss him. Feldman composed a eulogy in Hebrew in memory of Mielziner, *HUC Monthly*, vol. VII, no. 5 (February 1903).

35. See Raisin, *Dappim mi-pinkaso shel Rabbi*, *HUC Journal*, Vol. III, no. 6-7 (March 1889).
36. This first annual was a single volume and preceded the current *HUCA* series which began in 1924.
37. 'The entire trend of our work at the College is such as to lead us away from Zionism', *HUC Journal*, IV, p. 114, as quoted by Michael Meyer, op. cit., p. 45.
38. *Proceedings of the Union of American Hebrew Congregations*, V, 4002. An editorial in the monthly criticizes that declaration, vol. III, no. 3 (December 1898).
39. Ibid., pp. 61-2.
40. Vol. III, no. 8 (April 1899), p. 167.
41. Vol. IV, no 3 (December 1899). Wise, pp. 45-7, Deutsch, pp. 58-70, Grossman, pp. 71-6, Felsenthal, pp. 48-53 and Gottheil, pp. 54-5.
42. Vol. V, no. 3 (November, 1900), pp. 81-2; no. 4 (December, 1900), pp. 176-70, and Vol. VI, no 4 (January, 1902), pp. 74-7.
43. *Leon Gordon* (Philadelphia, 1910).
44. Ibid., p. 7.
45. Vo. V (1900-01), pp. 89-90.
46. On Rapoport, vol. V (1900-01), pp. 89-90; on Ahad Ha-'am, ibid., pp. 65-8, on Brainin's Mapu, ibid., pp. 224-9.
47. The revised book was published before his graduation (Warsaw, 1902). Cf, Raisin's *Toledot hayyai*, p. 53 and Kressel, *Lexikon* etc. vol. II, s.v. Raisin, pp. 861-2.
48. Vol. VII, no. 3 (December, 1902), pp. 97-102.
49. Ibid., no. 4 (January, 1903), pp. 133-5.
50. Ibid., vol. IV, no. 5 (February, 1900), pp. 109-18
51. Philadelphia, 1910, Jacob Raisin was Max's brother.
52. Among them Richard Gottheil who served as the first president of the Zionist Federation, (1897-1904), Judah Magnes as its secretary (1905-1908), Stephen Wise, Max Heller, Bernard Felsenthal, Gustav Gottheil and Max Raisin.
53. *HUC Monthly*, vol. XVII, no. 6 (June, 1930), p. 9.
54. Wise in his early attack on Zionism in 1897, *CCAR Yearbook VII*: 'That new messianic movement over the ocean does not concern us' and that American Jewish sentiments opposed 'the idiosyncracies of those late immigrants' (pp. XI-XII).
55. *Proceedings of the Union of American Hebrew Congregations*, VI, 4977.
56. *HUC Monthly* (June, 1914), p. 8.
57. Meyer, op. cit., pp. 56-9.
58. Ibid., p. 58.
59. Ibid., p. 62.
60. There is no evidence that Magnes was forced out. It is most likely that Kohler's blatant anti-Zionism was one of the major factors which prompted his resignation. Both Louis Liepsky (*Thirty Years of American Zionism*, New York, 1927, p. 35) and Norman Bentwich, *For Zion's Sake*, p. 35, indicate that this was the case. See, however, the minutes of the HUC Board of Governors in the *Union of American Hebrew Congregations Proceedings*, VI, 5228.

61. See his correspondence with David Neumark written in 1902 and printed in *Ha-toren* (July, 1925), pp. 61-72. Michael Meyer has translated key phrases from the Hebrew, op. cit., p. 258, note 40.
62. 'Backwards and Forwards', vol. VII (October, 1902—June, 1902), pp. 32-41, 75-82, 116-25, 176-86, 236-42.
63. See Louis Lipsky, op. cit., p. 35; E. R. Malachi, 'Olam hafukh', *Ha-doar*, vol. XXII (Feb. 26, 1943), p. 27. Kohler had a low opinion of Levias' scholarship, Meyer, op. cit., p. 63 according to Meyer, p. 66 Levias had only a Master's degree but Malachi claims he earned a Ph.D.
64. On this controversy see Naomi Wiener Cohen, "The Reaction of Reform Judaism in America to Identical Zionism (1897-1922)" in *Publications of the American Jewish Historical Society* vol XL (June 1951) pp. 372-82; cf. Meyer, op. cit., p. 66.
65. See Meyer, op. cit., pp. 66-7. For reactions in the Anglo-Jewish press in the United States see Naomi Wiener Cohen, op. cit., pp. 376-81 and her footnotes ad. loc.
66. David Philipson in 'History of the Hebrew Union College' (Cincinnati, 1925), p. 44. 'The issue was really loyalty to the president...particularly on the part of one of the professors.' He means Margolis, so too does Samuel S Cohon in 'The History of the Hebrew Union College', *Publications of the American Jewish Historical Society*, XL (1950-51), pp. 17-55.
67. Ibid., p. 65.
68. See Naomi Wiener Cohen, op. cit., pp. 376-81 and the recent data culled from the Max Heller-Magnus correspondence by David Polish, 'The Changing and the Constant in Reform Judaism' in *The American Rabbinate* edited by Jacob R. Marcus and Abraham Peck (Ktav, Hoboken, 1985).
69. 'Siman she'elah', *Ha-shiloah*, vol. XVII, no. 2 (Heshvan 5468 = 1907): 'Even the elders of Cincinnati's College (Beit Ha-midrash), the bastion of the "yesteryears", will not succeed in driving away the national question which bangs upon their doors by shouting.' Reprinted in *Kol kitvei Ahad Ha'-am* (Tel Aviv, 1947), p. 399.
70. The reference is to Malter.
71. Schloessinger and Margolis.
72. *Mi-keren zavit* (New York, 1917). Cf. *Ha-toren*, vol., 1925, no. 4.
73. Henry Englander in 1909, Jacob Marcus in 1921 and Solomon Freehoff in 1915.
74. Board of Governors Meeting of Feb. 23, 1915. See David Polish, op. cit., p. 191.
75. Ibid., pp. 190-91. The sermon 'Home of the Jewish Spirit', appeared in the *HUC Monthly*, vol. II, no. 6 (March, 1916), pp. 188-9.
76. No. 6, January 16, 1916, pp. 199-205.
77. 'Internationalism and Nationalism', no. 7 (April, 1916), pp. 229-33.
78. 'The Student Body Today and Yesterday', vol.XVII, no.6 (June,1930), p.8.
79. Vol. IV, no. 7 (April, 1918), p. 195.
80. Vol. V, no. 6 (May, 1919), p. 192.
81. Vol. VI, no. 3 (January, 1920), pp. 65-7.
82. 'Why I became a Zionist at the HUC', Vol. VI (May-June, 1920), pp. 187-90.
83. Ibid., p. 187.
84. Horace Kallen in 1915.

85. Ibid., p. 189.
86. Vol. XII, no. 6 (June, 1927), p. 9.
87. Vol. XIII, no. 1 (November, 1927), p. 5.
88. Vol. XV, no. 5 (May, 1928), p. 6.
89. Vol. IV, (June, 1918), p. 150.
90. Ibid., p. 153-5 with references to *Ha-shiloah*, vol. 3, pp. 392-3 and vol. 5, p. 102.
91. Ibid., Vol. XVI, no. 2, p. 2 (December 1, 1928).
92. *HUC Monthly*, Vol. XVI, no. 2, p. 7 (December, 1928).
93. *HUC Monthly*, Vol. XVI, no. 4 (March, 1929), p. 16. Following the deaths of Professors Jacob Mann and Zvi Diesendruck it was renamed the Mann-Diesendruck Society.
94. Ibid. Englander, however, expresses doubts as to the viability of spoken Hebrew in America.
95. Vol. XV, no. 6, p. 3.
96. On Neumark's significance as a Hebrew author see: Fischel Lachower, *Mehkarim ve-nisyonot*, vol. II (Warsaw, 1928), pp. 168-83; *Rishonim ve-'aharonim*, vol. II (Tel Aviv, 1935), pp. 78-94, and *Toledot ha-sifrut Ha-'ivrit ha-hadashah*, vol. III, part 2, pp. 177-89; Reuben Brainin; *Kol kitvei R. B.* (New York), pp. 231-5; Joshua Bloch, 'David Neimark mishnato ve-dei'otav', *Sefer ha-shanah li-yehudei Amerikah* (New York, 1951), pp. 256-68; Samuel S. Cohon, 'Rabbi David Neimark', *Ha-doar*, vol. VII (1937), no. 20, pp. 233-4, no. 21, pp. 359-;60; Aharon Ben-'or, *Toledot ha-sifrut ha-'ivrit be-doreinu*, vol. III (1956), pp. 267-77.
97. 'Mavo le-torat ha-'adam ha-'elyon', Vol. I (Vienna, 1894).
98. A full bibliography of his works was published by his disciple and his successor at the College, Samuel S. Cohon in Neumark's posthumous *Essays in Jewish Philosophy* (Cincinnati, 1929), pp. 369-76. Besides three books in Hebrew, *Toledot ha-'ikarim be-Yisrael* (Moriah, 1912-19), *Toledot ha-filosofiah be-Yisrael*, Vol. I, Stybel (New York, 1921), Vol. II, (Philadelphia, 1929) and *Mi-keren zavit* (New York, 1917), he wrote over seventy articles in Hebrew, a three-volume history of Jewish philosophy and ten articles in German, one book and at least two articles in English.
99. See his letter to Joshua Bloch of 24 March 1917 in *Igrot Ahad Ha-'am*, vol. V, p. 29. See also op. cit., vols II, p. 64; III, pp. 141, 180-82; IV, pp. 101-2 and VI, pp. 25-8.
100. *Luah Ahiasaf*, 1905, p. 30.
101. 'Ha-yahadut va-'atidoteha', *He-'atid*, Vol. IV (1913), p. 131.
102. See 'Ha-tziyyonut ve-ha-'am', *Ha-shiloah*, Vol. V (1899), p. 103. See his English article 'Reform Jews and Nationalists' reprinted in his *Essays*, pp. 91-100.
103. *Ha-shiloah*, Vol. V, pp. 103-4.
104. 'Reform Jews and Nationalism' in the *American Jewish Chronicle*, Vol. II, September 22-29, pp. 535-7 and October 19, 1919, pp. 1-8.
105. The interview was given to the London correspondent of the *American Jewish Chronicle* who recast it and issued it as an article written by Ahad Ha-'am in English! See *Igrot Ahad Ha-'am*, VI, p. 82.

106. *Kol kitvei* (1947), p. 40. Neumark later published an article in Hebrew on the subject of Ahad Ha-'am's Judaism in Hebrew: 'Yahaduto shel Ahad Ha-'am' reprinted in *Mi-keren zavit*, pp. 35-96.

THE *MASKIL* AS *LAMDAN*:
THE INFLUENCE OF JEWISH EDUCATION ON *HASKALAH* WRITING TECHNIQUES

Tova Cohen

Analyses of *Haskalah* writing techniques conventionally emphasise the dominant European influences in *Haskalah* literature. Attention is usually concentrated on the effects exerted on its composition by different schools (from the neo-classical to the realist), or by the *maskil's* conscious imitation of the principal genres of European literature—be they the sublime ode and epos or the prose romance. The purpose of the present article is to suggest an alternative approach. Specifically, it will examine the role of traditional Jewish relationships to the text as influences on two particular characteristics of *Haskalah* writing.[1]

(i) *The attitude towards Hebrew*: Although Hebrew was esentially 'the language of the book' and not a means of daily discourse, *Haskalah* authors regarded it as a living language—not a dead and 'classical' one. This approach explains many of the linguistic phenomena in *Haskalah* prose.

(ii) *'Simultaneous reading'*: Early *Haskalah* poets suggested this technique as a code for the understanding of their works. They directed their audience towards the concurrent reading of two texts: both their own poems and the biblical passage to which they themselves referred either in their notes of their work's opening motto. Readers could not fully appreciate the poem unless they read both sources side by side.

Elsewhere, I have discussed the centrality of both elements to *Haskalah* modes of writing. This article will focus on two allied aspects of the subject. One is the importance of the links between the *maskil* and his Jewish intellectual background. The second is the manner by which the traditional Jewish attitude towards textual reading served as a source for the writing techniques to which I have referred.

Stanley Fish has suggested that 'interpretive communities...are made up of those who share interpretive strategies...for consituting the properties [of texts] and assigning their intentions....These strategies exist prior to the act of reading and therefore determine the shape of what is read.'[2]

According to this theory, the writer, together with his audience, are constituents of a specific interpretive community. Both share the same reading strategies, which are founded on mutual cultural conventions. Hence, modes of textual composition are largely determined by common modes of textual interpretation. The reconstruction of such 'interpretive strategies' provides a key to an appreciation of the manner by which a defined interpretive community both reads texts and influences their formulation.

Haskalah literature is particularly amenable to analysis along those lines. Its authors were so intent on maximising their communication with their readership that they tended to place special emphasis on the shared cultural reading strategies of the Jewish interpretive community to which they themselves belonged. Consciously or otherwise, the modes of interpretation of that community thus continued to characterise even the 'new' maskilic literature.

In examining how the *Haskalah* interpretive community approached texts, I have adopted the following working hypothesis: fundamental attitudes towards books and language, together with modes of reading and basic cultural conceptions, are all forged during the very earliest years of study, when children first begin to engage in such activities.[3] True, *maskilim* did adopt the ideas of the European Enlightenment with considerable enthusiasm at a fairly young age.[4] Nevertheless, they could not free themselves of the basic attitudes instilled in them much earlier, when they first began to learn. It was within the traditional Jewish framework and under the influence of its educational system that the *maskil*—like his audience—first became sensitized to the language and form of written texts. Even when his self-image was that of an innovator and a 'European', his relationship towards texts, books and the language in which he wrote remained inherently 'Jewish'. That is why an understanding of the modes of textual absorption characteristic of the traditional *heder* and *yeshivah* are so important for an appreciation of both *Haskalah* writing and reading.

Fundamental to the argument that follows is the fact that the *Haskalah* interpretive community (particularly until the mid-19th century) was comprised of persons belonging to the intellectual élite of traditional Jewish society. Historians designate that group as 'the circle of *lomdim* [learners]', which consisted of 'talented young people who sought to become *talmidei hakhamim* (talmudic scholars), whose profession was Torah study'.[5] Reading strategies inculcated into all Jews by elementary education in the *heder* were intensified within those circles, all of whose members had furthered their religious studies at either a *beit midrash* or *yeshivah*.

Portraits of *Haskalah* authors provided by external sources (biographical sketches and the like) show this to have been a common pattern. Its ubiquity is confirmed in the maskilic autobiographies, for example those of Solomon Maimon, Ginzburg, Lilienblum and Gotlober.[6] Notwithstanding the diversity of their personalities and places of residence, all had devoted their youth to learning for its own sake (*torah li-shmah*), as was demanded by the conventions of their social circle.[7] Judged by his basic education, each was therefore a *lamdan*. Moreover, I suggest that he remained so throughout his life, despite undergoing the ideological transformation which resulted in his becoming a *maskil*.

It is, of course, impossible to be precise about the individual biographies and education of the entire *Haskalah* readership. However, that too seems to have been a small and élite circle,[8] probably also composed of *lamdanim*. As much is indicated by *Haskalah* narration of the mid-19th century, several of whose protagonists represent the *Haskalah* audience. Typically, they are young *lamdanim*; they become *maskilim* when, instead of devoting all of their time in the *yeshivah* to Torah study, they begin to read *Haskalah* works (initially surreptitiously, afterwards openly). Such is the case with Zerah in Mapu's *Ayit tzavu'a*, Shim'on in Abramowitz's *Ha-'avot ve-ha-banim*, Ya'akov Hayyim in Smolenskin's *Kevurat hamor,* Shemu'el in Braudes' *Shetei ha-ketzavot* and Mordechai in Branstätter's *Mordechai Kizevitch*. The process which they underwent is described in Mapu's portrait of a small *bet midrash* in a Lithuanian shtetl:

> The *bet midrash* located in Ovadiah's courtyard served both as a synagogue and a seat of learning. Poor young *lamdanim* study there, their food provided bythe local grandees...The light of day penetrated through these windows, too...when volumes of poetry and *Haskalah* sneaked into this building. These closet lovers of poetry hide the books to prevent them from being revealed.[9]

Within the present context, the importance of such depictions lies in the implication that the *Haskalah* writer and his readership comprised a single interpretive community. Moreover, it was one in which author-audience familiarity with the same interpretive strategies was particularly pronounced, by virtue of the level of traditional Jewish education which both had attained. The *Haskalah* writer could adopt those strategies in his own works in the knowledge that they would be fully appreciated by his readers.

I would argue that such strategies remained dominant until the last third of the 19th century, when *Haskalah* authors were subjected to two pressures. One was an expansion in the Hebrew readership to the less élitist and closed circles. The second was the growing influence of Russian Positivism, which required literature to appeal to a mass audience. Although most *Haskalah* writers were thereafter still *lamdanim* (as was much of their audience), their writing techniques adapted to changes in their interpretive community.[10] Consequently, the 'learned component' of their technique was weakened. As J.L. Gordon put it: 'I taught my tongue to speak an easier and simpler language, so that I could be heard by common people, since it is them that I wanted to reach.'[11]

The relationship to books as living entities is deeply embedded in Jewish tradition. The roots of that attitude lie in a mixture of religious concepts and historical processes. The first projects intellectual and spiritual activity as the apex of Jewish existence; the second defines book-learning to be the only activity open to independent pursuit by a people otherwise condemned to exile and persecution. *Halakhah* gave those expressions concrete form, expanding the requirement to revere learning and to include reverence for the Book in which learning is to be found. Thus, the *Shulhan Arukh* requires a Jew to honour all holy books ('it is forbidden to sit on a bench on which they are placed') and enjoins him to 'purchase the holy texts from which we learn, such as the Bible, *Mishnah*, the *Gemara* and its commentators, so that he may study them and lend them to others'.[12] Indicative of the crucial importance attached to books is that in subsequent periods some of the most respected rabbis and exegetes of Eastern Europe became known by the titles of their works: for example 'the Shalah' (*Shenei luhot ha-brit*); the 'Sha'agat aryeh'; and the 'Hafetz hayyim'.

One result of the extraordinary status accorded to the Book in the world of traditional Judaism, as well as of the religious and educational emphasis placed on the importance of Torah study, was that the Jew 'actualized' texts. The Book and the events it portrayed become more realistic than the physical and external circumstances of life. The Bible stories which the child absorbed at an early age in the *heder*, and which he re-read throughout his life when reviewing the weekly portion of the *humash* did not therefore constitute external 'literary' works. Rather, they provided the internalized prism for his experience of his physical surroundings.

This is reflected in descriptions of the thought patters attributed to traditional Jews. Thus, Reb Yudel, the hero of Agnon's *Hakhnasat kalah*, draws on talmudic depictions of 'the wolf and the lion and the bear and the leopard and the panther and the snake' to describe the animals which he fears he might encounter on his travels.[13] Bialik provides another example when depicting the manner in which textual pictures and reality are interwoven in the mind of a child:

> And you can find nothing in the Torah which is not explicitly illustrated or broadly hinted at in that part of the countryside. Which constituted the source for the other?—it's impossible to decide. Perhaps God read the *humash* and Rashi's commentary and created the countryside in accordance with those texts; or maybe things were the other way round...and perhaps they were always thus interwoven and neither was prior to the other.[14]

More critically, Berdiczewski and Ahad Ha-'am make the same point:

> The world into which we were born, in which we breathed life and in which we learned to think and live, to see and hear, to feel and sense, is solely the world of the book and its folios. Our lives are those of the script and the text, our questions are those of the text...other than the words of the text we have neither matter nor spirit.[15]

> But the nation of the Book is the slave of the Book, a people whose soul has departed and entered entirely into written words.... In every question of life, it is not the people who decide, but 'let's see what the Book says'.[16]

Since the *lamdan*, as a *yeshivah* student, spent far more time than most Jews in the company of books, his susceptibility to such traits was particularly marked. For him, controversies between 'former' and 'latter' authorities (*rishonim ve-'aharonim*) over the interpretation of a talmudic sentence were as vivid as an argument to which he might himself have been witness. They constituted immediate experiences, not dissections of historical events. One consequence was the phenomenon known as 'the war of the Torah'. Such was the vividness and critical importance which the world of the *yeshivah* attached to the Book, that disputes over its interpretation bore no relation to the fact that 'in reality' nothing more was at stake than the minutiae of exegesis. As Papirna recalled:

> In the *kloize* there was a constant hubbub created by the voices of dozens of young men... the books were laid out before them and they studied and argued amongst themselves diligently, living at peace with each other. But sometimes they would disagree about a difficult passage in the Talmud or its commentaties. Although the dispute began quietly enought and in good spirit, it gradually increased in intensity and the boys began to quarrel.... The other students also joined the disputants, some supporting one side, the rest the other. And the *beit midrash* was transformed into two warring camps.[17]

A second, and complementary, consequence of the vividness of the Book was that its study blurred all distinctions between present and past. Significantly, analyses of halakhic texts—mishnaic, talmudic or subsequent—were (indeed, still are) conducted in the *yeshivah* in the present tense: 'Abayye says'; 'the Tosafists ask...' and so on. Thus, the narrator in Feierberg's *Le-'an* deliberately shifts from the narrative past tense into the present tense when describing study from Nahman's point of view:

> He studied incessantly for three hours; the issue was deep and very complicated. The commentators *are waging* the war of Torah with ferocity and strength; [*one*] *resorts* to the weapons of proficiency; [*the other*] *employs* those of astuteness. How much he *enjoys and loves* this war.[18] [Italics mine.]

Since the talmudic text comprises a current event its study constitutes a realistic experience.

The role of the Hebrew language in Jewish reality is a consequence of the role of the Book. If the Book itself constitutes reality, then its language cannot be 'dead', even though it is not the idiom of ordinary Jewish discourse in the street and the home and despite the fact that it does conform to several of the characteristics of a 'classical' (that is a 'dead') language.

The claim that the Jew's attitude towards Hebrew might be analogous to that of other peoples to classical languages was contested by J.L. Gordon as early as 1858. In a letter to *Ha-maggid* (Vol. 2, no. 13, p. 49), Gordon launched a bitter attack on the thesis put forward by the historian I.M. Jost. The latter had maintained that, since Hebrew was as 'dead' as Latin or Greek, no modern literature in Hebrew could be developed. Gordon, however, argued that every Jew regarded Hebrew as a living language and that, even in the contemporary period, it could consequently constitute a medium for modern literature.

Gordon's argument is still valid. Admittedly, and as Even-Zohar claims, Hebrew served only as 'the language of the Book' in what he terms the 'diglossia'.[19] Contrary to other instances, however, that fact did not render Hebrew a 'dead' language. For the *lamdanim*, especially, it was presumably very much alive. After all, they spent most of their time in the intense study of books written in Hebrew and, as we have seen, engaging in what was for them an essentially 'realistic' activity. Their intimate acquaintance with Hebrew's nuances did not simply reflect their scholastic interests. It also prompted their relationship to the language as a vigorous means of communication in what they considered to be the most vital of all their 'realistic' activities.

Moreover, it is important to note the uniquely early age at which the Jewish child began to become acquainted with Hebrew. This, too, set him apart from his non-Jewish European counterpart, who did not generally begin studying Latin until he went to school. John Stuart Mill, who was taught Latin by his father when only three, is an exception which does much to prove the rule. For the average Jewish child, however, an introduction to Hebrew at that age was the norm. In Gordon's words: 'The Jewish child imbibes Hebrew virtually with his mother's milk.' Hebrew had become an integral component of his vocabulary at the most formative stage of his linguistic development.[20] Even before the Jewish child began to learn to read in the *heder* (when three years old) he had gained some familiarity with Hebrew letters and words on various occasions at home, particularly if he came from a family of *lamdanim*. He heard them in the daily blessings and in the various quotations which laced common speech.

Some Jewish parents even tried to instil a knowledge of the language into their children as soon as they could talk. Indeed, the duty to do so was enshrined in classic Jewish sources. *Devarim Rabbah*, an early rabbinic commentary on Deuteronomy, mandates (11:19): 'When a child begins to talk, his father speaks to him in the Holy Tongue and teaches him Torah. If he does not teach him Torah it is as though he had buried him.' Later halakhic injunctions are equally specific. 'As soon as the child begins to talk, he should be taught the verses "Moses commanded us the Torah..." and "Hear O Israel..." His father should also teach him snatches of other verses, until he reaches the stage when he goes to school.'[21] Fathers who were *lamdanim* would also sometimes sit their small sons on their knees while they were themselves engaged in study. Thus, from an early age, babies became accustomed to hearing the sound of Hebrew words and to seeing the graphic form of Hebrew letters.[22]

The mode of linguistic instruction adopted in the *heder* constituted what appears to have been an extension of the child's 'natural' absorption of

Hebrew in his home. Only the younger children were taught word-by-word translations of the verses they studied; as they progressed in the classroom, none but the most difficult of words was translated. Moreover, although translation did dominate the elementary level,

> the mode of heder instruction was akin to the natural form in which languages are acquired. The heder system did not arrange words and grammatical rules in mechanical tables, and in fact did not even formally teach the language itself. Rather, it introduced the child to the sources...his soul absorbed the words involuntarily and his mind structured the rules piecemeal and of its own volition. The words were not absorbed individually but as component units in a series of verses, with all their associated emotions.[23]

Taught thus, the language of the Book was not dissociated from everyday life. Instead, the approach was integrative. This played a crucial role in forming the Jew's basic attitude to Hebrew as an integral part of his life, and stands in contrast to an attitude based on the conception of language as an independent entity.[24] The manner in which Hebrew was woven into Yiddish provides further evidence of its vividness and its links with the vernacular.[25] Particularly noteworthy is the frequency with which original Hebrew citations are directly translated into Yiddish. This is evidence of the degree to which Hebrew phrases had come to constitute at least part of the Jews' linguistic framework. It also indicates that, for the Jew, Hebrew remained vivid in a sense not commonly applicable to 'dead classical languages'.

In the traditional Jewish world from which the *maskilim* emerged, therefore, Hebrew was indeed the language of the book. Because that world regarded the Book as a 'living' entity it endowed the language of the Book with the same attribute. The *maskilim* shared that attitude, and for most of the *Haskalah* period their use of language was characterised by a conviction that Hebrew was not extinct but alive. That explains why N. H. Wessely and Adam Ha-kohen, for instance, frequently resort to literary similes, for as far as they were concerned, such similes were more vivid than was their actual physical environment. Mapu's language exhibits similar influences in his use of shades of Hebrew to express the various characteristics of his heroes and their degrees of status.[26]

All such techniques were made possible by the attitude of the *lamdanim* towards the language of the Book. It was precisely the same attitude which ensured the receptivity of the *Haskalah* audience to works written in Hebrew. Today, the situation is very different. Massive shifts have taken place in the strategies of the Hebrew interpretive community. Consequently, the contemporary reader considers the poetry of Wessely and Adam Ha-kohen to be colourless,[27] and fails to appreciate the multiplicity of linguistic shades in Mapu's prose.[28]

As I have already suggested, the requirement that two parallel texts be read simultaneously provides a key to the understanding of *Haskalah* poetry. This is particularly true of such early examples of the genre as the works of Wessely and Adam Ha-kohen. 'Simultaneous reading' compels the reader to compare the poem with the biblical passage to which he is referred and illuminates the differences between the outlooks articulated in the two texts. This facilitates a full understanding of the poems. Only when readers adopt this technique can they truly appreciate the revolutionary implications of the ostensibly 'traditional' texts composed by Wessely and Adam Ha-kohen.

As first-generation *Haskalah* poets, Wessely and Adam Ha-kohen had to overcome several problems. Not only did they have to create new Hebrew poetic forms virtually from scratch, they had also to establish a means of contact with their readership. After all, the audience for Hebrew *Haskalah* writings was embryonic and could only be 'mobilized' by an approach to the traditional orthodox community to which most potential readers of *Haskalah* still belonged. That is why the writings of Wessely and Adam Ha-kohen are so much dominated by argumentation designed to legitimize *Haskalah* thought and methods. Wessely's essay *Divrei shalom ve-emet* (1782), for instance, constitutes an attempt on his part to convince his readers of the importance of the European Enlightenment, of the new education, and of the need to integrate within European society.

The technique of persuasion employed by the earliest *maskilim* was bilateral. While projecting their approach as entirely consonant with traditional Judaism, they blurred the extent to which it was revolutionary. The poetry of Wessely and Adam Ha-kohen exemplifies that technique. Ostensibly its character is traditionally Jewish: the subject matter is drawn from either the Bible or the world of religious experience; the poems are laced with phrases which express Divine worship. Such techniques enable the poet to establish a basis of communication with his contemporary reader who still has two feet firmly planted in the world of religion. Concurrently, however, the poet also supplies interested readers with a code for an alternative reading of the work, to be gained by its close comparison with a parallel Biblical passage. A simultaneous reading of the two texts reveals the extent of their difference. It illustrates, in a way not as apparent from an independent reading of the poem itself, the revolutionary nature of the *maskil's* approach.

What allows the poet to rely upon his readers' appreciation of the requirement for 'simultaneous reading' is his knowledge that this is the way they conventionally study *all* texts. Like them, he too belongs to the interpretive community of *lamdanim* and he is able to exploit for his own purposes his acquaintance with its dependence on 'simultaneous reading' as a primary reading technique.

Simultaneous reading involves interrupting the linear reading of a single text by frequent references to another source. The roots of that technique, like those of the traditional Jewish attitude to Hebrew, can be traced to the earliest years of a Jewish child's education, when children first began to study the Pentateuch (*Humash*).

Two educational tools explicitly incorporated simultaneous reading into elementary instruction in the Pentateuch. The first—and, from the child's standpoint, the earliest—involved translating passages of the Pentateuch verse-by-verse into Yiddish:

> The teacher [*melamed*] reads a verse, translating each word individually...Once he has completed the entire verse he repeats its content in Yiddish. Sometimes, the teacher supplements his interpretation of the words by reference to rabbinic parables.[29]

In other words, the child has not absorbed the biblical text straightforwardly. Linear reading is interrupted by comparison with the translation, and sometimes by added references to other (midrashic) sources.

The second, and more advanced, instructional tool which incorporated simultaneous reading into elementary education was the study of the *Humash* together with Rashi. The latter text was read side by side with each Biblical verse. Indeed, 'the people felt Rashi to be the brother of our Holy Torah; schoolchildren, together with all Israel, learn the Torah only with his commentary.'[30]

The two methodologies of textual reading became ingrained. So much so that the Jew continued to employ this methodology when, as an adult, he reviewed the weekly Pentateuchal portion every Sabbath. 'And the adults review it twice in the original Hebrew and once in translation, and study it again on the Sabbath with Rashi and other commentaries.'[31]

The 'simultaneous' mode of reading was further intensified through the study of the Talmud, especially amongst the *lamdanim* for whom study of that text was a primary occupation. No page of Talmud was ever studied in linear fashion; instead, each of its sentences or short paragraphs was interpreted by simultaneous references to later rabbinic commentaries. When those commentaries supplied conflicting interpretations of the passage, simultaneous reading had to involve concurrent comparisons of three or more different texts.

The very layout of classical Hebrew books itself encouraged the traditional Jewish predisposition towards simultaneous reading. In all the standard printings, the talmudic text never stands in isolation; it is surrounded by various interpretive commentaries and super-commentaries (by Rashi, the Tosafists, Rabbenu Hananel, and so on) and several marginal glossaries and references (for example: *Ein mishpat*; *Masoret ha-shas*; *Hagahot ha-bakh*; *Hagahot ha-grah*). *Lamdanim* would supplement all of these by consulting additional sources, some of which were appended to the end of the talmudic volume (the *Rif*, the *Maharshah* and so on), others located in independent works (notably, Maimonides and the *Shulhan 'arukh*). Similarly, standard editions of the *Humash* appended at least Rashi's commentary to the biblical text; more scholarly versions, such as those used by *lamdanim*, also printed alongside or beneath the source several other commentaries such as *Metzudat David*; *Metzudat tziyyon*; Ibn-Ezra; Ramban and Sforno.

For the *lamdanim* the strategy of simultaneous reading must have been second nature. They would not have thought it at all possible to attain a full understanding of a source-text simply by a linear reading and without recourse to additional texts with which it had to be read simultaneously. I suggest that such was also the basic predisposition of the *Haskalah* interpretive community. It determined the mode of *Haskalah* reading and composition, even when the text was no longer religious or halakhic in content, but modern and literary.

Haskalah literature must be read in the light of its own assumptions, just as it was originally read and understood by the interpretive community from which it emerged. Such a reading reveals a denominator common to several primary techniques of *Haskalah* composition: it reflected and was dependent upon the conventional reading strategies of the *lamdanim*. In the light of this I suggest that the 'lamdanic code' provides an additional key to *Haskalah* literature, and one which is essential if we are fully to comprehend it.

Admittedly, this suggestion does raise problems. As a result of the vast cultural divide which separates them from the interpretive community of the maskilim, most contemporary readers of Hebrew literature are totally unfamiliar with that code and can therefore hardly be expected to make full use of it. Hopefully, however, merely to indicate the existence of such a code is to make some small contribution to a more accurate appreciation of the literature to which it has to be applied.

Notes

1. After writing this article, I heard the subject independently alluded to in lectures delivered by Professor B. Harshav (at the 1991 inter-university congress on Hebrew Literature, Bar-Ilan) and Dr. David Patterson (at the 1991

Smolenskin conference held in Oxford). My own discussion is somewhat more expansive.
2. S. Fish, *Is There a Text in This Class?* (Cambridge, Mass, 1980), p. 171. In the same work, the concept of the 'interpretive community' is summarised in the chapter entitled: 'Interpreting the Variorum'. See also the article 'Change' in Fish's, *Doing What Comes Naturally* (Duke, 1989).
3. See, P. Mussen, et. al., *Child Development and Personality* (6th edition, New York, 1984), p. 186-7.
4. D. Biale, 'Childhood, Marriage and the Family in the Eastern European Jewish Enlightenment', in S. M. Cohen and P. Hyman, eds, *The Jewish Family: Myths and Reality* (New York, 1986), pp. 45-61. Biale shows that the *Haskalah*, like all contemporary ideological movements, was generated by young people.
5. I. Etkes, 'Marriage and Torah Study Among the *Lomdim* in Lithuania in the Nineteenth Century', in D. Kraemer, ed., *The Jewish Family: Metaphor and Memory* (New York, 1989), p. 154.
6. Analysis of the biographical materials provided by Klausner, for instance, shows each of the *maskilim* to have been born into a family of *lamdanim*. Moreover, while still young, each had shown himself to be an unusually talented student in the *heder* and *yeshivah*. That particular trait among the *maskilim* is also emphasised in Biale's depiction (above n. 4, p. 48).
7. On learning as an ideal in all Jewish societies, and especially in that of the élite comprised of 'fine Jews' (*sheine yidden*), see the chapter entitled 'The Eastern Wall' in M. Zborowski and E. Herzog, *Life is With People* (9th edition, New York, 1972), pp. 71-87.
8. D. Meron, 'Le-reka ha-mevukhah ba-sifrut ha-'ivrit be-reishit ha-me'ah ha-'esrim', in B. Bashevitz and M. Peri, eds., *Sefer ha-yovel le-Shim'on Halkin* (Jerusalem, 1975), p. 447.
9. *Ayit tsavu'a* in *Kol kitvei Mapu* (Tel Aviv, 1964), p. 322.
10. Fish, *Doing What Comes Naturally*, pp. 141-60.
11. In the introduction to the new edition of his works, 1884.
12. As summarised in *Kitzur shulhan 'arukh* (S. Ganzfried; Jerusalem, 1975), 28:2.
13. S. J. Agnon, *The Bridal Canopy* (trans. I. M. Lask; London, 1968), p. 52.
14. 'Safiah', chap. 13, *Kol kitvei Bialik* (Tel Aviv, 1957), p. 159.
15. 'Al ha-sefer', *Kitvei M. Y. Bin-Gurion*, Part 2 (Tel Aviv, 1936), p. 62.
16. Ahad Ha-'am, 'Torah she-ba-lev', *Al parashat derakhim*, Part I (Berlin, 1921).
17. Translation from the Yiddish into Hebrew in: Z. Sparstein, *Toledot ha-hinukh be-Yisrael*, Part I (New York, 1945), p. 92.
18. *Kitvei M. Z. Feierberg* (Tel Aviv, 1949), p. 92.
19. A. Even-Zohar, 'Le-birur mahutah ve-tifkudah shel lashon ha-sifrut ha-yafah ba-diglossia', *Ha-sifrut*, 2:2 (1970), pp. 286-302. In that article, Even-Zohar identifies pre-twentieth century Hebrew as a classical - and hence dead—language. A contrary view, which summarises the claim that Hebrew was a living language in the diglossia of the traditional eastern European Jew in B. Harshav, 'Al tivah shel leshon Yiddish be-hekshereihah ha-historiyim. Masat mavo', *Ha-sifrut*, new series, 10:3-4 (Summer, 1986), pp. 5-45.
20. Mussen, *Child Development*, p. 212.
21. *Kitzur shulhan 'arukh*, 165:10.

22. Zborowski and Herzog, *Life is With People*, p. 85.
23. A. M. Lifshitz, 'Ha-heder: tekhunato ve-shitato', *Ha-tekufah*, 7 (Spring 1920), p. 315.
24. The two approaches are contrasted in M. Nahir, 'Gishah holistit le-hora'at ha-lashon ha-'ivrit', in E. Elstein, ed., *Ha-'ivrit ke-koah me'ahed ba-hinukh ha-yehudi ba-tefutzot* (Tel Aviv, 1989), p. 31-44.
25. Yiddish is laced with many Hebrew words. In *Ha-psykhologiyah shel ha-keriyah* (Jerusalem, 1977), p. 97, R. Belgoor cites Mehlman who lists some thousand common Yiddish words whose form and meaning correspond to that of Hebrew. Moreover, between 3-4,000 Yiddish expressions are unknown in European languages, and derive from Hebrew sources. For examples, see W. Chomsky, *Hebrew. The Eternal Language* (Philadelphia, 1957), p. 226.
26. This issue is discussed in the chapter entitled 'Givun leshoni ke-bitui le-kotviut romansit be-'ayit tzavu'a', in my book, *Tzevuyim ve-yesharim, eliliyot ve-liliyot* (Tel Aviv, 1991).
27. See, for example, the description of Wessely's poetry in A. Sha'anan, *Ha-sifrut ha-'ivrit ha-hadashah li-zrameihah*, vol. 1 (Tel Aviv, 1967), p. 66.
28. Even-Zohar depicts 'the use of a diachronic framework as though it were a synchronic one' as one of the *Haskalah* modes of compensation for the absence of a Hebrew vernacular. In my opinion, Mapu's clever and rich use of this mode is not 'compensatory'; rather it illustrates the vividness of the language of the Book for both the author and his readership.
29. Sparstein (above, n. 17), p. 101.
30. R. Nahman of Bratslav, cited in Lifshitz (above, n. 23), p. 335.
31. Lifshitz, p. 325.

NOTIONS OF YIDDISH

Dovid Katz

'A language' is a social, psychological and political notion. Socially, the term implies group identity and a sense of belonging ('speak the same language'). Psychologically, the word evokes self-confidence, collective ego and a sense of security. Politically, it implies power and authority (nations have 'languages'). The old adage that 'a language is a dialect with an army and a navy' is not far off the mark.

In the usual historical progression, the political victors or the powers that be in a society create 'The Language' from the myriad varieties actually spoken and written, give it a name, standardise it, and teach it to successive generations. The policy becomes a success when a population accepts 'its language' as one of the natural givens of the universe, along with the sun, the moon and the stars. The incredible degree of political manipulation required has been exposed and chronicled by Roy Harris, with special reference to the rise of the notion 'English'.[1]

The circumstances which come into play in the history of Yiddish are inherently different from those of most documented languages. Yiddish may therefore offer an intriguing case history of what can happen where there is a highly elaborate verbal and written culture, but no army, no navy, and steep competition from other languages.

Yiddish is unique to the Jewish civilization known as Ashkenaz, which rose along the banks of the Rhine and the Danube around a thousand years ago. Until the eighteenth century, all Ashkenazim were by definition Yiddish speakers. The notion Ashkenaz, originally a geographic concept akin to 'Germany', became a Jewish cultural concept encompassing all of the territories of central and eastern Europe settled by Ashkenazim. During the sixteenth and seventeenth centuries, that territory stretched from Amsterdam at its northwest and Italy at its southwest, deep into Russia in the east, making for one of the largest speech territories in the history of Europe. But that is linguistic history. Here I shall attempt to chart the course not of Yiddish but of the notion 'Yiddish'. This essay is affectionately dedicated to Dr David Patterson, who convinced me some years ago that to establish Yiddish studies at Oxford would serve to enhance that notion internationally in the late twentieth century. But that is a matter for twenty-first century Yiddish scholarship.

Ashkenaz had (and in traditional, principally, hasidic communities, continues to have) not one, not two, but three Jewish languages (all in addition, of course, to varying degrees of command of one or more local non-Jewish languages). The internal trilingualism of Ashkenaz comprises Yiddish, Hebrew and Aramaic.[2] Yiddish was everybody's native language and the universal vernacular used in the intimacy of the home at one end of the language-use spectrum, and in the *yeshivah* and rabbinical court at the other. In contrast with Christian Europe, there were no Hebrew or Aramaic speaking schools or academies to parallel Latin-speaking schools. In short, only Yiddish was spoken. Hebrew and Aramaic were prayed, recited, quoted, declaimed and written.

The ability to write Hebrew (as opposed to the ability to read from the Pentateuch or the prayer book) was limited to a small minority of educated males who used it in communal documents, responsa, works on Jewish law and custom, and so on.

The ability to write Aramaic was even more limited to a smaller minority of top scholars who wrote treatises on the two culturally 'highest' endeavours in the eyes of the society in question: talmudic works on the intricacies of Jewish law, and kabbalistic works on Jewish mysticism.

It would be tempting to use trendy sociolinguistic concepts, such as High (or 'H') and Low (or 'L') to characterize the functional and conceptual interrelationships, but to do so would miss the point. We want to discover, or at least to hypothesise, how these notions were viewed through the eyes of the society in question. To start with, the presence of 'High' does not imply the presence of 'Low'. Yiddish was universal, Hebrew more limited and used for more prestigious purposes, Aramaic more limited still, used for more prestigious purposes still. But these highs did not correspond to any lows. The everyday vernacular, with stylistic differentiation, of course, was used by the simplest member of society and the greatest scholar alike.

The point of all this is that Ashkenazic trilingualism was natural. No governments, no language academies, no armies and no navies. The roles of Hebrew and Aramaic were inherited from the ancient near east into Ashkenaz.

The new vernacular, Yiddish, an intricate linguistic fusion of these Semitic elements with a uniquely modified Germanic component, was 'just spoken' and 'just written'. Initially, it did not have a fixed name.

Sadly, no records of the vernacular survive from the earliest centuries of Ashkenazic settlement. There are, however, proper names from 1096 (appearing in martyrs' lists following the first Crusade), a single sentence dated 1272 (in the famed Worms festival prayer book, now in Jerusalem), and an extensive literary manuscript dated 1382 (the Cambridge Codex, brought to England by Solomon Schechter as part of the Cairo Genizah collection). These and other monuments tell us precious little of attitudes toward the vernacular.

The earliest comments on the language occur in rabbinic legal treatises where the vernacular is at issue for this or that legal reason. The natural, prepolitical state of affairs is evident from the lack of rancour. Zalmen of St. Goar, faithful pupil of the Maharil (Yankev ben Moyshe Molin, c. 1360-1427), reports that his master complained about Yiddish songs on the thirteen Maimonidean principles of the Jewish faith:

> And he [the Maharil] said: As for stanzas and rhymes in *Loshn Ashkenaz* ['the language of Ashkenaz'] on the Unity [of God] and on the Thirteen Principles [of Maimonides], I wish they would not be written! For most of the ignorant people think that all the commandments hinge on this and they forego a number of positive and negative commandments, such as *tsitsis* [fringed garment worn under the shirt], *tfiln* [phylacteries], the study of the Torah and more, thinking they have fulfilled their obligation by singing these rhymes with conviction. But in these rhymes, no more is implied than the central point of the Jewish religion, and not a single one of the 613 commandments which Jews are obliged to fulfill.[3]

At first glance, the Maharil's complaint seems to suggest the existence of some sort of 'non-orthodox Yiddish culture' (to phrase it anachronistically) of which he does not approve. It is, however, the replacement that is offensive, not the linguistic medium. That is treated neutrally.

As for the name of the language, the Maharil uses *Loshn Ashkenaz*. One also encounters *leshoyneynu* ('our language'), *taytsh* ('translation language'), and, at least from 1597, *yidish* ('Jewish', 'Yiddish') as well.[4] The variety of names suggests the absence of the kind of unanimous linguistic consciousness that is implied by the political notion 'a language'. Now it is known, of course, that the linguistic variety used by the most remote tribe is structurally speaking every bit as sophisticated as Oxford English. The primeval state of 'Yiddish consciousness' in early Ashkenaz is then one of neutral recognition of 'what it is that everyone speaks', with no champions and no opponents. Early ambiguities about the concept 'Yiddish literature' strengthen this perception.[5]

An emerging Yiddish consciousness becomes evident from the vast number of comments on specific Yiddish words or phrases in two contexts which gave the rabbis occasion to write of Yiddish. One concerns the need, according to Jewish law, to transcribe a witness's testimony in a Jewish court of law in his exact words, making way for the preservation of linguistically accurate renderings of Old Yiddish. These have often been hailed as the oldest monuments of colloquial Yiddish.[6] They stand in sharp contradistinction to 'literary works' whose authors did their best to approach local or literary German, albeit in Jewish script.[7]

The second rabbinic context entails discussion of the precise forms of personal names to be used in writs of divorce, where Jewish law demands the writ include the name used in everyday life alongside the classical Hebrew name of the individual (e.g. 'Dov known as Ber'). This concern made way for the beginnings of Yiddish dialectology.[8]

The need for guidance on the precise morphology and spelling of names in writs of divorce also led the rabbis to pioneer the standardization of written Yiddish. Principles of modern Yiddish spelling, often praised for being nearly perfectly 'phonetic',[9] go back to the sharp legal minds of the rabbis. In standardizing the spelling of a Yiddish name, Isserlin (Yisroel ben Pesakhye, c. 1390—1460) weighed and counterweighed the univalency principle (one letter for one sound) against the dialectological principle (readability in all dialect areas).[10]

The rabbis frequently had to decide, again, in writs of divorce, how to write local variants of names that differ markedly from versions popular in other areas, or from the usual written versions. The Levush (Mordechai Yafe, c. 1535-1612) recorded that female forenames Rekhlin and Freydlin turn up elsewhere as Rekhl and Freydl and took note of the variants *Leyb, Leybe* and *Leyve* of the male forename. He ruled in favour of the local variant.

> One follows the language of the people in the country in which the divorce is issued and there is no need to be concerned with the way these names or nicknames appear written in books.[11]

The Levush's ruling in favour of local morphology was balanced by his finding in favour of standardization where differences are limited to spelling. He noted, for example, that names that do not derive from Hebrew and end in a vowel, should be written with aleph word-finally.

Issues interrelating dialectology and standardization were bound to result in the emergence of 'prestige dialects'. The Maharil was asked how to spell the name of the river Danube in a divorce writ, with *vov* at the end, giving *Donou* or *Donau*, or with double *yud*, giving *Donay*. He had before him one writ from Austria using vov. Another, sent from Regensburg to Prague with double *yud* had been 'returned to sender' with the query 'But I have seen that the wise men of Austria write Donou! What should in fact be written?' The Regensburg rabbis sent it back confirming double *yud*, 'as we have written it'. The Maharil ruled in their favour on the grounds that 'the people of Regensburg have a more correct language than the people of Austria'. Old Yiddish thus had its 'Regensburg Yiddish' just as modern Yiddish has its 'Vilna Yiddish'.[12]

In legal literature, *Loshn Ashkenaz* became the most frequent term for Yiddish. Hence the language 'had a name' and therefore 'existed' in group consciousness, and crucially, in the consciousness of the writers who were, after all, the intellectuals and cultural leaders, to use modern words, of the society in which they lived.

From the sixteenth century onward, there was a distinct movement for the expansion of Yiddish functions into realms traditionally reserved for Hebrew and Aramaic. The chief battleground was prayer, and the argument, often quoted from the *Seyfer khasidim*, the classic work attributed to Judah of Regensburg (c. 1150-1217), was that whoever does not understand Hebrew should preferably pray in a language he understands.[13] This theme recurs in prayer and ethical works from the sixteenth, seventeenth and early eighteenth centuries. The most famous introduction to a Yiddish prayerbook is probably Yosef bar Yokor's, in 1544. He went so far as to say that 'Those who want to pray in Hebrew without understanding a single word are in my view plain fools'.[14] The 1629 Prague festival prayer book contains the following introduction, printed on the reverse side of the title page:

> Prayer without meaningful intent is like a body with no soul. Therefore, when one prays before God blessed be He, and does not pray with all his heart, then that prayer is likened to a body of a person that has no life in it. Our sages of blessed memory therefore said that every Jew who wishes his prayers to be heard on the High Holy Days should read the prayers before the New Year and Yom Kippur to become accustomed to them and know what he is saying. Everyone should take as an example the case of a man who has to speak to a king (who is mere flesh and blood) concerning his life or property. He makes sure to consider carefully what he will say so that he does not stumble, and that

> he understands what it is he is saying. All the more so before the King of all kings, the Holy One blessed be He. Where the concern is every person's body, property and soul, it is of the utmost importance that a person knows what he is saying [...].[15]

Yiddish prayerbooks, and especially *tkhines* for women, were used extensively in Ashkenaz, and Yiddish did indeed 'capture' a considerable portion of the erstwhile Hebrew-and-Aramaic-only realm of prayer.[16]

One fellow went too far. He was Aaron ben Shmuel of Hergershausen who published a lame translation of the prayers in 1709. In his preface, in which he admitted his lack of Hebrew education, he argued that prayers should be in the mother tongue, citing the use of Aramaic in the Talmud. Everything about the book, including its appearance (the use of square Hebrew characters with vowel points rather than the special pre-nineteenth century Yiddish mashkit font) flew in the face of tradition. In 1830 a huge stock of copies was found in an attic. Rabbinic authorities apparently forbade its use. Viciously torn copies have also turned up.[17]

One of the most complex sagas is the century-long attempt to publish a Yiddish translation of the *Zohar*, the central work of Jewish mysticism, traditionally limited to learned Jewish males over the age of forty. Zelig, a rabbi near Lublin, began his translation in 1601. His son Yosi sought to publish it and accumulated a large number of rabbinic approbations, which were apparently lost during the Chmielnitzki pogroms of 1648 and 1649. Yosi's grandson Tsvi-Hirsh Khotsh finally published an edited version of his great grandfather's work, with the most 'secret' passages omitted, in 1711.[18]

The popular kabbalist Yekhiel-Mikhl Epshteyn devoted a chapter of his *Book of the Upright Path to the World to Come* (1704), to a spirited defense of prayer in Yiddish for those who do not understand Hebrew. His arguments include the following:

> When a man does not understand Hebrew and prays in a language that he understands with all his heart [...], such a prayer is for God, blessed be He, much more pleasing because it comes form the heart [...] One word that is understood does more good than a hundred that are not understood [...] People who do not understand Hebrew should say everything in Taytsh, for what one understands [...] one offers with complete devotion. That prayer will certainly be accepted. Moreover, women have meek hearts and are apt to start weeping immediately.[19]

On the level of psychological and spiritual sanctity, I for one believe that Epshteyn and all the others are wrong. To pray in an ancient hallowed language, to believe in the sanctity of every word and every letter, to believe that one is praying from the same sacred text and in the same pronunciation as one's forefathers, make for a spiritual 'high' vastly in excess of using the unromantic blasé of everyday life. Sprucing up the vernacular with *you*-to-*thou* type devices cannot compete with 'the real thing', although Yiddish prayers were generally composed in a highly specific sacred Yiddish style, which came to be known as *Ivri-taytsh*. It revelled in archaisms and neologisms crafted to consciously remove the text from the everyday. The special variant used for Bible translations has been the subject of several studies.[20] There is potential for fieldwork. How many learned Jews in traditional communities, who are capable of understanding Hebrew and Aramaic, actually concentrate during most of a prayer service, on the dictionary meaning of words rather than overall devotional expression?

Some modern scholars have seen 'a movement for Yiddish' in the various defenses of prayer in Yiddish.[21] Others have disputed this, charging anachronistic application of late nineteenth and twentieth century notions of 'Yiddishism' back onto Old Ashkenaz.[22] My own feeling is that there was no pre-modern 'Yiddishist movement'. There were, rather, converging religious, social and economic factors in favour of Yiddish moving in on turf previously exclusive to Hebrew, and, like all natural languages in steady use in a community over many centuries, functions expanded in the course of things. On the front of religion, many rabbinic figures saw in prayer and ethical books in Yiddish a potential replacement for the secular books, based on medieval European epic romances, that had been so popular for centuries. Socially, many non-learned authors wanted status for themselves and for simple people, a sort of participation in sanctity beyond the carrying out of commandments. Economically, authors and publishers wanted to make profits, which by the very nature of the mass readership, would have vastly exceeded those for rabbinic books.

The anti-Semitic view of Yiddish is traditionally traced to Martin Luther's 1528 introduction to an edition of the *Liber vagatorum*. The first, undated, edition of that work appeared around 1510 under the title *Liber vagatorum. Der betler orden*. It is an anonymous guide to various sorts of beggars and vagabonds that sought to protect an unsuspecting public from deceitful beggars. It concludes with a brief vocabulary of Rotwelsch, the German underworld language, which did in fact draw heavily upon Hebrew and Yiddish. In the 1528 edition, entitled *Von der falschen Betler büeberey / Mit einer Vorrede Martini Luther*, Luther made the damning accusation that the Jewish elements in Rotwelsch demonstrate that the underworld language stems from the Jews.[23] This theme was picked up in some later dictionaries of *Rotwelsch*, but it was not until the eighteenth century that a copious anti-Jewish literature obsessed with Yiddish emerged.[24]

Dozens of pseudonymous German anti-Semitic works of the eighteenth century, many written by apostate Jews, focused on Yiddish. They were founded upon the premise that Yiddish is some sort of 'anti-Christian plot', and they set out to 'expose' Yiddish and the 'secrets of the Jews'. One of the earliest, an undated book that appeared around 1714 by one 'J.W.' is a bilingual dialogue (in transcribed Yiddish and German on facing pages to enable the reader to follow) between a simple Jew, 'Joune' (=Youne, modern Yiddish Yoyne, i.e. Jonah) and 'Rebbe Itzick', a corrupt rabbi who progressively leads him down the path of lust, sin, and anti-Christianity. The book is replete with the heartiest curses of early eighteenth century Western Yiddish.[25] Other authors used rather more imaginative pseudonyms. The 1733 dictionary published by 'Philoglottus' concludes with an epilogue (true to form, in Yiddish and German, both in German script) condemning the contemporary Jewish faith.[26] Bibliophilus's 1742 effort ends with a series of dialogues translated from 'Hebräo-barbarisch' into German.[27] German anti-Semitism looked upon Yiddish as the embodiment of Jewish cultural barbarism, the encapsulation of anti-Christian propaganda, the backbone of the underworld language, and in practical terms, a secret language created to cheat Christians. These claims surface and resurface throughout this eighteenth century literature.

There is probably no hate as intense as the self-hate inspired by one's haters, and when the Ashkenazim of Germany moved toward the non-Jewish culture of their country in the late eighteenth century, they moved away from being Ashkenazim and toward being 'German Jews', or, 'Germans of the mosaic faith', and the obliteration of Yiddish became a primary goal of the Berlin-centred *Haskalah* ('Enlightenment') movement. The Western Yiddish dialects of the German speaking lands were every bit as vilified as the Eastern Yiddish varieties in the Slavonic and Baltic countries. The various older names of the language, Yiddish included, were eschewed. A name, any name, conveys notions of existence and identity, both of which were being denied, and the language came to be described by the verb *mauscheln* and the noun *Jargon*, both lifted, cheerfully and without hesitation, from anti-Semitic parlance. Both terms are 'non-names' that avoid the ethnic or geographical properties of names of languages. Even these non-names were avoided in a second stage of battle where the description is reduced to something in the order of 'poor speech'. Naphtali Herz Wessely (1725-1805) had this to say:

> We ruin our reputation among the nations by being stammerers.
> It is well known that even a wise man well educated in the

sciences, who does not have a pure language, and does not know how to place his words into a sentence, is made into a mockery. All the more so the common man when he deals with officials and merchants and speaks a castrated language like us, the Jews of Germany and Poland. For he will attract mockery and scorn in their eyes, and he will be treated as a peasant and one who is despised by people. This is not the case for a man who knows how to speak properly and in good taste. He will find grace and honour in all who see him.[28]

Hopes for social and political integration were linked with linguistic assimilation, and the ultimate fate of German Jewry reflects all too tragically upon these hopes. Although most Western Ashkenazim did in fact become German speakers of the Jewish faith, pockets of Western Yiddish survived well into the twentieth century.[29]

Haskalah opposition to Yiddish was transplanted to the Hebraist movement in Eastern Europe, where, in the early years of this century, the proponents of Yiddish and those of Hebrew were engaged in the bitter language controversy (the *riv leshoynes* to the Yiddishists, *riv leshonot* to the Hebraists), which flared with particular bitterness in the years immediately following the Chernowitz conference of 1908. That conference proclaimed Yiddish to be a national Jewish language and was followed by polemics on all sides.[30]

In Palestine, and later in Israel, a massive campaign was centrally coordinated to eradicate Yiddish, which became for Hebraists an object of hate vastly in excess of the German-Jewish antipathy. Anti-Yiddish measures included laws against Yiddish newspapers and periodicals, and gangs known as *gedudei meginei ha-safah* ('Regiments of Defenders of the Language') which stoned Yiddish writers, firebombed Yiddish publishers and broke the windows of shops selling Yiddish papers.[31] One of the curiosities of the battle was the Yiddish literary journal in Tel Aviv that 'beat the law' against Yiddish periodicals, in 1929, by calling the first issue *Eyns* ('One'), the second *Tsvey* ('Two'), and the third (after the authorities got wise to the scheme), *Tsvishn tsvey un dray* ('Between Two and Three'). The Hebraist movement, alongside its astounding success in establishing modern spoken Hebrew, succeeded in creating a national feeling of shame about Yiddish, fostering notions that it was ugly, dead, a ghetto-language, did not exist, had no literature and more. The greater degree of hate stemmed from the circumstance that nearly all the scholars and cultural and political leaders who revived modern Hebrew were themselves native Yiddish speakers, whose early years had been spent in the linguistically thriving Yiddish speaking civilization of Eastern Europe. This triggered characteristic self-hate reactions, in contrast to their German-Jewish Haskalah forebears who were born into communities where Yiddish was very weak or had largely disappeared.

As Freud often pointed out, hate and love are kindred emotions given to ambiguity and, at times, interchangeability. When the ideas of the *Haskalah* moved eastward, they found their champions in the East European Pale of Settlement. Among them was Yitskhok-Ber Levinzon (Isaac Baer Levinsohn), who, like Wessely before him, cited a Talmudic parallel of those who advocated Hebrew or Greek as opposed to the Jewish Aramaic then spoken. Levinzon went on to ask: 'And so we must say in this country: 'Why Judeo-German? Either pure German, or Russian!'[32]

But history is full of ironies, and the beginnings of the use of Yiddish as a modern literary language, go back to one of Mendelssohn's pupils who went back east to spread Haskalah. He was Mendl Lefin, also called Satanover, whose anonymous Yiddish translation of the book of Proverbs appeared in Tarnopol around 1814. Unlike anything that had appeared before then, the translation was penned in the local Ukrainian dialect of East European Yiddish. For the first time, a kind of written Yiddish capable of being a modern literary language, appeared in print. Previously, Yiddish books were written in special forms of the language much more removed from everday use than the usual writing-to-speaking gap.[33] Moreover, Lefin's book appeared in square Hebrew type and, unlike Aaron ben Shmuel's experiment a century earlier, Lefin's work signalled the death knell of the old *mashkit* typeface which was psychologically associated with the premodern genres of Yiddish literature.

The *maskilim* attacked Lefin bitterly. The assault was led by Tuvia Feder who compiled a pamphlet in Hebrew, challenging Lefin to explain why he had exchanged his silk robe (i.e. German) for rags (i.e. Yiddish), and why he had hurled King Solomon's Proverbs 'into the mud'. Feder's pamphlet proceeds to a mini-drama providing a glimpse into Heaven, where an incredulous, otherworldly Mendelssohn finds it difficult to believe that his faithful pupil so betrayed the cause after his death by publishing in Yiddish. The play is entitled 'Conversation in the Land of the Living' and duly includes an intervention from the 'Voice of God'.

Various appeals to Feder from Lefin's friends, plus a hundred ruble 'reimbursement for expenses', led Feder to withdraw the pamphlet from the press. It did not appear until long after the death of the protagonists.[34] It was, however, in wide circulation in maskilic circles and attracted a reply from Yankev Shmuel Bik, who leapt to Lefin's defense. Bik compared Lefin's achievements to Benjamin Franklin's in Philadelphia, and noted that the greatest rabbinic minds of Ashkenaz including the Gaon of Vilna 'spoke, thought, and taught' in Yiddish. He went on to argue that English and French were equally mixed and derived from various other languages.[35]

The *Haskalah* embraced modernization, participation in the culture of the country where one resided, and of course, social and political reform that would provide Jews with equal rights. It was in the context of striving for all these goals, that the strategy evolved of ridding Jews of their culture (language, clothing, and so on) while enabling them to retain their religion. What the Berlin *maskilim* could not have foreseen was that the very hated language they sought to eradicate, was itself capable of rapid transformation into a language of world literature whose works would rival or surpass those of the host nations. In all fairness, it took a *Haskalah* outlook to accomplish that feat too.

Lefin was followed, in the first half of the nineteenth century, by others who used East European Yiddish in their didactic books on everything from medicine to the story of Christopher Columbus.[36] Now these *maskilim* saw they needed Yiddish to reach the millions of Jews in the Pale of Settlement. The most momentous single turnaround from using Yiddish to 'enlighten the masses' to developing it as the language of a new literature was that of Sh. Y. Abramovitsh. The Hebrew-writing *maskil* became Mendele Moykher Sforim, known as the 'grandfather of modern Yiddish literature'. He made his Yiddish début in Alexander Zederbaum's *Kol mevaser*, in the issue of 24 November 1864, which is regarded as the symbolic birthdate of modern Yiddish literature.

Tradition has it that it was Yehoyshue-Mordkhe (or Shie-Mordkhe) Lifshitz who talked Zederbaum into launching a modern Yiddish weekly in 1862, and Abramovitsh to turning his pen to Yiddish in 1864. To the point here is that Lifshitz was the first conscious 'Yiddishist' who had in his own mind centered the notion 'Yiddish' as a cultural object inspiring love and respect. Lifshitz went on to compile the first two sophisticated dictionaries of modern Yiddish.[37]

Sublimation of hate and love relationships vis-à-vis language is of course not unique to Yiddish, but Yiddish is an unusually salient example. For the Berlin *maskilim*, Yiddish was the hated parent. For some of the east European followers of *Haskalah*, it was more of a 'logical rejection' than a true hate; hence the easterners were able to modernize and refine the language as an instrument of modern literary and cultural movements. The difference between west and east stemmed in part from the very different objective status of the language in each of the areas. In the west, Yiddish had been in demographic and literary decline well before the Berlin *Haskalah*.

In the Slavonic and Baltic lands, Yiddish was experiencing unprecedented demographic and literary growth.

The reaction to the *Haskalah* position was a pro-Yiddish stance, which was, in its own way, itself an offshoot of *Haskalah* insofar as it advocated a 'modern' (that is, Western style) culture, entailing the notions 'literature', 'education', 'press', and more. The title of Lifshitz's classic 1863 defense of Yiddish was, innocuously enough, 'The Four Classes'. After going through inanimate objects, plants, animals and humans, he shifts to the human attribute of speech and introduces his bombshell (in the terms of the day): use of the term *di yidishe shprakh* ('the Yiddish language') in a *Haskalah* newspaper. Lifshitz went on to say:

> The Yiddish language is our mother tongue [...], and in the end all I hear is people insulting her and making fun of her. People say: She is corrupt! I must confess that I do not begin to understand with what sort of logic one can call 'corrupt' a language, in which many thousands of people, an entire nation, live and thrive. It is appropriate to use the word 'corrupt' of a thing which was once better and has been ruined. But whence it is inferred that other languages were at their beginning better? Were they then given on Mount Sinai? They too, like our language, derive from various other languages. Why are they not called 'corrupt'?[38]

The movement for Yiddish gave rise to a new field of scholarship. Polemics gradually turned to linguistic science in a succession of seminal works, including a pamphlet in Hebrew by Alexander Harkavy in 1885, a study in German by Philip Mansch in 1888-1890, and finally, the sensational paper in Yiddish read by Matisyohu Mieses at the first Yiddish language conference in Chernowitz in 1908.[39] The turning point came in 1913 when the conceptual 'centering' of Yiddish was completed by Ber Borokhov, the founder of modern Yiddish linguistics. He proclaimed philology to be a 'national science', that is, the scholarly component of the sociocultural rise of Yiddish.[40] To put the finishing touch on 'modern languagehood', he declared that standard Yiddish pronunciation was based upon the dialect of Vilna, thereby codifying the dialect that has, in most of its features, become the equivalent of 'Queen's English'. And thus, in a stroke, 'Yiddish' had all the attributes of 'English' or 'French' or 'Russian'.[41]

The notion 'Yiddish' was evolved from an early history of neutrality through to functional expansion, to an object of hate and an object of love. Today the notion 'Yiddish' is often accepted uncritically but even in the

1990s, its existence is occasionally denied. The proportion of deniers in Israel is probably much higher than anywhere else in view of the relative recency of an intense campaign to eradicate the language. This last claim can only be substantiated or refuted by fieldwork.

Traditional Orthodoxy (a term intended to exclude 'neo-Orthodoxy', the combining of observance of religious precepts with linguistic and cultural assimilation) went about, and continues to go about its life, largely oblivious to many of the battles and emotions of the modernisers. The pro-Yiddish ideology of traditional (and today, principally, hasidic), Orthodox groups has two historical sources. The first is traditional hasidism with its emphasis on every person's direct communication with God and its implicit elevation of Yiddish to a status of sanctity. The Yiddish versions of two of its most treasured works became classic (Nakhmen Bratslaver's *Sipurey mayses* and the *Shivkhey habesht*, both first published c. 1815).

The second strand, especially strong among Hungarian-origin hasidim, goes back to the Khsam Soyfer (Rabbi Moyshe Shrayber / Moses Sofer, 1762-1839), who led the battle against both the reform movement and neo-Orthodoxy. In a book in Yiddish, he went so far as to say:

> And you must not think that what is written in this book reflects only hasidism. It is, as all the books we have written, no more than is written in the *Shulkhn orukh* [*Shulkhan 'arukh*, Joseph Karo's Code of Jewish Law]. We bring evil upon the world by abandoning the Yiddish language and conducting ourselves as the Gentiles. It says in the *Shulkhn orukh, in Yoyre deyo* (§175), that the Jews must be separate and separated from other peoples [...].
>
> And one must not God forbid change Yiddish names [...] (Leyb Chaim, not 'Leopold Heinrich' etc.). And in accordance with 'they did not change their language' [said of the Children of Israel in Egypt] we must not forsake our Yiddish language. Do not go, God forbid, to a rabbi or preacher who replaces the Yiddish language. From him and his children one must run as from a fire.[42]

In his Hebrew responsa, the Khsam Soyfer claimed that Jews consciously transformed their language so as to adhere to the commandment of not walking in the way of Gentiles.[43] He went so far as to compare rabbis who speak non-Jewish languages with those who would place an Asherah in the Temple.[44]

The traditionalist pro-Yiddish position is very different from the secular one (although in the history of ideas, it too must perhaps be regarded as *Haskalah* provoked). The secularist pro-Yiddish position, which came later in the nineteenth and most prominently in the twentieth century to be associated with various Jewish socialist, anarchist, communist and territorialist movements, derived from elevation of the notion 'Yiddish', in its own right, to a major component of modern Jewish culture. The traditional Orthodox position is that Yiddish is the language of the Ashkenazic Jewish way of life, and serves as a preserver of Jewish life and faith. It was most recently eloquently set out by the Sulitser Rebetsin in an American orthodox journal.[45]

Intriguingly enough, the various polarically opposed notions of Yiddish have survived, in greater or lesser degrees, even after the Holocaust, and right down to our own times. There are traditional hasidic families (a demographically increasing group) for whom Yiddish just 'exists' as the vernacular, alongside Hebrew and Aramaic and local non-Jewish languages. There are secular Yiddishists (a demographically collapsing group) who view Yiddish as the embodiment of quintessential (albeit secularized) Jewishness and Jewish values. There are some, mostly Israelis, who deny its existence. Many diaspora Jews regard Yiddish as unnecessary in the light of Hebrew and Israel. There are, as always, thousands of shades of opinion about Yiddish, ranging from love through to hate. Finally, there are several thousand young Jews and non-Jews who since the 1960s have become devotees of Yiddish. A number have taken the time, trouble and expense to master the language and one of its associated academic disciplines at university level. The trend of the 1990s seems to be toward the consolidation and expansion of Yiddish at institutions of higher learning, a development which has included the emergence of writers and teachers as well as scholars. Its future as a living language in actual speech communities is, however, secure only among Hasidim).

There is however one position that the exotic history of Yiddish seems to have eluded in modern times: neutrality.

Non-neutrality brings us back to the inherent relativity of such notions as 'a language', and the acceptance by people of 'natural objects' which are in fact constructs of political and social power. There is a usual and an unusual sequence of events. The usual sequence entails a nation state or region, wherein the population accepts that it speaks 'Xish' as a matter of the natural order of the universe.

The unusual circumstances of the rise of the notion 'Yiddish' are many. They include the absence of the nation state and political power, participation in Ashkenazic internal trilingualism, hate from outside and self-hate by its very speakers, and ultimately (derivatively, I have argued) love and elevation to high status by select groups of its speakers and others.

The contribution of Yiddish studies to the debate on the existence and definition of 'languages' is to expose empirically, not just theoretically, the relativity and subjectivity of the concept. That one and the same variety of human speech is for one member of a group (in this case, the Jewish community in the wider sense) a highly cultured language, and does not even exist for another, demonstrates the latent ideological input to the rise and acceptance of 'a language'.

Within Jewish history, the ever-changing and coexisting notions of Yiddish are correlates of a variety of situations: the civilization Ashkenaz, anti-Semitism, Hasidism, *Haskalah*, Yiddishism, Hebraism, the Hebrew-Yiddish conflict, and a post-Holocaust reorganization of ideas whose contours will become clear only in the next century.

Notes

1. Roy Harris: *The Language Makers* (London, 1980); *The Language Myth* (London, 1981); The Language Machine (London, 1987).
2. Dovid Katz: 'Hebrew, Aramaic and the Rise of Yiddish' in J. A. Fishman, ed., *Readings in the Sociology of Jewish Languages* (Leiden 1985), pp. 85-103, see pp. 96-97.
3. Zalmen of St Goar: *Maharil* (Sabionetta 1556), p. 113a.
4. Nokhem Shtif: '"Loshn Ashkenaz" — "taytsh", "leshoyneynu", "yidish", "undzer shprakh"' in *Yidishe filologye* 1 (1924), pp. 386-388; Max Weinreich, *Geshikhte fun der yidisher shprakh* (New York 1973), vol. 1, pp. 321-333; vol. 3, pp. 332-343.
5. David Neal Miller: 'Transgressing the Bounds: On the Origins of Yiddish Literature' in D. Katz, ed., *Origins of the Yiddish Language* (Oxford 1987), pp. 95-103.
6. Zalman Shazar: 'Gviot 'edut bilshon yidish be-she'elot u-teshuvot mi- tehilat ha-me'a ha-hamesh 'esre 'ad sof ha-me'a ha-sheva 'esre' in his *Ure dorot* (Jerusalem 1971), pp. 239-319.
7. Dovid Katz: 'The Proto Dialectology of Ashkenaz' in D. Katz, ed., *Origins of the Yiddish Language* (Oxford 1987), pp. 47-60; see p. 47-48.
8. Dovid Katz: 'Origins of Yiddish Dialectology' in D. Katz, ed., Dialects of the Yiddish Language (Oxford 1988), pp. 39-55, see. pp. 39-42.
9. Uriel Weinreich: 'Tsu der frage vegn a normirter oysshprakh' in *Yidishe shprakh* 11 (1951): pp. 26-29.
10. Isserlin (Yisroel ben Pesakhye): *Seyfer trumas hadeshen* (Venice 1519), §231.
11. Levush (Mordechai Yafe): *Seyfer levush habuts veargomon* (Krakow, 1599), §129.33-34, pp. 80b-81a.
12. Zalmen of St Goar: *Maharil* (Sabionetta 1556), p. 89b.

13. Judah of Regensburg: *Seyfer khasidim*, ed., R. Margoliot (Jerusalem, 1957), §785.
14. Yosef bar Yokor: *Siddur* (Ichenhaussen, 1544).
15. *Kroyvets. Dos iz roshey teyves koyl rino vishuo beoholey tsadikim* (Prague, 1629), p. [2].
16. Devra Kay: *Women and the Vernacular. The Yiddish tkhine of Ashkenaz* (Oxford University DPhil thesis, 1990); David E. Fishman: 'Mikoyakh davnen af yidish: a bintl metodologishe bamerkungen un naye mekoyrim' in *Yivo bleter* n.s. 1 (1991), pp. 69-92.
17. Yisroel Tsinberg: 'Der kamf far yidish in der alt-yidisher literatur' in *Filologishe shriftn* 2 (1928), pp. 69-106, see pp. 100-103; Hermann Süss: 'Di tfile in kheyrem' in Oksforder yidish (forthcoming).
18. Maks Erik: *Di geshikhte fun der yidisher literatur fun di eltste tsaytn biz der haskole tkufe* (Warsaw, 1928), pp. 239-242.
19. Yekhiel-Mikhl Epshteyn: *Seyfer derekh hayoshor leoylom habo* (Frankfurt, 1704), §31, pp. 67b-68a.
20. Nechama Leibowitz: 'Die Übersetzungstechnik der jüdisch-deutschen Bibelübersetzungen des XV. and XVI. Jahrhunderts dargestellt an den Psalmen' in *Beiträge zur Geschichte der deutschen Sprache und Literatur* 55 (1931), pp. 377-463; Shlomo Noble: *Khumesh taytsh. An oysforshung vegn der traditsye fun taytshn khumesh in di khadorim* (New York, 1943).
21. Yisroel Tsinberg: 'Der kamf far yidish in der alt-yidisher literatur' in *Filologishe shriftn* 2 (1928), pp. 69-106; Shlomo Noble: 'Reb Yekhiel-Mikhl Epshteyn — a dertsier un kemfer far yidish in zibetsntn yorhundert' in *Yivo bleter* 35 (1951), pp. 121-138; 'A tshuve Khayim Libermanen' in *Yivo bleter* 36 (1952), pp. 319-321.
22. Mendl Pyekazh: 'Vegn "yidishizm" in sof fun zibetsntn un der ershter helft fun akhtsntn yorhundert' in D*i goldene keyt* 49 (1964), pp. 168-180; Khayim Liberman, 'Bamerkungen tsu Shloyme Nobls artikl: "Reb Yekhiel-Mikhl Epshteyn — a dertsier un kemfer far yidish in zibetsntn yorhundert"' in *Yivo bleter* 36 (1952), pp. 305-319.
23. Martin Luther: 'Vorrede Martini Luther' in *Von der falschen Betler büeberey. Mit einer Vorrede Martini Luther* (Wittemberg, 1528), p. 1.
24. Dovid Katz: 'On Yiddish, in Yiddish and for Yiddish: 500 Years of Yiddish Scholarship' in M. H. Gelber, ed., *Identity and Ethos. A Festschrift for Sol Liptzin on the Occasion of His 85th Birthday* (New York, 1986), pp. 26-27.
25. J.W.: *Jüdischer Sprach-Meister* [...] (± 1714).
26. Philoglottus [= J. P. Lütke?]: *Kurze und gründliche Anweisung zur Teutsch-Jüdischen Sprache* (Freiberg ,1733).
27. Bibliophilus: *Jüdischer Sprach-Meister, oder Hebräisch-Teutsches Wörter-Buch* (Frankfurt & Leipzig, 1742).
28. Naphtali Herz Wessely: *Divrey sholoym veemes* [transcribed *Diwré Schalom Weemes* on title page] (Vienna, 1826).
29. Dovid Katz: 'Zur Dialektologie des Jiddischen' in W. Besch et al. eds., *Dialektologie. Ein Handbuch zur deutschen und allgemeinen Dialektforschung*, 2, (Berlin 1983), pp. 1018-1041, see. pp. 1025-1028.
30. [Nathan] Birnbaum: 'Di konferents far der yidisher shprakh. Efenungs-rede fun Dr. Birnbaum' in *Dr. Birnboyms vokhnblat 1* (1908). pp. 3-7; [Max Weinreich & Zalmen Reyzen: eds.], *Di ershte yidishe shprakh konferents.*

Barikhtn, dokumentn un opklangen fun der tshernovitser konferents 1908 (Vilna 1931); Emanuel S. Goldsmith: *Modern Yiddish Culture. The Story of the Yiddish Language Movement* (New York, 1987).
31. Redaktsye *Nayvelt* ['editors of the journal *Nayvelt*']: *Tsi vert yidish in Erets Yisroel geroydeft?* (Tel Aviv, 1935); Zrubovl [= Yankev Vitkin]: 'Mir bashuldikn un monen akhrayes!' in *Yidish in Erets Yisroel* (1936), 7-18; Mordechai Kosover: 'Materyaln tsu der geshikhte fun kamf kegn yidish in Erets Yisroel' in *Erets Yisroel shriftn.* Zamlbikher (Tel Aviv, 1937), pp. 139-164; Joshua A. Fishman: ed., *Never Say Die! A Thousand Years of Yiddish in Jewish Life and Letters* (The Hague, 1981), p. 21.
32. Yitskhok Ber Levinzon: *Seyfer teudo beyisroeyl* (Vilna & Grodna, 1828), p. 59.
33. Dov-Ber Kerler: *The Eighteenth Century Origins of Modern Literary Yiddish* (Oxford University DPhil thesis, 1988; forthcoming: Oxford University Press).
34. Tuviohu Feder: *Kol mekhatsetsim* [transcribed *Kol Mechazezim* on title page; with introduction by A. M. Mohr] (Lemberg, 1853).
35. Yankev-Shmuel Bik: '[Letter no.] 28' in *Kerem khemed 1* (1833): 96-99; Tuviohu Feder: '[Letter no.] 29' in *Kerem khemed 1* (1833): 99-102.
36. Zalmen Reyzen: *Fun Mendelson biz Mendele. Hantbukh far der geshikhte fun der yidisher haskole literatur mit reproduktsyes un bilder* (Warsaw, 1923).
37. Yehoyshue-Mordkhe Lifshits: *Rusish-yidisher verterbukh* (Zhitomir, 1869); *Yidish-rusisher verterbukh* (Zhitomir, 1876).
38. Yehoyshue-Mordkhe Lifshits: 'Di fir klasn' in *Kol mevaser 21* (6/18 June 1863), pp. 323-328, see page 326; 23 (20 June / 1 July), pp. 364-366; 24 (27 June / 8 July): 375-380; 25 (4/16 July), pp. 392-393.
39. Dovid Katz: 'Alexander Harkavy and his Trilingual Dictionary' in A. Harkavy, *Yiddish-English-Hebrew Dictionary* (New York, 1988), pp. vi-xxiii, see p. xiv; Robert D. King: 'Matisyohu Mieses' in D. B. Kerler, ed., *History of Yiddish Studies* (Chur, 1991), pp. 25-38, see pp. 28-29.
40. Dovid Katz: 'Ber Borokhov, Pioneer of Yiddish Linguistics' in *Jewish Frontier* 47 (no.6/105; 1980), pp. 10-20.
41. Ber Borokhov: 'Di ufgabn fun der yidisher filologye' in Sh. Niger, ed., *Der pinkes* (Vilna, 1913), pp. 1-22, see. p. 18.
42. Khsam Soyfer [Moyshe Shrayber]: *El hoadorim sheyni* [transcribed *El huadurem Hascheni* on title page]. *Der tsveyter ufruf on yidishe kinder* (Lemberg, 1869).
43. Khsam Soyfer: *Seyfer Khsam Soyfer. Kheylek even hoezer,* 2 (Pressburg, 1859), p. 6b, §11.
44. Khsam Soyfer: *Seyfer Khsam Soyfer. Kheylek khoyshen mishpot* (Vienna, 1872), p. 74b, §197 [misnumbered '179'].
45. Shifra Rubin, Sulitser Rebetsin: 'Shtayg hekher — redt mame loshn!' in *Dos yidishe vort* 302 (1992), p. 52.

THE TEACHING OF JEWISH LAW IN BRITISH UNIVERSITIES

Bernard S. Jackson

It is a privilege to publish this lecture (which was delivered under the joint auspices of the Oxford Centre for Postgraduate Hebrew Studies and the Institute of Advanced Legal Studies) in a *Festschrift* in honour of David Patterson, whom I am proud to count as one of my teachers (I recall with pleasure my attendance at his class in Mishnah *Avot*, in the mid-sixties), and who has done more than anyone else in this country to foster the institutional development of Jewish Law. From the early days of the Oxford Centre for Postgraduate Hebrew Studies, David promoted lectures in Jewish law: first through an Associate Fellowship, later with the Littman Fellowship and ultimately through the sponsorship of a Jewish Law Fellowship, the principal fruits of which will become apparent in the next few years. In addition to these appointments, David has given significant support to international scholarship in the field. The 1978 conference sponsored by the Centre on 'Jewish Law in Legal History and the Modern World'[1] prompted the formation of The Jewish Law Association, which has met biennially ever since. *The Jewish Law Annual*, published from 1978 by E. J. Brill of Leiden and since 1985 by Harwood Academic Press in association with the Boston University School of Law, has also benefited from the academic sponsorship of the Centre.

The interest of the Oxford Centre for Postgraduate Hebrew Studies in the advancement of study and research in Jewish Law is obvious, necessary, natural, and inevitable. That flows from the centrality of Jewish law within Jewish culture: to conceive of Jewish Studies without the *Halakhah* is to conceive of western music without the symphony. However, the interest of the Institute of Advanced Legal Studies is not quite so obvious. One could, indeed, conceive of an Institute of Advanced Legal Studies which failed to take an interest in Jewish Law—even though, it must be said, such an Institute would find itself in increasingly isolated company, since the teaching of Jewish Law is to be found, nowadays, at Harvard, New York University, Boston University, Stanford, The Sorbonne (with its Centre de Droit Hebraïque), and Bologna. Nevertheless, Jewish law can hardly claim the same centrality to legal studies as it can to Jewish studies, outside the State of Israel. True, one may find some relatively esoteric legal systems taught in British law schools, but in most cases the reasons are not too far to seek: Japanese Law, to serve the commercial world; Soviet law (which no doubt will revert to Russian Law) to serve the needs of politics and diplomacy; French law, no doubt for its gastronomic delight. Doubtless there are other reasons for teaching these systems of foreign law; for the purposes of the present argument, it suffices to say that Jewish law could hardly justify a place on the basis of the traditional criteria for the teaching of these, individual systems of foreign law.

My purpose in this lecture is to sketch, partly by way of examples, some of the academic claims of the study of Jewish Law in British universities. I shall not seek to present a survey of present practice: regrettably, the results would hardly justify a lecture. Nor shall I restrict myself to the teaching of Jewish law in law faculties. Indeed, I suggest that faculty boundaries should not be rigidly deployed in the teaching of Jewish Law within our universities. And to conclude this gloss upon the title of my lecture, I do propose to speak of the teaching of Jewish Law in *British*, not merely English universities. I have had the pleasure of teaching in one of the ancient Scottish universities, the structures of which may turn out to be particularly congenial for our purpose.

Let us now consider some possible paradigms for the teaching of Jewish law in British universities. I offer the following list of approaches: dogmatic, historical, comparative, apologetic, culturo-historical, ethno-historical, anthropological, theological and philosophical. In each case, I shall try to sketch both the nature of the teaching and the educational objectives which it should serve, as well as providing some examples of the kind of material which might be used in this context. My list should not be read as a prescription—so many doses per day of each particular medicine—but rather as a menu, available to the teacher to choose for the appropriate audience and occasion, and to adapt and re-create in accordance with his or her abilities and resources.

Legal Dogmatics

I start with legal dogmatics. What are the applicable legal rules in Jewish law on particular topics? What legal institutions in Jewish law are of particular interest to the jurist? To answer these questions, of course, we have to adopt a view on the dogmatic foundations of Jewish law: what are the sources of Jewish law, or what are the rules of recognition which allow us to identify a binding rule?

At a different point on our menu we may have occasion to question the pertinence of this approach—the appropriateness of talking about 'binding rules' or 'rules of recognition' in the context of Jewish law. We may conclude that these questions themselves derive from an alien intellectual environment, from the context of modern western systems of law viewed through the lenses of legal positivism. Nevertheless, in many academic contexts it is indeed appropriate to use an external approach, provided that we are aware that we are doing so, and are doing so for a particular purpose. There may well be such a purpose in the dogmatic presentation of Jewish law: there are many conflict of law situations, not the least important of which is found in the relationship between Jewish law and Israeli law in the State of Israel, where such a dogmatic presentation of Jewish law—even though it might not be historically 100% authentic—is required for practical purposes. (It is no accident, perhaps, that this type of dogmatic presentation of Jewish law has flourished especially in recent years in the research institutes of the Israeli Universities.)

To some, it may seem strange to present the dogmatic approach to Jewish law as primarily related to its presentation to *foreign* jurisdictions. Surely, the primary purpose is to know what will be applied in a Jewish court, a *bet din*. But there is a powerful argument (one which would appeal to legal realists) that the *bet din* uses legal doctrine as a starting point, not as a definitive means of resolving the individual case.

Of course, the dogmatic presentation of Jewish law is of interest for reasons which go beyond practical application, whether in Jewish or other courts. Dogmatics, particularly in its continental sense, is concerned not merely with the outcome, but with the manner of arriving at that outcome. Legal argument may take many forms, but Jewish legal dogmatics has a particular interest, for the following reason: at an early stage in the history of Jewish law, the basic conceptual building blocks became, if not rigidly fixed, at least highly privileged. There was a presumption that new legal institutions should be created through deployment of traditional concepts, rather than through conceptual innovation. I think here particularly of the fascinating study of insurance by Stephen Passamaneck, in which he shows how the traditional categories of bailment—the gratuitous guardian (*shomer hinam*), the guardian for reward (*shomer sakhar*), the gratuitous borrower (*sho'el*) and the hirer for reward (*sakhar*)—were used in order to build up insurance institutions of a high degree of commercial flexibility, particularly adapted for use in maritime trade.[2]

On other occasions, perhaps, ancient conceptual resources have not, or not yet, proved adequate to meet the needs of modern circumstances. I think here of the modern problems of divorce, where, despite the panoply of conceptual tools available to assist a court in releasing a chained wife (*'agunah*) from the bonds of a dead marriage, the husband's veto—sometimes resulting from spite, sometimes from greed—continues to override all other considerations.[3] Despite the mountains of modern halakhic literature discussing the relative merits of agency, of pre-nuptial agreements, of extension by analogy of the areas of legitimate coercion[4]—despite all this, a consensus as to the way ahead is still lacking. It is true, of course, that here we are dealing with a matter which, from the internal dogmatic point of view within Jewish law, falls not within our categories of 'civil law' or even 'family law', but within that of *hetter ve'isur*, permission and prohibition, rather than *dinei mamonot* (rules of compensation). Here, a stricter view has often been taken on matters of interpretation and innovation, particularly where, as here, the rule at stake is one which has the status of *de'orayta* (deriving from the Bible) rather than *derabbanan* (deriving from rabbinic enactment). Nevertheless, the biblical text in Deuteronomy 24:1-4 is one which, even on its grammatical construction, is capable of more than one interpretation.[5] The teaching of the dogmatics of Jewish law in British universities needs to be critical: not only to present successes but also to assess failures.

The Historical Approach

The second item on my menu is the historical approach, the one with which the school of David Daube,[6] to which I am proud to belong, is most closely associated. Jewish law has a history which spans, on almost any view, at least 3,000 years. Despite the influential advocacy, by Supreme Justice Professor Menachem Elon, of 'all-period' research in Jewish law[7]—an approach which seeks to trace the history of any particular institution from its inception, often in the Bible, through all its periods, right down to modern responsa, in order to demonstrate the (assumed) bedrock of principle which informs that institution throughout its history, notwithstanding the layers of detailed elaboration and local variation which are to be found—and despite the appearance of a number of monographic works, such as Elon's own treatise on personal freedom of the debtor[8]—I hesitate to ascribe true historical expertise to any one scholar in all periods of the history of Jewish law. I have never, myself, for example claimed an expertise which goes beyond the biblical and tannaitic periods. Nevertheless, a course which concentrated upon the features of this period of Jewish legal history (including, of course, internal historical development within it) would, to my mind, be worth teaching in British universities.

An historical approach is not to be understood as a dogmatic approach applied to some period or other of Jewish law in the past. Rather, it is an attempt to place the dogmatics of an earlier period within an historical context. Thus, for example, the study of biblical law has to take account of the relationships—political and cultural—between ancient Israelite society and its neighbours (frequently, its conquerors). In some cases, we can study such questions as jurisdictional autonomy from actual official, or semi-official, documents.[9] More important, very often, is the comparative study of the 'legal cultures' of the societies concerned. To what extent was law a matter of state symbolism?[10] To what extent was it informed by the 'wisdom' of literary groups located in the King's court or the Temple?[11] And of course, equally interesting questions arise in the halakhic literature of the Spanish golden age, with its intimate relationship to Islamic legal culture.[12] The recent history of Jewish law affords further examples of opportunities for this kind of historical approach. Norman Solomon has pioneered the analytical approach to the legal reasoning of the Lithuanian school of the late 19th and early 20th century, where some echoes of Germanic *Pandektenrecht* appear to be evident.[13] Nor should we turn away from grappling with the responsa of the Holocaust, notwithstanding the difficulties of academic detachment.[14]

But are such courses appropriate in British universities, and if so, do they have a place in British Law Schools? The latter really depends upon the orientation and objectives of the particular Law School. I frequently hear lip-service paid to the ideal of a 'liberal arts education in law'. Regrettably, once decoded, this often means no more than a desire to expand or maintain the range of dogmatic legal subjects which may be taught, despite the effective control which the profession enjoys over the content of approximately half the courses taught in a typical English law degree. There are, however, some law schools which more genuinely aspire to a 'liberal arts' education in law, and for them, the historical approach is unproblematic. From *this* vantage point, the historical teaching of Jewish law is no less valuable (but also no more valuable) than the study of Roman Law in the period of the Republic, or of the French law of the ancien régime. I stress, from *this* vantage point. There are also others, as we shall see.

The Comparative Approach

I turn now to the comparative approach. Perhaps its most systematic expressions are found in Boaz Cohen's *Jewish and Roman Law* [15] and Rabbi Dr. Isaac Herzog's (sadly incomplete) *Main Institutions of Jewish Law*.[16] Anglo-American law reviews have for many years carried occasional articles seeking to compare modern American law with Jewish law on particular topics. Torts seems to have been particularly favoured in this context.[17] This is not an item on the menu which I myself would frequently be inclined to choose. All too often, it seems, the dish is either over-cooked or prepared without the appropriate set of ingredients. 'Over-cooked' here means that there is an assumption, frequently unstated, that the Jewish 'solution' is either inherently better than the Anglo-American or of particular interest simply because it is Jewish. 'Preparation without the proper set of ingredients' means that the cook has not had adequate training, or has failed to use all the ingredients necessary for the recipe. To produce the Jewish 'solution' for comparative purposes involves full evaluation of the sources of Jewish law, not a selective approach or one based primarily on secondary sources. It also involves asking a basic theoretical question: whether the two systems perceive the problem in the same way, since only then is it meaningful to compare their solutions. I should add that many would recognize in these strictures characteristics of the practice of comparative law in general. But let me add: provided that the criteria implied in these strictures are satisfied, comparative study can be very rewarding. Its reward lies not so much in the answers it might provide to the question: 'what does Jewish law do about X?', but rather in the differences it may reveal between Jewish law and modern western law, differences at the level of basic structure and values. I do not see, for example, how a comparative study of a topic like easements could be pursued—if the dish is properly cooked—without casting light upon notions of community within the two cultures. The immense value of this kind of study is not what it tells us about Jewish culture (a matter which may be regarded as of relatively parochial concern) but rather what it tells us about the legal culture of the western society with which comparison is made—and this is a vital concern for the non-Jewish audience of Jewish law courses.

Particularly important, in this context, is the comparative study of legal argument, a topic on which there are some excellent studies—I think particularly of the work of Louis Jacobs for Jewish law[18]—but relatively few genuinely comparative treatments, Robert Brunschvig's Jewish-Islamic comparison representing an important starting point.[19] The reason for this lack is not too difficult to find. A western-trained lawyer will readily sink in the sea of the legal argument of the Talmud, and may have difficulty in floating even in such simpler commentaries upon legal texts as may be found in the *Mekhilta*. Indeed, even the great Jewish master of Islamic law, Joseph Schacht, suggested a distinction between the 'analytical' approach of Western law on the one hand with the 'analogical' approach of Islamic law on the other, with the implication that the latter was somehow a looser, less scientific or advanced form of legal reasoning.[20] Now that we observe the march of literary criticism into the formally pure temple of legal reasoning—and even, I should say, without this apparent intrusion—Schacht's view on this matter may appear superficial. For the issue here is the range of permissible modes of analogy, and the basis of analogizing. The Common Law processes of construction of precedent have themselves been regarded by some as analogical, though without too precise a definition of this term. Translators of Jewish legal dogmatics tend to restrict the term 'analogy' to one particular form of Jewish legal reasoning, *hekesh*—equivalent to the Islamic *qiyas*.[21] This form of reasoning is regarded, itself, as somewhat extreme, perhaps even marginal. Nevertheless, forms of comparison—such as the *gezerah shavah* —are used in Jewish law which, even if not described by the term 'analogy', do appear to be quite different from acceptable modes of reasoning in the West.

I would suggest that this is a puzzle well worthy of academic attention, and indeed of teaching to certain types of law student—perhaps the more jurisprudentially oriented. For a deeper examination of it will reveal that these differences in rationality stem not from degrees of intellectual capacity (a view seemingly favoured by some traditions of social evolutionism) but rather from a combination of theological and linguistic assumptions. Not even the secular lawyer can ignore the fact that the biblical text has been regarded, by the vast majority of those involved with Jewish law throughout its history, as a divinely dictated text. The question then arises: what language was God supposed to speak? Self-evidently, Hebrew—*leshon hakodesh*. But that was only the beginning of the problem. What kind of Hebrew did God speak, and particularly what kind of language was used when dictating the Pentateuch to Moses? For the answer to this question will significantly affect the nature of permissible—even, required—interpretation of the biblical text. Like modern linguists who ask what are the peculiar features of the language of modern statutes, and who in some cases even go so far as to claim that 'legislative language' should be conceived as a special, partially autonomous, language, and not merely a register of natural English,[22] so too the Rabbis had to find linguistic models which would serve on the one hand to explain how divine language reflected divine omniscience, while on the other hand how it succeeded in communicating to a human audience.[23] And even within the latter conception of the function of divine language, encapsulated within the famous dictum: *hatorah nikhtevet bilshon benei 'adam*,[24] there was still room for discussion. Was the Torah written so as to be intelligible—even, fully intelligible—to the *average* person, or was it written in a semi-technical, or allusive language which would be accessible to the scholar, but not to the lay-person? This is just one sense given to the famous distinction between *peshat* and *derash*. But leaving aside questions of classification, it is clear that the Rabbis identified *themselves* as the *benei 'adam,* as having a unique capacity to interpret the meaning of the divine words to the lay audience.

In proceeding from the theological assumption of the perfection of the divine text, the Rabbis adopted three postulates: first, that there could be no contradiction in the text; second, that there could be no redundancy in the text; third, that nothing in the text was accidental. This conception of the perfect text extended to literary features which even a modern parliamentary draftsman might regard as unimportant, and therefore capable of being decided arbitrarily. Suppose, for example, that you were the draftsman of a new criminal code—one which, unlike the present draft of the Law Commission,[25] purported to be truly comprehensive, not only of general principle but also of all the substantive criminal offences. Certainly, you might group a number of offences together, under such categories as offences against property, offences against the person, sexual offences, etc. But within each group you might have some difficulty in arriving at a rational basis of arrangement. Not so, for the Rabbis. For them, even such decisions as these could not have been arrived at by the divine draftsman arbitrarily. Simple collocation therefore became a basis for analogical argument—a form of analogy quite foreign to our way of thinking, being based upon *literary* positioning, rather than *substantive* similarity.[26] If, then, we are to adopt a comparative approach to the teaching of Jewish legal reasoning, we cannot do so without paying attention to such systemic and theological underpinnings. To misuse the currency of modern linguistics, we have to look at the deep structure of legal argument and not merely at its surface manifestations.

The Apologetic Approach

Somewhat tendentiously, I have included an apologetic paradigm in my list. This is *not* to suggest that there is any place in an academic institution for the teaching of Jewish law motivated either by a desire to demonstrate its superiority, or through its teaching to fortify the ethnic or religious identity of Jewish students. Indeed, my assumption throughout is that the audience for Jewish law in British universities is mixed, if not predominantly gentile. Yet there is one very special sense in which issues which have been used polemically in the past, and which still inform the cultural subconscious in its image of Jews and Jewish law, do call out for proper academic study—even if the result may be, in a certain sense, apologetic. I realise that I tread here on very sensitive ground. But let me use an historical parallel. The medieval disputation was not initiated by Jews. It was a forum within which Jews were required to defend themselves and their culture. The records of such disputations—as both modern scholarship[27] and some dramatic representations indicate—were not without didactic interest. The modern teaching which would correspond to this is not unconnected with the medieval disputation. For the whole history of Jewish-Christian relations is informed by Christian perceptions of Jewish law, and the views taken of it in the New Testament. The New Testament takes a view—several, in fact—of the operation of Jewish law in the trial of Jesus, generating an image then given popular form in the deicide charge, which even the scholarly diplomacy of Vatican II cannot, of its nature, suddenly remove from the popular consciousness.

I include an analysis of the trial of Jesus in my course on Jewish law. The object is not to show, as has been done with perhaps over-brilliant advocacy by Justice Haim Cohn of the Israel Supreme Court,[28] that it was the Romans, not the Jews, who did it, but rather to display the immense complexity of the problem, and the huge gaps and uncertainties in our knowledge.[29] This is not to say that the New Testament is a valueless document for historical purposes. Quite the contrary; in some respects, it is the best—even the only—direct evidence we have for the state of Jewish law in the first century C.E. But on this issue, as many Christian scholars now recognize, the account given by some of the New Testament writers was necessarily informed by the post-70 relationship of the early church to both the Roman empire on the one hand and the by then disempowered priestly Jewish leadership on the other.

Another aspect of the problem is the relationship of the 'trial' before the Sanhedrin (if that it be) with normative statements of criminal procedure found in the Mishnah and other early Jewish literature. But how do we know that the rules contained in the rabbinic documents, none of which reached their final form before the early third century, do actually date back to the period of Jesus? In some respects, it is possible to argue that Jewish law underwent internal modification *precisely in response* to the events associated with the birth of Christianity. The argument has been made, for example, that the rabbinic downgrading or diminution of the powers of the 'prophet' was a response to the claims made by Jesus under that very title.[30] In short, the trial of Jesus presents perhaps the most difficult problem of ancient legal history, and here, to prove what we do not, and cannot, know is at least as valuable—for both academic and inter-faith purposes—as the making of more positive claims.

Of course, not everyone is still fighting the battles of the first century C.E, even though it is not so long since these battles had their deleterious effect on universities, and not only in Germany. Just as significant is the modern secularization of these very issues. Frequently, we speak about the difference between interpretation according to the letter of the law, and interpretation according to its spirit. There remains an impression that Jewish law is characterised by interpretation according to the letter (which somehow sounds rather different from the 'literal interpretation' which most Common Law judges regard as the norm). But it is, as I tried to show in a lecture some years ago,[31] a blatant misunderstanding of the theological context and import of the original distinction. When Paul discarded his Pharisee background, and attacked Jewish law in the name of the 'spirit' rather than the 'letter', this was not a plea for some 'Grand Style' of interpretation of the biblical text (and indeed, some of the analogical interpretation of the biblical text, to which I have already alluded, could hardly be grander in the Llewellyan sense); rather, it was an argument for the continuation of direct revelation from God into the heart of the individual subject, rather than revelation by means of *any kind of* interpretation of the written word. I doubt that this conception of interpretation according to the spirit would appeal to many modern judges, even those blessed with a highly self-conscious sense of justice, such as Lord Denning.

The Culturo-Historical Approach

The next item on my menu is labelled, somewhat pretentiously, 'culturo-historical'. Jewish law can be presented as a kind of golden thread which links together much of the legal history of the Western world. As such, it is part of English legal history, of Scottish legal history, even of Irish legal history. I do not wish to overemphasise this feature; indeed, it is a phenomenon which I find difficult to evaluate. In very general terms, the story is this. The biblical roots of Jewish law emerged within the culture of the ancient Near East. The nature of the biblical codes bears remarkable resemblance to, as well as important differences from, those of Hammurabi and his lesser-known predecessors and successors. Indeed, there are some striking substantive parallels, such as the almost verbatim adoption by Exodus 21:35 of a rule found in the Laws of Eshnunna regarding an ox which is *tam* goring to death another ox.³² But the cultural focus of Jewish law naturally changed, in the wake of the conquests of Alexander and his Seleucid successors. Hellenistic culture brought an interest in Hellenistic rhetoric and modes of interpretation,³³ and eventual Roman rule brought daily contact with Roman jurisdiction (and generated some fascinating conflict of law rules).³⁴ In all these cultural relations, Jewish law was largely the recipient rather than the donor. But then the situation changed. *Judaea vincta victorem vinxit*, one might say. The Roman empire did not turn Jewish (though at one point it was not too far from doing so), but it did turn Christian. The church fathers were not averse to consulting Rabbis on matters of scriptural interpretation, though I would take this normally to have been consultation in a rather weak sense. Just as significant, the Roman conquest gave immense impetus to, if it did not entirely create, the Jewish Diaspora, and the possibility of cultural contact, at first hand, between Jewish lawyers and the legal authorities of the host nations. The example of Maimonides, and the relationship between his code and those of the contemporary Islamic world, is only one example.³⁵

It was, however, through Canon law, rather than through Roman law, that the major influence of Jewish law has been brought to bear upon the West. It is a story best told from detailed examples. I shall allude to just two. The first is the goring ox, which we first know from the laws of Eshnunna, then in Hammurabi and the Bible, and which reappears as the kicking horse in the Code of Justinian and the biting dog in the Laws of Alfred (to name but a few). Of course, we might expect any early code to deal with kicking horses and biting dogs. It is not, however, inevitable that every society will adopt a rule comparable to the Jewish distinction between *tam* and *mu'ad*, nor that they will do so in words which indicate continuing *literary* dependence. Indeed, the Roman formulation in the example of the kicking horse runs so far counter to classical Roman doctrine as to have been labelled an interpolation by modern scholars.³⁶

Again, the two-witness rule of the Bible has been widely adopted in countries influenced by Canon law, as indeed have some of the necessary means of avoiding its rigours. When the medieval Canon lawyers sought to construct an institution of corroboration by similar fact evidence (*testes singulares*), they justified their argument by analysis of the facts of the story of Susannah, found in the Apocrypha to the Hebrew Bible. True enough, they said, Susannah could not be rightly convicted when one elder said that she committed adultery under an oak tree while the other said it was under a holm tree. But that was only because the two elders had claimed to have observed the event *together*. Had they not made this claim, their evidence would not have been regarded as logically contradictory: for though adultery may not be committed simultaneously under two different trees, it may be so committed successively. Moreover, we all know (so the Canon law doctors argued) that adultery with the same lover is an act which is prone to be repeated—*factum iterabile*—unlike some other crimes against Canon law, such as the murder of a Bishop (especially the same Bishop). I have traced the use of this argument for corroboration by similar fact evidence from a Canonist *Summa* of the mid-12th century, written in Bologna, to English treason trials of the 17th century, and a famous Scottish divorce case of the same period, which then became one of the principal foundations for the so-called *Moorov* doctrine, which Lord Hailsham so fully read into his speech in the House of Lords in the modern leading case of *Kilbourne*.[37]

I do, as I indicated, have some difficulty in evaluating such phenomena. They are threads of literary transmission, comparable perhaps to the intertextuality one would find in the literary world. But are they only this? Were the writers of these legal texts concerned only to show their own cleverness, to make literary allusion for the sake of literary allusion, or did their choice of that to which they alluded show something deeper, about not only their own cultural values but also those of the milieu in which they wrote? The study of Jewish law, viewed in this way, becomes part and parcel of our overall cultural history, the study of which needs no justification in British universities, nor even—I speak perhaps as an optimist—in British law schools.

The Ethno-Historical Approach

By contrast, the next item on my menu is particularist. Within Jewish studies, the teaching of Jewish law has a crucial part to play, not merely as an element of Jewish culture (and it is, I re-emphasize, a central facet of Jewish culture, which no degree of modern secularization can obscure); it is also a crucial indicant of the history of Jewish identity on the one hand, and of the nature of Jewish relations with the outside world on the other.

It is not only in the modern state of Israel that the question 'Who is a Jew?' has come to be important;[38] indeed, one of our leading historians of Jewish antiquity recently published a book entitled *'Who Was a Jew?'*, dealing with Jewish identity in the early Rabbinic period.[39] It may not have been the pressures of emancipation and secularization which prompted identity crises in the ancient world; nevertheless, conversion was a recurrent issue (and a central one, of course, in the rupture between Judaism and the early church), and the modern argument about patrilineal as against matrilineal descent quite naturally arises when one considers the marital history of some of the Biblical figures, not least Moses.

Jewish attitudes to the outside world also receive some of their most concrete expressions in the context of the *Halakhah*. It is not merely a matter of *dina demalkhuta dina*, and the manner in which it was interpreted and applied in particular contexts.[40] There is also the Jewish tension between particularism and universalism: how could the Jews on the one hand proclaim their status as a 'special people', while seeking at the same time to get on with the rest of humanity? There are some rules of Jewish law which are discriminatory: according to Jewish law, the owner of a Jewish ox (if I may so put it) which was killed by a gentile ox could claim full damages whether the gentile ox were *tam* or *mu'ad*, while the owner of a Jewish ox which killed a gentile ox would pay only half damages, if the ox were *tam*.[41] Yet immediately, such discriminatory rules, perhaps based upon a conflict of law rule which favoured the defendant's law, were perceived to be problematic in the context of inter-communal relations, and the overriding principle of *kiddush hashem* was brought into play. But such legal principles, as Dworkin would remind us, are merely guides; they do not determine outcomes, and they do not necessarily ensure consistency. It therefore becomes necessary to look at such rules within the context of the particular historical context of inter-communal relations in each case.

The Anthropological Approach

Next, the anthropological approach. At its most general, the argument might proceed thus: Jewish law is different and esoteric, and that in itself is good enough reason to study it. But of course, many systems of law are strange and esoteric, but we do not include them all within the curriculum. Yet I dare to suggest that Jewish law has something which is of particular interest to the anthropologist. Its origins go back to a largely pre-literate era, but its elaboration became immensely scholastic; its origins were associated with small-scale political autonomy, but much of its subsequent history was in the context of dispersion within an alien environment. Not surprisingly, perhaps, modern structural anthropologists have found plenty within Jewish law to manifest a particular interest in boundaries: the boundaries between the holy and the profane, between the pure and the impure, between the permitted and the prohibited as reflections—so Mary Douglas has argued[42]—of a heightened concern with the boundaries of the social. The tendency has been to apply this approach primarily to the ritual law. The object is not to provide some simple 'decoding' of individual symbols, but rather to gain access thereby to the deeper values of the society, of which the particular rules are manifestations. There is a difference between a 'rationalist' search for legal principles—as reflected in the work of Moshe Greenberg in Biblical law or Ronald Dworkin in modern western law—and the approach of the structural anthropologist or semiotician. The latter is not content with the principles which reside within the consciousness of the legal culture concerned, whether made explicit or not, but rather with deeper, taken-for-granted unarticulated values which reside—if one may use this metaphor—in the collective unconscious.[43] I believe that this approach is fruitfully applied also to the civil law and have tried to demonstrate this in relation to the Biblical laws of slavery.[44] Others have done the same as regards the status of women in Jewish legal texts—a problem prone to attract apologetics on the male side and hysteria on the female, both of which, however, have been successfully avoided in what I regard as the best of the modern studies, that by Judith Romney Wegner.[45]

The Theological Approach

Jewish law may also be taught within a theological framework. I have already commented, in the context of the comparative approach, upon the vital importance of appreciation of the theological assumptions of rabbinic interpretation of Biblical legal texts. But the theological agenda goes far beyond this. I am not thinking here of such works as Louis Jacobs, *Theology in the Responsa*[46]—which seeks to extract theological observations from the corpus of the responsa literaure, but rather of the influence upon the *halakhah* of such theological concepts as *imitatio dei*, personal redemption, and messianic restoration.[47] These may appear at first sight rather remote from the concerns of the lawyer, especially the one who arbitrarily reduces the *halakhah* to *mishpat 'ivri*, to civil law as against religious law, in order to construct Jewish law in parallel to a modern secular legal system. Yet even in the civil law, theological concepts cannot be excluded. Lamm and Kirschenbaum have argued, for example, that *kedoshim tiheyu* is used in Jewish legal argument as a kind of Dworkinian principle,[48] and Ben Zion Wacholder has shown how messianic beliefs shape the rabbinic conception of time itself, such that the present becomes merely an instant in the gap between the ideal state (with both a small and a capital s)—identified with the period of the first Jewish commonwealth—and its ultimate restoration.[49] This has its effect not merely in the concern to prepare for the legal constitution of the future commonwealth, but also in the definition of some present institutions. The literary representation of Jewish law in different periods is also informed by a temporality which looks forward to restoration. Repetition of the ideal (even in the non-literal conception of repetition which is implicit in the use of the title *Mishneh torah* for both Deuteronomy and the Code of Maimonides), becomes a sacred moment in both reviving the past and anticipating the future.

The Philosophical Approach

Such theological concerns merge into the final item on our menu, the philosophical approach. The relationship is necessarily a close one, at least if one is to view Jewish law in the context of the philosophical claims of its own culture. For the philosophy of Jewish law is to be found, for the most part, in the pages of the *Aggadah*, itself conceived as part of the Oral Torah. I believe, and have argued, that there is much value to be found in a comparative approach to the philosophy of Jewish law, one which addresses questions posed both within the system and by modern western philosophy.[50] In some cases, and perhaps for reasons which are readily explained on historical grounds, such concerns readily converge: Jewish law, like Western legal philosophy, asks what is the source and status of the universal in law, and offers its own solution in terms of the elaboration of the aggadic concept of the *mitzvot bnei noah*, Noahide Commandments—a topic sensitively treated in a recent book by David Novak.[51] Equally, we can use western jurisprudential models to elucidate aspects of Jewish legal practice, and this has been done to some extent in the field of legal reasoning. Such activities are useful provided that we remain conscious of what we are doing. If we apply a western philosophical model to Jewish law, it must be either because we have good reason, independent of Jewish law, to assert the universality or other pertinence of that model, or because we are using Jewish law as one area of field work within which to test such general claims. Otherwise, the Western model merely has the status of hypothetical description, which—even if we find facts to fit it—may turn out to be quite inauthentic.

This is why the use of a casebook seems to me to be inappropriate for the teaching of Jewish law. Jewish law is not structured in the same way as Common Law. It lacks a comparable doctrine of precedent. Its courts are largely private rather than public, and there is no general system of law reporting. Sometimes, an eminent halakhist may publish a *responsum* based upon a decision in a particular case, but such a *responsum* derives its authority (not as a precedent, but as contributing to the consensus of halakhic views) not because the decision was made in a case, but because the argument has been published by this particular halakhic jurist. To construct a casebook from that *genre* of halakhic literature is both to misconceive its nature and to extract it artificially from its overall place in the Jewish legal system. For Jewish law is primarily a system of texts, not of cases.

Some Practical Considerations

It is right, perhaps, that I should conclude with such practical concerns. What steps now need to be taken? In my view, there are three broad issues which need to be addressed: human resources, material resources, and course structures.

There are very few 'experts' in Jewish law teaching in British universities, whether in law schools or outside. Undoubtedly, the endowment of posts—provided that they are genuinely integrated into their academic environment—would be of enormous assistance. But there are already many scholars who have a good part of the background necessary to teach Jewish law from one or more of the vantage points outlined in this paper. A practical step would be to institute an intensive summer school. A similar approach was successfully adopted in the United States a few years ago for the teaching of Roman law. It attracted both classicists and lawyers. The desired result, of course, is not to produce instant experts, but rather a mutually supportive group of teachers with the basic competence and confidence to offer first-level courses.

Secondly, we need material resources, particularly the sponsorship of a number of Jewish law collections in British university libraries. Such collections would concentrate primarily on material in English, though the basic Hebrew texts would have to be present. The compilation of appropriate lists has recently become much easier, with the publication of Rakover's *Multi-Language Bibliography of Jewish Law*,[52] and Weisbard and Schonberg's *Jewish Law: Bibliography of Sources and Scholarship in English*.[53] A number of the classics of modern Israeli scholarship in Jewish law, Urbach's *Ha-halakhah* and Elon's *Ha-mishpat ha-'ivri*, are or are about to become available in English. But resources are also required in order to translate a whole range of monographic literature produced in the last 20 years by younger Israeli scholars—literature, I may add, much of which falls within the 'dogmatic' paradigm and is immensely superior to anything available in English in that *genre*. Equally, a range of textbooks needs to be commissioned, appropriate to Jewish law courses of different kinds. Despite the recent books of Aaron Schreiber[54] and of Dorff and Rosett,[55] there is an urgent need, in particular, for an historical textbook, with chapters written to a single plan by experts in each of the different periods—a project espoused for a number of years by the Jewish Law Association. The resources needed for these purposes are not vast. Some Jewish communities ought to be able to endow Jewish law collections in their local universities, and courses in Jewish law ought to be open to interested members of the public (Jewish and non-Jewish). The commissioning of textbooks is a more substantial problem. A charitable trust has been established for this purpose, but as yet we lack a Maecenas.[56]

Finally, there is the question of course structure. Universities find themselves under pressure either to reduce the length of the degree, or to cram more professional training into it. Many of us consider that this is shortsighted in the extreme, and that it will put us at a disadvantage as against lawyers trained in the universities of other European countries. On the other hand, we hear increasingly of 'modularization' of courses, leading to the possible introduction of half-year courses, more akin to the American semester model. The structure of legal education in Scotland has always appeared to me to be far superior, in affording the option of a four-year honours degree to those who want it, and indeed in allowing for a modicum of specialization within that degree, so that students may take second-level courses in areas of the curriculum which particularly interest them. It would not, perhaps, be appropriate to argue the case for a four-year degree in England purely in terms of the needs of Jewish law teaching. But I venture to suggest that the type of teaching in Jewish law which I have advocated in this lecture is but an example of a properly academic approach to legal studies in general, which it is the role of our universities to foster. For the academic value of the teaching of Jewish law in British universities is the same as the academic value of any subject worthy of university teaching, namely that it leads to a better understanding, both of others and of ourselves.

A recent experience of this was quite striking. At Kent I taught Jewish law to a small group of Shi'ite Muslims. Their openness and interest—even where, as was inevitable, the subject matter impinged on contemporary politics—was remarkable. I have had few more rewarding experiences as a teacher.

Notes

1. Its proceedings published in a volume of that title, ed. B. S. Jackson, Leiden: E. J. Brill, 1980 (Jewish Law Annual, Supplment II).
2. S. M. Passamaneck, *Insurance in Rabbinic Law* (Edinburgh, 1974).
3. The Chairman of the B'nai Brith Canada National *Get* Committee was reported recently in the Canadian press as claiming that 15% of Jewish males involved in divorce cases (most of them non-practising Jews) use the *get* as a

'bargaining chip'. I have not yet been able to ascertain precisely how this figure was arrived at.
4. For an important symposium on the topic, see *The Jewish Law Annual*, vol. IV (1981). Bleich's proposed pre-nuptial agreement at JLA IV (1981), pp. 184-7, may be compared with that in Shlomo Riskin, *Women and Jewish Divorce* (New York, 1988).
5. The procedure of delivery of the *get* by the husband is mentioned in a series of clauses introduced by vav-conjunctive, which are generally (though not inevitably) regarded as a continuing protasis (leading to the apodosis which rules against restoration of the original marriage). The passage thus mentions the procedure incidentally, implying it to be the normal procedure, but not stipulating that it is the only possible procedure. The rabbinic reading of the text does, however, regard the procedure as normative. See now R. Gordis, *The Dynamics of Judaism* (Bloomington and Indianapolis, 1990), pp. 149, 227, n.9.
6. See particularly his *Studies in Biblical Law* (Cambridge, 1947); *The New Testament and Rabbinic Judaism* (London, 1956); *Ancient Jewish Law* (Leiden, 1981).
7. 'More about Research into Jewish Law', in *Modern Research in Jewish Law*, ed. B. S. Jackson (Leiden, 1980), pp. 66-111 (and see also the contrary views in that volume).
8. *Herut ha-perat be-darkhe geviyat hov ba-mishpat ha-'ivri* (Jerusalem, 1964). Elon's monumental introduction to the sources of Jewish law, *Ha-mishpat ha'ivri* (Jerusalem, 1973) is shortly to appear in English translation.
9. E.g. the Persian decrees relating to the restoration under Ezra and Nehemia, recorded in the biblical book of *Ezra* (1:2-4, 4:17-22, 5:9-17, 6:3-12, 7:12-26) and the Apocryphal *1 Esdras* (2:3-7, 25-29, 6:24-26, 8:9-24). See E. Bickerman, 'The Edict of Cyrus in Ezra I', *Journal of Biblical Literature* 65 (1946), pp. 244-75; Daniela Piattelli, *Concezioni giuridiche e metodi costruttivi dei giuristi orientali* (Milan, 1981), pp. 11-21.
10. B. S. Jackson, 'The Ceremonial and the Judicial: Biblical Law as Sign and Symbol', *Journal for the Study of the Old Testament* 30 (1984), pp. 25-50.
11. An issue to which I have devoted considerable attention in recent years: see 'Law' in *Harper's Bible Dictionary*, ed. P. J. Achtemeier (San Francisco, 1985), pp. 548-51; 'Some Semiotic Questions for Biblical Law', *The Oxford Conference Volume*, ed. A. M. Fuss (Atlanta, 1987), pp. 1-25 (Jewish Law Association Studies III); 'Ideas of Law and Legal Administration: a Semiotic Approach', in *The World of Ancient Israel: Sociological, Anthropological and Political Perspectives*, ed. R. E. Clements (Cambridge, 1989), pp. 185-202; 'Legalism and Spirituality: Historical, Philosophical and Semiotic Notes on Legislators, Adjudicators, and Subjects', in *Religion and Law, Biblical-Judaic and Islamic Perspectives*, ed. E. B. Firmage, B. G. Weiss and J. W. Welch (Winona Lake, 1990), pp. 243-61; 'Law' in *A Dictionary of Biblical Interpretation*, ed. R. J. Coggins and J. L. Houlden (London and Philadelphia, 1990), pp. 383-6.
12. See José Faur, *Golden Doves with Silver Dots: Semiotics and Textuality in Rabbinic Tradition* (Bloomington, 1986).
13. See 'Hilluq and Haqira: A Study in the Method of the Lithuanian Halakhists', *Dinei Israel* 4 (1973), pp. lxix-cvi, and other articles listed in Phyllis

Holman Weisbard and David Schonberg, *Jewish Law: Bibliography of Sources and Scholarship in English* (Littleton, 1989), pp. 189-90.
14. Irving J. Rosenbaum, *The Holocaust and Halakhah* (New York, 1976); H. J. Zimmels, *The Echo of the Nazi Holocaust in Rabbinic Literature* (New York, 1977).
15. New York, Jewish Theological Seminary of America, 1966, 2 vols.
16. London, Soncino Press, 1965-7, 2 vols.
17. Going back as far as B. B. Lieberman, 'Torts in Jewish Law', *Journal of Comparative Legislation and International Law* 9 (1927), pp. 231-40. As early as 1929, George Webber (later Reader in English Law at University College London and himself a contributor to the JCLIL on Jewish law), compiled a 'Bibliography of Recent Works on Jewish Jurisprudence', *The Law Journal* 69 (1929), pp. 82-3. The recently-established *National Jewish Law Review*, in its first four issues (1986-89), has shown a particular bias towards torts questions. See further Weisbard and Schonberg, *supra* n.13, at pp. 437-43; N. Rakover, *The Multi-Language Bibliography of Jewish Law* (Jerusalem, 1990), ch. 13.
18. *Studies in Talmudic Logic and Methodology* (London, 1961); *The Talmudic Argument* (Cambridge, 1984).
19. 'Herméneutique normative dans le Judaïsme et dans l'Islam', *Accademia Nazionale dei Lincei*, 8th Ser., 30 (1976), fasc.5-6, pp. 1-20.
20. 'Law and the State—(a) Islamic Religious Law', in J. Schacht and C. E. Bosworth, *The Legacy of Islam* (Oxford, 1974), p. 397.
21. See. L. Jacobs, 'Hermeneutics', *Encyclopedia Judaica* (Jerusalem, 1972), VIII, p. 368.
22. See further B. S. Jackson, *Semiotics and Legal Theory* (London, 1985), pp. 46-50.
23. B. S. Jackson, 'The Concept of Religious Law in Judaism', *Aufstieg und Niedergang der römischen Welt* (Berlin, 1979), Bd. II.19,1, pp. 51-2.
24. *Sifre Bamidbar*, on *Numbers* 15-31 (R. Ishmael).
25. *A Criminal Code for England and Wales* (London, HMSO, 1989), 2 Vols., Law Com. No. 177.
26. B. S. Jackson, 'Analogy in Legal Science: Some Comparative Observations', in *Legal Knowledge and Analogy,* ed. P. Nerhot (Dordrecht, 1991), pp. 145-64.
27. *Encyclopedia Judaica*, VI, pp. 79-103, and literature there cited.
28. Haim Cohn, *The Trial and Death of Jesus* (London, 1967).
29. See also S. G. F. Brandon, *The Trial of Jesus of Nazareth* (London, 1968); E. Bammel, ed., *The Trial of Jesus* (London, 1970); J. D. M. Derrett, *Law in the New Testament* (London, 1970), ch. 17; Jean Imbert, *Le Procès de Jésus* (Paris, 1980); B. S. Jackson, 'The Prophet and the Law in Early Judaism and the New Testament', *Cardozo Studies in Law and Literature* 4/2 (Fall 1992), 123–166.
30. B. S. Jackson, 'Jésus et Moïse: le Statut du Prophète à l'égard de la Loi', *Revue historique de droit français et étranger* (1981), pp. 341-60.
31. B. S. Jackson, 'Legalism', *Journal of Jewish Studies* 30 (1979), pp. 1-22.
32. Discussed in B. S. Jackson, *Essays in Jewish and Comparative Legal History* (Leiden, 1975), pp. 130-41.

33. See, e.g., David Daube, 'Alexandrian Methods of Interpretation and the Rabbis', *Hebrew Union College Annual* 22 (1949), pp. 239-64.
34. See note 40, below.
35. On Maimonides' codification, see the articles in Vol. I (1978) of *The Jewish Law Annual*.
36. B. S. Jackson, *supra* n. 35; for the medieval reception of this distinction see 'On the Origins of *Scienter*', *The Law Quarterly Review* 94 (1978), pp. 85-102, xvi; 'Travels and Travails of the Goring Ox: The Biblical Text in British Sources', *Studies in Bible and the Ancient Near East Presented to S. E. Loewenstamm*, ed. Y. Avishur & J. Blau (Jerusalem, 1978), pp. 41-56.
37. 'Susanna and the Singular History of Singular Witnesses', *Acta Juridica* (1977), pp. 37-54 (Essays in Honour of Ben Beinart).
38. A recent semi-popular treatment is Oscar Kraines, *The Impossible Dilemma: Who is a Jew in the State of Israel?* (New York, 1986).
39. L. H. Schiffman, *Who Was a Jew? Rabbinic and Halakhic Perspectives on the Jewish-Christian Schism* (Hoboken, New Jersey, 1985).
40. See the monograph of S. Shilo, *Dina demalkhuta dina* (Jerusalem, 1974).
41. Tosefta Baba Kamma 4:2; see B. S. Jackson, 'Liability for Animals in Roman Law: An Historical Sketch', *The Cambridge Law Journal*, 37 (1978), pp. 138-140.
42. *Purity and Danger* (London, 1966).
43. As argued in 'Some Semiotic Questions for Biblical Law', *The Oxford Conference Volume*, pp. 1-25, at 16-18; more generally, 'Conscious and Unconscious Rationality in Law and Legal Theory', in *Reason in Law, Proceedings of the Conference Held in Bologna, 12-15 December 1984*, ed. Carla Faralli and Enrico Pattaro (Milan, 1988), III. pp. 281-99.
44. 'Biblical Laws of Slavery: a Comparative Approach', in *Slavery and other Forms of Unfree Labour*, ed. L. Archer (London and New York, 1988), pp. 86-101 (History Workshop Series).
45. *Chattel or Person? The Status of Women in the Mishnah* (New York and Oxford, 1988).
46. (London, 1975).
47. On the relationship of the *Aggadah* to the *Halakhah*, see the stimulating writings of David Novak: *Law and Theology in Judaism* (New York, 1974); *Law and Theology in Judaism* (second series, New York, 1976); *Halakhah in a Theological Dimension* (Chico, Ca., 1985).
48. N. Lamm and A. Kirschenbaum, 'Freedom and Constraint in the Jewish Juridical Process', *Cardozo Law Review* 1 (1979), pp. 132-3; see also B. S. Jackson, 'Secular Jurisprudence and the Philosophy of Jewish Law: A Commentary on Some Recent Literature', *The Jewish Law Annual* 6 (1986), p. 32.
49. *Messianism and Mishnah: Time and Place in the Early Halakhah* (Cincinnati, 1979) (The Louis Caplan Lecture on Jewish Law); Jackson, *supra* no. 48, at pp.39-41.
50. 'Secular Jurisprudence...', *supra* n. 48.
51. *The Image of the Non-Jew in Judaism, An Historical and Constructive Study of the Noahide Laws* (New York and Toronto, 1983) (Toronto Studies in Theology, 14).
52. *Supra* n. 17.

53. *Supra* n. 13.
54. Aaron Schreiber, *Jewish Law and Decision-Making: A Study Through Time* (Philadelphia, 1979).
55. E. Dorff and A. Rossett, *A Living Tree: Materials on the Jewish Legal Tradition with Comparative Notes* (Albany, 1987).
56 It was in response to this remark, at the delivery of the lecture in June 1990, that a Maecenas—Mr. David Landau—*was* found for the Jewish Law Association's Textbook, *An Introduction to the History and Sources of Jewish Law*. The Textbook will be published by Scholars Press in 1994 in the Association's series, *Jewish Law Association Studies*. Further support for textbooks devoted to particular areas of Jewish Law, and for the translation of leading monographs published in Israel, is now being sought.

JEWISH EDUCATION IN THE BYZANTINE EMPIRE IN THE TWELFTH CENTURY

Nicholas de Lange

Jewish education in Byzantium is a subject which still remains cloaked in deepest darkness. Very little research has been done, and it must be admitted that the raw materials on which such research might be based are not, at first glance, promising. The invitation to contribute to this volume in honour of a loved and respected teacher and colleague presented a challenge which the present writer, rashly no doubt, could not resist. What follows, then, should be read as a tentative exploration of unfamiliar paths. There are three main elements: a consideration of the general issues involved; some thoughts about the syllabus; and, by way of an appendix, a list of 12th-century Judaeo-Byzantine scholars known by name.[1]

The Jewish culture of Byzantium, like its Christian counterpart, is characterised generally by a high regard for literacy and learning. The twelfth-century Christian historian Niketas Choniates complains of the Latin Christians that 'they ridicule us as scribes and scriveners, who ostentatiously carry reed pens and inkwells, and hold books in their hands'.[2] In similar vein in the 1140s a Byzantine Jew living in Egypt, one Elia son of Caleb son of Leo, writing to the Nagid Samuel in Fostat, deplores the contempt for learning shown by the Jews of Benhe, where he is living,[3] while in another letter written a few years earlier a scholarly Jew from Baghdad, Samuel ben Judah Ha-bavli, indicates his intention of leaving Egypt, where he is residing, and settling in the Byzantine Empire because of the superior opportunities for study which are available there.[4]

How was the high rate of literacy achieved, and how was learning transmitted? On the Christian side we have a certain amount of information.

The Greeks had inherited from antiquity a three-tiered system of education not inherently different from that prevailing in western countries today. The institutions of secondary education and higher studies were, however, severely disrupted following the reforms of the emperor Justinian in the sixth century and a general collapse of urban life. For a long time the classical tradition only really survived, in an attenuated form, in the metropolis, and elsewhere we should probably imagine only some kind of primary instruction conducted by private teachers. From the ninth century there was a gradual recovery of learning, but it was not until the eleventh century that we can speak of a real revival, which is probably to be associated with a restoration of urban life.

To what extent Jewish education shared this pattern of decline and recovery we can only surmise, but the Jews cannot have been immune to the effects of the collapse of the cities, and we must suppose also that the concentration of higher learning in the hands of the Church from the fifth century on, and particularly from the reign of Justinian,[5] was severely damaging to their tradition of scholarship. What is certain is that all indications point to a serious decline in literacy from about the sixth century, after which time we have no datable inscriptions, whether public or private, in Greek, and very few indications of the copying of Greek manuscripts, let alone the creation of new works, by Jews. Jewish writing only recovers, very slowly, from the ninth or tenth century in Byzantine South Italy and from the eleventh century in Byzantium proper. (At this time, as we shall see, education was based on the Hebrew language and script, and evidence of literacy in Greek becomes very rare among Jews.) The Jewish evidence is thus broadly in line with that from the Christian *milieu*.

The revival of Christian learning in the eleventh century is accompanied by the creation of new institutions, both permanent secondary schools, attached to churches, and also institutes of higher study, enjoying state support. Clearly it would not be appropriate for the state to support an analogous Jewish university, nor would our sources have left us in the dark had this been attempted or even so much as suggested. It is, however, tempting to imagine the creation at this time of permanent Jewish schools attached to synagogues, in the same way as the Christian school was attached to churches or the Muslim *madrasa* was attached to mosques. And indeed the letter of Samuel ben Judah ha-Bavli, mentioned above, lends support to this idea. Samuel writes as follows:

> ...And I should inform you that someone who came to Alexandria told me that in the land of the Byzantines, in Thebes and Salonica, there are permanent schools [*midrashot kevu'ot*] and respectable scholars [*vetalmidei hakham(im) hagunim*] who are

fond of those who study the Torah. I have made up my mind to go there after Pesah, God willing, for my sole desire is for the Torah. And I have made up my mind to give up my life to its study. Before I do this I shall come up to Fustat to fetch the books that have been purchased for me, God willing, or else to put them in store. If you also wish to go with me to study Torah, tell me so and make me happy. As for me, God willing, my mind is made up.

[T-S 16.301, verso, lines 11-21]

The letter can be placed approximately in the 1130s.[6] Although it is written in Arabic, the words we have given in the original ('permanent schools and respectable scholars') are in Hebrew, perhaps because they represent the original words of the (Byzantine) informant. (The Hebrew term *midrashah* corresponds exactly to the Arabic *madrasa*.) Although this is, to the best of my knowledge, the only explicit mention of such permanent schools, their existence at this time is inherently probable. It is particularly interesting that Samuel is interested in going to Thebes or Salonica, and not to Constantinople or to some other provincial centre. There may, of course be personal reasons for the choice. But we should remember that both cities had substantial Jewish populations in the twelfth century. The Spanish traveller, Benjamin of Tudela, who visiting Byzantium around 1168, gives this information:[7]

...the great city of Thebes, where there are about 2,000 Jews. They are the most skilled tailors of silk and purple garments in Greece. They have scholars learned in the Mishnah and the Talmud, including some prominent figures [*gedolei ha-dor*]... There is none equal to them in all of Greece, except in Constantinople...

...the city of Saloniki... is a very large city with about 500 Jews. Here live R. Samuel and his sons, who are scholars...

For Thebes the Spaniard's testimony stands in frustrating isolation. However in the case of Salonica the Cairo Genizah has yielded even earlier confirmation of the essential picture in a letter which can be dated c.1090.[8] The writer is an Egyptian Jew who has settled in the Byzantine Empire because 'he despaired of the Muslim lands', at first in the east and then, after the Battle of Manzikert, in Salonica. Despite going blind, he is happy in Salonica:

> I am liked and respected by every God-fearer and every man of understanding and intelligence. ... And even though the community of Salonica are impressive people, not one of them can find fault with me in property law or capital cases or any other branch of the law.
>
> [T-S Ar.53.37, recto, lines 8-15]

Thus we can see that Salonica, now a burgeoning city with an important fair,[9] is just the sort of place that we might expect to have a Jewish school of its own. Indeed the Christian school there which was directed by Archbishop Eustathius, a considerable scholar, was so popular that it even attracted pupils from Constantinople.[10]

Leaving aside the intriguing question of permanent schools, we must imagine that for most students education took place with a private teacher, either individually or in a class. Several writers inform us that they were educated, at least in part, by their own fathers,[11] but children could also be farmed out to teachers. The Cairo Genizah, which provides us with abundant information about Jewish education in Egypt, gives us several examples of advanced scholars who took jobs as teachers of children so as to gain an independent livelihood, despite the contempt with which this occupation was often viewed.[12] In Byzantium we may suppose that a similar situation prevailed.

Jewish education in Byzantium was presumable organized, like its Christian counterpart, on three levels, as we know was the case in other Mediterranean Jewish communities. In a document from the Genizah, a Jewish scholar from Iraq, writing in Egypt around the middle of the twelfth century, gives us a succinct account of the three levels: the broad masses study the Pentateuch and the prayerbook; the next level, what he terms the scholars, study the rest of the Bible and a code of Jewish law; the highest level, that of the 'doctors', master the Mishnah and Talmud with their commentaries.[13] The main practical goal of elementary education, which involves learning to read and write in Hebrew, as well as a good deal of memorizing, is to be able to participate fully in the services of the synagogue. More learning than this would hardly be required by most classes of Jews; but communal functionaries (judges, teachers and so forth) would require more advanced study, both of the 'written' and of the 'oral' Torah.

The Genizah, which sheds such an abundant light on Egypt, offers us very little material of assured Byzantine provenance. But here and there we do find fragments of school books (whether textbooks, aids to study, or a teacher's or pupil's notes) from approximately our period which are either written in a

Jewish education in 12th century Byzantine Empire 119

mixture of Hebrew and Greek or carry annotations by a Greek-speaking Jew. These give us some indication of the subjects of study, as do the works written by Byzantine Jewish scholars, whether extant or known to us only indirectly.

The first point to emerge is that, whatever the spoken language might have been, the only written language, which clearly occupies pride of place as the object of all grammatical and textual study, is Hebrew. Although this may seem obvious to anyone accustomed to Jewish texts of the Middle Ages, it marks Byzantine Jews off very sharply from Byzantine Christians, who studied Greek grammar, strove to write classical Greek, and read even the Bible in Greek. There are very few indications in the Genizah of Jews being able to read and write Greek, and generally they use Hebrew characters for writing Greek words, which are normally taken from the vernacular language.

This state of affairs is presumably linked to the use of Hebrew in the synagogue liturgy and the use of the Hebrew Bible in synagogues. We do not know precisely when this usage was adopted, but it was standard from the end of the tenth century and probably much earlier, even if the Greek Bible continued to be used as a sort of *targum* and for educational purposes.

We have examples from the Genizah of various ways in which the Greek could be used to help the student to learn and understand the Hebrew. At the most basic level we find odd Greek glosses written into biblical manuscripts, between the lines or in the margins.[14] In another type of compilation, a list of difficult words may be followed by their Greek equivalents: a sort of lexicon, except that the words are arranged not in alphabetical order but following the order of their occurrence in the text of the Bible.[15] At a more complex level, the biblical lemma may be followed by an explanation in Hebrew, as well as one or more Greek equivalents.[16] And finally we may find a continuous commentary, in which Hebrew explanations predominate but Greek glosses are used occasionally to make the meaning clearer.[17] Some of these commentaries are carefully written out and may be considered as finished texts; others are presented in such a way as to raise a suspicion that they are informal notes or drafts. The fragments identified so far range over most of the Hebrew Bible, from Genesis to Job. There is no indication that any particular part (such as the Torah) is more highly favoured than any other: the sample is a small one, and it is due to chance presumably that there are fragments of two different compilations on 1 Kings while there is nothing at all on the Psalms.

Outside the Genizah, copies have been preserved of other Byzantine compilations from our period. To judge from what survives, and supposing it to be typical also of what is lost, we can identify biblical commentary as a particular predilection of Byzantine Jewish scholars, whether of the Rabbanite or the Karaite persuasion. The sources of these commentaries are various, and include both *midrashim* and recent scholarly commentaries such as those of Rashi and Ibn Ezra.[18]

Hymnography (*piyyut*) was another favourite *genre* of Byzantine Jewish authors, encouraged no doubt by the place it enjoyed in the religious ritual of the dominant faith. The Byzantine Jewish ritual is very rich in hymns, which are commonly marked by a playful obscurity of language and a richness of allegorical reference which would certainly baffle anyone not initiated into their inner thought-world. Some kind of education in the appreciation of the hymns will have been necessary, therefore, and it is hard to imagine this as proceeding further than a very superficial initiation at the primary and even the first stages of the secondary education. More advanced students were apparently instructed in the elaborate rules of composition, to judge by the very large numbers of hymns surviving, of very different artistic and philological standards, and issuing not only from large centres but even from more obscure Jewish communities, such as Kastoria.[19] A stray Genizah fragment of a learned commentary on a hymn from the Byzantine ritual for the Fast of Av[20] provides just a hint of the importance of this heritage in Byzantine Jewish study.

Little need be said here about Midrash, which was, together with hymnography, one of the very richest elements in the Byzantine Jewish tradition.[21] Suffice it to say that, even if there is no clear indication that new midrashic texts were composed in Byzantium in our period, the old *midrashim* continued to be copied, and, as we have already observed, they were exploited by Byzantine scholars. They will not doubt have provided a useful teaching resource.

Talmudic study was the backbone of Rabbinic Judaism, and it was evidently important in Byzantium. We have already remarked the words of the letter from Salonica in the late 11th century: the author is admittedly an Egyptian Jew, who is delighted to discover that he can hold his own in halakhic discussion with the natives, but clearly traditional Halakhah constituted a subject of common interest. Students probably commenced with the study of the Mishnah, before moving on to the much harder Gemarah. The Cairo Genizah has preserved fragments of a number of aids to study, normally consisting of lists of difficult mishnaic words together with their Greek equivalents.[22] If these are sometimes focussed on the names of plants and their correct identification, this may reflect an interest in medical education, or at a more mundane level the importance of textile production in the life of the Byzantine Jews.[23] The Genizah has also given us a number of manuscripts, from both the Palestinian and the Babylonian Talmud, bearing notes by Byzantine readers, sometimes written in a mixture of Hebrew and Greek.[24]

Byzantine Karaites, of course, did not view the Talmud in the same light, although some of them clearly did have a knowledge of it. They had their own traditions and their own preoccupations (among which theology and law are uppermost), which emerge from their abundant surviving literature. This subject need not detain us: it has been fully discussed elsewhere.[25]

This survey of Byzantine Jewish education in the twelfth century has of necessity been somewhat discursive: in the present state of the raw material, that is inevitable. In particular there are two topics which have had to be passed over entirely. One is the place of secular studies in Byzantine Jewish education: this is a very complex subject on which little work has been done even of an exploratory character. The Greek philosophical and scientific heritage was in any case apparently exploited only by a small élite of advanced scholars: it did not form any part of the basic education for Jews.[26] The other topic that, sadly, has had to be omitted from consideration is the important one of the education of women, on account of the silence of our sources. The few letters from or to Byzantine Jewish women preserved in the Genizah come from Egypt,[27] and they do not allow us to make any deductions about the situation prevailing in Byzantium.

Appendix

The state of the evidence makes it very difficult to draw up an inventory of Byzantine Jewish scholars at this period. Benjamin of Tudela mentions a few names, but he does not elaborate, and his testimony cannot be checked. For Crete, I have relied also on the earliest statutes of the Jewish community, dated 1228, which were edited by Elia Kapsali in the early sixteenth century (see ARTOM and CASSUTO, TK, pp. 3-7). It seemed legitimate to include established personalities mentioned in sources of the early 13th century, who presumable studied in the 12th, and also some figures who are mentioned in sources of the late 11th century but presumably continued to teach into the following century. Colophons in manuscripts, a useful source of information about scholarly activities at a later period, are rare for Byzantium before the beginning of the 14th century. The main and most solid evidence for this period consists of actual written work, either surviving or mentioned in other sources. In the list that follows I have not attempted to give full bibliographical information, but refer to the fullest or the most recent modern discussions.

Constantinople

Aaron Bekhor Shor: mentioned briefly by Benjamin of Tudela.

Abtalion: Chief Rabbi in 1168 according to Benjamin of Tudela.

Caleb Korsinos: Author of a lost supercommentary on Abraham Ibn Ezra, mentioned by Judah Ibn Moskoni in the 14th century, who praises his mastery of grammar. His date is uncertain: according to ANKORI (*KB*, p.199 n.110) he may well have lived in the 13th, rather than the 12th, century.
STARR, *JBE*, pp. 64, 236.

Eliakim: Leader (*parnas*) of the Rabbanite community, according to Benjamin of Tudela.

Jacob b. Reuben: Karaite author of an extant compilation on the Bible, the *Sefer ha-'osher*.
POZNANSKI, *KLO*, pp. 66-8.
ANKORI, *KB*, pp. 196-8.

Jacob b. Simeon: Karaite translator. He studied in Jerusalem and translated into Hebrew a treatise on incest by his master Yeshu'ah b. Judah.
ANKORI, *KB*, pp. 188-9.

Joseph: Author of the *Sefer 'adat deborim*, a treatise on the text of the Bible. It is not certain whether he was a Rabbanaite or a Karaite. Benjamin of Tudela mentions a Rabbi Joseph in Constantinople in 1168.
STARR, *JBE*, pp. 63, 240f.
BOWMAN, *JB*, pp. 217f.

Judah b. Elijah Hadassi: Karaite author of the encyclopaedic compilation *Eshkol ha-kofer*, begun in 1148.
STARR, *JBE*, p. 244.
ANKORI, *KB*, index, s.v. 'Yehuda Hadassi'.

Meyuhas b. Elijah: Biblical commentator.
STARR, JBE, pp. 63f., 225f.

Ovadiah: Mentioned briefly by Benjamin of Tudela.

Solomon: Royal physician, mentioned by Benjamin of Tudela.

Crete

Anatoli b. David Kazani: Hymnographer, and author of the work *Ruah hen*. A number of his compositions survive.
E.g. WEINBERGER, *HUCA* 39 (1968) [Hebrew section], pp. 27-9; *RPP*, pp. 52-4; *JPC*, pp. 25-40.

Baruch b. Isaac: Rabbi whose name figures in the statutes of 1228. He is described as *gaon* and *ha-rav ha-gadol* (*TK*, p. 3).

Benjamin b. Joseph Bonifaccio: Rabbi whose name figures in the statutes of 1228. The name also occurs in some colophons.

Eleazar b. Mattathias: Rabbi whose name figures in the statutes of 1228.

Elijah b. Reuben: Leader (*parnas*) whose name figures in the statutes of 1228.

Isaac b. Joseph: Rabbi whose name figures in the statutes of 1228.

Ishmael Maimon: Communal leader and physician whose name figures in the statutes of 1228.

Joshua b. Ovadiah ha-Levi: Leader whose name figures in the statutes of1228.

Judah Anatoli b. Harav: Leader whose name figures in the statutes of 1228.
Mattathias b. Eleazar: Rabbi whose name figures in the statutes of 1228. He bears the title *hasid*, TK, pp. 3, 7.
Menahem b. Jacob: Leader (*parnas*) whose name figures in the statutes of 1228.
Menahem b. Joel: Rabbi whose name figures in the statutes of 1228.
Parnas Kapsali b. Solomon b. Joseph: Communal leader whose name figures in the statutes of 1228. *Parnas* was perhaps his title, in which case his personal name is missing, Kapsali being a surname.
Samuel b. Gamliel b. Shemtov: Communal leader whose name figures in the statutes of 1228.
Shemariah b. Shelahyah: Scholar. His name figures in the statutes of 1228.
Shemariah b. Solomon b. Isaac ha-Kohen: Rabbi whose name figures in the statutes of 1228.
Simeon (or Samson?) Agora: Rabbi whose name figures in the statutes of 1228.
Elia Romanos b. David: Known to us only from the genealogy of his great-great-grandson Shemariah b. Elia of Negroponte (Paris, BN, MS héb. 897 fol. 12r). From the fact that he is given the title *harav* (unlike his son and grandson) we may assume that he had some claim to be considered a scholar. His father, a Roman Jew, is called *rabbenu*. From his surname Romanos and the fact that his father is specifically described as a Roman it is to be deduced that Elia had left Rome, and we may presume that he settled in Crete, where his great-grandson, also called Elia, occupied a position of prominence in the latter part of the 13th century.
Zerah b. David Kazani: Hymnographer. Thought by some to be identical with Anatoli b. David Kazani (Zerah being a possible Hebrew translation of the Greek Anatoli): see STEINSCHNEIDER, *Mosè* 2 (1879), p. 415.

Salonica

Eliezer b. Judah: Hymnographer, believed to be a nephew of Tobias b. Eliezer.
   WEINBERGER, *RPP*, pp. 165-7.
   Cf. J. MANN, *Hatekufah* 23 (1925), p. 256; STARR, *JBE*, p. 204.
Elijah: Brief mention by Benjamin of Tudela.
Michael: Briefly mentioned by Benjamin of Tudela.
Samuel: Head of the Jews of Salonica by royal decree, according to Benjamin of Tudela, who adds that his sons were scholars. Benjamin also mentions his son-in-law Shabbetai.
   S. D. GOITEIN, *Sefunot* 11 (1971/77), pp. 14, 17.
Tobias b. Eliezer: Biblical commentator, author of the influential commentary *Lekah Tov*. Although a native of Kastoria, where he taught for a while, Tobias apparently mainly lived and wrote in Salonica (see A. MARMORSTEIN in *REJ* 73 (1921) pp. 92ff.).
   S. BUBER (ed.), *Midrash Lekah Tov* (Vilna 1880) (with very full introduction).
   STARR, *JBE*, pp. 63, 215-7 (with bibliography).
   BARON, *SRHJ* vol. 6, pp. 173-5 and notes, pp. 411 f.
   One of his hymns is republished by WEINBERGER, *BSP*, pp. 20-24.

Thebes

Abraham Zutra: His lost writings included a number of commentaries on rabbinic texts: *Sifra*, Babylonian Talmud tractate *Shabbat*, and the whole order *Tohorot*. They are quoted by Isaiah of Trani in the 13th century and by Elijah Mizrahi in the 15th. He may well be the earliest supercommentator on Rashi (BARON, *SRHJ* vol. 6, p. 278).
    S. SCHECHTER, *JQR* 4 (1891), p. 94.
    STARR, *JBE*, pp. 62, 226f.
Elijah Tirutot: Brief mention by Benjamin of Tudela.
Hiyya: Brief mention by Benjamin of Tudela.
Michael b. Caleb: Poet. According to al-Harizi he studied in Spain. It is not certain whether any of his compositions survive, but cf. WEINBERGER, *HUCA* 39 (1968), 52.
    BOWMAN, *JB*, p. 220.
Quti: Chief rabbi in 1168: briefly mentioned by Benjamin of Tudela, together with his brother, Moses.
Yoktan: Brief mention by Benjamin of Tudela.

Other Centres

Abraham b. Marino ha-Kohen: Hymnographer, thought to have lived in Corfu.
    WEINBERGER, *ESP*, p. 9.
Joseph: Leader (*parnas*) in Halmyro, according to Benjamin of Tudela.
Meir: Pupil of Tobias b. Eliezer from Kastoria, author of a lost work quoted by Judah Ibn Moskoni.
    STARR, *JBE*, pp. 63, 218.
Menahem b. Elijah: Hymnographer in Kastoria.
    WEINBERGER, HPG, p. 24; RPP, pp. 46-8, 72-6, 81-3, 155-9; BSP, pp. 66-99; ESP, pp. 1f.
Shiloh Lombardo: Chief Rabbi of Halmyro according to Benjamin of Tudela.
Tobias b. Eliezer: Scholar of Kastoria: see above, under Salonica.
Yohanan b. Reuben: Halakhist of Ohrida. His date is uncertain.
    KRAUSS, *Studien*, p. 136.

Locality Unknown

Avishai of Zagora: Author of several lost works, including a commentary on Abraham Ibn Ezra's *Commentary on the Pentateuch*. Our only information about him comes from the mid-14th century scholar Judah Ibn Moskoni (Introduction to *Even ha-'ezer*, ed. A. Berliner, *Otzar Tov* (Berlin, 1878, p. 6), who dates the supercommentary on internal grounds to 1170.
    STARR, *JBE*, pp. 64, 236.
    BOWMAN, *JB*, pp. 283-5, cf. p. 66.
Baruch: Halakhist.
    KRAUSS, *Studien*, p. 136.
    Y. N. EPSTEIN, *Tarbiz* 16 (1944-45), pp. 49-53.
Caleb b. Solomon: Hymnographer.

Caleb Nenni b. Shabbetai: Hymnographer.
David Peppi: Hymnographer.
Eleazar b. Hanukkah b. Eleazar b. David b. Abraham: Scribe. Copyist of a Torah scroll, of which only the last three columns remain, dated 1192 (Bodleian MS Heb. c. 6, Neubauer 2616.4. Neubauer describes the hand as 'Greek'.)
Hillel b. Eliakim: Rabbinic scholar, whose commentaries on *Sifra* and *Sifre* survive. He is said to have originated from, or lived, in, Selymbria, but it is not clear that this is where he mainly lived and wrote.
    STARR, *JBE*, pp.61 f., with bibliography.
    The commentary on *Sifra* is edited by S. Koleditzky, 2 vols, Jerusalem, A. M. 5721 [1961]; that on *Sifre* by id., 2 vols in one, Jerusalem, A. M. 5708 [1948].
Isaac: An author named 'Isaac of Romania' is quoted by Isaiah of Trani (see BOWMAN, JB, p. 61 n. 30).
    An 'Isaac Zutra' is mentioned by Elijah Mizrahi (ibid., p. 130, n. 3), but according to STARR (*JBE*, p. 226) this may be a mistake for Abraham Zutra (of Thebes—see above).
Isaac b. Judah: Hymnographer.
    Cf. WEINBERGER, *ESP*.
Isaac b. Melchizedek: Rabbinic scholar, associated with Siponto. He is quoted by Isaiah of Trani, and referred to as 'the Greek rabbi' by Abraham b. David of Posquières.
    See WEINBERGER, ESP, p. 8.
Joseph b. Isaac: Hymnographer.
    Cf. WEINBERGER, *RPP*, pp. 100-101, 103-107.
Joseph b. Jacob Qalai: Hymnographer, 24 of whose compositions have been recovered from the Genizah. He follows Spanish models in his work, and may even have been born in Spain.
    WEINBERGER, *HUCA* 39 (1968) [Heb.], 11; *RPP*, p. 129f.; cf. *ESP*.
Judah b. Jacob: Karaite scribe. In one colophon he mentions the name of the city where he was working (in 1207) as GGRA, which has been variously identified as Gagry on the Black Sea or Gangra (Germanicopolis) in Paphlagonia. See ANKORI, *KB*, pp. 125-8; BOWMAN, *JB*, pp. 217-18.
    For a hymnographer of the same name, see WEINBERGER, *RPP*, pp. 171-3.
Mordecai b. Isaac: Hymnographer.
    See WEINBERGER, *RPP*, pp. 130-33.
Moses Daba: Mentioned briefly by Isaac b. Abba Mari of Marseilles, c. 1180.
    STARR, *JBE*, p. 214.
Moses b. Abtalion: Hymnographer. Mentioned approvingly by Judah al-Harizi, c. 1218.
    BOWMAN, *JB*, p. 220.
Moses b. Hiyya: Hymnographer. Mentioned by al-Harizi, who says he studied in Spain. More than twenty of his hymns survive.
    BOWMAN, *JB*, p. 220.
    Cf. WEINBERGER, *HUCA* 39 (1968) [Heb.], pp. 41-4; *RPP*; *ESP*.
Yehiel b. Eliakim: Scribe. He copied the commentary on the *Sifra* by Hillel b. Eliakim (see above) in Alexandria in 1212 (Frankfurt UB MS Heb. 4o 2), and it has been suggested that he was the brother of the author.
    BOWMAN, *JB*, pp. 218f.

Zedekiah b. Abraham: Hymnographer, and author of the halakhic compendium *Shibbolei ha-leket* (edited in part from an Oxford manuscript by M. Z. HASIDA, Jerusalem, A. M. 5729 [1969]).

Notes

1. This last feature owes an obvious debt to Robert Browning's study, 'The Patriarchal School at Constantinople'. (Full references for all abbreviated titles will be found in the bibliography at the end of this article.) I should add that the idea for this article as a whole evolved from a stray remark of Professor A. P. Kazhdan concerning the Cambridge Genizah fragment T-S 16.301, during the 24th Spring Symposium of Byzantine Studies.
2. See A. P. Kazhdan and Ann Wharton Epstein, *Change in Byzantine Culture*, p. 120.
3. Starr, *JBE*, p. 220 (Cambridge UL, T-S 10J.9.14).
4. T-S 16.301. Arabic text with Hebrew translation and discussion by S. D. Goitein in *Sefunot* 11 (1971-77), pp. 23-31.
5. It is sometimes held that a law of Justinian dated 529 bans Jews (in common with pagans and heretics) from teaching Christians, but this is by no means certain: see A. M. Rabello, *Giustiniano, Ebrei e Samaritani alla luce delle fonti storico-letterarie, ecclesiastiche e giuridiche*, vol. 2 (Milan 1988), pp. 726f.
6. See Goitein, *Education*, p. 185 and his more detailed arguments in *Sefunot* 11 (1971-77), p. 23f.
7. Starr, *JBE*, pp. 229-30.
8. T-S Ar. 53-37, cf. Goitein, *Sefunot* 11 (1971-77), pp. 11-22.
9. See the vivid description from a 12th century source in Kazhdan and Epstein, *Change in Byzantine Culture*, p. 236.
10. Ibid., p. 121.
11. E.g. Tobias b. Eliezer (fl. c. 1100): see Starr, *JBE*, p. 216. At a later date, Shemariah b. Elia (fl. c. 1300) describes how, as part of his son's education, he wrote out for him a condensed version of the Talmud with a commentary: see Bowman, *JB*, p. 257.
12. See Goitein, *Community*, p. 189, and more generally on education ibid., pp. 171-211, *Education*, pp. 75ff.
13. T-S K3.1, see Goitein, *Education*, pp. 148f., *Community*, pp. 205f.
14. E.g. M. C. Davis, *Hebrew Biblical Manuscripts in the Cambridge Genizah Collections*, vol. 2 (Cambridge 1980), p. 267 and pl. 9.
15. An example is T-S NS 309.9, published by me in *Vetus Testamentum* 30 (1980), pp. 291-4.
16. E. g. T-S K24.14, published by me in *Interpreting the Hebrew Bible. Essays in Honour of E. I. J. Rosenthal*, ed. J. A. Emerton and S. C. Reif (Cambridge 1982), pp. 75-83.
17. E. g. T-S K25.288, K27.47, both unpublished.
18. S. Buber, in his introduction to the *Lekah Tov* on the Torah by Tobias ben Eliezer (Vilna 1880), pp. 36-45, lists the sources of that important and influential work. They run to 38 distinct headings, some comprising several

works. The sources listed include the Targum, both Talmuds, a wide range of Midrashim, the Heikhalot, *Sefer yetsira*, *seder 'olam*, halakhic compilations of the Geonic period, Saadia, the Masoretes Ben Asher and Ben Naphtali, the *Yosifon*, Shabbetai Donnolo, and various other sources both named and unnamed. On the use of Ibn Ezra in Byzantium see my article 'Abraham Ibn Ezra and Byzantium' in *Abraham Ibn Ezra y Su Tiempo*, ed. Fernando Díaz Esteban (Madrid 1990), pp. 181-92.

19. L. J. Weinberger has published a number of volumes of editions of Byzantine Jewish hymns, including one entirely devoted to Kastoria: *Bulgaria's Synagogue Poets: The Kastoreans* (Cincinnati, Ohio 1983). See also his other collections listed in the Bibliography.
20. Published by L. Ginzberg in *Ginzei Schechter* vol. 1, pp. 246-97. Ginzberg attributed it on insufficient grounds to Tobias ben Eliezer: see the remarks of Starr in *JBE*, pp. 217f.
21. See further my remarks in *Revue d'Histoire des Religions* 206 (1989), pp. 171-81.
22. See, for example, J. Starr, 'A Fragment of a Greek Mishnaic Glossary', *PAAJR* 6 (1934/35), pp. 353-67.
23. See Bowman, *JB*, pp. 119-121.
24. See for example S. Morag, *Vocalised Talmudic Manuscripts in the Cambridge Genizah Collections*, vol. 1 (Cambridge 1988), pp. 26, 31 and plate 7.
25. Ankori, *KB, passim*.
26. On the situation in Muslim lands, see Goitein, *Education*, pp. 195ff.
27. E. g. Cambridge UL Or. 1080 J1, T-S 8J.19.33 (both unpublished). See also Goitein, *Education*, pp. 63ff.

Bibliographical References and Abbreviations

A. Ankori, *Karaites in Byzantium. The Formative Years, 970-1100*. New York/Jerusalem, 1959. (*KB*)

E. S. Artom and H. M. D. Cassuto, *Statuta Iudaeorum Candiae eorumque memorabilia* [Hebrew]. Jerusalem, 1943. (*TK*)

S. W. Baron, *A Social and Religious History of the Jews*. 17 vols to date, 1952-80. (*SRHJ*)

S. B. Bowman, *The Jews of Byzantium, 1204-1453*. University of Alabama, 1985. (*JB*)

R. Browning, 'The Patriarchal School at Constantinople in the Twelfth Century', *Byzantion* 32 (1962), pp. 167-202; 33 (1963), pp. 11-40.

S. D. Goitein, *Jewish Education in Muslim Countries, based on records from the Cairo Geniza* [Hebrew]. Jerusalem, 1962.

S. D. Goitein, *A Mediterranean Society*, vol. 2, *The Community*. Berkeley/Los Angeles/London, 1971.

A. P. Kazhdan and A. W. Epstein, *Change in Byzantine Culture in the Eleventh and Twelfth Centuries*. Berkeley/Los Angeles/London, 1985.

S. Krauss, *Studien zur byzantinisch-jüdischen Geschichte*. Vienna, 1914.

S. Poznanski, *The Karaite Literary Opponents of Saadiah Gaon*. London, 1908. (*KLO*)

J. Starr, *The Jews in the Byzantine Empire, 641-1204*. Athens, 1939. (*JBE*)
J. L. Weinberger, 'New Poems from the Byzantine Period', *HUCA* 39 (1968) [Hebrew section], pp. 1-62.
Id., *Anthology of Hebrew Poetry in Greece, Anatolia and the Balkans*. Cincinnati, 1975. (*HPG*)
Id., *Romaniote Penitential Poetry*. New York, 1980. (*RPP*)
Id., *Bulgaria's Synagogue Poets, The Kastoreans*. Cincinnati, 1983. (*BSP*)
Id., *Jewish Poets in Crete*. Cincinnati, 1985. (*JPC*)
Id., *Early Synagogue Poets in the Balkans*. Cincinnati, 1988. (*ESP*)

CRITERIA OF MODERNISM IN EARLY HEBREW *HASKALAH* LITERATURE

Moshe Pelli

Historians and critics of Hebrew letters—from Klausner to Lahover, from Shapira to Sha'anan, and onward—have attempted to identify the beginning of modern Hebrew literature with a certain writer or a group of writers. Underlying the respective selections of these literary historians is the notion that their choice represents the beginning of modernism in Hebrew literature. The beginning of modern Hebrew literature is said to have coincided with the beginning of modern times in Jewish history.[1]

A detailed analysis of all these theories will not be undertaken here as it extends beyond the scope of this study. Such analysis may be found, however, in several of the studies which I cite below, especially those by Avraham Holtz, Arnold Band and Uzi Shavit. Nevertheless, reference will be made to some of them in order to point out their orientation and some of their inherent weaknesses. Subsequently, several alternative avenues will be suggested for further attempts to define the concept of modernism in Hebrew literature.

At the outset, we should note that criteria for modernism in literature may be classified according to extra-literary as well as literary classifications. The extra-literary criteria are based on disciplines such as the history of ideas, or religion, rather than literature. Undoubtedly, they were adopted to reflect changes in literature as well, and thus it can be argued that they may be used also for literary purposes.

The literary classification refers to discussions of major trends toward modernism in strictly literary terms. This approach may be further subdivided into European or Judaic orientations. The former relies on European trends which found their way into Hebrew literature, a phenomenon that is said to represent the modern inclination in Hebrew letters. The other orientation is inclined to define the new trends in Hebrew literature from within the confines of the Jewish literary corpus without reference to European literary criteria. While the concept of 'modernism' in Hebrew literature has not been defined satisfactorily, if at all, it was generally believed to be represented by a major shift from normative Jewish tradition to secularism.

Thus Joseph Klausner defines modern Hebrew literature as 'essentially secular' in that 'it started a new direction—to enlighten the people and resemble in its form and contents more or less the literature of all European peoples.'[2] Apart from the criteria of setting a new direction and enlightening the people, the concept of secularism is taken for granted as a term which needs no definition.

The notion that secularism epitomizes the modern trends, as advocated by Klausner and others, was generally accepted in *Haskalah* historiography. Both Lahover[3] and Sha'anan[4] used the notion without defining it.

As with modernism, the concept of secularism was originally presented in an intuitive fashion. Historians and social historians such as Bernard (Dov) Weinryb, Jacob Katz and Azriel Shohet later identified certain social trends prevalent among West-European Jews which were said to represent an emerging secularism.[5] There was, however, hardly any attempt to define secularism in strictly literary terms.

It was Barukh Kurzweil who dwelt most upon the concept of secularism in modern Hebrew literature. He identified a radical gap between traditional Jewish literature and modern Hebrew literature, claiming that the latter represents a complete discontinuity from the former. Traditional Jewish literature, he said, has acted throughout its history from within a background of a sanctified world. Modern Hebrew literature, however, was said to have possessed 'secularism. . . [which] emerges from a spiritual world that became void of the primordial certainty with a backdrop of sanctity encompassing the totality of life's phenomena and providing a criterion for their evaluation'.[6]

Klausner's theory of modernism identifies Naphtali Herz Wessely as the person who initiated modern Hebrew literature. He considered Wessely 'a new man', someone who 'fought for a new life, a new education, and a new Hebrew style'.[7] Although Klausner's criteria for modernism now becomes clearer, his selection of Wessely to represent secular modernism in Hebrew letters is problematical. His choice is based on Wessely's *Divrei shalom ve-'emet*. However, Wessely's other writings, before and after this controversial treatise on education, lean very heavily on the traditional aspects of Judaism. While there is something to be said for Klausner's choice of Wessely, it is not entirely satisfactory. For more than any other writer in the early Hebrew

Haskalah, Wessely epitomized in most of his writings—with the exception of *Divrei shalom ve-'emet*—the traditional values in Judaism.[8] He represented the very norms of traditional Judaism rather than a still-to-be defined modern secularism. Paradoxically, his writings contained a major innovation which Klausner failed to discern, and which will be discussed below.

Lahover identifies signs of a modern literature in the writings of Moshe Hayyim Luzzatto even though he, too, accepts the criterion of secularism as identifying modernism.[9] The selection of Luzzatto as a modernist is questioned by Klausner and other scholars. H. N. Shapira, for example, asserts that the beginning of modern Hebrew literature should be identified with the *me'assfim*, the writers and editors of *Ha-me'assef*.[10]

Kurzweil's definition of secularism as applied to the *Haskalah* is too broad and too general. His concept of *Haskalah*, while fitting the late phenomenon of Hebrew Enlightenment, is nevertheless incongruous with regard to the early Hebrew *Haskalah*.

Another theory was offered by Simon Halkin. His major criterion for identifying 'modernism' was 'humanism'. Accordingly, modern Hebrew literature is characterized by the shift from the theocentricity of traditional Judaism to an anthropocentricity modelled on European tendencies. Halkin borrowed this concept from the European Enlightenment, but stressed that European humanists were religious people. Thus, according to Halkin, modern Hebrew literature's inclination towards anthropocentricity does not represent a revolutionary trend, as suggested by Kurzweil, but rather an evolution.[11]

Classifying these theories according to the literary or extra-literary classifications, it seems that Klausner's definition is both extra-literary as well as literary, for he identified the new trends in modernism as attempts to emulate European literatures in form and content. Employing the second classification, European or Judaic, his orientation is definitely European.

Kurzweil, on the other hand, dealt mostly with the context of religion in an extra-literary fashion which nevertheless had a major bearing on literature. He seemed to concentrate on the Judaic—rather than the European—milieu, although by implication, the new trends were European-inspired.

While Halkin keeps referring to modern Hebrew *literature*, his criteria are basically extra-literary in origin, and are European-oriented. Although his terminology did not originate in the sphere of literature, he applied it to Hebrew literature.

A more recent attempt to define the modern trends of *Haskalah* was made by Uzi Shavit. Rejecting Kurzweil's notion of secularism, Shavit presented a concept which he had borrowed from Brenner. Accordingly, *Haskalah* literature is characterized not by its 'secularism', but by its *'hofshiyut'*—its 'freedom' or 'freethinking'.[12]

Ironically, Shavit's argument with Kurzweil's definition may also be applied to his own concept of *'hofshiyut'* which, I believe, does not generally characterize the early Hebrew enlighteners. Although one may find a high degree of clandestine 'freethinking' in the writings of Isaac Euchel, Saul Berlin and Isaac Satanow—some of the extremists among the early *maskilim*—they were in no way 'free Jews', as may be deduced from Shavit's definition. They were functioning either within, or at the periphery of organized Jewish life and organized institutions, which, indeed, they tried to change. Euchel tried to form an Enlightenment substitute for the traditional structure of the *kehillah*, while Saul Berlin officiated as a rabbi, but was clandestinely involved in the *Haskalah*.[13]

Noting the inability to present modern trends of the *Haskalah* by a single concept, Shavit suggests three fundamental principles of the Hebrew *Haskalah:* Belief in the human mind (*sekhel*), in reason and in science, belief in God and in a revealed religion, and belief in the power of aesthetics.[14] He considers these principles as the common denominators of both early and late *Haskalah*. Even though his definitions are broad enough, one may question whether these criteria have the same weight and significance in both the early as well as the late *Haskalah*. One may also question whether all three principles carry the same weight, and whether the first two cancel or complement one another in the mind of the *maskilim*. Shavit's criteria combine both extra-literary and literary orientations, and capitalize on European Enlightenment concepts that also prevailed in medieval Jewish philosophy.

Recently Arnold Band has examined the question of modernism and the beginnings of Hebrew literature. He has scrutinized past theories, and has applied Hans Robert Jauss' theory of literary reception 'of a work of art by certain audiences' to both Wessely's *Shirei tif'eret* and Moshe Hayyim Luzzatto's *Layesharim tehillah*. Both works exerted a seminal influence on subsequent *Haskalah* writers. But Band argues that as no one has regarded these literary works as modern in the sense of being secular, or rationalist, he suggests caution in the use of the term 'modern', and proposes Berdiczewski as the herald of modernism in Hebrew literature.[15]

It indeed seems that Berdiczewski was considered to be *aher*—'other'—by his contemporaries. But his 'otherness' vis-à-vis Ahad Ha-'am, Bialik, Tchernichowsky, and Frischmann, I submit, does not make him a modernist in contradistinction to them. Both Berdiczewski and his contemporaries were products of the *Haskalah* and experienced its aftermath, the advent of a national movement, differently. To some, Frischmann represents some degree of this 'otherness' which is found in Berdiczewski. Unquestionably, the 1890s represent modernism at its peak. However, the beginnings of modernism are to be found, as I shall presently show, in the early *Haskalah*.

In assessing previous theories, one notes that they contain insightful observations and intriguing generalities, but on the whole lack textual proof based on the literature itself. Thus, it is often easy to question some of these observations and even to refute them. This was done quite successfully by successive Hebrew critics as they reviewed their predecessors' comments on the subject while attempting to present a new notion of modernism in Hebrew letters.

In addition, some of these observations are inherently weak because they attempt to address a complex issue in a simplified manner. They attribute a complicated process of social and ideological changes to a single individual or to a single idea which was purported to have represented the new trends.

Furthermore, while some of the observations seem to be correct, that is to say, that they do represent phenomena which indicate aspects of a new trend, they do not necessarily in themselves represent the only answer, or the only criterion, as they were purported to. Thus, each single criterion, such as disrespect for the religious authority, or skepticism, rationalism, humanism, emphasis on man, utilitarianism, or freedom of thought, etc., is only a part of the picture. Other criteria, and some of the above, have been arrived at by answering the question 'What are the common characteristics of *Haskalah* writers?'[16] The answer, then, identifies social, cultural, religious and/or literary phenomena which are alleged to represent the change to modernism.

It is my contention that these common denominators only appear to represent the change towards modernism. They did indeed occur with the change; however, they were, in effect, the result of an occurring change, symptoms of a transitional process leading towards modernism. Many of these criteria are correct, but they do not represent the essence of 'modernism', which may be said to consist of mega-trends, or major shifts, encompassing the variety of phenomena, some of which are the result of modernism.

A definition of modern Hebrew literature is predicated on the following premise: first, on the occurrence of change and on our ability to distinguish the difference between the two periods of literature. However, it is not accepted universally that change had occurred in the first generation of Hebrew *Haskalah* writers in Germany. Ahad Ha-'am, for example, believed that early Hebrew *maskilim*, such as Wessely and Solomon Maimon, did not want to create a new literature on a new basis, but to continue the development of an old literature which had stopped developing.[17] A more modern critic, Dov Sadan, broadens the scope of 'modern literature' to include hassidic and mitnagdic literatures, and not only *Haskalah* literature. He even expands the scope of the discussion beyond Hebrew to include Yiddish and other modern European languages.[18] Thus, according to Sadan, the question of modernism disregards the major criterion of secularism as epitomizing the modern age.

Second, we should take into consideration the gradual process of that change and its relative scope, whether in society, within the individual, or in literature. It was limited in size and in scope, and did not encompass the totality of Jewish experience, or the totality of the Jewish people at any given time or place. Nor did the change appear to be uniform and universal even within a given group of writers which considered itself to be 'enlightened'.

Third, we must discard attempts to arrive at a one-sentence definition of modernism in Hebrew literature. We are dealing here with a very complex issue, and with a process which covers a number of areas of human endeavour, and thus has had its impact on society, religion and culture as well as on literature.

In the same vein, we must acknowledge the multiplicity of *Haskalah* phenomena as an essential premise for its study. The term *Haskalah* is used to refer to diverse individuals and groups in different localities and at different times.[19] Even with a given group in the same locality and of the same period, *maskilim* may differ from one another in their interpretation of what *Haskalah* means and in their implementation of it.

In order to identify modernism in Hebrew literature we should bear in mind the need to examine the very early period of the *Haskalah* in order to distinguish aspects of the new period and its literature from those in the earlier period. This premise presupposes, for the sake of discussion, that the early period of the Hebrew *Haskalah* in Germany contains sufficient inherent signs of change which may—or may not—signal the beginning of different, or yet to be defined, modern Hebrew literature.

Last, and more importantly, any definition of modernism in literature should come from the literature itself. In other words, contemporary Hebrew *Haskalah* literature itself should convey to us its own sense of modernism. If possible, it should lead to its own definition. Thus, we must search the literary works for a definition, or else look for literary phenomena which represented these new trends in Hebrew letters. However, we should not confuse symptoms of modernism—which are of importance and indeed quite relevant—with major shifts in *Weltanschauung* leading to modernism. Those major shifts in outlook, unlike symptoms of the change, were mega-trends, representing the all-encompassing transformation which in effect radically changed the Jewish outlook on life and the Jews' view of themselves vis-à-vis their tradition and their surrounding society and culture.

The need to find a definition from within the corpus is especially proper in literature which, due to its unique sensitivity, is prone to register overt as well as covert expressions of awareness concerning the changing spiritual and cultural trends. One may thus argue that literature may contribute a better insight into modernism than some social and historical records.

Based on the above, we may hypothesize that modernism began in Hebrew literature from the time that the awareness of modernism permeated the Hebrew writings. Consequently, it is the role of the literary historians or critics to identify, trace and locate this ostensible sense of modernism and the literary and linguistic expression of this change as manifested in the writings of the early Hebrew *maskilim*. They should then interpret and assess them critically as they would any other literary text or phenomenon for accuracy and insight. They should especially question the writers' ability to discern their own historical, cultural, or spiritual process of transformation.

Looking for this kind of awareness, we find several overt expressions enunciated by the early Hebrew German *maskilim* in *Ha-me'assef*. They indicate a deep awareness of the changes that had emerged on the European scene. These expressions were followed by statements of the need to emulate these trends. It was believed that the changing times necessitated a change from a traditional way of life and thought to a more current (modern?) orientation. Many of these expressions announced the advent of a new age of reason which indeed serve as a litmus paper for modernism. They may sound euphuistic, expressed as they were in *melitzah*, or even naive, yet they clearly represent the literary and linguistic awareness of the changing times.

Consider, for example, the modified quotation from Proverbs 1:20, 'and behold wisdom now sings outside', which was used by the editors of *Ha-me'assef* to indicate the nature of the new times. Behind the thrust of this observation one may detect the use of the sacred biblical idiom to convey an updated concept. It signals the linguistic trend of employing the sacral Hebrew language for secular use. Thus, the very language reflects in a subtle way the complex transition into modernism. These writers detect the emerging new epoch in Europe, referring to it as 'the days of the first fruits of knowledge and love in all the countries of Europe.'[20] Let us note that the two components of the new epoch are knowledge and love, namely tolerance, and that the two are related to one another.

These Hebrew writers further argued that this change among European nations also necessitated a similar change among the Jews: 'The era of knowledge has arrived in all nations; day and night they do not stop teaching their children [both] language and book. And we, why should we sit idle? Let us get up and revive [those] stones from the heaps of dust.'[21]

Undoubtedly, the *me'assfim* discerned a major change taking place in Europe, and they advocated its adoption by European Jewry. Their continuous efforts to introduce changes in all spheres of Jewish endeavour helped bring about these changes among the Jews. Thus, if our assertion is correct, these expressions—and many others which should be explored—indicate that the writers and editors of *Ha-me'assef* were the exponents and the proponents of modernism in the eighteenth century.[22]

Simultaneously, some contemporary writers displayed their sensitivity through covert expressions of the ensuing transformation. Unlike the overt expressions, as cited above, these were subconscious expressions; they indicate a subterranean sensitivity to the budding changes and they foreshadow the new trends. They may be even more important than the overt expressions because of the covert message which they carry concerning Judaism and the Jewish religion in modern times. Those subtle signals in Hebrew literature conveyed the notion that traditional Judaism, as practiced and transmitted, was no longer self-sufficient and self-contained. They implied that Judaism in the modern age could no longer be a self-contained entity upon which its adherents could exclusively rely. There was a feeling that traditional Judaism was inadequate for the needs of modern man. This expression signaled a major turning point in Jewish history.

This change took place in the minds of some *maskilim* as they projected the sense that traditional Judaism was, moreover, subservient to Western civilization. Thus, they believed that in order to survive, modern Judaism had to adapt and adjust to its surrounding culture. For if it did not, Judaism would be doomed.

I believe that this awareness represented a new phenomenon in eighteenth-century Judaism. It shattered the age-old notion that Judaism was an all-encompassing way of life, which addressed all relevant issues and gave satisfactory answers to all the needs of the individual Jew and Jewish society.

Halkin has already observed that the total sufficiency of a Jew in his inner Judaic life typified his confines 'within the walls' until the eighteenth century. Afterwards, the Jew is inclined more towards more worldly issues.[23] Additional study should be directed at this transitory period to ascertain whether these aspects of modernism had not occurred earlier.

What is so impressive about this new awareness is that it was first detected in the writings of a moderate *maskil*, Naphtali Herz Wessely. In other words, even traditionalist *maskilim* were aware of some inadequacy of Judaism vis-à-vis European culture in modern times, and manifested this attitude in their writings. As I have shown elsewhere,[24] this traditionalist *maskil* seemed to have subordinated Judaism to Western civilization in his controversial book *Divrei shalom ve-'emet* (1782). In this educational treatise Wessely discusses two major concepts related to his view of Judaism. He makes a distinction between *Torat ha-shem*, which literally translates as the laws, or teaching, of God, and *Torat ha-'adam*—the law of man. He expands the first term, *Torat ha-shem*, to mean not only the laws of God, but also Judaism in general. Similarly, *Torat ha-'adam* is broadened to include not only the laws of man, but social customs and manners, and more importantly, secular knowledge and Western civilization. Wessely believes that *Torat ha-shem*, that is, Judaism, is subordinated to *Torat ha-'adam*, namely to Western culture in the modern age, and that it is completely dependent on it. Thus, even a traditional *maskil* such as Wessely sensed the changes affecting Judaism in his day and age. Accordingly, he felt that Judaism in modern times was subservient to Western culture, and it could not exist as an entity by itself. Judaism, he considered, was no longer as self-sufficient as it had been until the age of Enlightenment. Significantly, these observations were made by a Hebrew writer, a devout Jew, who was proud of his heritage. Unquestionably, this represents a major shift from traditional Judaism to the modern period in Jewish letters. Modernism in Judaism may then be construed as reflecting a shift from total reliance on Judaism and its values as self-sufficient and all-encompassing towards placing it in an inferior position to Western civilization.

The *Haskalah* has also manifested its orientation toward modernism through the concerted efforts of its writers to re-define Judaism. In a desire to reject the phenomenon of contemporary rabbinic Judaism, a major spokesman for the *Haskalah*, Isaac Satanow, searched for a historical model of his vision of authentic Judaism which could and should be emulated in the Enlightenment. Interestingly, he found the epitome of authentic Judaism in *early* rabbinic Judaism. The mishnaic and talmudic periods were conceptualized by Satanow as representing Judaism at its highest degree of wisdom, knowledge and scholarship. It was then—he felt—that the Jewish people made its lasting contribution to science and humanism. Satanow thus selected early rabbinic Judaism, as opposed to contemporary rabbinic Judaism, as the model for Judaism in modern times.[25]

Modernism, then, may reflect not only the secular tendency, as is asserted by literary historians, but also a desire to re-define modern Judaism in terms of a past model. Replacing the existing tradition with a re-defined, neo-traditional, modern version of Judaism was definitely the goal of many *maskilim*. However, one should not be misled by various pronouncements made to appease the contemporary rabbinic authorities. On the other hand, the accepted notion in *Haskalah* historiography that the early *maskilim* rejected the Talmud must, as I have shown, be re-examined and revised.[26] Hebrew scholarship must examine aspects of modernism within the neo-traditional, cultural elements of *Haskalah* Judaism. Admittedly, the term 'neo-traditional' may *not* be construed in a religious, observant fashion, or as 'modern Orthodoxy', as it is conceptualized nowadays. In this respect, Kurzweil's view of modern Hebrew literature as a complete break from the past must be questioned.

There was yet another subtle awareness of a major shift in modern Judaism. Its covert manifestation emerged from questioning accepted fundamentals and values of normative Judaism. Isaac Satanow asserted that love of God (*'ahavat ha-shem*) and trust in God (*bitahon ba-shem*)—major tenets in traditional Judaism—were no longer binding in the age of Enlightenment. He even questioned the very faith in God (*'emunah*). Instead, these essential Jewish values were replaced by skepticism as the fundamental value and vital principle of modern Judaism in modern times.[27] Significantly, these extra-literary observations are found in Satanow's *belles lettres*, in *Mishlei Asaf* (1789-1802), and are therefore related to literary phenomena within *Haskalah* literature.

Modernism may be further identified by significant changes in the conceptualization of major historical processes in Judaism by the early *maskilim*. There emerged an important change in the view of, and attitude towards, Jewish history. For the first time, as far as I know, a Jewish writer questions the inevitability of Jewish history and the course it had taken. It was an attempt to fathom the meaning of Jewish historical existence. The effort of the *Haskalah* to change the course of Jewish history reflects this modern aspect of eighteenth-century Judaism.

The *Haskalah* exponent of this new attitude was a rabbi and a *maskil*, Saul Berlin. His views on Jewish historiosophy were presented in a satirical piece entitled *Ktav Yosher* (1795). Berlin's objective was to shatter accepted notions and major concepts in Jewish historiosophy and to destroy some normative values in Judaic tradition. He questioned the sacred attitude towards *kiddush ha-shem*, martyrdom, and the ostensibly predestined fate of Jews in history. Among other fundamental phenomena in Judaism, Saul Berlin scrutinized the phenomenon of *galut* (state of exile), the nature of *ge'ulah* (divine redemption), the chosenness of Israel, and gentiles' hatred of the Jews.[28]

Behind the satire, Saul Berlin gave voice to ideas which, I believe, represent a watershed in Jewish history and Hebrew literature. They mark a shift in view of Jewish history. No longer was there passive acquiescence to, and acceptance of, the tragic consequences of Jewish history. A bitter protest now emerged against Jewish fate. Moreover, the Hebrew *maskil* protested against the Jewish mentality which accepted Jewish history as a God-given gift to be welcomed in the past as in the future. Saul Berlin expressed a changing attitude towards the concept of *galut*: it was no longer viewed as inevitable, or as reflecting the nature of Jewish existence in modern time. *Ge'ulah*, on the other hand, was no longer conceptualized as being confined to the Divine, and the alleged chosenness of Israel was questioned.[29] From a Judaic point of view, these changes reflected substantial shifts in Jewish outlook that may be said to reflect modernism.

Another mega-trend of the shift in conceptualizing Judaism was asserted in the writings of two major writers of the early *Haskalah*: the editor of *Hame'assef*, Isaac Euchel, and Saul Berlin, cited above. For the first time in the modern age, the question arose as to whether traditional Judaism could bring happiness to the individual Jew and to Jewish society as a whole.

Aware of the centrality of *mitzvot* (precepts) and *kiyyum mitzvot* (observing the *mitzvot*) to traditional Judaism, Euchel and Berlin doubted whether the modern Jew could achieve happiness through observance of *mitzvot*.[30]

The major shift seemed to be a natural development of Wessely's view of the revised relationship between Judaism and Western civilization. With the abandonment of traditional Judaism as the exclusive, unique provider of happiness for the Jew, the door to modernism seemed to be wide open even for those who continued to observe the precepts of Judaism.

Both Euchel and Berlin touched upon the most significant aspect of the change towards modernism in that period: the desire of the modern Jew to achieve worldly happiness. They manifested a mega-trend towards secularism—prevalent in modern Judaism to this day—in its inception.

Our discussion so far has concentrated on criteria of modernism borrowed from non-literary disciplines and applied to literature. To address the issue fully, we should also attempt to define modernism in strictly literary terms. One prospective avenue is the study of emerging new literary genres and new literary phenomena in the *Haskalah*. It will, I hope, lead to a different concept of modernism in Hebrew literature. Accordingly, a new definition of modernism may be based on the shift from traditional Hebrew literature to modern Hebrew literature by noting the changes in literary genres.

Regrettably, as of now, Hebrew criticism has not produced a detailed, thorough and comprehensive study of the *Haskalah's* literary genres. Until such time that the whole of *Haskalah* literature is dissected and classified it will be difficult, perhaps even impossible, to arrive at any satisfactory definition along these lines. For the time being, however, we may use some working hypotheses to guide us in our endeavours.

We may nonetheless hypothesize that the literary genres of the Hebrew Enlightenment indicate a dual trend.[31] There is certainly a noticeable element of continuity in *Haskalah* literary genres. Many of the Hebrew *maskilim* continued to use accepted genres in the traditional Jewish literary corpus. Parables, fables and aphorisms, for example, represent a continuity. Of course, their contents reflected contemporary preoccupations.

There was also a tendency to revise accepted Judaic genres, or rather to search for established genres in the Judaic corpus. These genres were then re-presented either in the appearance of the old cast, such as in Satanow's *Mishlei Asaf*, or as a re-introduction of a genre, such as the religious disputation in Satanow's *Divrei rivot*. A student of modernism must then take into account the neo-literary genres which were re-introduced into *Haskalah* literature.

On the other hand, modernism is manifested by the introduction into Hebrew literature of European literary genres such as satire, epistolary writing, the travelogue, the biography and autobiography. These often show a strong European influence, with different degrees of Hebraic colouring, indicative of some background in past Hebrew literature.[32]

It may be suggested that modern Hebrew literature began with the introduction of a sufficient number of new literary genres. They represent a substantial literary shift which we can refer to as a shift towards modernism.

The search for literary definitions of modernism would be incomplete without the necessary probe into the subtle changes that affected the Hebrew language. The process of secularization of Hebrew should be part of a study of modernism for it reflects—and it affects—the inner *Weltanschauung* not only of literature but also of the Jewish people at that time.

Many sacred concepts, terms and words, which had been venerated for centuries, underwent acute, albeit subtle, changes, and were pressed into a secular, that is, modern use. The topic of language as well as others which I have touched upon in this paper indicate the need to re-examine the complex issue of modernism in Hebrew literature closely from within the *Haskalah* literature itself.

Notes

1. See F. Lahover, *Toldot ha-sifrut ha-'ivrit ha-hadashah*, I (Tel Aviv, 1963), p. 1: '...it [modern Hebrew literature] echoes the modern times.' Joseph Klausner, *Historiah shel ha-sifrut ha-'ivrit ha-hadashah*, I (Jerusalem, 1952), p. 9: 'The term "Modern Hebrew Literature" should be changed to the Hebrew literature of modern times... .' Shimon Halkin, *Derakhim ve-tzidei derakhim ba-sifrut*, I (Jerusalem, 1970), p. 155: 'Modern times in the history of the

world and the nation gave birth to modern Hebrew literature' (the above quotations originally in Hebrew).
2. Klausner, *Historiah*, p. 9.
3. Lahover, *Toldot ha-sifrut ha-'ivrit ha-hadashah*, I, p. 4: 'The inclination was now towards secularism.' It was presented earlier by Yaakov Rabinowitz, *Maslulei sifrut*, I (Jerusalem, 1971), p. 5 (originally published in 1919). See also: Isaac Barzilay, 'Li-vdikat mahut ha-haskalah u-vikortah', *Hadoar*, 43 (No. 19, March 13, 1964), p. 320.
4. Avraham Sha'anan, *Ha-sifrut ha-'ivrit ha-hadashah li-zrameha*, I (Tel Aviv, 1962), p. 18: '...penetration of secularism to the Jewish world of opinions and faiths'. Avraham Holtz comments on the ambiguity of the term as used by the Hebrew literary historians in his 'Prolegomenon to a Literary History of Modern Hebrew Literature', *Literature East and West*, XI (No. 3, 1967), p. 261, as does Arnold Band, twenty years later, in his elaborate article 'The Beginnings of Modern Hebrew Literature: Perspectives on "Modernity"', *AJS Review*, XIII (Spring-Fall 1988), pp. 1-26. The question of secularism as indicative of the beginning of modern Hebrew literature was discussed in 1947 by Hayim Bar-Dayan, 'Li-she'elat reshitah shel sifrutenu ha-hadashah', *Ha-kinnus ha-'olami le-mada'ei ha-yahadut*, 1947 (Jerusalem, 1952), pp. 302-306.
5. Dov Weinryb, 'Gormim kalkaliyim ve-sotzialiyim ba-haskalah ha-yehudit be-germaniah', *Knesset*, III (Tel Aviv, 1938), pp. 416-436; Jacob Katz, *Masoret u-mashber* (Jerusalem, 1958), ch. 20, 21, 23, 24; Katz, *Tradition and Crisis* (New York, 1977). Azriel Shohet, *Im hilufei tekufot* (Jerusalem, 1960); Shohet, 'Reshit ha-haskalah be-yahadut germaniah', *Molad*, XXIII (203-204, September 1965), pp. 328-334.
6. Baruch Kurzweil, *Sifrutenu ha-hadashah: masoret 'o mahapekhah* (Tel Aviv, 1960) p. 16; also: p. 44: '. . . modern Hebrew literature is secular because it comes out of a world void of divine holiness that had been hovering over the unit of Jewish culture' (translated from the Hebrew).
7. Klausner, *Historiah*, p. 10.
8. See Moshe Pelli, *The Age of Haskalah* (Leiden, 1979), ch. VI; Pelli, *Be-ma'avkei temurah* (Tel Aviv, 1988), pp. 47-55.
9. Lahover, *Toldot ha-sifrut ha-'ivrit ha-hadashah*, p. 4.
10. For example: H. N. Shapira, *Toldot ha-sifrut ha-'ivrit ha-hadashah* (Ramat Gan, 1967), pp. 57-58. This notion was presented earlier by Yaakov Rabinowitz, *Maslulei sifrut*, I, p. 16 (see note 3 above for the date of publication).
11. Simon Halkin, *Zeramim ve-tzurot ba-sifrut ha-'ivrit ha-hadashah*, I (Jerusalem, 1984), p. 31. Halkin had formulated his views earlier in his *Modern Hebrew Literature* (New York, 1970 [first published in 1950]), p. 36.
12. Uzi Shavit, 'Masat mavo', *Shirah ve-'ideologiah* (Tel Aviv, 1987), p. 16; published previously in *Be-fetah ha-shirah ha-'ivrit ha-hadashah* (Tel Aviv, 1986), p. 9.
13. See the respective chapters on Euchel, Berlin and Satanow in my book *The Age of Haskalah*. Also: Shmuel Feiner, 'Yitzhak Eichel—Ha-'yazam' shel tenu'at ha-haskalah be-germaniah', *Zion*, 52 (4, 1987), pp. 427-469.
14. Shavit, *Shirah*, p. 25.
15. Band, 'The Beginnings of Modern Hebrew Literature', pp. 25-26.

16. See ibid., p. 15.
17. 'Ha-lashon ve-sifrutah', Li-she'elat ha-lashon, *Kol kitvei Ahad Ha-'Am* (Tel Aviv, 1956), p. 95.
18. Dov Sadan, *'Al sifrutenu—masat mavo* (Jerusalem, 1950), pp. 1-9; first chapter published earlier in ' 'Al tehumei sifrutenu ha-hadashah', *Molad*, II (1948-9), pp. 38-41. Sadan reiterated his views in other articles and recently in ' 'Al sifrutenu—masat hitum', *Yerushalayim*, XI-XII (1977), pp. 162-171.
19. On the concept and term 'haskalah' see Uzi Shavit, 'Ha-"haskalah" mahi', *Mehkerei yerushalayim be-sifrut 'ivrit*, XII (1990), pp. 51-83.
20. 'Nahal ha-bsor', Prospect of *Ha-me'assef*, bound with vol. I (1783-4), p. 3.
21. *Ibid.*, p. 13.
22. An observation made, on other grounds, by H. N. Shapira, in his *Toldot ha-sifrut ha-'ivrit ha-hadashah*, p. 58.
23. Halkin, *Derakhim ve-tzidei derakhim*, pp. 156-157; Halkin, *Zeramim ve-tzurot*, p. 11.
24. Pelli, *The Age of Haskalah*, p. 121-124; Pelli, *Be-ma'avkei temurah*, pp. 54-61.
25. See *The Age of* Haskalah, ch. VIII; *Be-ma'avkei temurah*, ch. III.
26. *The Age of* Haskalah, ch. III.
27. *The Age of* Haskalah, pp. 166-169; *Be-ma'avkei temurah*, pp. 120-122.
28. *Be-ma'avkei temurah*, pp. 14-17. See also *The Age of* Haskalah, ch. IX, and my two additional articles on Saul Berlin published in *Leo Baeck Year Book*, XX (1975), pp. 109-127; XXII (1977), pp. 93-107.
29. *Be-ma'avkei temurah*, pp. 17, 144.
30. *Be-ma'avkei temurah*, pp. 13-14.
31. Avraham Holtz has lamented this phenomenon in the article cited in note 4, p. 268. Note also Shmuel Werses' comprehensive review of the study and research of the haskalah, 'Al mehkar sifrut ha-haskalah be-yameinu', *Megamot ve-tzurot be-sifrut ha-haskalah* (Jerusalem, 1990), pp. 356-408, published previously in the *Newsletter* of World Union of Jewish Studies, 25 (Summer, 1985) and 26 (Winter, 1986).
32. In the published studies on the genres of the *Haskalah* I have discussed the following genres: satire, biography, autobiography, epistolary writing, dialogues of the dead, religious disputations, travelogues, utopian and wisdom literature, and pseudo-Halakhah.

THE CONTROVERSY BETWEEN M.L. LILIENBLUM AND THE WORLD OF THE *YESHIVOT* AS DEPICTED IN 'MISHNAT ELISHA BEN AVUYAH' (1878)

Yehuda Friedlander

> 'Elisha Aher will be saved through the merit of his [study of the] Torah,' (Talmud of the Land of Israel* (hereafter T.I.), *Hagigah*, (2:1).

Elisha Ben Avuyah is depicted in the Talmud and the *midrashim* as a Promethean, tragic, complex and schizophrenic character, information on whom is more enigmatic than explicit.

The reaction of the Babylonian Talmud** (hereafter B.T.) to the death of Elisha Ben Avuyah clearly reflects three different attitudes to this anomalous character. The first was bewilderment due to the dilemma of judging Elisha Ben Avuyah as a *tanna* and regarding him as Aher[1,] the second was hatred and the desire to erase his name from living memory [2], and the third was admiration and the desire to acquit him and to clear his name[3].

The 'acceptance' of Elisha Ben Avuyah as a literary character, both in aggadic literature, in Jewish studies and in modern Hebrew literature, is a fascinating subject for research. His character has continuously exercised the intellectual curiosity of scholars[4] as well as the imagination of writers[5].

Lilienblum was attracted to the controversial character of Elisha Ben Avuyah from the time he began to write. In a letter to J.L. Gordon in 1871 he proposed changing the name of the poem 'Rabbi Meir'[6] to 'Elisha Ben Avuyah,' contending that the fanatics claim that Rabbi Meir (like all the

---

* This and other quotations are from *The Talmud of the Land of Israel*, translated by Jacob Neusner, Chicago and London 1986.
** Quotations from B.T. are from *The Babylonian Talmud* edited by Rabbi Dr. I. Epstein, The Soncino Press, London, 1935

143

tannaim) belongs to *them* [emphasized in the original], and the heretics want no part of him; and when they see a heretic honouring his name they boast that the heretics are also overcome by awe of the *tanna'im* and in veneration of their sagacity; thus every *maskil* who speaks well of one of the *tanna'im* or *amoraim* is, in my opinion, one who aids and abets a transgression![7]. It was for this reason that Lilienblum willingly acceded to Aharon Shmuel Liberman's request to write an article on Elisha Ben Avuyah, which would be in keeping with the socialist bias of the periodical *Ha-'emet* which he intended to publish in 1877. In fact, Lilienblum deviated from Liberman's original concept[8,] and 'Mishnat Elisha Ben Avuyah' assumed a different form in certain aspects[9.]

'Mishnat Elisha Ben Avuyah' therefore constitutes a further phase in the controversy between Lilienblum and the world of Orthodox Jewry, as it developed in the Lithuanian yeshivot in the nineteenth century.

Lilienblum's work 'Mishnat Elisha Ben Avuyah' consists of four sections and is written in the conventional form of the satirical parody of eighteenth and nineteenth century Haskalah Hebrew literature. It opens with the 'short introduction' by the editor, as found in the satirical works of Aharon Wolfssohn of Halle, Joseph Perl, Judah Leib Mises and others. The satirist in the guise of the editor explains to the reader how that particular work came into his possession. He had participated in a séance during which the ghost of his maternal grandfather had passed to him the manuscript of Elisha Ben Avuyah containing a personal missive, the 'Tractate *Yishuv Olam* ' together with a 'commentary'. These works were addressed to 'the overseer of the good of his people'[10,]of whom no trace has been found to this day. It was in this way that the manuscripts remained with the editor. The grandfather's ghost was not summoned by chance, since this character is well known to readers of Lilienblum's works. The writer states that he was the priest of God the Most High, erudite and pious and never spoke an untruth throughout his life.[11] This truthful man was therefore chosen to be the emissary of Elisha Ben Avuyah and to bring his tidings from the world to come to this world. In deference to the sender and out of respect for the emissary the editor was bound to ask for 'halakhic justification in order to dispel any amazement that may arise in the reader's mind, and to undermine the integrity of the authors and the sincerity of the intentions of the 'innocent' editor ...

The astonishment expressed at the fact that Elisha Ben Avuyah's letter was written on the Day of Atonement is explained away by the editor with expressly satiric sophistry containing a double meaning: When Elisha Ben Avuyah inhabited this world he defiled the Sabbath, a graver transgression than on the Day of Atonement, and even more so now after his death, when the dead are exempt from keeping the precepts (*Shabbat*, 151b) and with even stricter inference as regards the ministering angels, where writing is carried out every New Year and the Day of Atonement.[12] This explanation is aimed both at those readers wishing to see Elisha Ben Avuyah as a man of principle dedicated to following his customary way, and those readers at whom, in fact, the satire is aimed — those very 'fanatics', as Lilienblum terms them on various occasions. And if it seems surprising that in his letter Elisha Ben Avuyah shows little respect for his colleagues the *tanna'im*, that, too, is no wonder, because he himself was a *tanna* and we have found that the *tannaim* and *'amora'im* did not respect each other.[13] Say from now on: He is not Aher, but one of them and acts as they do.

The 'letter', the second section of Lilienblum's work, could in fact constitute a satire in itself. Its main aspect is the presentation of Elisha Ben Avuyah's confession, following a very long silence, before a Hebrew author named 'the overseer of the good of his people,' whose work[14] had reached the *Bet ha-midrash* in heaven. The reading of this work aroused Elisha Ben Avuyah to come forth and identify himself.

The satirist's purpose in presenting this letter was twofold: (a) the exoneration of the character, and presenting it to the reader as his conception of the stereotype of the ideal *maskil*, that is to say, according to the outline presented in the Mishnah; (b) a satirical disputation with the outlook of the Orthodox rabbis, the absolute negation of their lifestyle and that of those who come under their aegis, and a proposal for an alternative way of life. The letter opens with an apology for the delay in replying, and the two tendencies clearly evolve from the text itself:

> I wanted to write to you from the earliest hour, [...] but I was not at liberty to do so until now, the Day of Atonement, since I was occupied in my work with Metatron.[15] At first, at the time when Israel were fulfilling their will according to the demands of time and place, and the majority were engaged in tilling the soil and in all sorts of occupations, their adversaries were unable to arraign them to any great extent, and one hour each day sufficed for Metatron to sit and write down the merits of Israel [.] [...] when the times were in disarray and the children of Israel were dispersed to many lands [...] and their adversaries increased and Metatron was able to argue no more, [...] when the ministering angels saw that it was thus, they appointed me to assist him, and thus they said unto me: Ben Avuyah! you are learned in Greek Wisdom [...] go forth and minister to them as a guardian against those that hate them. [...] And from that moment until now I have been constantly occupied in writing down the merits of Israel as against those who denounce them.

> For this reason I was unable to write to you, but now on the Day of Atonement, the majority of the children of Israel are engrossed in prayer and are not involved in their regular pursuits, they are fasting throughout the day and do not benefit from the labour of others, and Satan is not permitted to accuse them (*Yoma* 20a) and I do not have to write down the merits of Israel — thus I write to you.[18]

This fragmented text, extracts of which are presented here, contains four satirical elements, characteristic of the entire work: (a) Elisha Ben Avuyah was appointed to work under the aegis of Metatron to plead Israel's cause; (b) the appointment was made because he was learned in Greek; (c) the People of Israel were 'protected from their adversaries because they are fulfilling their will according to the demands of time...' (d) the uniqueness of the Day of Atonement is that it is the only day of the year on which the children of Israel 'do not benefit from the labour of others'. These four elements are in complete contrast to Elisha Ben Avuyah's character as portrayed in the aggadic and midrashic literature. From an ostracized traitor, from Aher, in this world, he has become the defender of Israel in the world to come.

Let us examine these four elements:

(1) In B.T. (Hagigah, 15a) the Gemarah explains the meaning of the Baraita which states 'Aher mutilated the shoots'[17]:

Aher saw that permission was granted to Metatron to sit and write down the merits of Israel. Said he:

> It is taught as a tradition that on High there is no sitting and no emulation, and no back, and no weariness. Perhaps — God forbid!—there are two divinities! [...] Permission was then given to him [Metatron] to strike out the merits of Aher. A *bat kol* went forth and said: 'Return ye backsliding children' [Jeremiah 3:22] except Aher.

Elisha Ben Avuyah entered the 'Garden' and his encounter with Metatron became a fierce confrontation between them. Ben Avuyah's arrogance resulted in the loss of all his privileges, and his removal from among all those entitled to repentance and forgiveness. However, in the above mentioned 'letter' Elisha Ben Avuyah and Metatron have been jointly assigned the task by a command from above, and 'he who has no rights' is responsible for the rights of Israel.

(2) The Gemarah (ibid.) asks: What of Aher? Greek song did not cease from his mouth. It is told of Aher that when he used to rise [to go] from the schoolhouse, many heretical books used to fall from his lap. At various times the sages were sensitive towards a preoccupation with 'Greek

wisdom.[18] While in the 'letter' Aher tells us that by virtue of his knowledge of 'Greek Wisdom' he acquired a prestigious position with the ministering angels.

(3) In B.T. *Berakhot* (35b) the two basic approaches towards the desirable lifestyle of the Children of Israel are compared:

Our Rabbis taught: 'And thou shalt gather in thy corn' (*Deut.* 11:14). What is to be learnt from these words? Since it says, 'This book of the law shall not depart out of thy mouth' (*Joshua* 1:8), I might think that this injunction is to be taken literally. Therefore it says,

> 'And thou shalt gather in thy corn,' which implies that you are to combine the study of them with a worldly occupation. This is the view of R. Ishmael. R. Simeon B. Yohai says: Is that possible? If a man ploughs in the ploughing season, and reaps in the reaping season, and threshes in the threshing season, and winnows in the season of the wind, what is to become of the Torah? No; but when Israel *perform the will of the Omnipresent*, their work is performed by others, as it is said, 'And strangers shall stand and feed your flocks, etc.' (*Isaiah* 61:5), and when Israel do not perform the will of the Omnipresent their work is carried out by themselves, as it is said, 'And though shalt gather in thy corn.'

The author of the 'letter' replaces the phrase 'perform the will of the Ominpresent' by 'fulfilling their will according to the demands of time and place,[19] namely, living according to the spirit of the times and the demands of ordinary life. Secularism, and not the keeping of the precepts of the Torah, is therefore certain to bring about the annulment of the defence of the People of Israel. It is in this manner that the writer of the 'letter' interprets the attitude of R. Ishmael who dealt with them with respect in the spirit of the nineteenth century *Haskalah* movement. On the other hand, the attitude of Orthodox Jewry is reflected in the words of R. Simeon Ben Yohai which are not accepted by the Gemarah: Said Abaye: Many have followed the advice of R. Ishmael, and it has worked well; others have followed R. Simeon b. Yohai and it has not been successful.

(4) The Mishnah on B. T. tractate *Yomah* (85b) stresses:

> For transgressions between man and the Omnipresent the Day of Atonement procures atonement. But for transgression between man and his fellow the Day of Atonement does not procure atonement until he has pacified his fellow.

The writer of the 'letter' places all the precepts between man and his fellow upon the negation of commerce and affirmation of creative labour: ....are not involved in their regular pursuits, and ... do not benefit from the labour of others. The Day of Atonement is for him indicative of the special day in the year on which the people of Israel do not transgress by exploiting others, and thus Satan does not have the right to arraign them. The writer of the 'letter' hints at the Gemarah in B. T. *Yomah* (20b) as support for his opinion: Rama b. Hama said, *Ha-satan* in numerical value is three hundred and sixty-four, that means:

> on three hundred and sixty-four days he has permission to act as accuser, but on the Day of Atonement he has no permission to act as accuser.

This assertion constitutes the central motif of the 'letter,' as well as the third section of the work 'Tractate *Yishuv Olam.*'

Elisha Ben Avuyah's confession in his letter is a combination of apologetics and polemics, and its satirical character is expressed by the language, Elisha Ben Avuyah considers it his duty to give to his readers—who have been educated in the tradition of antagonism against him—a convincing explanation about his way and the sense of mission animating him:

> I have mutilated the shoots of the inferior vines that were planted within me by mistake by my mentors in order not to stunt the growth of the good trees I found in the Garden [...] I have resolved to live according my new-found and authentic beliefs and to be another person. I have thus resolved: Whereas I was driven away from the world of tradition, the world of my people, it behoves me to partake of the joys of this world and to look upon it and its requirements, because it is a real and dynamic world, and it cannot be said to be fictitious.[20]

This fragmented quotation reveals the satirical pattern of Lilienblum at its best. The first part expresses the deep affinity between the speaker, 'Aher,' and the writer, author of Ways of the Talmud (1868). On the face of it, this is a declaration of a *Maskil* demanding 'reform' of the religion while not negating it. However, the phrase mutilating the shoots sends us to the well-known *Baraita* in B. T. *Hagigah* (14b) Our Rabbis taught: Four men entered the 'Garden,' namely, Ben Azzai and Ben Zoma, Aher and R. Akiba. [...] Aher mutilated the shoots. This analogy is negative, whether it is in the interpretation of the Gemarah in T. I. (2:1): 'Who slew the young scholars of the Torah,' or whether it is explained in the manner of Judah Halevi in the *Khozari*: 'He scorned the fulfilling of the precepts after he had examined their rationality, saying to himself: the fulfilling of precepts is no more than a means towards this spiritual level, and I have already attained it'.[21] Whatever approach we take, whether it be mystic-kabbalist, philosophical-rationalist or even psychological, mutilating the shoots expresses Elisha Ben Avuyah's grave sin for which he was expelled and given the ignoble appellation of 'Aher.' However, in the 'letter' this analogy, expressed by Elisha Ben Avuyah who decided to be 'ish Aher', is given a manifestly positive connotation — cropping or pruning by a responsible 'gardener', eradicating the misconceptions from the 'Garden of Halakhah'.

The continuation of the excerpt intensifies the contrast between the character of the talmudic 'Aher' and that of the letter: And thus I said unto myself: 'Whereas I was driven away from the world of *Halakhot*, the world of my people, it behoves me to partake of the joys of this world and to examine it and its requirements.' This is a deliberate deviation from the text in B.T. *Hagigah* (15a): A *bat kol* went forth and said: 'Return, ye backsliding children' — except Aher. Thereupon he said: Since I have been driven forth from yonder world, let me go forth and enjoy this world. So Aher went forth into evil ways. He went forth, found a harlot and demanded her.

Gaining pleasure from this world here refers to the pleasure of transgression. The visit of 'Aher' to the harlot expresses the deterioration of a person who has been punished with the gravest of all punishments: the closing to him of the gate of repentance. However, in the letter before us, gaining pleasure from this world is derived from examining it and its requirements, that is to say, pleasure is not the satisfaction of desire, but the spiritual pleasure of one who studies the laws of nature in order to live by them and not by the world of *Halakhot*. The world of *Halakhah* in general is identified in this context with the 'lesser planting' (the non-religious world) while the 'good trees in the garden of knowledge' symbolize the 'new-found and authentic beliefs', the nature of which is explained in the 'letter', and in the 'Tractate *Yishuv Olam*'. The polemical undertone becomes more acute because the 'world of *Halakhot*' is the 'world of my people', and is in fact 'fantasy', and therefore fantasy must be replaced by reality in a 'real and dynamic world'. Elisha Ben Avuyah's approach in his 'letter' is thus that of a militant not a moderate *maskil*, content with the introduction of a number of 'reforms' in the *Halakhah*. This extract also alludes to the positivist basis of Lilienblum's *Weltanschauung* at the end of the nineteenth century.

The apologetic undertone is, in effect, a thin facade for a compelling message which intensifies towards the end of the 'letter'. Elisha Ben Avuyah directs his assertion towards a very specific audience: I would ask you, students, youth of Israel who have not tasted the sin of perversion, and learned men who have become corrupt! Read these words with great intent and do everything so that you too will be able to labour in an occupation so that you will not live at the expense of the community [...] so that you will not have to seek worldly delights and abominations with which to pass the time.[22] The 'lesser plantings' are therefore not only fantasy but 'delights and abominations'.

Elisha Ben Avuyah's letter is a fictional and satirical confession written as an adjunct to his main 'work' with the purpose of attracting the nineteenth-century reader.

The Tractate Yishuv Olam — combination of satire and parody.

The 'Tractate *Yishuv Olam*' and Rabbi Ovadia Bartenura's pseudocommentary[23] appended to it, constitute the third and fourth sections of Lilienblum's 'Mishnat Elisha Ben Avuyah'. References from the Mishnah have been added to this contrived tractate as is common in the presentation of texts of the Babylonian Talmud. Here, too, Lilienblum uses conventional means as employed in earlier Talmudic parodies. On the face of it, it can be said that these two sections are satires in parodic form, but this rather simplistic definition is the subject of controversy. There are certain scholars who claim that parody is one of the forms of satire, and one of its main instruments.[24] On the other hand, some scholars endevour to make a clear distinction between the two, and relate to parody as an art form of its own, with no mandatory dependence on satire.[25] These divisions of opinion reflect the principal differences in the approach and the type of satire and parody at different periods, in different literatures and cultural climates.[26] I doubt that Lilienblum was aware of the nuances definition of these terms. I have no reasonable basis to believe that Lilienblum read, for example, the important essay on parody by Octave Delepierre.[27] 'Mishnat Elisha Ben Avuyah' can be construed according to Delepierre's basic assumptions, but such an interpretation would be nothing more than 'academic casuistry'. On the other hand, a more realistic surmise is that Lilienblum, who read and wrote Russian, was familiar with the satirical and parodic writings of Mikhail Saltykov-Shchedrin. In nineteenth-century Russian, and needless to say, in Hebrew literature, parody served as one of the means of expressing satire, a sort of sub-form, and both jointly constitute the mode in which the ideological struggle has been presented.

Lilienblum's choice of the parody as the form for his polemic-satirical work deserves careful scrutiny. His intention differed from that of Lieberman who considered the socialist content to be the essential aspect and the character of Elisha Ben Avuyah as the external framework. On the other hand, Lilienblum was referring to gently moving the lips of 'Aher',[28] and the views of the *tannaim* have been passed down to us in the form of *mishnayot* and not in the form of treatises. The simulation of mishnaic form was designed to give the work a semblance of authenticity. To this end, the satirist 'interspersed' fictional *mishnayot* into the genuine *mishnayot*, *beraitot* and well-known *'aggadot* in the tractates of *Ta'anit, Hagigah, Kidushin, Sanhedrin, Avot, Avot Derabbi Natan, Oktsin,* and so on.

From the viewpoint of the satirist, the authentic *mishnayot* interspersed in the fictional text have an additional task: overtly it is not Lilienblum's prupose to negate the world of *Halakhah* completely, but rather to change it 'a little' by means of a few 'additions': but covertly 'Mishnat Elisha Ben Avuyah' is designed to be the complete antithesis of traditional *Halakhah*, and to undermine it. Let us look at the first Mishnah:

> Upon three things the world is based: upon the Torah, upon *Avodah*, and upon the practice of charity, Elisha Ben Avuyah said: on the Torah and Avodah. The reformation of the world is as in its creation: its creation is based on Torah and *Avodah*, and its reformation is also based on Torah and *Avodah*.[29]

The first part is quoted from Simon the Just in the B. T. *Avot* (1:2), and the author of the 'Tractate *Yishuv Olam*' sends the reader to the source (*Masoret ha-shass*). However, Elisha Ben Avuyah diverts from the first part, eliminates the principle of the practice of charity, arguing that 'the reformation of the world is as in its creation'. This expression is a satirical distortion of what is stated in the T. I., tractate *Ta'anit* (1:3). The Gemarah comments on the verse in Isaiah (45:8): Drop down, ye heavens from above, and let the skies pour down righteousness; let the earth open, and let them bring forth salvation, and let righteousness spring up together; I the Lord have created it. And it continues, saying among other things: 'And let righteousness spring up also' (*Isaiah* 45:8). This refers to rain. 'I the Lord have created it (*Isaiah* 45:8): for this purpose did I create it, for the good order and settlement of the world. The Gemarah therefore stresses that the world was created in both righteousness and charity, and this combination was a sort of design for the creation of the world and a formula for the reformation of the world. Now Elisha Ben Avuyah comes along and eliminates the principle of charity, basing himself through astute elision on that very quotation from the T. I.

Rabbi Ovadia Bartenura's 'commentary', appended to these *mishnayot*, 'elucidates' Elisha Ben Avuyah's intention. He adds: On Torah and Avodah. But not on the practice of charity; we have not found that nature behaves according to the criteria of the practice of charity, as is written (*Avodah Zarah*): "the world pursues its natural course." This addition is not a parodic adjunct, but breaks down a further level in the world of the Halakhah by negating the providence of the Creator. The commentary deals with the conduct of nature and its laws, as a permanent and immutable phenomenon, as a clear antithesis of Divine Providence over the world, but it presents as support a homily of the sages which specifically explains the essence of Divine Providence. The B. T. tractate *Avodah Zarah* (54b) states:

> Our rabbis taught: philosophers asked the elders in Rome, 'if your God has no desire for idolatry, why does He not abolish it?' They replied, 'If something for which the world has no need was worshipped, He would abolish it; but people worship the sun, moon, stars and planets; should He destroy the Universe on account of fools! The world pursues its natural course, and as for the fools who act wrongly, they will have to render an account.'

This example is enlightening from two points of view: that of the internal relationship between the *mishnayot* to Ovadiah Bartenura's 'commentary', and that of the function of the Halakhah and Aggadah throughout his work.

This double negation of belief in the concern of Divine Providence for his children, and of the principle of the practice of charity, alluded to in the covert layer of 'Tractate *Yishuv Olam*', is stated specifically and precisely formulated in Elisha Ben Avuyah's letter appended to the tractate:

> ... the laws of nature and the way of the world are not known to him who seeks explanation for the work of creation [...] he who stands against the arrow will be killed, whether he stands of his own will having summoned his comrade to battle to preserve his honour, or whether he has been taken prisoner and falsely charged; and he who has not made preparation is the same as he who has gone walking in gardens and orchards, and is the same as he who has broken his arm and is unable to prepare anything: he will not eat on the Sabbath! This is my method, and it was to this end that I laboured when I was still alive.[30] From now on say 'The 'Tractate *Yishuv Olam*' is based on the concept that there is no room in the world for compassion and justice, but for the laws of nature alone, and there is no belief in Divine Providence and in his involvement after the creation was completed.'

One of the basic principles in 'Mishnat Elisha Ben Avuyah' is that of utility, and from this we learn that divine *Avodah* according to Halakhah and the practice of charity cannot be changed, nor has it any use since by the absence of Providence there is no additional cost.

Elisha Ben Avuyah's approach in this respect is superficial and shallow, and Joseph Klausner justly defined it as 'primitive socialism.'[31] It contains a veritable mixture of ideas. As Avraham Sha'anan stated, 'It is a mixture of Voltairian rationalism and the cult of positivism in its various manifestations,' [32] and it reveals a gap in the internal logical structure of the work. If there is no need for Providence nor the practice of charity, there is no need for reward and punishment; and if there is no need for recompense, why is Elisha Ben Avuyah occupied with Metatron in writing down the merits of Israel? This internal breach derives directly from Lilienblum's usage of a hybrid of satire and parody and impairs the internal connection between the sections, between the 'letter', the 'Tractate *Yishuv Olam*' and Ovadiah Bartenura's 'commentary'.

A good example of a blend of texts in a parodic-satirical context, and the distinct contrast between their various levels, is the fourth Mishnah in the first chapter of the 'Tractate *Yishuv Olam*':

> R. Meir asked Elisha Ben Avuyah: and is it possible that all mortals could learn the entire Torah, for it states: the measure thereof is longer than the earth and broader than the sea, and when will their labour be done? He said unto him: from where are the labourers as against the wayfarers in this world. After he had pondered he replied: Rabbi! He who abandons you is as though he abandons life.[33]

The first part of the Mishnah is presented in the form of the Aggadah in B. T. *Hagigah* (15a), except that the roles have been reversed. In the tractate *Hagigah*, Aher asked Rabbi Meir 'after his apostasy,' a question the teacher puts to his pupil, whereas here it is a question put by the pupil to his teacher. The association of B. T. Tractate *Hagigah* leads directly to T. I. Tractate *Hagigah* (2:1). There it is Elisha Ben Avuyah who is concerned with teaching a trade instead of Torah, saying to the children in the *Beit ha-midrash*: 'What are those doing here? This one should be a mason; this one should be a carpenter; this one should be a fisherman; this one should be a tailor. When they heard this they would leave [the teacher] and go [and become workmen]. 'Here it is Rabbi Meir who is concerned that the multiplicity of scholars would lead to a dearth of tradesmen. Rabbi Meir's question leads to a third association, which is a parody on the words of Rabbi Simeon Ben Yohai in B. T. *Berakhot* (35b)[34], except that once again the objects have been exchanged. In the tractate *Berakhot* Rabbi Simeon is concerned about the multiplicity of trades, and asks: 'What is to become of the Torah [?],' and here it is Rabbi Meir who is concerned about the multiplicity of those learning Torah, and asks: 'Their labours, when will they be done' [?]

Elisha Ben Avuyah's reply is vague, and the conclusion arrived at by Rabbi Meir was not explained in the Mishnah. Ovadiah Bartenura's 'commentary' comes to fill this disparity when he states:

> ... After he had given it some thought. As we read in the Tosefta, he reflected and found that more than half of the world travels, and on his return lamented and said: 'Woe to mankind for contempt of themselves, that they are engaged in reforming it.'[35]

Here the fourth association is introduced, where Rabbi Meir's comment parodies Rabbi Yehoshua ben Levi in B. T. *Avot* (6:2): 'Every day a *bat kol* goes forth from Mount Horev, and makes a proclamation and says: Woe unto men on account of [their] contempt of the Torah.' Rabbi Meir's words in the latter part of the Mishnah bring forth the fifth association with B. T. Tractate *Kiddushin* (66b), except that there the words are attributed to Rabbi Tarphon who spoke them to Rabbi Akiva, and here they are said by Rabbi Meir about Elisha Ben Avuyah.

In this short sentence uttered by Rabbi Meir lies the key to understanding the Mishnah, and in fact to understanding the entire work, and it links the restrained and even amusing parodic layer and the revolutionary, provocative satirical layer. Rabbi Tarphon's emotional outcry about Rabbi Akiva was made in excitement in the course of a profound discussion of a most complicated Halakhic problem, where the word 'life' is a metaphor for Torah, as stated in B.T. *Yoma* (72b): 'If he is meritorious, it tests him unto life, if not, it tests him unto death.' The significance of Rabbi Meir's comment on Elisha ben Avuyah presented here is the acceptance of his teachings as expressed in his 'Mishnah', where life refers to secular life without the Halakhah, but according to the laws of nature alone...

It would seem that in this case the satirist has succeeded in combining all the sections of his work and justifying the use of a combination of parody and satire. Furthermore, the superficial and disappointing thesis has been presented in a brilliant literary style in the form of a Mishnah and commentary.

NOTES

1. B.T., *Hagigah* (15b)
2. Ibid.
3. Ibid.
4. See Yehuda Liebes, *Heto shel Elisha (The Sin of Elisha — four who went into the 'Garden' and the nature of the Talmudic mysticism)*, second edition, Jerusalem, 1990, and the bibliographical references there (hereafter: *The Sin*

of Elisha) See also: Bin Gurion [Micha Joseph Bin Gurion] the entry 'Aher: *Hagoren, Anthology of Jewish Learning*, ed. Shmuel Abba Horodetski, VIII, Berdichev 1912, pp. 76-83.
5. Ibid., pp. 82-83. See also Milton Steinberg: *As A Driven Leaf.* New York: 1939: Sh. Shalom: *Shabbat ha-'olam (The Sabbath of the World, a dramatic poem in five scenes and a prologue).* Tel Aviv: 1945; Moshe Shamir: *Al suso be-shabbat* (On his horse on the Sabbath), in Sippurei ha-'even, ha-hut ha-meshulash. Tel Aviv: 1959, pp. 240-253.
6. See '*Gam 'eileh mishlei Yehuda*,' in *Ha-shahar*, Second Year, Vienna 1871, pp. 354-356.
7. *Letters from Moses Leib Lilienblum to Yehuda Leib Gordon* [Heb.], edited with an introduction by Shlomo Braiman, Jerusalem, 1968, pp. 110-111. Letter dated 6 February 1871.
8. Lilienblum described the difference in outlook between bim and A.S. Lieberman in his letter to Mordekhai Ben Hillel Hacohen (1894). See: Moses Leib Lilienblum: *Katavim 'autobiografiyim (Autobiographical works),* edited and introduced by Shlomo Braiman, vol.3, Jerusalem 1970, pp.190-192 (hereafter *Autobiographical Works).* See also the detailed explanation in the editor's introduction, ibid., vol.1. pp.47-49. Cf. Joseph Klausner: *Historia shel ha-sifrut ha-'ivrit ha-hadashah (History of Modern Hebrew Literature),* vol.4, Jerusalem, 1972, pp.284-285, and the references quoted.
9. Published anonymously by the author in the periodical *Assefat hahamim*, 1878, pp.76-77, 96-99, 108-113, 125-127. Only the 'Short Introduction,' the 'Letter,' and the first chapter of the 'Tractate *Yishuv Olam*' were printed there and the last part appeared in the periodical *Me'assef le-ha-kol*, 1879. The work in its entirety was published in *Kol kitvei Moshe Leib Lilienblum (The Collected Works of Moshe Leib Lilienblum),* vol.2, Krakow 1912, pp.180-220 (hereafter: *Collected Works).*
10. Lilienblum, *Collected Works,* vol.2, p.182. In my opinion this appellation refers to Lilienblum himself.
11. '*Hata'ot ne'urim*' (Sins of youth), part 1, 1876, *Autobiographical Works,* vol.1, p.81.
12. Ibid., Lilienblum was adamant that Elisha Ben Avuyah's letter should bear the date, the Day of Atonement 1878. See Lilienblum's letter to Aharon Shmuel Liberman of September 24, 1877. Lieberman was not comfortable with this date, fearing that it would arouse the ire of the Orthodox. See Zevi Karol: introduction to *Ha-'emet (The Truth),* Tel Aviv, 1938, pp.35-36. See also Joseph Klausner (above n.8, p.285). See B.T., *Shabbat* 151b: 'Once a man dies he is free from all obligations, and thus R. Johanan interpreted: "Among the dead I am free': once a man is dead he is free from religious duties."'
13. Lilienblum, *Collected Works,* vol.2, p.181.
14. Apparently an allusion to Lilienblum's essay 'Orhot ha-talmud' (Ways of the Talmud) and 'Nosafot la-ma'amar, "Orhot ha-talmud" (1868), *Collected Works,* vol.1, pp.7-52.
15. The angel Metatron defends the rights of Israel (B.T., *Hagigah,* 15a), teaches schoolchildren Torah (ibid., *Avodah Zarah* 3b), mourns the destruction of the Temple (introduction to *Eikha rabbati.)*
16. *Collected Works,* vol.2, pp.182-183.

17. See detailed discussion on the significance of the expression in Y. Liebes, *The Sin of Elisha*, chapter 3, pp.29-50.
18. See B.T., *Baba Kamma* 82b: 'There was, however, an old man [among the besiegers] who had some knowledge of Greek Wisdom and who said to them: "So long as the other party [is allowed to] continues to perform the service of the sacrifices they will not be delivered into your hands." On the next day when the basket of *denarii* was let down, a swine was sent up. When the swine reached the centre of the wall it stuck its claws into the four hundred parasangs. It was proclaimed on that occasion: [...] and cursed these words at face value and asks: 'But was Greek Wisdom proscribed?' Further on (83a) the Gemarah distinguishes between the Greek Language five hundred children who were learning Greek Wisdom in the home of R. Simeon Ben Gamliel, and replies: 'The family of R. Gamliel was an exception, as they has associations with the government.' See the discussion on the entire matter, ibid. Cf. B.T. *Sanhedrin* (90a):
'But the following have no portion therein: [...] R. Akiba added: One who reads uncanonical books.' See also ibid. (100b): 'A *tanna* taught: [this means], the books of the Sadducees.'
19. Cf. Lilienblum's comment in 'Nosafot la-ma'amar 'Orhot ha-talmud', Collected Works, vol.1, p.41: 'All their comments [of the *tanna'im* and *amora'im*] have been stated according to place and according to time!
20. *Collected Works*, vol.2, p.184.
21. R. Judah Halevi, Sefer ha-kuzari (*The Khozari*), art. 3, 65, Cf. Rambam: *Moreh nevukhim*, part 1, chap.32.
22. Lilienblum, *Collected Works*, vol.2, p.190.
23. A parodic allusion to the commentary of the Mishnah of Rabbi Ovadia of Bartenura.
24. A survey of the various opinions on the subject will be found in Joseph A. Dane: *Parody, Critical Concepts Versus Literary Practices, Aristophanes to Sterne*, Norman and London, 1988, pp.10-13.
25. See Dane, *ibid.*, and Linda Hutcheon: *A Theory of Parody, The Teachings of Twentieth-Century Art Forms*. London, 1985, pp.30-49.
26. See M.M. Bakhtin, 'From Prehistory of Novelistic Discourse,' *The Dialogic Imagination, Four Essays*, edited by Michael Holquist, Translated by Caryl Emerson and Michael Holquist. Austin, 1981, pp. 71.
27. See Octave Delepierre, *La Parodie chez les Grecs, chez les Romains, et chez les modernes*. Londres, 1870.
28. *Autobiographical Writings*, vol.3, p.157.
29. Lilienblum, *Collected Works*, vol.2, p.192.
30. Ibid., p.183.
31. Joseph Klausner (above n.8), p.288.
32. Avraham Sha'anan, *Hasifrut ha-'ivrit ha-hadashah le-zrameha (Modern Hebrew Literature and its Trends)*, vol.2. Tel Aviv, 1962, p.27.
33. Lilienblum, *Collected Works*, vol.2, p.193.
34. See above, p. 5.
35. Lilienblum, *Collected Works*, vol.2, p.193.

RELIGIOUS EDUCATION IN ISRAEL: A PERSPECTIVE

Noah Lucas

As pointed out by David Patterson in 'Religion and Life'[1], the Jews of Europe in the 19th century were obliged to compress into a few decades the processes of modernization that had engaged their host societies in Europe for centuries. In Israel a comparable accelerated upheaval, in which the young generations are confronted with a 'glittering panorama of fresh ideas and aspirations' (*Phoenix*, p.53) that are incompatible with traditional Judaism or any of the other diverse cultures of origin of which their parents partook, is reflected in the constant ferment of ideological discourse.

The most poignant expression of the resulting flux of identity is perhaps the quest for self-definition as acted out in the political arena, and particularly as it affects the younger generation of oriental origin. The place of religion in life, which is largely shaped if not entirely determined by education, is the very crux of the quest. This may be a universal fact. Be that as it may, so far as Israel is concerned the quality of equilibrium established between Judaic-religious and Israeli-national values at the core of personal and national identity, is perhaps the very test of the society's ideological integrity and viability.

In 1859, when Jewish philanthropists in Austria, wishing to bring their brethren in Palestine the advantages of secular knowledge, established the Laemmel School in Jerusalem[2], the Orthodox Jews of the city pronounced a ban of excommunication on any parents who sent their children there. The school was therefore patronised in the main by Sephardi children, whose parents and leaders were more moderate. The Alliance school at Mikve Israel came under the same ban in 1882, in spite of its distinguished origin in the initiative of Rabbi Kalischer.

Heder continued to be the dominant educational institution in Jerusalem and the primary purpose of education continued to be understood as the formation of character through religion, rather than the acquisition of skill for material advancement. As Rabbi Kook put it in 1909,

> The aim of education is to fashion man in his right form, of which the essence is that he shall be honest and good ..... Practical training in the struggle of life we have always regarded as of secondary importance.

When the Zionists began to settle in Palestine they aimed to reconstruct Jewry to befit it for survival and success in the modern world. They came as modernizers who aimed to render Jewry economically productive by educating the young for material success, while the religious continued to pursue the perfection of man through religious service. The religious Zionists in the spirit of Modern Orthodoxy sought to combine secular and religious study, but the majority of the Orthodox continued in their traditional way to defy or ignore modernity.

When Theodor Herzl, the visionary founder of political Zionism, nearly a century ago published *Der Judenstaat* in German, the title was translated into English as *The Jewish State*. That is only a correct translation if the meaning of Jewish state is understood to be the state of the Jews, or the Jewish people or Jewry, but not if it is taken to mean the Jewish state in a religious sense with Judaism as its official religion.

Israel's very establishment and its development as the Jewish state, in the sense of the state of the Jews, from the beginning required it to rearrange and stabilize its relations with Judaism the religion. Before the state was established, Zionism, the Jewish aspiration to political independence and the whole experience of political organization to that end, was associated with a divergence between Jewish belonging and Jewish belief.

Belief and belonging were for centuries two sides of the same coin, inextricably intertwined in the ethno-religious heritage. As is to be expected in a tribal religion, the believers were the belongers, being Jewish meant both to practise the religion and to belong to Jewry. The communal traditions and customs, the social institutions, schools and charities, these were derived from the religious practice. The community was created by the religion. In the course of time, the society of Jewry became a coherent web of institutions and relations with a reality of its own. If indeed derived from religious practice, the Jewish society and community existed nevertheless as a residual fact even when religious practice lapsed or ceased.

The impact of secularization and modernity in Europe created a separation between believing and belonging in such a way that Jewish identity was recast and new choices were presented to Jews. Once the total authority of the religion of command was undermined, beginning over two centuries ago, Jews could believe as much as they chose or belong as much as they chose. With the attenuation of faith, Judaism ceased to be all things to all Jews, and Jewish identity in effect bifurcated.

The modern world began to spawn varieties of Judaism such as Reform and Orthodox, with various shades of obedience to the law in between, and varieties of belonging, with infinite variations in the extent of assimilation to the wider secular society and in the intensity of identification with the Jewish people. Individuals decided for themselves according to taste, and undoubtedly under the influence of the social pressures they experienced as members of a minority, to what extent and in what manner to be Jewish. As often as not, the religious conception of being Jewish was displaced by a social conception which was primarily ethnic and cultural in content.

Zionism was avowedly a secular and secularist movement which abandoned the religion and stressed the belonging. It sought to parlay the tribal or ethnic foundations of the people into the national. In other words it stood for the modernization of the form of Jewish belonging, to enable it to conform to the universal European norm of the nation. It wanted to translate Jewry from the pre-modern traditional form of association known as peoplehood to the respectable modern form known as the nation-state.

The religious leaders of the time in eastern Europe, a century ago, fiercely fought Zionism as a sinful secular movement that undermined the education of the young. To the religious establishment, except for a tiny minority, Zionism was not merely heresy, it was blasphemy and virtual apostasy. The idea of a return to the ancient holy land of Judaism through human political effort was the antithesis of the religious expectation of a messianic return at a time and in a manner of divine choosing. In the Orthodox religious view Zionism was just another of the seductive ideologies of modernity which would inevitably leave its deluded followers stranded without Jewish bearings.

This historical fact—of intense religious hostility to political Zionism—needs to be stressed as a reminder of the background, because in recent years the religious are more familiar as a nationalistic group than as opponents of statism. The religious have moved from downright antagonism through halfhearted acceptance and finally to halfhearted cooperation with Jewish sovereignty. But the religious Zionists, who are wholeheartedly nationalist and who consider that the political events associated with Zionist endeavour are religious in significance, are still a minority amongst the Orthodox. The majority of the religious are at best ambivalent towards Jewish statehood and hostile to its ideological claims if not always so antagonistic to its practical results such as settlement of the land.

In fact it has taken a generation for the religious to come to terms with Jewish statehood. The Orthodox have, in the course of their adjustment to Israel, come to accept the State with greater or lesser enthusiasm. This is a process which began in the late 1930s as the power of the Nazis spread. After the Second World War, in the aftermath of the Holocaust, the anti-Zionist Agudah rabbis were reduced in repute and authority and were in no position to stand against the tide of Zionist opinion by opposing Jewish statehood. This was doubly so considering that Jewish Palestine rescued many of them from the European debacle. Ben-Gurion, for his part, was concerned to avoid a situation in which the religious authorities within Judaism would publicly oppose Jewish statehood at a time when all Zionist diplomatic efforts were being concentrated at the United Nations to persuade the world that the Jews unanimously considered statehood the only solution adequate to the plight of the people.

It was in these circumstances that the famous agreement was drawn up between Ben-Gurion and his colleagues on the Zionist Executive, on the one hand, and the Agudah rabbis on the other, known as the Status Quo agreement of September 1947.[3] In this agreement the rabbis undertook not to oppose statehood, in return for which the Zionists agreed that the status quo in religious matters would be maintained in the future state. This status quo was a legacy of British rule, which in turn had been based on the Ottoman Turkish system in which religious minorities enjoyed a considerable measure of self-rule. And so, just as the state finds it necessary to reconsider and redefine its relationship to Judaism, so too Judaism, as interpreted by its sages, has had to reformulate its attitude to Jewish statehood.

Thus it is that from one direction, from a position of vigorous secularist ideology, the state reconsiders its relation to the Jewish religion, while from the opposite direction, from religious antagonism to secular nationalism, Orthodox Judaism comes to grips with the material facts of statehood. The paths of the two interests cross in the struggle for collective definition of the Israeli national personality. Somewhere between the two poles of identity, defined respectively by religious devotion and national culture, the Israeli identity forms. The problem is that there is no real possibility of compromise between theocracy and democracy, or between divine sovereignty and popular sovereignty.

The political outcome of the clash of world-views is an equilibrium reflecting the position of the majority, which is neither ultra-Orthodox nor ultra-secularist, but merely traditionalist. This outcome mitigates the abrasiveness of a marriage between two incompatibles, bound to each other by history and sociology. It is not that the clash between them yields some synthesis, or that in the future the conflict will in some way with wisdom be resolved for all time, by a creative synthesis of values. Nor can it any more probably be resolved by divorce, along the lines that had been advocated by the Canaanite movement. The national identity of the Israeli is a marriage of incompatibles which cannot be resolved in a divorce, because the marriage itself, the bi-polarity, *is* the essence of the identity. Israel as a sovereign state, the very author of the new identity, is obliged to write the marriage contract in fine detail in legislation and then in bureaucratic administration. A new national identity cannot be fashioned without developing general rules which fix the boundaries of status in legislation. Nor is it possible to escape from the constant need, day by day, to interpret and administer the rules. The political explosiveness of the encounter is to some extent neutralised by the affinity for tradition which is characteristic of the majority of the secularists. And this result is the fortuitous product of demographic change, following the mass immigration of Oriental Jews, that is, Jews from the Middle East and North Africa, who have become, with their offspring, the majority of the population of Israel today.[4]

In reference to the historical background, only Europe, where political Zionism originated, has been considered. The Jews of Islam are a different case because they did not undergo modernization in the European manner. Their exposure to modernity took place in Israel itself, in a climate of 20th-century politics very different from that of Europe in the late 19th century. The Jewish immigrants to Israel from the countries of the Middle East, who came mainly in the early 1950s and 1960s, played a role in the politics of religion and state very different from that of their European immigrant predecessors.

All modern states have undergone adjustment of church-state relations in response to the new values of modernity and new patterns of citizenship and administration derived from modern philosophical systems. In Israel the matter is complicated because there is no Jewish church, in the conventional sense, to deal with, only a body of religious commandments whose observance determines the lives of the Orthodox. How can the state relate to a body of laws that governs every detail of existence, operating quite apart from the laws of the state and which draws its authority from different and indeed incompatible rival sources?

The secularist Zionist founders of Israel, wishing to normalize Jewish identity according to the norms of nationality, thought that they could do this simply by sustaining those Jewish traditions which pleased them, without reference to rabbinic authority. They thought that in any case within the new national culture that they were establishing, religious belief would gradually atrophy. But they discovered that they had a problem. How could traditions be maintained and transmitted to succeeding generations without the respect and reverence which accompanies and informs religious devotion? Could this be done without belief in God or in the truth of the Bible? Of course this question is not uniquely Israeli in its reference, since it equally exercises Jewish 'belongers' everywhere. But it is only in Israel that the State itself is crucially involved, since its own very legitimacy as a link in the continuity of Jewish history is at stake.

The Jews of early 20th-century eastern Europe who created and led the national movement and became Israel's founding fathers were secularists in rebellion against the religious authorities and the religious way of life which seemed to them to have brought the people to a desperate pass. By contrast, the immigrants of the 1950s and 1960s who came from the Middle East and North Africa retained their commitment to religious practice and tradition, and did not display the polarization characteristic of East-European and indeed Western Jewry. In the Orient it was uncommon to meet extremes of commitment to ritual or total rejection of it. The Oriental Jews of Islam were much more relaxed about their religion. They practised traditional customs and sustained their traditional beliefs easily, while allowing for a fair measure of deviation. They did not have the defensive attitude of European Orthodoxy, since they had not come up against the challenges of modernity, that is, not until they immigrated to Israel. They did not come to Israel as Zionists rebelling against the Rabbis, but as refugees from Arab nationalism coming to their ancient homeland in what to them appeared as a fulfilment rather than a denial of religious promise.

The experience of modernity which the immigrants from the Middle East underwent was their resettlement in Israel under the auspices of a modern bureaucratic state. In the 1950s the State impinged on the Oriental immigrants in an abrasive way, undermining their religious values, subverting and breaking down their religious culture in the course of their induction into the modern economic, social and political system. This was most keenly felt in the process by which the children of the newcomers were directed into secularist rather than religious schools. This was an experience which the Orientals resented, and they exacted political punishment when they came into their own as an electoral force, that is when they dislodged the socialists from power in 1977.

A generation after their arrival their religious culture in a modified version prevails as the civil religion of the country. The civil religion, so-called by the sociologists, is secularist in nature, but is friendly towards traditions of Judaic provenance, and it represents the world-view of the majority of Israelis today. There are Orthodox and there are anti-religious in the manner of polarization, but there is a secularist-cum-traditionalist majority, underpinned by the numbers of the Orientals and the vigour of their religious affinities, who want to maintain lucid continuity with the Jewish religious past. The new national identity of Israel has in effect recovered some of its Jewish content from the ideological ferment associated with the melting-pot of immigration. The dominant bias is still undoubtedly secularist, but there is a leavening of religious flavour as though of Oriental spice.

It is a happy coincidence for Israel that the demographic change due to the Oriental influx has produced a national culture which both the secularists and the Orthodox can live with, because they both think it affords a useful platform for the eventual triumph of their own version of the desirable. The religious, although at first they were suspicious of traditional practices conducted under secularist auspices, now see them as no bad thing, which may even assist the return to the religious fold of the majority of lapsed Jews, while equally, the secularists see them as forming the basis of a national culture which in due course could dispense with the influence of the rabbinate.

The socialist Zionists who built the foundations of Israel came to see that Jewish traditions were extremely important as a social cement for a population drawn from a tremendous variety of cultures. National culture had replaced divine authority as the source of legitimacy for the allegiance of the great majority. But, increasingly as the centre of gravity of the population moved in the direction of Oriental culture, religious tradition came into its own as the primary source of national culture. A Judaic reservoir nourishing secularist attitudes gradually replaced the faltering liberal and socialist sources of public values. The national culture increasingly took on a religious tone, by the choice of the secularists and in the name of secularist national values. This is the paradox of Israeli public ideology today, as it matures. It is secularist in its very foundations, the product of a secularist challenge to religious authority, but the content of the secularist national myth is increasingly supplied by and dependent upon religious traditions for its sustenance and transmission to the younger generation.

Countries that are not based on mass immigration are less dependent on ideological harness, because national identity is largely naturalistic, given by geography and history without effort. In an immigrant society—and the United States for a century had the same problem until its national life was firmly established—it is necessary to provide an ideology that helps to weld the immigrants into a nation while at the same time it justifies their arduous migration. In the case of the United States the 'American dream' of freedom, wealth and opportunity served very well. In Israel, which is so burdened by military service and other privations exacting a penalty in sacrifice, universal values which could be pursued elsewhere with greater ease and more promise of success, do not suffice to compensate for the penalties of the national revolution. Continuity with Jewish history, which can be established only by reversion to the religious sources of the culture, comes into its own as a belief system and value system capable of justifying sacrifice and anchoring a new nation in the land.

The choice of heightened Jewish content of the secularist civil religion is evidence of a weakness at the heart of the Zionist revolution such as had been addressed by Ahad Ha-'am with great prescience. It should be understood that this trend is not the same thing as a religious revival, but is truly in the spirit of Ahad Ha-'am's attempt to provide for a modern Judaic national culture that would not be governed by the rabbinate. It is secularist in origin and spirit, as is the very argument that halakhic law should be an integral part of the law of the land as an essential foundation for a cohesive society. Utilitarian reasons do not qualify as religious reasons. So if there is friction between secularists and rabbis, this should not be blamed on the rabbis. The minutiae of social regulation based on considerations of religious ritual are sponsored by the secularists of their own free will and institutionalized by their own decisions.

The Israeli government kept its part of the bargain of 1947, and established Judaic decorum in the public realm: national holidays, Sabbath observance, *kashrut* in public institutions, exclusive rabbinic jurisdiction in matters of personal status, state-funding for religious education and indeed for synagogues, all these were organized in a way that took full account of religious sensibilities.

If the status quo has changed since 1947, and changed in favour of religious expansion, this is not due to any discernible religious revival, but rather to a number of general conditions, such as the political strength of the religious in a segmented political system lacking a majority, which enables the religious to negotiate material benefits in excess of their numerical weight, a situation not caused but reinforced by the electoral mechanics; or the proven quality of the religious schools, and the large families of the religious community which helps to sustain them. The socialist or labour ideology lost its transmission belt when the old educational trends were abolished by the education law of 1953, but the religious trends, publicly funded, were nevertheless effectively allowed to continue in full vigour. But surely more important than these considerable technical advantages, is the prevalent traditionalist bias of the population, which results in the secularists giving favour to religious demands. If the major competitive political parties pursue the religious bearing gifts this is because they know that the public is willing to pay for them, within reason.

Bibliographical note

The general issue of religion has become widely recognised among Israeli scholars as perhaps the most important key to the understanding of Israeli political and social development. Quite apart from philosophical and literary discussion which is not so accessible to social scientists abroad, this is reflected in a superb body of political sociology which has reached the proportions of a literature. Among the pacemakers are the works of Charles Liebman and Eliezer Don-Yehiya, Menahem Friedman and Daniel Elazar, as well as a host of original analysts including the late U. Tal, M. Samet, A. Ravitsky, S. N. Lehman-Wilzig, G. Weiler, B. Kimmerling, E. Ben-Rafael and S. Sharot, E. Schweid. A. Fishman, Y. Leibowitz, E. Luz, to name but a few at the risk of invidious omission.

Notes

1. David Patterson, *A Phoenix in Fetters: Studies in Nineteenth and Early Twentieth Century Hebrew Fiction*, Savage, Maryland : Rowman & Littlefield Publishers Inc. (1988 i.e. 1990), chap. 5 and also the Introduction.
2. Joseph S. Bentwich, Education in Israel, London : Routledge & Kegan Paul(1965).
3. Menahem Friedman, using new archival evidence, shows that the status quo agreement contained less substance than has been generally assumed, and he casts doubt on the importance and supposed origins of the letters exchanged. Friedman demonstrates that the pattern of religious-secular relations which prevailed for more than a generation as the "status quo" was in fact hammered out between religious and secularist military commanders on the battlefields of the War of Independence in 1948. See M. Friedman, 'The Structural Foundation For Religio-Political Accommodation in Israel: Fallacy and Reality', in S. Ilan Troen and Noah Lucas (eds), *Israel: The First Decade of Independence*, SUNY Press, New York, Forthcoming 1994.
4. The recent mass immigration from Russia and other countries of the former Soviet Empire has reduced the Oriental majority. If the immigration continues, European Jews could quite soon balance and eventually exceed the Oriental. It remains to be seen how the overwhelmingly secularist C.I.S. immigrants may adjust to or influence the religious *modus vivendi* that has formed in Israel.

JEWISH ATTITUDES TO GREEK CULTURE IN THE PERIOD OF THE SECOND TEMPLE

Martin Goodman

The curriculum favoured in Jewish academies of learning has been influenced in most periods of Jewish history by the intellectual concerns of surrounding cultures. The Jewish element in such curricula can rarely be distinguished from outside influences without begging questions about a hypothetical Jewish core. In practice, such questions are sometimes left on one side by historians: Jewish civilization is defined simply by what Jews do and write. It is thus an unusual aspect, in the context of the modern historiography of the wider Jewish past, that the culture of the Second Temple period is so often analysed in terms of the acceptance or rejection of Hellenism.[1] I hope that a study of some aspects of this curious phenomenon may be an appropriate tribute to David Patterson, who has done so much to foster the pursuit of Jewish knowledge within the wider academy.

Scholars' concentration on the relationship between Jewish and Greek culture in the history of this period has been prompted above all by theological concerns. If Judaism in the last centuries B.C.E. was profoundly affected by hellenistic ideas, the claim of hellenized Christianity to represent the true inheritance of Israel is much enhanced; conversely, rabbinic Judaism can be portrayed as a reaction against Hellenism.[2] It will not be my concern here to investigate such claims, although in fact they are open to more than a little doubt.[3] I intend only to look at the simpler issue of Jews' own awareness of their cultural predicament as it is attested in the literature which survives. What did Jews say that they thought about Greek culture?

This issue has attracted remarkably little attention. It is logically quite separate from analysis of the *actual* adoption of Greek culture by Jews.[4]

Awareness of a cultural threat can increase or decrease almost regardless of the extent of contact or influence. Indeed, foreign cultures may be attacked most strongly precisely by those most under their influence, such as the deeply hellenized aristocrat Cato the Censor, who launched bitter attacks on Greek culture in Rome in the mid-second century B.C.E.[5] No one has ever asked whether Jewish writers such as Ezekiel the Tragedian or the philosopher Philo thought of themselves as introducing Greek culture into Jewish education or whether Jews like the sectarians at Qumran consciously rejected the same culture. Just as recent studies on Greek attitudes to Jews have enhanced understanding of the period by concentration on the explicit statements of ancient Greek writers about Jews and Judaism,[6] a study of Jews' explicit comments about the Greek culture in their midst may also be enlightening.

The most striking aspect of Jewish references to the prevalence of Greek culture among Jews is their rarity. If there existed any Hebrew word in antiquity for 'acting Greek', like the Latin *pergraecari*, no trace of it survives.[7] Post-biblical Jewish literature contains numerous attacks on Greek rulers and against paganism and idolatry, but Jews might in theory heartily dislike such things and yet enjoy reading Homer. Jews in the second century B.C.E. expressed much hostility to gentiles *qua* gentiles, but the non-Jews singled out were no more likely to be Greeks than Ammonites and Gileadites (I.Macc. 5. 6-54), or Samaritans, Edomites and Philistines (Ben Sira 50. 25-6). Attacks on the 'ways of the gentiles' may often have been deliberately theoretical, like the non-Jewish behaviour forbidden in the later rabbinic formulation of the Noachide Laws,[8] and if authors in this period had any particular non-Jews in mind, it might quite plausibly be their non-Greek neighbours in the regions which surrounded the land of Israel. It is only in the mind of modern scholars that the attack in Ben Sira (41.8-9) on Jews who 'forsake the covenant' is taken to describe capitulation specifically to Hellenism; Ben Sira himself did not explicitly mention Greek culture at all.[9]

Most of the major changes which took place in Judaism in this period could have occurred regardless of the spread of Hellenism in the Near East. Ezra's injunctions against mixed marriages, the notion of sacred scripture and the concept of a biblical canon owed nothing to the Greeks.[10] The emergence of distinct sects, trends and philosophies within Judaism owed more to the adoption of divergent calendars and different ways of interpreting biblical texts than to the influence of Hellenism.[11]

Most evidence for explicit awareness by Jews of Hellenism as a cultural phenomenon which might affect Jews was written in the Hasmonaean period and specifically with reference to the events of the Maccabaean revolt from 175 to 164 B.C.E. According to I Macc. 1. 14-15, in the 170s B.C.E., 'the wicked left the ancient laws, joined themselves to the gentiles, and built a gymnasium according to the customs of the nations'; in the parallel account in II Macc. 4. 7-13 about the same incident, the author claimed that the 'acme of Hellenism' was the wearing of the broad-brimmed hat in the gymnasium. It is evident that the authors of these works saw (correctly) that the gymnasium was a distinctively Greek phenomenon. Elsewhere in the same books the antithesis between 'ancestral honours and Greek notions' (II Macc. 4.15) was left vague: in II Macc. 6.9, it was simply stated that the wicked among the Jews decided to kill those not prepared to go 'to Greek things'.

References from the time of the Second Temple to the influence of Greek culture on Jews are rare outside this context of the revolt of the Maccabees, but a few can be found. So, for instance, Josephus wrote (*A. J.* 15. 267-8) that some Jews opposed the entertainment plans of Herod the Great in Jerusalem on the grounds that athletic games, the theatre and the amphitheatre were 'foreign customs' which 'destroyed the ancient way of life'. Athletics and theatre performances were distinctively Greek (although theatres could have other uses in Syria in this period),[12] but the more violent entertainments found in the amphitheatre represented a Roman custom only recently imported into the Eastern Mediterranean.[13] Josephus argued that some Jews felt particularly strongly opposed to wild beast shows because 'it is wicked to kill for pleasure' (*A.J.* 15. 274), and to athletic games specifically because of the trophies (178-9), even though other Jews simply disliked all practices which were 'not from custom' (281, cf. 365).

Such titbits provoke interest more by their scarcity than their force. If Jews were paranoid about encroaching Greek culture in the first centuries B.C.E. and C.E., they wrote remarkably little about it. Nothing in the Dead Sea Scrolls hints that imitation specifically of Greeks is wicked. Even literature which might be expected to contain explicit opposition to Greek culture in fact lacks any such attack. Nothing can be found in Ben Sira or Jubilees. There survives no record of any attack on those Hasmonaean rulers, like Aristobulus I in 104 B.C.E., who styled themselves 'philhellene' (Jos. *A.J.* 13. 318); since, according to I Maccabees, the Hasmonaeans claimed credit for the expulsion of hellenizers from the control of Temple, such a self-description should have been embarrassing, even if its prime intention at the time was political alliance rather than cultural integration. But in fact, and despite the *tendenz* of the accounts in the books of Maccabees, there is little evidence that the Hasmonaeans did *constantly* stress the wickedness of hellenizing practices: at any rate, the festival of Hannukah, which was in existence in something like its present form in the first centuries C.E. and presumably dated back to Hasmonaean times (cf. John 10:22; m. B.K. 6.6), stressed only the repurification of the Temple and focussed antagonism not on wicked Jews but on the evil king Antiochus.

It is likely that this lack of concern about encroaching Hellenism was reinforced by a general feeling among Jews in the Hasmonaean period that Greek culture was not really wholly alien. Hence the remarkable acceptance by the ambassadors sent by Judas Maccabee to Sparta that Jews had a distant family relationship with Spartans (II Macc. 5:9; the claim was taken at least semi-seriously since it formed the basis of an alliance). Jewish historians like Malchus-Cleodemus claimed that Jewish history could be integrated into Greek myth.[14] Other Jews went even further, asserting that Greek culture was derived from the Jews. Thus Eupolemus taught that the Greeks got their alphabet from the Phoenicians who in turn got it from the Jews (Euseb. P.E. 9.26), and Artapanus asserted that Moses, 'who is Musaeus', brought the arts of astrology, navigation and architecture to the Egyptians, and hence to Greece (Euseb. P.E. 9. 27). Such writers' self-confident views presupposed the desirability and excellence of Greek culture - all the more desirable insofar as Hellenism was derived from Judaism.

Such easy co-existence was not to survive, and I shall spend the rest of this essay endeavouring to suggest why it collapsed. The clearest contrast to such views may be found in the writings of Josephus in the late first century C.E. His explicit attitude to Greek culture seems to me entirely different from those attested previously. For Josephus, Jewish culture was separate from, and markedly superior to, Hellenism, a view which he laid out in full in his long apologetic treatise, *Contra Apionem*.

Josephus disclaimed any suggestion that Jews are preoccupied with Greek culture: 'Greeks', he wrote, 'are not the only people with whom our laws come into conflict' (*C.Ap.* 2.99). Ordinary Jews, 'do not desire to emulate the custom of others' (*C. Ap.* 2. 261). Greek culture leaves them indifferent, feeling neither enmity or envy (*C. Ap.* 2. 123). It is true that Jews have some things in common with some aspects of the culture of some Greek states, but Jewish culture is far superior to all (*C. Ap.* 2. 225-7, 258-68); Josephus showed no interest in the alleged family relationship with Spartans, and he omitted all reference to it even in his paraphrase of the correspondence in I Macc. 12.6-23 (Jos. *A.J.* 12. 225-8; 13. 165-70). In sum, for Josephus, Greek culture was irretrievably alien - and, to a proud Jew, inferior.

The origins of this shift in attitude over two and a half centuries were presumably complex. Four possible main sources seem worthy of investigation. I suggest that this change in Jewish attitude may have been brought about primarily by a combination of the attitudes of the Seleucid state, the Hasmonaean rulers of Palestine, and the non-Jewish inhabitants of the cities adjacent to Judaea. One further factor, which is not often taken into account by modern scholars, may have emerged only in the time of Josephus himself, when Jews came to define themselves in relation to the outside world not by reference to Greeks, but by reference to Romans.[15]

First, the attitude of the Seleucid state. No one knows for certain what stimulated Antiochus IV Epiphanes to seek to abolish the Jewish cult in Jerusalem, but rather more can be said about the way he chose to portray his actions. In II Macc. 11.24 is preserved the decree of his son Antiochus V by which he rescinded his father's attempt to bring the Jews to *ta hellenika*. In terms of practical politics, the decree constituted recognition of Judas' success in recapturing the Temple, but it was presented as a gracious about-turn, 'to permit Jews to practise their ancestral customs'. One can see why Antiochus Epiphanes had needed to portray his attack on Jerusalem in the guise of a cultural mission. Attacking cults of the gods was a dangerous activity in the eyes of polytheists, so Antiochus justified his actions by claiming that the Jewish cult was uncivilized and thus did not deserve to exist. The rape of the sanctuary could be passed off in the anodyne phrase used in describing these events by Tacitus in the second century C.E: 'Antiochus changed the Jews to Greek ways' (*Hist.* 5.8.2). In the first century C.E. the anti-Semitic Alexandrian Greek Apion preserved a story which probably went back to such Seleucid propaganda, about the Jews' habit of swearing an oath to preserve their enmity against the Greeks, which they confirmed by the annual sacrifice of a Greek foreigner (Jos. *C.Ap.* 2.95).[16]

The Maccabees had initially no need to adopt this image of Judaism as at odds with Hellenism, since their original aim was simply to purify the Temple and restore the cult (see above). I suspect therefore that their eventual presentation of their revolt as a revulsion against hellenizing Jews owed much to the opposition within Jewish society which they faced when they usurped the high priesthood from the families which had long held it. The new dynasty was on weak ground when it took over this position, which had central importance in Jewish cult. Hence the seven-year interregnum after the death of the High Priest Alcimus which preceded Jonathan's self-elevation to this position on the dubious authority of the Seleucid Alexander Balas (I Macc. 10.15-21; Jos. *A.J.* 20.237). The later myth that Judas himself had been High Priest (even though there is no hint of it in I or II Macc.) testifies to the existence of Hasmonaean propaganda to justify their occupation of the office. The Hasmonaean Simon even invented a procedure of acclamation by the people to confirm his right to the role (I Macc. 14.25).

This is the context which explains the attempt by the author of I Macc. 1: 11-15 to slur the reputation of the high priests who had governed Jerusalem and the Temple before Antiochus' attack on the shrine. I Maccabees is a history of the revolt composed as dynastic propaganda in the style of the historical books of the Hebrew Bible. Within a biblical view of reward and punishment, the hellenizing habits of the Jewish priests in the 170s fulfilled a historiographical purpose as the aspect of Jewish society which deserved the punishment meted out by Antiochus. The author made no attempt to show quite how in practical terms their predeliction for Greek athletics could have caused Antiochus' attack on the Temple, which, as priests of the cult, they can hardly have welcomed. Perhaps the reason was that there was in fact no connection, and that the author included mention of the 'wicked' high priests before 168 B.C.E. only to justify the exclusion of their descendants from office in the time when he was writing.[17]

The third participant in the process by which Jewish and Greek culture came to be seen as mutually exclusive were the gentile inhabitants of the cities which bordered the Hasmonaean state. The hatred felt by such cities for the Jewish state is evident from the decision by some of them to begin new eras of 'liberty' from the date of their transferral from Hasmonaean rule to Roman 'protection'.[18] Some neighbours of the Jews, such as the Idumaeans, adopted Jewish customs and were incorporated into the state (Jos. *A.J.* 13. 255-8, 318-19), but the city-dwellers remained distinctively apart; the inhabitants of Pella in Transjordan even allowed their town to be destroyed 'because they did not promise to convert to the native customs of the Jews' (Jos. *A.J.* 13. 397). Inhabitants of such cities saw themselves not just as gentiles but specifically as Greeks, and at least by the first century C.E., Jews shared their perception. The gentile inhabitants of Beth Shean were described as Greeks by Josephus in a reference to the massacres in the city in 66 C.E. (Jos. *B.J.* 7.364). This was not a question of ethnicity, for it is unlikely that any of these people had Greek ancestors;[19] hence also the remarkable designation in Mark 7: 26 of a woman who approached Jesus as a 'Greek, a Syrophoenician by race'. Nor was it a question of language use. It is likely that the Jews of Caesarea spoke as much Greek as their gentile neighbours,[20] but when Josephus referred to those gentiles, as he did frequently in his two accounts of the events which preceded the outbreak of the great revolt in 66 C.E., he referred to them sometimes as 'Syrians', sometimes simply as 'Greeks' (*A.J.* 18. 183; 20. 173-8; *B.J.* 2. 266-8; 3. 409).

For Josephus, it seems, 'Greek' could simply be synonymous with 'gentile'. The clearest case of such a usage may be *Vita* 74, where he referred to the effects on Jews in Caesarea Philippi of their taboo against the use of non-Jewish olive oil. In other references in Jewish texts to this prohibition, and in Josephus' own narrative of the same events in *B.J.* 2. 591, concern was expressed about all oil produced by any gentile,[21] but in the *Vita*, written at about the same time as *Contra Apionem* in the nineties C.E., Josephus explicitly described the oil that must be avoided by Jews as 'Grecian'. It seems that Josephus' agenda, however much it built upon Seleucid, Hasmonaean and other traditions of the Hellenistic period, was different from those of earlier writers.

The basis of this agenda lay in the events of his own time, for the historian Josephus had a double identity. He was not only Joseph ben Mattatiyahu, a Jerusalem priest; he was also Flavius Josephus, a Roman citizen.[22] Witness, victim and participant in exciting times, he explained the destruction of Jerusalem society in his days as evidence of God's favour to Rome. According to his theology, Roman power had been achieved through the goodwill of the God of the Jews (*B.J.* 3. 354; 6.300). He knew that other peoples dominated by Rome contrived to preserve national and cultural identities while simultaneously merging themselves into Roman society, and hoped that Jews could do the same.

It is unlikely that Josephus was the only Jew who wore his Roman citizenship with pride and hoped (in vain, as it turned out) that Jews could be accepted in Roman society as Jewish Romans. But it may well be that, even if he was the sole example of the phenomenon, it was that self-image which encouraged his picture in *C.Apionem* of *Greeks* as fickle, prone either to forget (e.g. *C.Ap.* 2. 227) or to change (2. 273) their laws, sexually immoral (2.275), unduly enthusiastic about innovation (2. 182), inclined to value rhetorical style above historical accuracy (1. 27), unable to put their fine words into practice (2. 172), lacking any real regard even for their own nation's writings (1. 44) and contradicting each other even about their own history (1. 15). As Josephus put it, 'among the Greeks, everything is new, dating, so to speak, from yesterday or the day before' (1. 6-7). Such qualities not only contrasted neatly with the Jews' proud opposition to innovation (2. 182), love of sobriety (2. 195, 204) and serious attitude to life (2. 271-2), and so on. More importantly, they also coincided with the self-image of *Romans* when they compared themselves to Greeks.[23] For Josephus, busily insinuating himself into another, more powerful culture, Hellenism had not just ceased to be a threat to Judaism, it no longer really mattered at all.

If any Jews had ever defined themselves primarily in relation to Greek culture, this Jew at least did so no more. In the eyes of Josephus, the Jewish schoolboy who devoted himself to the study of Homer might be wasting his time, but he could hardly be accused of sin.

Notes

1. The classic discussion is M. Hengel, *Judaism and Hellenism*, 2 vols, E.T., 1974. The same assumptions permeate W. D. Davies and L. Finkelstein, eds., *The Cambridge History of Judaism*, vol. 2, *The Hellenistic Age* 1989; see my review in *London Review of Books*, 14.2 (1992), 13–14, in which some of the ideas in this essay are given a preliminary airing. See also L. H. Feldman, 'How much Hellenism in Jewish Palestine', *HUCA* 57 (1986), pp. 83-111; M. Hengel, *The 'Hellenization' of Judaea in the First Century after Christ* (1990).
2. For criticism of Hengel's thesis on these lines, see F. Millar, 'The background to the Maccabean revolution', *JJS* 29 (1978), pp. 1-21.
3. For instance, on the Greek elements in rabbinic Judaism, see S. Lieberman, *Hellenism in Jewish Palestine* (1962).
4. This is not always appreciated by historians. Thus, the study by J. A. Goldstein, 'Jewish acceptance and rejection of Hellenism', in E. P. Sanders et. al., *Jewish and Christian Self Definition*, vol. II (1981), pp. 64-87, which begins by looking at the same issue as I have tackled here, diverges into a discussion of the actual penetration of Hellenism into Jewish society.
5. Cf. A.E. Astin, *Cato the Censor* (1978), pp. 157-81.
6. A. D. Momigliano, *Alien Wisdom: The Limits of Hellenization* (1975); M. Stern, *Greek and Latin Authors on Jews and Judaism*, 3 vols. (1974-84).

7. This is noted by Goldstein, 'Jewish acceptance', pp. 70-71.
8. D. Novak, *The Image of the Non-Jew in Judaism* (1983).
9. See Hengel, *Judaism and Hellenism*, vol. I, p. 151, for the claim.
10. Cf. J. Barton, *Oracles of God* (1986).
11. Cf. M. E. Stone, *Scriptures, Sects and Visions: a profile of Judaism from Ezra to the Jewish revolt* (1982).
12. Cf. Ed. Frezouls, 'Recherches sur les theatres de l'Orient syrien', *Syria* 36 (1959), pp. 202-27; 38 (1961), pp. 54-86.
13. L. Robert, *Les gladiateurs dans l'Orient grec* (1940).
14. C. R. Holladay, *Fragments of Hellenistic Jewish Authors*, vol. I, *Historians* (1983), pp. 245-59.
15. This list is not intended to exhaust all possibilities. It takes no account, for instance, of the special political significance of Greekness in Alexandria at the time when Philo lived and wrote there.
16. E. J. Bickerman, *Studies in Jewish and Christian History*, 3 vols. (1976-86), vol. II, pp. 225-55. Stern, *Greek and Latin Authors*, vol. I, p. 412, preferred to attribute the story to anti-Semites in Alexandria, but he admitted the plausibility of Bickerman's suggestion.
17. For the date of I Maccabees, see now S. Schwartz, 'Israel and the nations roundabout: I Maccabees and the Hasmonaean expansion', *JJS* 42 (1991), pp. 16-38.
18. On the cities, see E. Schürer, rev. and ed. G. Vermes et al., *The History of the Jewish People in the Age of Jesus Christ*, vol. II (1976), pp. 85-193; A. Kasher, *Jews and Hellenistic Cities in Eretz Israel: relations of the Jews in Eretz Israel with the Hellenistic cities during the Second Temple period (332 B.C.E. - 70 C.E.)* (1990).
19. On Beth Shean, see G. Fuks, *Scythopolis - Greek city in Eretz-Israel* (1983) (in Hebrew).
20. L. I. Levine, *Caesarea under Roman Rule* (1975).
21. M. Goodman, 'Kosher olive oil in antiquity', in P. R. Davies and R. T. White, eds., *A Tribute to Geza Vermes* (1990), pp. 227-45.
22. T. Rajak, *Josephus: The Historian and His Society* (1983).
23. N. K. Petrochilos, *Roman Attitudes to the Greeks* (1974), pp. 55-62.

THE CONTENT OF JEWISH EDUCATION AND ITS RESPONSIBILITY WITHIN THE JEWISH-CHRISTIAN ENCOUNTER

Alice and Roy Eckardt

Whenever Jewish education loses sight of historical concretion, it runs the danger of idealist ineffectiveness. It deteriorates into a series of truisms already known to all.

What ought to be the *content* of Jewish education respecting the Jewish-Christian encounter? What specific themes ought to be addressed within this all-important dimension of Jewish education? For there is little value in propagating the desired and desirable motivations behind the Jewish-Christian meeting, for example the 'need' for 'knowledge' of and 'sympathy' with another's traditions 'in a multicultural world' unless and until such interests are fleshed out via study of and research into concrete events and phenomena. That Dr. David Patterson should have developed the research and curriculum of the Oxford Centre for Postgraduate Hebrew Studies to encompass Jewish-Christian relations and (within that frame of reference) the study of the Holocaust, is a mark of his concern for educational concreteness and completeness. The essay that follows is a tribute to David Patterson's contribution to Jewish educational specificity and breadth vis-a-vis the two areas indicated.

Within the context of the Jewish-Christian dialectic, what elements ought at once to underlie and constitute the *curriculum* of contemporary Jewish education? The answer extends to:

(a) one abiding and indeed salient fact: anti-Semitism;

(b) two communities in their ongoing, vibrant character: the Jewish community and the Christian community; and

(c) two all-decisive events (shared by the parties, yet not shared by them): the European Holocaust of 1933-1945, and the reestablishing of Israel, power-politically speaking, in 1948.

This matrix, this series of five factors, does two opposite things: It offers the major pedagogical conditions and subject matter for a humanly challenging encounter; at the same time it sets significant limits upon the Jewish-Christian dialogue's fruition and moral possibilities.

The dynamic interaction of forces presupposed here is reminiscent of a not unusual form of sociological understanding—broadly speaking, a structural-functional way of thinking.[1] More precisely, the theoretical (though not the practical) thrust of the effort is toward a working phenomenology of the Jewish-Christian relation.[2]

Behind all the cooperativeness and good feeling that seek to penetrate planned meetings, the many conferences and even casual association between Jews and Christians, there lurks the spectre of anti-Semitism. It is the hidden agenda of all such encounters. While self-hatred is not unknown among Jews, it is a truism that the non-Jewish world bears the primary responsibility for the anti-Semitic condition—in both meanings of responsibility: involvement and culpability.

The social and historical reality of anti-Semitism creates a distinctive and repugnant profile for the Jewish-Christian dialogue and within the pedagogy that directs itself to a shared historical era. The determining quality of anti-Semitism is seen in the truth that both our historic events, the Holocaust and the rebirth of the State of Israel, for all their transcending and independent significance, can be apprehended within and under the fact of anti-Semitic vileness. For the Holocaust comprised the apocalyptic fulfillment of century upon century of Christian and extra-Christian *Judenfeindschaft*, the hatred of Jews as Jews, while the experiential meaning of the State of Israel is describable in comparably, but diversely, fulfilling ways. The late Pinchas Peli of Beersheva University asserted that the very 'essence of Israel's meaning' lies in its enabling Jews to fight for their lives.[3] A point to be noted is that Professor Peli was a fully Orthodox Jew. The usual stereotype would rather have him speak of his country Israel in 'pious' or at least 'religious' fashion. Preeminently, the State is the 'No' that can at last be said by Jews to the Jewish powerlessness that empowers anti-Semitic demonry.

A most important 'function' of the component of anti-Semitism, pedagogically and practically speaking, is to ensure a certain psycho-moral asymmetry within the dialogue—well before discrete dialogue activities ever get under way.[4] This is in no way to idealize the Jewish people. According to the classic Jewish and Christian understanding of humankind, all human beings have a proclivity for sinfulness and idolatry.[5] In principle, therefore, the shoe could have been placed on the other foot. Had the Jewish people of early Western history somehow been turned into a triumphant majority community, politically and socially speaking, that community, at least theoretically, could have come to dominate and persecute a Christian minority. But history had other plans. Nor did the nineteenth-century record of anti-Semitism in Christian Europe and elsewhere end with the Holocaust or the State of Israel. Jewry today is beset by continuing incarnations of anti-Semitism, including neo-Nazism, anti-Israelism, and ever-renewing Jew hatred in Eastern Europe and Russia. Anti-Semitism, a fateful constant intrinsic to the story of Western (and Middle Eastern[6]) society, persists as a chronic moral disease, the world's one eternal hatred,[7] indeed a universal religion, and hence it is the dominating, if sorry, component of the entire Jewish-Christian relation. Historically, symbolically, and psychologically, the Jew remains the victim, while the Christian serves and is rightly perceived as the victimizer. This fact works to produce marked psycho-moral unease within the dialogue. Not only do some Christian students seek to deny the perniciousness of the reality of anti-Semitism; often, Jewish students do the same. This situation makes the task of the teacher triply difficult: having to teach a history that is morally abysmal; trying to convince—or remind—Christians that it is their own faith that still carries a heavy burden of the 'teaching of contempt'; and endeavoring to convince Jewish students that not all Christians are as understanding as their own Christian friends. In addition, it has to be brought home to all that the horror of anti-Semitism is not merely a phenomenon of the past but persists today. Demands for simple justice and decency continue to come from the one (Jewish) side, while from the other (Christian) side come ideological expression, protestations of innocence, yet also occasional confessions of guilt. (The terms 'ideological' and 'ideology' are used in this analysis in the meaning, following Karl Marx, of thinking that advances collective self-interest.) All in all, the phenomenon of anti-Semitism is at one and the same time a most formidable barrier to Jewish-Christian understanding and reconciliation, and the single most weighty factor in motivating and perpetuating the dialogue on the part of those who are committed to the moral transformation of a dread state of affairs.

Of the several factors that here qualify for curricular attention, the categories 'Jewish community' and 'Christian community' are the hardest to encapsulate, for three reasons: their great age, their massive complexity, and the continually shifting features and fortunes of their world and the world about them. The very idea of 'dialogue' as it is today accepted was unthinkable before the modern era.[8] Authentic dialogue, along with pluralism as a whole, boasts essential secular roots, as well as religious ones.

Again, the two communities before us are themselves developing, changing realities—their vibrancy was mentioned before—and neither community is what it was as late as a hundred years ago. The upshot is that any short treatment of these two component factors cannot escape simplism.

Happily, however, our social and theological history, out of which the Jewish and Christian communities have come, has fashioned a handle for us to grasp in our quest for understanding. This history, a common inheritance but also a radically divergent one, suggests two analytical categories: continuity and discontinuity. The exploration of these two categories is crucial to any responsible pedagogical program. The overall continuity-discontinuity of the two communities rests, on the one hand, upon the component of religious faith that they both possess, and, on the other hand, upon the component of laic identity that they do *not* both possess, since it is peculiar to Jewishness. ('Laic identity' refers to 'peopleness' or 'peoplehood' in a much wider and deeper sense than ethnicity.) Christianness means Christian faith, and that is virtually or normatively all it means. Jewishness *may* entail religious faith, but it does not have to do so. Christian atheism is a contradiction in terms; Jewish atheism is not. That is to say, Jews who abandon the Jewish faith remain Jews, and they continue to be received as such by many believing Jews. The only traditionally operative requirement for Jewishness is birth by a Jewish mother, with the possible added proviso (much debated) of non-conversion to another faith.

The fundamental link between this singular feature of Jewishness and the *raison d'être* of the State of Israel is evident, or ought to be. A Jewish state is perfectly logical and perfectly normal. A Christian state, by contrast, is a theological anomaly, necessarily dependent for its presumed integrity upon extra-Christian props (cf. Vatican City).

Religiously considered, the infinite complexity of the relation between Judaism and Christianity can be probed with aid from the concept of *covenant*—more precisely, by means of the dialectic of oldness/newness, as in the concepts 'old covenant,' 'new covenant.' Generally speaking, from the Jewish side *oldness* signifies untramelled validity; from the prevailing Christian side *newness* has meant triumph and supersession. For the Jewish religious conscience, the Lord of Israel has never withdrawn the covenant-promises from the people of Israel, and will not do so. Despite any chastising acts by God or the hiding of the face (*hester panim*), God is identified as a God who keeps God's word; and despite the vicissitudes of their history, Jews remain heirs of the original bond with Abraham, Isaac, and Jacob. But the Christian church was very early to define itself as the new Israel, not in the sense of a partner with original Israel but as the God-given fulfillment and replacement of Israel because of, reputedly, the special sins of the Jewish people and the advent of the incarnation of God in Jesus Christ.

In Christian thinking today no issue is more paramount (normatively speaking), more controversial, or more in a state of crisis than that of the church's self-identification. How is the church to define itself? Jewishness can readily define itself without any reference whatsoever to Christianness. But there would appear to be no way for Christianness to define itself apart from Jewishness (even when it is trying to deny its Jewishness). The stubborn fact remains that the alleged incarnation took place in a Jewish human being. Is the Christian church in fact the successor of the old Israel, or is it instead an accession, somehow grafted into the trunk of Israel, the abiding people of God? (cf. Rom. 11:17ff.; Eph. 2:11ff.). We shall return to this question. For the moment, we might interject that if, as the church has claimed, 'later is better', why then is not Islam the seal of, and the successor to, previous revelations, including not Judaism alone but also Christianity? But by the same token, why is not Mormonism the successor to Islam, the Unification Church of Sun Myung Moon the successor to Mormonism, and on and on?

The Jewish-Christian dialogue of our time and the academic study of the entire Jewish-Christian complex are penetrated by the themes 'Holocaust' and 'State of Israel', the latter since the 1940s and particularly after 1967, the former, strikingly enough, only since the late 1960s.[9]

Each year observances of Holocaust Remembrance Day (*Yom Ha-shoah*) are held in unnumbered Jewish congregations. The same is now the case in large numbers of Christian churches across North America. Does this mean that the Holocaust is a Christian event as well as a Jewish one? One Christian spokesperson answers Yes, not respecting the Holocaust as such alone but also respecting the State of Israel:

> The cornerstone of Christian anti-Semitism is the superseding or displacement myth, which already rings with the genocidal note. This is the myth that the mission of the Jewish people was finished with the coming of Jesus Christ, that 'the old Israel' was written off with the appearance of 'the new Israel'. To teach that a people's mission in God's providence is finished, that they have been relegated to the limbo of history, has murderous implications which murderers will in time spell out. The murder of six million Jews by baptized Christians, from whom membership in good standing was not (and has not yet been)

withdrawn, raises the most insistent question about the credibility of Christianity. The existence of a restored Israel, proof positive that the Jewish people is not annihilated, assimilated, or otherwise withering away, is substantial refutation of the traditional Christian myth about their end in the historical process....[10]

For the above spokesperson, Israel and the Holocaust are what he calls 'alpine events' within the history of modern Christianity.

Two recent episodes may be introduced by way of further pointing up the interrelation of Holocaust and anti-Semitism. Several years ago Ernest O'Neill, pastor of a predominantly student church in Minneapolis, preached a series of sermons contending that the Holocaust-event was God's punishment upon the Jewish people for their iniquity in rejecting Jesus Christ.[11] The sermons produced a massive backlash of protests and meetings within the Christian and Jewish communities of the Twin Cities, Minneapolis and Saint Paul. The other episode occurred about the same time at the University of Notre Dame where a group of students (nuns and lay brothers) addressed an open letter to the eighteen members of the Theology Department. The students asserted that a course they had just concluded entitled 'Theology of the Holocaust' posed agonizing questions concerning the credibility of Christian doctrine. To quote from their letter: '[We have been made aware of the antisemitism that was regnant within] centuries upon centuries of Christian tradition. What disturbed us most, however, was the sense that this situation has not been completely remedied even today.' Referring to the use of the Gospel of John in the Christian Good Friday liturgy, the students asked if there were any way to modify 'the antisemitic elements present there.' Then they added a plea: 'We ended our course last Friday with the sense that something was terribly wrong and we were at a loss how to deal with it. We would appreciate any help you can offer. We ask you please to give this matter your prayerful consideration.'[12]

Scholars of the history of Jewish-Christian relations need to be made aware of this two-fold condition within today's Christian community: the abidingness of Christian supersessionist anti-Semitism, counterbalanced though probably not matched by ever-increasing acknowledgment of and concern with such anti-Semitism on the part of the Christian community and Christian scholarly endeavor. Jewish education has an important role to play in apprising students and the wider world of learning of such phenomena within the Christian church and Christian scholarship.

On the theme of Zionism and the State of Israel, our fifth component, Jewish education is obliged to make clear how the reimplementing of political sovereignty for Jews occasioned a crisis not only within the world Jewish community but within the Christian community and Christian thinking. The persuasion that Jews had been expelled from their land because of their sins, and were thereby fated to wander homelessly throughout the world,[13] was and even remains today a powerful ideological force within the churches. On that view, any State of Israel can only embody unbroken Jewish presumptuousness and sin. But, contrariwise, we are also witnessing at present, and increasingly so, the phenomenon of Christian Zionism, wherein the ideology that Jews have lost the right to their ancient land is being fought inside the churches themselves.

At least three variations within the Christian Zionist position vie for attention. The first is not wholly bereft of its own ideological taint (again to resort to Marxian terminology). That is to say, many Christian Zionists ground their support of Israel upon the Parousia, the expected Second Coming of Christ. According to this millennialist outlook, the return of the Jews to their land must take place before the Son of God reappears.[14] We might identify this type of thinking as instrumentalist, that is, Israel is reduced to a means to the end of Christian truth. The second variation is not instrumentalist. Israel's integrity is not subjected to Christocentrism. In keeping with a stress upon the authority of the Old Testament (so-called) as Word of God, many Christians relate the State of Israel to the intention and promises of the faithful God we referred to earlier. As the Anglican historian James Parkes describes this view, 'the whole religious significance of the Jewish Bible ... ties it to the history of a single people and the geographical actuality of a single land.'[15] The third variation within Christian Zionism is notably more cautious theologically than other views. It emphasizes secular-moral legitimation, concentrating upon the historic rights and juridical authenticity of the State of Israel.[16] 'Christian Zionism' is thus not the best phrase for describing the third possibility; that outlook restricts itself to the affirmation that *Jews* are entirely justified in *their* Zionism, a discretely Jewish phenomenon.

The foregoing Christian interpretations have counterparts within Jewish political and religious reflection. To make plain the great variety within both Christian thinking and Jewish thinking respecting Zionism and the State of Israel constitutes a further salient task for contemporary Jewish education.

A foremost source of tension within the Jewish-Christian encounter of today arises out of the Arab-Israeli conflict. The Governing Board of the National Council of Churches in the U.S.A. officially declared that the Palestine Liberation Organization is 'the only organized voice of the Palestine people and appears to be the only body able to negotiate a settlement on their behalf', and, further, that in exchange for an advocated

PLO recognition of Israeli sovereignty, Israel must agree to the 'option' of a sovereign Palestinian state 'apart from the Hashemite Kingdom of Jordan' and must accept the PLO as 'a participant in the peace negotiations.'[17] The prevailing ongoing and contemporary rejoinder to this position by Jews and others supportive of Israel is that the PLO remains a terrorist body that has never in truth accepted Israel's legitimacy (despite propagandistic promises beamed to the outside world but never to the inner-Arab world), that there is already a Palestinian state (Jordan) and that a second such state could only be counted upon to persist in Israel's total effacement.

Continuing Christian criticism of Israel and failure to criticize Arab policy and behaviour, together with out-and-out Christian opposition to the Israeli cause, have led many Jews and others to doubt whether contemporary Christian education and Christian participation in the dialogue can be, on balance, received as genuine, sincere, or worthwhile—this against a background of still-vivid Jewish memories of the church's contribution to the Holocaust, and of more recent memories of the dominant failure of the Christian community to speak out against threats to Israel's life in 1967, 1973, and ensuing years. However, it is essential to recognize that the debate over the Arab-Israeli conflict is by no means drawn only along Jewish and Christian lines. Thus, for example, in the United States the National Christian Leadership Conference for Israel (NCLCI) is unreservedly non-accepting of the PLO, not just because of that organization's savage terrorism and its unrepresentativeness of Palestinian welfare, but for its purpose *sine qua non* to destroy Israel. Accordingly, the NCLCI has clashed head on with official National Council of Churches policy on the conflict.[18]

The other part of the task we have, with our five-fold paradigm in mind, is to focus upon a few very practical questions as they are being addressed today within Christian as also within Jewish, theological, moral, and scholarly effort. The issues to be covered lie implicit within our structural-functional model, and, accordingly, within every Jewish-Christian conversation and every Jewish educational venture.

The broadest and most profound question that confronts us—it has, in fact, underlain much of the analysis to this point—is: *How are we to relate faith and history?* How are we to connect religious affirmation to the events of time and place? Is faith to determine our judgment about events? Or are events to determine our faith? Or are the two categories to be mutually determinative?

Something deep within the Jewish-Christian *Weltanschauung* keeps this issue very much alive—unlike in the Graeco-Oriental conception of things, wherein historical event as such occupies an inferior place or perhaps even no place at all. Judaism and Christianity (Islam as well) are eminently historical religions, by which we of course do not mean that they have a history—all religions have histories—but rather that they construe certain historical events as ultimately decisive for the very meaning and destiny of human life, and indeed as intimately associated with the divine purpose itself. And so, traditionally, Jews concentrate upon such sacred events as the Exodus of the children of Israel from Egypt and the giving of the covenant at Mount Sinai, while Christians concentrate upon the crucifixion of Jesus and his resurrection.

But are we to stop with such events as these? What would be the justification for stopping with them?

Irving Greenberg puts his finger upon the whole issue involved when, writing of the Holocaust and traditional Jews, he states (parallel counsel could be given Christians), 'to ignore or deny all significance to [the Holocaust-] event would be to repudiate the fundamental belief and affirmations of the Sinai covenant [itself: the conviction] that history is meaningful, and that ultimate liberation and relationship to God will take place in the realm of human events.' And Greenberg goes much farther than this general affirmation when he summons all previous faith-claims to stand before the bar of judgment of the Holocaust-event. He declares: No statement, theological or other, can be legitimately made today 'that would not be credible in the presence of the burning children' of Auschwitz.[19]

To illustrate how the Holocaust-event can influence current Christian reflection, let us turn to an essay by Rolf Rendtorff, a Protestant professor of Sacred Scripture at the University of Heidelberg. Rendtorff's contribution is titled, 'The Effect of the Holocaust on Christian Mission to Jews.'[20] He is referring to the *Judenmission*, as the phenomenon is called on the European Continent, a traditional organized and concerted effort to 'bring Jews to Christ.' Proponents of the *Judenmission* have usually argued in a twofold way: If God's gift of the Christian gospel is a truly saving one intended for any and every human being, how could it ever be withheld from Jews? And where it does get withheld from the Jewish people, and the church is not opened to Jews, is this not an embodiment of anti-Semitism, inexcusable discrimination against the Jewish people?

Rendtorff answers representatives of the *Judenmission* by pointing out that the real question is the way in which the Christian church is to identify itself (a question to which we earlier alluded). There are two possibilities: if the church is inherently anti-Jewish (as the Holocaust testifies) and hence immoral, there is no possible *moral* justification to bringing the Christian gospel to Jews. If, by contrast, the church is not inherently anti-Jewish but is distinguished by being appended to the people of God, there is no possible *religious* justification to bringing the Christian gospel to Jews. As Rendtorff puts it, 'the addition of the gentiles to the people of God ... shows the impossibility of a Christian mission to Jews.'[21] On this alternative, the mission to Jews is, all unwittingly perhaps, a self-destructive attack upon the church's true foundation, namely, the covenant with the people of God. Jews are not meant to be Christians; Christians are, in a compelling sense, meant to be Jews. It is from within this perspective that Krister Stendahl of the Harvard Divinity School has spoken of the Christian as a 'peculiar kind of Jew.'[22]

We may be permitted one critical *midrash*. Professor Rendtorff is of course correct, historically speaking, that it took the horror of the Holocaust to expose the untenability of the *Judenmission*. Yet if the Christian effort to evangelize Jews is wrong in a post-Holocaust world, and if, as Rendtorff argues, it is wrong on the theological principle that the church has not superseded Israel but is conjoined to Israel, then it was wrong as well in the pre-Holocaust world, and, accordingly, its wrongness today has nothing to do with the Holocaust-event. This does not mean that we are to dissociate Holocaust and *Judenmission*. Rudolf Pfisterer of Schwäbisch-Hall, another contemporary German thinker and Protestant churchman, brings the two realities together, perhaps more tellingly than Rendtorff. Pfisterer asserts that there is no real difference between the German Nazi physical Final Solution, *die Endlösung der Judenfrage*, and *die geistliche Endlösung der Judenfrage*, the attempted spiritual liquididation of Jews by Christian missionaries.[23] In both cases, the outcome is the same: there are to be no more Jews. As J. Coert Rylaarsdam of the University of Chicago describes (and completely opposes) the long centuries of the Christian tradition, the only 'good Jews' are either dead ones or Christians.[24] Nevertheless, Rolf Rendtorff's essay exemplifies very helpfully how, within contemporary Christian theology, a determining historical event sometimes enables Christians to stand in judgment upon their own particular faith-claims and religio-moral policies.

In ways not unlike those to be found within the Christian community and Christian education, yet in radical contradiction of the recent massive Christian reversal regarding the traditional *Judenmission*, the Jewish educational enterprise of today is called to enquire into possible theological and moral foundations of the Jewish mission to Christian and other communities. Within a world riddled with catastrophe, crises, and moral breakdown, is there not a basis for rethinking and perhaps reinstituting a Jewish missionary enterprise? This question has recently been asked, and responded to positively, within Reform Jewish circles in the USA.

Our next practical question is a variation upon the first one: 'How are we to relate theology and politics?' What is the rationale for including this question within a curriculum of Jewish studies that is concerning itself with the Jewish-Christian relation? What does it mean to offer a 'theology of politics'? We are brought back again to our fifth component, the State of Israel.

One way to approach this question is via the challenge to surmount a twin temptation: *the theologizing of politics* (a subjecting of the political order to the demands of faith), and/or *the politicizing of theology* (a subjecting of faith to the demands of the political order).

The theologizing of politics is vividly exemplified in a statement of the General Synod of the Reformed Church of Holland. The document is called *Israel: People, Land and State.* The Dutch churchpeople determine that alone among the peoples of this world, Israel is summoned to achieve a peculiar righteousness. They assert that 'the land was the place allotted to this people in order that they might realize their vocation as God's people to form a holy society', and the synod goes on to insist that 'the Jewish people now, as in the time of Jesus, are in danger of falling victim' to 'nationalistic self-assertion.' The writers go so far as to contend that 'the special place of the Jewish people' makes highly problematic 'the right of existence' of the Jewish state.[25]

Is there a point of view that does not fall into this kind of theologizing of politics and yet can offer a tenable theology of politics? The challenge is a formidable one; only a few suggestions will be tendered.[26] The challenge to avoid both a theologizing of politics and a politicizing of theology is as vital to Jewish education as it is to Christian education.

A first suggestion is the need to exorcise all double standards from political decision-making. Recognition of this need is found in a statement issued by a continuing colloquium of Catholic and Protestant scholars in the United States that devotes itself to the theology of the Christian-Jewish relation and is known as the Christian Scholars Group on Judaism and the Jewish People. One paragraph of this group's 'Statement to Our Fellow Christians,' as their document is titled, stands in direct opposition to the pronouncement of the Reformed Church of Holland: It is 'quite unrealistic and unjust to expect Israel to become a sort of heavenly society of which more is demanded than of other nations ... Christians must refrain from the type of criticism that would use Israel's failures, real or imagined, to live up to the highest moral standards as an excuse to deny its right to exist. Such a view would be a double standard, one not applied to any other nation on earth.'[27] From the standpoint of this Catholic-Protestant document, perhaps the most revealing thing about the Dutch Synod's statement is its total failure to make special moral demands (in the unavoidable context of the Arab-Israeli conflict) of Syria or Jordan or Iraq—or, for that matter, of its own country, Holland. Its attempt to religionize or spiritualize the Jewish people is rather typical of

Christian ideology. The laying of special demands upon the Jewish people is particularly reprehensible in coming from the Christian church, which helped bring to pass the annihilation of the Jews of Europe.

A second suggestion to the end of achieving a tenable theology of politics is the insistence that political claims be desacralized and relativized, in the interests of peace and justice for all. The theologizing of politics and the politicizing of theology are, in the end, but two sides of the one coin. [28] To try to transform a political state into a church that is an exclusively 'spiritual' or 'religious' reality is no different in kind from trying to transform a church into a state. The effort to identify human collective interests with the standards and will of God and with divine right is as old as human culture. Once collective claims are relativized, usually through the power and influence of secularity, the peculiar genius of politics is given a chance. That genius is the art of compromise. Today, fortunately, any theologizing of Israel remains a minority exercise within that country and is kept under effective public control. The last thing most Israelis would tolerate is a theocracy. (Most Israelis are not very religious.) Out of a long and bitter history these people know well that the nation-state is anything but a law unto itself. Political sovereignties are subject to the universal norms of justice. Were this not insisted upon, we should find ourselves subject to the error of many Christian Zionists and even of some Jewish Zionists, both of which groups often put forward their own particular brands of a theologizing of politics. A genuinely secular theology will never sanction more than relative and partial claims respecting political sovereignty.[29]

This leads to one added suggestion in the search for a theology of the political dimension. The journey from theology to politics may be nourished by religious anthropology, the understanding of the nature of human beings as such. The concrete possibility here is political democracy. Israel is a democracy, the only one in the entire Middle East.

According to Judeo-Christian anthropology, humankind, morally and spiritually apprehended, is a creature of infinite heights and infinite depths. Humankind is fashioned in the very image of God, is barely below the angels, crowned with glory and honour, and has been put in charge of the entire world (Ps. 8:5-6). Yet humanity is also an incorrigible idol-maker who falls into radical self-deification and in the process subjects itself and the whole creation to its self-destructiveness.

Democracy is the political instrument that takes most seriously this dialectical anthropology. Reinhold Niebuhr, foremost political theologian of this century, gave voice to the aphorism, 'Man's capacity for justice makes democracy possible; ... man's inclination to injustice makes democracy necessary.'[30] Democracy is a middle path between and beyond political absolutism and political anarchy. The absolutist pretends that ordinary human beings are not fit to govern themselves; the anarchist pretends that there is no need for humanity to be governed at all. Absolutism means tyranny, anarchism means chaos. In truth, assert biblical Judaism and biblical Christianity, human beings are not so evil that they cannot achieve tolerable levels of justice and self-government, and human beings are not so good that they can be counted upon to serve the commonweal. The American system of institutional checks and balances, as also the Israeli and British ones, know that human beings are not to be trusted, but they also know that the very same human beings are peculiarly trustworthy. The biblical doctrine of humankind escapes the twin maladies of utopianism and cynicism. The cynic is an idealist who has had to learn something from experience. The Jew and the Christian, insofar as they are nurtured and sustained by biblical anthropology, are neither cynics nor idealists but realists, in politics as in everything else.

And now a final practical question : *Where, if anywhere, does the problematic of Christology enter and gain a justified and integral place in Jewish education?* This question takes its origin, of course, from the Christian side; its only licitness here lies in the fact that it is constituent to Jewish studies once the latter grapples fully and openly with the Jewish-Christian encounter.

The issue of Christology is particularly difficult, sometimes even grievous, for Jewish students, not wholly unlike, to mention a parallel, the problem raised for Christian students (most especially, Arab Christians) by political Israel as wholly intrinsic to Jewish reality, insofar as that issue appears as alien to the Jewish tradition of strict monotheism and the proscription of idolatry. And with respect to the Christian student who is engaged in Jewish studies, any questioning of traditional Christological affirmation may seem to comprise an attack upon the foundation of the church and the student's own faith. The problem is compounded when the subject is introduced—as it must be—within a context that is not only interfaith but academically neutral. Yet there is no way to escape such complications; this type of challenge confronts all those who undertake to teach and learn within a strictly academic setting.

Christology—the effort to understand what it means to speak of Jesus as the Christ—can and does very often entail Christian triumphalism vis-a-vis the Jewish people and Judaism. A noted current representative of such triumphalism is the Protestant theologian Wolfhart Pannenberg of the University of Munich. Pannenberg grounds his case upon the resurrection of

Jesus. He writes that Judaism as a religion is done away with 'from the perspective of Jesus' Resurrection.'

The point is, for Pannenberg, that the resurrection comprises God's personal intervention within the controversy between Jewish claims and Christian claims. God himself testifies that the Christian is right and the Jew is wrong. For Jesus' claim to an authority that supersedes Judaism was, Pannenberg declares, 'visibly and unambiguously confirmed by the God of Israel' in the singular act of raising his own Son from the dead.[31]

The question Pannenberg faces, along with unnumbered Christian theologians and lay people of like mind, is how to avoid the Christian supersessionism that paved the way to the death camps. Pannenberg does more than hinder the dialogue, he *destroys* it—by destroying the Jewish partner. One American Catholic theologian who recognizes this consequence is Rosemary Ruether, who, in *Faith and Fratricide* as in other writings, attests that anti-Jewishness is, inevitably and immorally, 'the left hand' of traditional Christology.[32]

Must Christology always constitute a hindrance to intergroup understanding, or can it, contrariwise, foster dialogue and reconciliation? In alternate terms, is it possible for Christians to be objective and self-critical respecting their own beliefs and truth-claims? James Parkes, our late redoubtable British mentor in the history and theology of the Christian-Jewish encounter, often repeated a favourite watchword: 'It is impossible to build true theology upon false history.' Historical truth is an instrumentality, not only for achieving objectivity and marshalling self-criticism, but for discriminating between sound doctrine and heresy.

What does all this have to do with Christology? In the nature of the case, food for thought comes perforce from the Christian side, or, put differently, there is no existential challenge here to the Jew, only to the Christian. And the Christian scholar and student of today has little real alternative but to choose—his or her choice obviously has implications for Jewish understanding within the sphere of Christology—between the majority of the surface records of the New Testament and the independent findings of historical research, simply because these two levels of authority conflict gravely and decisively. This is not to imply that the New Testament materials are devoid of all truth. Most of what we know concerning Jesus is to be found therein, although not apart from careful study and scholarly checking. Available methods for assessing the New Testament books duplicate those utilized everywhere in historical work. Given passages are set against other sections of the total corpus and against what is known of life in the first century through other writings, the findings of archaeology, and general historical knowledge and inference. A working principle often called upon by historians is to entertain prima facie validity for passages that somehow managed to remain in the record despite their conflict with the known aims of the author or authors. Thus, for example, in the Gospel of Luke, but only there, Jesus (after the Last Supper) counsels his disciples to purchase swords (22:36).

The crucial question, at once scholarly and human, for all who are not themselves expert historians of the first century, is, Whom or what are we going to trust? The fact is that the New Testament writers tendentiously transform Jesus of Nazareth from the loyal Pharisee Jew that he was into the enemy of Pharisees and of the Torah, and into a virtually divine figure sent into the world to suffer and die to atone for sin and save humanity. The historical researches of such scholars as S. G. F. Brandon, Hyam Maccoby, and others tell us something quite different. The difference is epitomized in the ending to Maccoby's study, *Revolution in Judaea: Jesus and the Jewish Resistance:*

> [Jesus] was to fall among those [the Gentile Christian church] who did not understand that to turn him into a god was to diminish him. He tried [through revolution against Rome] to bring about the kingdom of God on earth, and he failed; but the meaning of his life is in the attempt, not the failure. As a Jew, he fought not against some metaphysical evil but against Rome. Yet the [Christian] movement which denied his life by deifying him misrepresented him as being opposed to the people whom he most loved and on whose behalf he fought [his own Jewish people]. It was an entirely fitting outcome that this movement, Gentile-Christianity, made a successful accommodation with Rome and became the official religion of the Empire which crucified Jesus.[33]

The vocation of Jesus of Nazareth extended to that of opposition to the Roman occupation. He was a religious freedom fighter, a resistance leader of apocalyptic persuasion. In the prevailing Jewish life and thought of the time, a Messiah (Christ, *Christos*) was called to bring liberation to his people from the oppressor—anything but a purely 'spiritual' business. In the course of this struggle, Jesus of Nazareth was apprehended, tried, and found guilty as a seditionist, 'King of the Jews'—and of course he *was* guilty, of subversion and rebellion against Rome.[34] Jesus was a Christ all right, even if, with other Christs until today, he remained a personal failure. But he was not a total failure in the political and moral sense, the sense that counts in life, because together with previous and subsequent Christs, he helps keep us vigilant to the demonic character of human tyranny. He became assured that tyranny is to be fought not just with the sword of the spirit (whatever that may mean) but with force and violence, in the hope of a responding intervention 'by the hand of God.'[35]

Jesus learned for himself that in a world after the Fall the only answer to the suffering made inevitable by powerlessness is the weight and authority of preponderant power. In certain all-compelling respects, therefore, the life of Jesus was to be vindicated, slightly over 1900 years afterwards, when the Third Jewish Commonwealth was begun and the people of God at last gained their temporal freedom.

Hope for the effectiveness of Jewish education, within the broad province of Jewish studies, rests upon the capability of scholars to come to grips—in the train of David Patterson—with highly discrete and momentous problems of our time, in ways that redeem students (Jews but also non-Jews) from realms of abstraction and instead engage them responsibly with the world of concretion in which they are called to live.

Notes and References

1. The Gestalt of a society—what Talcott Parsons calls 'the structure of social action'—is here assumed to arise out of a congeries of dynamically interrelated structures and functions, or subsystems of human action, in conjunction with two environments: physical nature and ultimate reality. The latter-mentioned element refers to the human effort to validate patterns of behaviour through reference to ultimate or transcendent principles that often assume a religious form. See W. Richard Comstock et al.: *Religion and Man: An Introduction*. New York: Harper & Row, 1971, p.15; Talcott Parsons: *The Structure of Social Action*. New York: McGraw-Hill, 1937; Parsons: *Essays in Sociological Theory: Pure and Applied*. Glencoe: Free Press, 1949; Parsons: 'General Theory in Sociology' in Robert K. Merton, Leonard Broom, and Leonard S. Cottrell, Jr., eds.: *Sociology Today: Problems and Prospects*. New York: Basic Books, 1959; Daniel Bell: 'Talcott Parsons: Nobody's Theories Were Bigger', *The New York Times*, 13 May 1979; and Gerhard Lenski: *The Religious Factor: A Sociological Study of Religion's Impact on Politics, Economics, and Family Life*, rev. ed. Garden City: Doubleday Anchor, 1963. However, the overall orientation of the present essay is cross-disciplinary. Any partisan mixture of social, historical, ethical, and theological reflection may eventually assign different weights to one or another approach. The present effort contents itself with an assumption that each method has an equal right to be heard and can be applied to any and every raw material.
2. On the general subject of Jewish-Christian relations, consult, e.g., James H. Charlesworth, ed: *Jews and Christians: Exploring the Past, Present, and Future*. New York: Crossroad, 1990; David Novak: *Christian-Jewish Dialogue: A Jewish Justification*. New York: Oxford University Press, 1989;

and Peter von der Osten-Sacken: *Jewish-Christian Dialogue: Theological Foundations.* Philadelphia: Fortress Press, 1986; also Michael Shermis: *Jewish-Christian Relations: An Annotated Bibliography and Resource Guide.* Bloomington: Indiana University Press, 1988.
3. Pinchas Peli: 'The Future of Israel', *Proceedings of the Rabbinical Assembly 74th Annual Convention* (5-9 May 1974), Lake Kiamisha, N.Y., p.15.
4. A. Roy Eckardt: *Jews and Christians: The Contemporary Meeting.* Bloomington: Indiana University Press, 1986, pp. 8-9, 126-127.
5. However, the history of Jewish and of Christian anthropology suggests that Judaism is relatively more optimistic about human nature and Christianity relatively more pessimistic.
6. Consult Bernard Lewis : *Semites and Anti-Semites.* New York : W. W. Norton, 1986 and Ronald L. Nettler: *Past Trials and Present Tribulations: A Muslim Fundamentalist's View of the Jews.* Oxford: Pergamon Press, 1987. The protestation is often heard within Arab circles, 'We cannot be anti-Semitic, because we are ourselves Semites.' Apart from the unproven exclusion here of any possibility of self-hatred, everything depends upon the relation of language to actual attitudes and behaviour. 'Anti-Israelism' is not anti-Semitism, or it may not embody anti-Semitism, when it fully acknowledges the right of Israel to exist, and is content simply to raise questions about this or that condition or policy within Israel. In such a case, it is perhaps inappropriate to use the term 'anti-Israelism.' Where there is radical or true anti-Israelism, meaning the rejection of the right of Israel to exist, we are faced with anti-Semitism. 'Anti-Semitism' should be used in its objective meaning. The remanding of Jews to non-existence in a collective sense is identical with anti-Semitism in an individual sense, where the person of the Jew is rejected and destroyed. In addition, on the basis of a recognition of human sinfulness, we cannot exclude the possibility that the protestation cited above is a verbal stratagem to hide the party's *Judenfeindschaft,* enmity to Jews as Jews. Anti-Semites may very well find it to their political and social advantage to get others to believe that they are not in truth anti-Semitic. In such situations, those who are taken in by the ploy become hostages to anti-Semitism in a rather diabolical form. It is well to recall that, traditionally, the devil is known for his cleverness, which includes the persisting assurance that no devil is in fact present.
7. In the fourth century John Chrysostom dubbed the Jews 'a nation of assassins and hangmen' (cited in Malcolm Hay: *Thy Brother's Blood: The Roots of Christian Anti-Semitism.* New York: Hart Pub. Co., 1975, p.30). In the propaganda of the twentieth-century Arab world identical descriptions are fabricated. See A. Roy Eckardt: 'Antisemitism Is The Heart', *Theology Today* 41, 1984, 301-308; Shmuel Almog, ed., *Antisemitism Through the Ages.* Oxford: Pergamon Press, 1988.
8. Hans Joachim Schoeps of Erlangen University argues that genuine dialogue did not exist until the twentieth century. Professor Schoeps observes that only within an 'atmosphere of external freedom can that inner freedom develop ... [which allows] questions to be asked in complete openness ... [in] expressing its own point of view, it [takes] seriously the concern of the other, understanding itself from the other's point of view, without ... relativizing the position of either' (*The Jewish-Christian Argument: A*

History of Theologies in Conflict, trans. David E. Green. [New York: Holt, Rinehart and Winston, 3rd ed., 1963, pp. 125-126.])

9. Consult Alice and Roy Eckardt: *Encounter With Israel: A Challenge to Conscience.* New York: Association Press, 1970; Alice L. Eckardt and A. Roy Eckardt: *Long Night's Journey Into Day: A Revised Retrospective on the Holocaust.* Detroit: Wayne State University Press; Oxford: Pergamon Press, 1988. The concern of Christian thinking with the Holocaust has been largely brought about through the influence of Jewish experience. On the question of why the Holocaust did not come explicitly to the fore within the Jewish community and Jewish thinking until the late 1960s, see, e.g., Reeve Robert Brenner: *The Faith and Doubt of Holocaust Survivors.* New York: Free Press, 1980, pp. 4ff. Brenner seeks to account psychologically for the sudden readiness of countless survivors to speak of the Holocaust by means of the events of the Six Day War (1967) and the Yom Kippur War (1973). These events taught Jews 'the significance of that new era in which so many have begun to realize and assimilate the message that each one is a fellow survivor' (p. 9).

10. Franklin H. Littell: *The Crucifixion of the Jews.* New York: Harper & Row, 1975, p. 2.

11. Ernest O'Neill, as cited in 'An Antisemitic Preacher', *Christian Jewish Relations* (London) 72 (Sept. 1980): 46-47.

12. The authors have on file a copy of the letter.

13. Cf. Luke 21:23b-24: 'For great distress shall be upon the earth and wrath upon this people; they will fall by the edge of the sword, and be led captive among all nations; and Jerusalem will be trodden down by the Gentiles, until the times of the Gentiles are fulfilled.'

14. Overall (attempted) support of this notion is found in the Book of Revelation. For example, before the (presumed) Parousia, thousands of the sons of Israel are to be gathered together (7:4ff.); cf. 1:7a: 'Behold, he is coming with the clouds; and every eye will see him, every one who pierced him'; cf. also Acts 1:6-11.

15. James Parkes: *Whose Land? A History of the Peoples of Palestine.* New York: Taplinger Pub. Co., 1971, p. 136. Cf., e.g., Gen. 17:8: 'As an everlasting possession I will give you and your descendants after you the land in which you now are aliens, all the land of Canaan, and I will be God to your descendants.'

16. See A. Roy Eckardt: 'Toward a Secular Theology of Israel', *Religion in Life* 48 (Winter 1979): 462-473.

17. *Middle East Policy Statement, Adopted by the Governing Board, National Council of Churches of Christ in the U.S.A.,* 6 Nov. 1980, New York: National Council of Churches, p.11.

18. For recent statements by Christian bodies upon Judaism and the Jewish people, including in some instances upon Zionism, the State of Israel, and the Arab-Israeli conflict, consult Helga Croner, comp.: *Stepping Stones to Further Jewish-Christian Relations.* London-New York: Stimulus Books, 1977; Croner, comp. and ed.: *More Stepping Stones to Jewish-Christian Relations.* New York: Paulist Press, 1985; and *The Theology of the Churches and the Jewish People: Statements by the World Council of Churches and its*

Member Churches, with commentary by Allan Brockway, Paul van Buren, Rolf Rendtorff and Simon Schoon. Geneva: WCC Publications, 1988.
19. Irving Greenberg: 'Cloud of Smoke, Pillar of Fire: Judaism, Christianity, and Modernity After the Holocaust', in Eva Fleischner, ed.: *Auschwitz: Beginning of a New Era? Reflections on the Holocaust*. New York: Ktav, 1977, pp. 24, 23.
20. Rolf Rendtorff: 'The Effect of the Holocaust on Christian Mission to Jews', *Sidic* (Rome) 14 (1981): 20-25.
21. Ibid., p. 24.
22. Krister Stendahl: 'Judaism and Christianity II—After a Colloquium and a War', *Harvard Divinity Bulletin* (New Series) 1 (1967): 5.
23. Rudolf Pfisterer, conference with authors, Schwäbisch-Hall, 24 Sept. 1975.
24. J. Coert Rylaarsdam, letter to editor of *The Christian Century* 83 (26 Oct. 1966): 1306.
25. The version of *Israel: People, Land and State* (adopted by the Dutch Synod in June 1970) that is cited here is a duplicated English translation circulated by the Department of Faith and Order, National Council of Churches.
26. A fuller discussion is found in Eckardt, 'Toward a Secular Theology of Israel'.
27. 'Joint Protestant Catholic Document,' Christian Scholars Group on Judaism and the Jewish People, as cited in Croner, comp., *Stepping Stones*, p. 154.
28. The practical difference is that the former is usually put forward by representatives of the religious order, the latter usually by representatives of the political order.
29. The second suggestion here is adapted from Eckardt, 'Toward a Secular Theology of Israel,' pp. 469-470; the section beginning 'Today, fortunately' is an amended passage from ibid., p. 471.
30. Reinhold Niebuhr: *The Children of Light and the Children of Darkness: A Vindication of Democracy and a Critique of its Traditional Defense*. New York: Charles Scribner's Sons, 1960, p. xiii.
31. Wolfhart Pannenberg: *Jesus—God and Man*, trans. Lewis Wilkins and Duane A. Fiebe. Philadelphia: Westminster Press, 1968, pp. 67, 255, 257, 258.
32. Rosemary Radford Ruether: *Faith and Fratricide: The Theological Roots of Anti-Semitism*. New York: Seabury Press, 1974.
33. Hyam Maccoby : *Revolution in Judaea: Jesus and the Jewish Resistance*. New York: Taplinger Pub. Co., 1980, p. 195. See also S. G. F. Brandon: *Jesus and the Zealots: A Study of the Political Factor in Primitive Christianity*. New York: Charles Scribner's Sons, 1967; *The Trial of Jesus of Nazareth*. London: B. T. Batsford, 1968. The New Testament scholar Walter Wink, in an important review-article of Brandon's *Jesus and the Zealots* (*Union Seminary Quarterly Review* 25 [Fall 1969]: 37-59), acknowledges that Brandon has succeeded 'in reviving the prospect that Jesus' eschatological convictions were really fleshed out in the form of Jewish nationalistic longings' (p. 54). Coming as it does from one who is seriously critical of Brandon's study, this is a significant admission. See also Haim Cohn: *The Trial and Death of Jesus*. New York-San Francisco: Harper & Row, 1971; Pinchas Lapide: *Israelis, Jews, and Jesus*. Garden City: Doubleday, 1979; and A. Roy Eckardt: *Reclaiming the Jesus of History: Christology Today*. Minneapolis: Fortress Press, 1992. The New Testament analyst John Townsend (Episcopal Divinity School) uses the oldest available Christian literature (the Apostle Paul's

writings) to argue that Jesus was crucified by the Romans for the crime of acting as a royal pretender who, having proclaimed himself King of the Jews sought to free his people from the Roman occupation of the Land of Israel. Further, the picture in the Gospels matches closely what we learn from Paul. Jesus was a political rebel, but one who failed in his rebellion (Townsend, 'Jesus, Land, Temple,' unpublished paper, 1981).
34. Maccoby, *Revolution in Judea*, p. 157.
35. Ibid., p. 145.

THE BERLIN HOCHSCHULE FÜR DIE WISSENSCHAFT DES JUDENTUMS
Marginalia—Personalities—Reminiscences

Edward Ullendorff

It is, perhaps, remarkable that, until the early 19th century, there existed in Europe no institution of higher Jewish learning comparable in aim and status to the secular universities. It was, almost certainly, the central position of the *yeshivot*, those traditional schools of rabbinical instruction which had survived, in one form or another, since talmudic times, that had stifled the rise of western-style academic institutes. But the advent of the emancipation of the Jews in central and western Europe and the impact of the *Haskalah* and the evolving *Wissenschaft des Judentums* produced a demand for secular learning and general studies to be added to rabbinical education—and indeed for Jewish learning to be made a discipline independent of the professional training of rabbis. In Eastern Europe traditional learning based on the *yeshivot*, combined with a different social, political, and demographic structure, remained the mainstay of Jewish education, while in central and western Europe (and later in the United States) institutions of modern academic studies were established that vied with universities in the rigour of their scholarly application.

It was in Italy that the first such seminary was founded in 1829 with S. D. Luzzatto among its principal professors. The Istituto (later Collegio) Rabbinico was somewhat peripatetic in moving its centre of activities from Padua to Rome, later to Florence and again back to Rome. The École Rabbinique was established at Metz as early as 1830, but subsequently found its permanent home in Paris. The Israelitisch-Theologische Lehranstalt of

Vienna (later the Rabbiner Seminar) and the Rabbinical Seminary in Budapest were not founded until the second half of the 19th century. By now oriental studies adjacent to Hebrew and Aramaic had become part of the curriculum, and famous names such as D. H. Müller and especially I. Goldziher could be found among the teaching body. In England Jews' College could boast such accomplished scholars as Adolph Buechler and I. Epstein on its staff.

In Germany it was at first Breslau's Jüdisch-Theologisches Seminar that established Jewish and Rabbinical studies on a secure footing and attained international fame with men like Graetz, Loew, Jacob Guttmann and Heinemann as members of the Faculty. Berlin did not follow until 1872, although the greatest exponents of the *Wissenschaft des Judentums*, men like Abraham Geiger and Leopold Zunz, had long advocated the establishment in Berlin of an independent centre of university status in the field of Jewish studies. When the Hochschule für die Wissenschaft des Judentums opened its portals, Geiger, Steinthal, and Cassel were among the foundation professors.

Only eleven years after its inception the *Hochschule* (i.e. a university-type institution) was forced by the Imperial Government to downgrade its designation to *Lehranstalt* (i.e. teaching institute), largely as a result of anti-Semitism rampant in Germany in the early 1880s and prominently associated with the name of the anti-Semitic politician Adolf Stöcker. After the first World War the *Hochschule* reverted to its original name until, in 1934, the Nazi authorities decreed the same diminution of its nomenclatorial status once again. It was at that time that the *Hochschule* (as it continued to be called—except in official contexts) experienced its greatest expansion: in subjects taught, in the teaching body, and in the number of students. With the exclusion of many Jewish university teachers from their positions, a few obtained temporary assignments at the *Hochschule*; Jewish studies were interpreted to include orientalia and even the classics; and students who failed to gain entry into the universities drifted towards Hebrew and cognate studies.

While the Berlin Orthodox Rabbinerseminar[1] and the Breslau Seminary were closed at the time of the *Kristallnacht*, the *Hochschule* was, curiously enough, allowed to continue its activities until July 1942 when Leo Baeck was ordered to cease teaching the handful of students who had survived until then. The demise of the *Hochschule* thus coincided with the virtual extinction of German Jewry.

During the seventy years of its existence the *Hochschule* (like most similar institutions in Europe during that period) managed its affairs on a shoestring. It was supported by a small endowment fund and through contributions by a society of friends. It was not until early this century that it acquired a building of its own where its fine library and lecture halls were accommodated.[2] The luxury of private rooms for professors and lecturers was unheard of in those distant days before the Second World War—and this was equally true of research and travel funds. I have referred elsewhere[3] to the remarkable fact that the budget of the Hebrew University of Jerusalem in the mid-1930s was £87,000—for all academic and administrative purposes! And similar indigence was manifest at most Jewish institutions of higher learning at that time. The *Hochschule* was administered by a 'curatorium' which appointed members of the teaching staff who, in their turn, elected a chairman from their ranks. What those great scholars lacked in material means they made up abundantly in the profundity of their learning and in their just renown and international fame.

Self-advertisement and exaggerated claims have nowadays pervaded even the cloisters of academe and suffused its vocabulary—deeds and words unthinkable in that ambience fifty or sixty years ago. If it is true that nobody has yet lost a fortune by underestimating public taste, it is probably equally true that, at any rate *sub specie aeternitatis*, genuine distinction requires no recourse to advertisement and no appeal to the arts of the public relations industry by which many aspects of academic life have become disfigured in the course of the last few decades. It was part of the glory of the great Jewish academies of Budapest or Breslau or Berlin that their light shone without any artificial illumination.

The foundation scholars of the Hochschule, to whom I referred earlier on, were followed by other נרות ישראל worthy successors of whom it can truly be said that בכל הארץ יצא קום ובקצה תבל מליהם (Ps. 19:5). Among them were S. Maybaum, E. Baneth (whose son, D. H. Baneth, became Professor of Arabic in the Hebrew University), A. S. Yahuda, and, for only a few years, J. N. Epstein who, in 1925, became the foundation professor of Talmudic philology in the Hebrew University. For obvious reasons I did not know Epstein at the *Hochschule*, but I became an occasional and admiring pupil of his at the Hebrew University in the 1930s. One of his principal and most brilliant students, Gedalya Allon, was my main Talmud teacher at Jerusalem (about him and J. N. Epstein see *The Two Zions*, pp. 28-9 and 51, respectively).[4] Epstein was succeeded at the *Hochschule* by Chanoch Albeck who remained there for ten years before joining the former as Professor of Talmud at the Hebrew University.

This takes me to the generation of my own teachers at the *Hochschule*. I ought to explain, perhaps, that I was permitted to attend lectures in Hebrew, Aramaic, Arabic, Bible, and Talmud for two years while still at school. After that I had only one semester as a properly registered student pending the arrival of my student's certificate of entry into Palestine. I owe the privilege of premature attendance to Professor Ismar Elbogen, who, after some persuasion by me and a fairly stiff oral examination set by him in the above-mentioned five subjects, allowed me to participate as a 'special auditor', although in normal circumstances only duly matriculated students with university-level educational qualifications were admitted. But he agreed that the times and circumstances were not 'normal' and that it was a good thing, in view of the close relations between the *Hochschule* and the University in Jerusalem, to prepare a prospective student of the Hebrew University (even though two and a half years in advance) for the exacting courses of study there.

I owe to Elbogen more than that. He was a demanding teacher, a sage counsellor, a polymath in all things Jewish and he could have taught, single-handed and with great competence, all subjects on offer at the *Hochschule*. By sheer coincidence we found ourselves on the same ship to Palestine, he to visit his daughter in Tel Aviv and I to start my studies at Jerusalem. During the journey and afterwards I had ample opportunity to experience his personal qualities and his exquisite tact. Proof of his singular position in Jewish scholarship was the call he received to serve as research professor simultaneously at the four premier Jewish institutes of higher learning in the United States: the Jewish Theological Seminary, Dropsie College, Hebrew Union College, and the Jewish Institute of Religion.

Ismar Elbogen (1874-1943) was not only a great scholar and teacher but also became a public figure of some renown.[5] He was an alumnus of the Breslau Seminary, and at the age of 25 was appointed lecturer in Jewish history and Bible exegesis at the Florence Collegio Rabbinico. In 1903 he transferred to the *Hochschule* where he remained until his move to America in 1938. At the *Hochschule* he was throughout the most central and influential personality, and for a long period he acted unofficially as the generally acknowledged head of the institution. What he was professor of had never been clearly stated; he was simply the most renowned representative of the *Wissenschaft des Judentums*, and as such he taught many subjects. During the one semester for which I was officially registered he lectured on 'The Beginnings of the people of Israel (including sources)' and on 'Selected sections of בבא מציעא.'[6]

His most important published work, which went through several editions and translations, was *Der jüdische Gottesdienst in seiner geschichtlichen Entwicklung*, but he contributed to many other branches of learning, such as a re-assessment of the Pharisees, a history of the Jews since the fall of the Jewish State, a history of the Jews in Germany, etc. His influence, either directly or through his students, on academic developments in the field of Jewish studies on an international scale was quite prodigious. When he settled in the United States, at the age of 64, he and his disciples expected that now that he was for the first time free of administrative duties he would have many years for the pursuit of his historical studies. Alas, he died, aged 69, while working on a supplement volume (from 1840 to 1940) to Graetz's *History of the Jews*.

Leo Baeck (1873-1956) was one of the ornaments of the *Hochschule* for close on fifty years, as student and as teacher. But his life did not revolve around the institution as did Elbogen's. Baeck was a practising rabbi, a philosopher and teacher of the philosophy and religion of Judaism, and for twelve fateful years, from 1933 until 1945, the outstandingly courageous leader of German Jewry, a duty unsought but bestowed upon him quite naturally and by general acclaim. He was, perhaps, the only Jew towards whom even the Nazis evinced a measure of respect amounting almost to awe.

Baeck came to the *Hochschule* in 1894 after three years of study at the Breslau seminary. He gravitated towards Berlin, firstly because the *Hochschule* was not just an institute for the training of rabbis but was a university centre for the study of Jewish tradition and culture with the same entrance requirements as any secular university; it was open to students—including non-Jews—who had no intention of becoming rabbis. Secondly, he was attracted to the University of Berlin, then at the acme of its fame, and particularly to its great professor of philosophy, Wilhelm Dilthey.

He joined the *Hochschule* in 1913, in its new home in the Artilleriestrasse,[7] as lecturer in homiletics. His inaugural lecture was delivered on the subject of 'Greek and Jewish Preaching' and provided eloquent testimony to his wide learning. Eight years earlier he had already published his *magnum opus* entitled *Das Wesen des Judentums*, a work of profound philosophical and theological erudition which went through many editions and was translated into many languages, including Hebrew and Japanese. The modifications introduced by Baeck into successive printings reveal his changing views and attitudes towards Judaism and its development. In contrast to Elbogen, Leo Baeck's life and achievements have been celebrated in many publications and in institutions dedicated to his memory. He was an exacting teacher and a truly saintly man. There is nothing I could add to the existing literature.[8]

H. Torczyner (later N. H. Tur-Sinai) had for many years been one of the luminaries of the *Hochschule*, particularly in the fields of Hebrew language and Biblical exegesis. He had long left for the Bialik Chair of Hebrew at Jerusalem by the time I joined the *Hochschule*, but he became one of my principal teachers in the Hebrew University, a man with a spark of genius, a somewhat erratic scholar, a passionate teacher, and a remarkable personality. I have written about him in *The Two Zions* (pp. 86-8) and also penned his obituary in *The Times* (10 November 1973—reprinted on p. 208 in my *From the Bible to Enrico Cerulli*, 1990).

Julius Guttmann (1880-1950), son of the Rabbi and distinguished philosopher Jacob Guttmann, served—like Torczyner—for some fifteen years at the Hochschule in the inter-war period until he, too, joined the Hebrew University of Jerusalem. He was an historian of Jewish philosophy as well as a philosopher in his own right. He wrote a good deal on Kant and also engaged in criticism of Sombart's work on the position of Jews in the economic life of Europe. But his magnum opus was *Die Philosophie des Judentums*, translated into Hebrew, in an amended and enlarged form, as הפילוסופיה של היהדות. Guttmann was a self-effacing and reticent man, essentially a scholar's scholar, highly respected, as savant and man, by colleagues and students alike. I did not know him well when I was an undergraduate at the Hebrew University, but I admired him from afar. When he heard that I had been a student of Elbogen's at the *Hochschule*, he invited me to tea. I was immensely impressed with so great a scholar talking with such modesty and humanity to one who was just at the beginning of his studies. Although the conversation was, of course, conducted in Hebrew, he would punctuate it with the occasional and excessively flattering 'Herr Kollege'.

Gershom Scholem, in the Hebrew version of his justly renowned *From Berlin to Jerusalem* (Tel Aviv, 1982, pp. 167-8), relates that he registered at the Hochschule in 1922 before leaving for Palestine and found a remarkably distinguished teaching staff consisting of such famous scholars as E. Baneth, H. Torczyner, Leo Baeck, Julius Guttmann, and Ismar Elbogen. Scholem himself was mainly interested in Guttmann's seminar, in the man as well as in those sitting at his feet. He describes Guttmann as

> ... a wonderfully clear thinker, strict in the interpretation of all problems arising from the study of a profound philosophical text that was, however, faulty in its printed version. G's analysis was thought-provoking and invited lively discussion among the participants who represented a select audience of a kind I had not seen before nor was to experience afterwards. Sitting there were men like Yitzhak Baer, D. H. Baneth, Chaim Borodianski (Bar-Dayyan), Fritz Bamberger and other young men who were destined to become well-known names in Jewish studies and Hebrew literature. It was obvious that Guttmann himself enjoyed his students and the interchange of ideas.

Some ten years later Scholem and Guttmannn were close colleagues and friends in the department of Jewish philosophy and Kabbalah at the Hebrew University of Jerusalem.

Guttmann's successor at the *Hochschule* was the highly respected rabbi and philosopher Max Wiener (1882-1950). Like his predecessor he was a man of profound learning and genuine diffidence, retiring in manner and not given to using words other than with the greatest care and deliberation.

To him Jewish philosophy consisted essentially of the teachings of the Hebrew prophets, and his first major work was indeed devoted to the ideas and notions of morality in the literature of the prophets. He later published a highly regarded book on Jewish religion in the age of emancipation. His study on Abraham Geiger appeared posthumously. He went to the United States in 1939 and taught at the Hebrew Union College.

It seems to me that no institution of higher Hebrew and Jewish learning nowadays—with the probable exception of the Hebrew University—can compare with the internationally celebrated calibre and standing of its teachers by which the pre-war Berlin *Hochschule* (or the seminaries of Breslau, Budapest, and Vienna) was distinguished. The constellation at one and the same time in a relatively small setting of men like Elbogen, Baeck, J. N. Epstein, Torczyner, J. Guttmann (and a few hardly lesser luminaries) might have been wellnigh unique since the days of חז"ל. Shortly after President Kennedy moved into the White House he gave a glittering dinner party for the most illustrious of American scholars, artists, and men of letters. He told them that this must be the most distinguished assembly of minds in the White House since Jefferson dined there on his own. This is a little how I felt about Elbogen and his colleagues in the 1930s.

Postscript: My friend, Professor Simon Hopkins of the Hebrew University of Jerusalem, has urged me, rightly, to draw attention to the fact that, though the justly renowned *Monatsschrift für Geschichte und Wissenschaft des Judentums* (*MGWJ*) was originally associated mainly with the Breslau Seminary, it later became the principal scholarly organ of the *Hochschule*—another important feather in that institution's collective cap. I am much indebted to Simon Hopkins for offering לקח טוב in criticizing a draft of this article. There is no greater joy in life than the *Pirqe Aboth* maxim

עשה לך רב וקנה לך חבר

especially when that *rav* and *haver* is a former *talmid*.

Notes

1. Founded not long after the *Hochschule* by Azriel Hildesheimer (hence usually referred to as 'Hildesheimer's Seminar') as the strictly orthodox training college for rabbis—in contrast to the much wider brief of the *Hochschule*.
2. Photograph in *Universal Jewish Encyclopedia*, vol. 5, p. 405; it was situated in close proximity to the magnificent Oranienburgerstrasse synagogue.
3. Edward Ullendorff, *The Two Zions* (Oxford University Press, 1988), p. 8.
4. See also *Encyclopedia Judaica*, vol. 2, cols. 654/5 and vol. 6, cols. 830/1, respectively.
5. Photograph in *Universal Jewish Encyclopedia*, vol. 4, p. 45.
6. In the *Universal Jewish Encyclopedia*, vol. 2, p. 212, is a photograph of an Elbogen seminar (to judge by the size and shape of the books on the table it was probably a reading of מקראות גדולות). To the best of my knowledge, I am now the only survivor of the class shown in that picture.
7. According to Leonard Baker (*Days of Sorrow and Pain: Leo Baeck and the Berlin Jews*, OUP paperback, New York, 1980, p. 58) the building still stands (1976) and is used as a nursery and a block of flats. The Artilleriestrasse was renamed Tucholskistrasse (should be Tucholsky, Kurt, the German-Jewish satirist) shortly after the Second World War. It is a curious coincidence that some of the principal Jewish institutions happened to be in streets with very similar military names: Artilleriestrasse (Hochschule), Exerzierstrasse (the main Jewish hospital), Grenadierstrasse (the principal quarter of Eastern Jewish immigration).
8. In Leonard Baker's book (see note 7) is a two-page photograph of Leo Baeck, Elbogen (together with his wife, incidentally the sister of the great conductor, the late Otto Klemperer), their academic colleagues, and of the entire body of students of the Hochschule. The photograph was taken in the 1930s. Happily, the caption that 'most of the persons in this photograph did not survive the Nazi savagery' is somewhat too pessimistic. At least fifteen of those shown in the picture and with whom I was acquainted did, in fact, survive, largely as a result of emigration.

CHAOS IN THE BIBLE?
Tohu vavohu

Terry Fenton

It might be felt that an *Alttestamentler* with a penchant for mythical and linguistic origins, most of which relate to the further end of the second millennium B.C.E. would seek but infelicitously to honour one concerned with the latter end of the corresponding millennium C.E. *Menschlichkeit*, however, demands a tribute of gratitude and esteem for a very dear tutor, guide, philosopher, friend and colleague of some three decades' standing, a scholar whose creative skill and vision have opened an entire new area of opportunity for men of Hebrew letters. I presume, therefore, to invoke an ancient *topos* which, however, has had its echoes down the centuries, is accepted in its original Hebrew dress in modern European languages, and has proved a potent source of ideas—beyond, perhaps, its creator's intention. David Patterson's broad and humanist outlook will not, I think, eschew an offering which falls outside the ד' אמות of his own field; one may indeed suspect that a treatment of *tohu vavohu* will tickle his fancy. The intention, however, is not to celebrate but to curtail confusion, תרתי משמע, and David has always demanded, practised and welcomed clarity and clarification in literary as in other matters. Accordingly our offering lies broadly within the purview of his scholarly and educational concerns, and that is what this volume is about. Should then, the topic itself find favour, the primary aim will be achieved: should, further, the argument be found to have made a point, the reward will lie in having presented a piece worthy of its recipient.

It will be argued that the original sense of the phrase תהו ובהו in Gen i 2 is 'nothing and emptiness' and not 'chaos' in the sense of 'disorder', 'confusion' or even 'unformed matter'. The original sense has been misunderstood as a result of contamination with a prior shift in the understanding of the 'Hesiodic' chaos (to which the Hebrew phrase was indeed related), the resultant confusion being exacerbated by the adoption of the phrase—*tohu vavohu*, *tohu-bohu* etc.—in modern languages. It is further held that precisely this semantic shift has given rise to recent notions of a chaos opposed to cosmos, of a 'non-creation' opposed to creation; of chaos as a threat to man's existence and an instrument of divine chastisement; of chaos as a primordial symbol of evil. An attempt has been made to trace at least the outline of this semantic shift in order to discover whether the French or German borrowing, in the sense of *'désordre'*, *'tumulte'*, *'Durcheinander'*, *'Wirrwarr'* has contributed, together with, perhaps more than, traditional exegesis to the rise of the theological idea adumbrated. This attempt has necessitated some journeyings in unexpected by-ways—relative to the stated topic—of literary history: the temptation to essay a footnote on odd matters, including Pantagruel's voyage past the isles of Tohu and Bohu, has not been resisted.

I

In seeking to establish the sense of *tohu vavohu* in Gen i 2 attention must be paid to the etymology of the words, to their usage elsewhere in the Hebrew scriptures and to the most ancient translations. Perhaps I should declare that, methodologically, my inclination is to give etymology the first say, though not necessarily the weightiest. (Following the excesses of a century to half-century ago it might seem that etymology is now undervalued, on the whole, as an exegetical tool. Though, happily, it is by no means defunct, it is still sometimes, unhappily, no better controlled). Naturally, all aspects of the matter have been treated often, sometimes at some length. This study would not have been undertaken were it not felt that nowhere are they treated together with the best results attainable for each of them, with the correct emphases and with a satisfactory overall conclusion: hence the attempt to make some progress towards that goal. Here I would note that in researching the subject after growing doubt concerning the 'current' view I find that objections to the chaos notion have indeed been raised before, particularly by E.F. Sutcliffe in 1934[1] and more recently by D.T. Tsumura in 1989[2]. Neither treatment, however, appears to me to result in a correct solution ('emptiness'—the earth has 'come into being'—היתה—in v.2 but is not yet stocked with vegetation and living beings, an interpretation which harks back, in fact, to quite traditional exegesis). In both cases the supporting argumentation seems to contain a number of difficulties. Some other treatments of a similar tendency, some of which will be mentioned below, are either restricted in scope or resist chaos only partially or pose other problems. They seem not to have affected current thinking, though Tsumura's work may not have had time to make an impact. One cannot refer merely to these voices in order to sustain the view propounded here.

The word תהו occurs fairly frequently in the Old Testament, given the limited size of the linguistic corpus, but it is often observed that its 'primary meaning', 'Wiedergabe' (now perhaps 'sense', that is *signifié*, 'signification', 'reference') is difficult to establish. This may be true in general though many instances benefit from contextual indications and, especially, parallelism. The Semitic languages, however, (Semito-Hamitic, if we include Egyptian) have a plethora of verbs and associated vocables with the root-consonantal phonemes THY/W and many evidently cognate combinations which express going astray, losing one's way, being at a loss, erring—first with physical then with mental and moral reference.

Egyptian, to use our oldest evidence first, has *thi* 'go astray, transgress, do evil', *th ib* 'misguided' ('erring of heart'). Arabic produces several closely related roots: $t\bar{a}ha$ (roots *twh* and *tyh*) 'lose the way, be perplexed' (note *'alqaytanī fī ttuūhi* 'you have plunged me into destruction', $y\bar{a}$ *mutawwahu* 'O misguided one'), *tawiya* 'perish, come to an end'. Since תהו is often said to mean, basically, 'desert' on the strength of Arabic $tīh^{un}$ and this matter is of some significance for the subsequent discussion, it will be as well to note here that $tīh^{un}$ seems not to be a basic or general term for desert but one essentially conditioned by the experience of the Syro-Arabian heartland. $tīh^{un}$ is essentially 'where one loses one's way' as shown by its use in apposition to words for territory and, indeed, desert: $'ard^{un}$ $tīh^{un}$, 'a land wherein one loses one's way'.[3] Now תהו may have developed a similar connotation despite the consideration noted above but if the primary reference of $tīh^{un}$ itself is not 'desert', the same is true *a fortiori* of תהו. Observation of usage will confirm this view of the matter. At any rate, J. Barth's comment[4] 'תהו "Oede, Wüste" muss zu $tīh^{un}$ ... gestellt werden, woraus *'istataha* "in die Irre führen" ... determiniert ist' bears reconsideration. S.Fränkel[5] indeed, agreed the general connection but adduced Aramaic—Syriac t^ewah 'be alarmed' and added 'wenn die Araber $tīh^{un} = mat\bar{\iota}hat^{un}$ als "den Ort wo man ängstlich umherirrt" erklären, so werden sie darin wohl Recht haben.' Exactly.

It has long been claimed that Ugaritic *thw* signifies 'desert'. In view of what has been said it would appear unlikely—Ugaritic has *mdbr*—that this hapax does mean 'desert'. If it did, the implication would be that the 'true', absolutely uninhabitable, desert is the natural habitat of lions as the sea is the home of dolphins (or sharks)![6]

Besides the Aramaic root mentioned, Aramaic–Syriac has a series of related and highly productive roots of the senses already mentioned—'err (literally and metaphorically), be frightened, astounded', and further, 'regret, hesitate' and so forth, usually in common with Biblical Hebrew, *th'/y*, *tw'*, *tmh*, etc. Thus the etymological field of תהו would appear to be well established.

The case of בהו seems simpler: the Arabic root BHW/Y (*baha, bahuwa, bahiya* etc.) refers to emptiness and this is the commonest traditional understanding of the Hebrew. *Bahw^{un}*, in form a perfect cognate for בהו, signifies 'vacant space'.

II

Modern dictionaries and discussions usually take 'desert' to be the basic sense of תהו. In his magisterial Genesis commentary[7] Westermann divides the occurrences into three groups: those where תהו means 'desert', those where it refers to the desert-like state to which the land will be reduced in 'judgement proclamations' and those, consequently, where it has the sense 'nothing', 'insignificant', 'in vain'. In this analysis Westermann is followed by most scholars, recently by Tsumura. Possibly all treatment of the matter over the past century is influenced by P. de Lagarde[8] whose starting point is Job xii 24 where, with the identical Ps. cvii 40 and Job vi 18, Dt. xxxii 10, תהו is said to be 'die weglose unbehagliche wüste'. The view to be propounded is that the diachronic development has been reversed: essentially תהו signifies the insubstantial, nothingness, the useless. In the few instances which de Lagarde and subsequent scholars regard as primary, we are, in fact, dealing with a secondary usage and even here the texts do not bear out the interpretation which has been put upon them. The pristine usage rather, is to be found in those passages of Deutero-Isaiah and Job where תהו appears, usually in hendiadys with, or as the parallel to, words such as בלי־מה, רוח, שוא, הבל, ריק, אפס, אין.

A highly significant text is Job xxvi 7,

נטה צפון על־תהו תלה ארץ על בלי־מה

'who stretches *tzafon* upon *tohu* suspends the earth upon nothing'.

Tzafon, the Canaanite Olympus, is here, within the context of v. 5f., parallel with 'earth' and, as the object of נטה, surely 'the heavens'. Contrary then, to the more ancient 'cosmology' and despite the introduction of more ancient conceptions at v. 11, this text talks of an earth suspended on nothing and, equally, of heavens stretched upon nothing: for what else might תהו signify in this context and as the parallel to בלי-מה? [9] Accordingly we have a text in which תהו refers to 'nothingness' in a 'concrete' or 'physical' sense and which is concerned, moreover, with creation. The consequences for our understanding of Gen. i 2 are considerable, but have not, so far as I am aware, been recognised.

Armed with one clear instance of the signification 'nothingness' for תהו we should consider the other occurrences in Job, especially since they are claimed for the 'desert' reference. At xii 24 we have: מסיר לב לראשי עם-הארץ ויתעם בתהו לא-דרך and the second colon is found again in Ps. cvii 40. Both contexts relate to the prevention of 'leaders' from fulfilling their essential function. They cannot lead their people for they themselves have lost their way: 'he makes them stray in a pathless תהו'. Now a desert is by no means the only environment in which one may lose one's way and there is nothing in the general context of either passage in which the colon occurs, certainly not in the parallel units, specifically to suggest a desert. In fact it may be asserted that a more general meaning would be more appropriate to those contexts and that a translation which captures the essential thought might be 'nowhere'. These ineffectual leaders take a course which leads their people nowhere: the pathless תהו is a 'non-direction'. The Targum rendering here, to anticipate, has 'nothing'. This again is the targumic version and, incidentally, that of AV, also at Job vi 18. Linguistic difficulties arise here despite the clarity of the general intention expressed in the fine image of the dried-up torrents from v. 15 to 20, the image which depicts the betrayal of Job by his comforters. What are the subjects of the verbs in ילפתו ארחות דרכם יעלו בתהו ויאבדו? Are the ארחות 'caravans', as in v. 19, or the 'courses'[10] of the torrents? What are the syntactic relationships of the components of this verse? Fortunately, the solution of these problems is not urgent for determining the sense of תהו. If ארחות is the subject of יעלו and if it signifies 'caravans' the sense would be 'the caravans lose (lit. 'twist') their way (or 'are confused in respect of their way' if the *niphal* of the text is retained), they get nowhere and perish' much as in the previous verse treated: if the ארחות are 'courses' it is they (or their torrents) which become 'twisted', 'get nowhere and run out'. However, despite assertions that the Israelites did not know what happened to water in hot sunshine, it seems to me that Ibn-Ezra was right to think of evaporation (יעלו, especially after v. 17) and in objecting to exegesis which anticipated v. 19 by finding 'caravans' in v. 18. In fact the 'caravan' verse seems to have occurred to the poet after his different use of ארחות in v. 18.

Ibn-Ezra's idea results in 'they (the streams) ascend into nothingness and cease to exist' which seems to be the idea of AV and, I would say, is a fair description of evaporation. Incidentally, the modern Hebrew idiom

עלה בתהו

derived from this verse and possibly from Ibn-Ezra's suggestion, means 'come to nought' of ideas or plans. The various possibilities raised, all pointing to the sense 'nothing' for תהו seem better than 'go up into the desert': why 'up' (עלה)?

In Job then, the basic signification 'nothing' is established for xxvi 7 and far more likely for the other occurrences.

The other text in which תהו is thought to mean' desert' is Dt. xxxii 10, ימצאהו בארץ מדבר ובתהו ילל ישמן. There are serious problems with respect to the second colon but if we consider the most usual understanding, literally, 'He found him in a desert-land, in a waste of a howling of a wilderness' it may be asked if תהו is not interpreted merely in the light of the verse as a whole, specifically in the light of the words מדבר and ישמן. The ancient versions, however, do not use words for 'desert'. Ibn-Ezra explains the word as referring to an absence of habitation which seems to be an important theme in association with תהו in passages to be discussed. If such is the function of the word here, if it is not merely a third synonym of מדבר and ישמן, a telling element is added which certainly remedies what would be a somewhat flat monotony in the poetic diction. It emphasizes the predicament of a people astray in an unpopulated and succourless environment. The notions of 'emptiness' and 'absence of life' suggested by some part of the exegetical tradition are readily understood if the basic sense of תהו is 'nothingness'—at least as readily as if 'desert' were the primary signification. In the context of Dt. xxxii 10 that signification, despite first appearances, would lessen the communicatory effectiveness of the language employed. Here the usage of תהו approaches most nearly the usage of $tīh^{un}$ in Arabic but this development is limited and marginal as the other usages will show.

It is maintained then that in those passages where 'desert' has been taken as the primary sense of תהו, 'nothing' fits the contexts better. Now such a sense lends itself to depictions of man's experience of the desert, especially in poetry. This tendency in Hebrew is similar to the Arabic development as discussed above, but owing to the different environments it is neither so pronounced nor so specific as that development. Arabic derivatives from the basic Semito-Hamitic root-morpheme remained bound to the notion of 'going astray': Hebrew, apart from the passages discussed, uses תהו essentially of 'nothing' and 'insignificance'. After a consideration of the other occurrences the question of derivation will again be raised.

Examples of the signification 'nothing' are found in Deutero-Isaiah though none, I think, is more unequivocal than the Job verse with its parallel בלי-מה. At Is. xl 17 both parallelism and hendiadys establish the sense, תהו‎:כל הגוים כאין נגדו מאפס ותהו נחשבו-לו is the equivalent both of אין and אפס. V. 23 of the same chapter reflects the same usage הנותן רוזנים לאין שפטי ארץ כתהו עשה.

Four verses are of interest because they have some bearing on Gen. i 2. Is. xlv 18 is concerned with the creation of heaven and earth and of the earth it is said לא תהו בראה לשבת יצרה. One may speculate on the relationship between the two verses and on the question of priority. If the Isaiah passage is not alluding to Gen. i 2 or to a tradition which lies behind it then the Genesis verse is responding in some way to the Isaiah passage. At any rate, the assertion of the Isaiah verse, within the context of the following verses, appears to be that territory was not created by the Deity to remain empty: the exiles will return to inhabit their land but this can be achieved only through the sole and omnipotent creator. תהו here is a 'vacuum', not chaos, nor 'desert', unless that sense had been established on other grounds. The other verses to be considered in this context refer to destruction, to the removal of conditions requisite for human habitation. Not much more can be learned from Is. xxiv 10

נשברה קרית תהו סגר כל-בית מבוא

the 'city of nothingness', where every house denies entry, and human habitation is annihilated. The idea is close to that of Is. xxxiv 11, which is set within a description of total destruction[11],

ונטה עליה קו-תהו ואבני-בהו

Instruments of construction are turned to the reverse of their natural function to 'create destruction' to 'produce nothing'. The territory is given over to the beasts and the birds, for mankind this land is 'nowhere'. Chaos or confusion is not the condition described, it is rather the total removal of the machinery of civilization, the dismantling of the apparatus of human existence. Absence, emptiness, non-being is the image evoked. This is the only place where תהו and בהו appear together (one of them has been interpolated at Jer. iv 23) apart from our Genesis text and it may well be that the debt lies with Genesis. If so, the implications for the intent of תהו ובהו are clear. The final example of this image is the Jeremiah text just mentioned.

ראיתי את-הארץ והנה תהו ובהו ואל השמים ואין אורם:
ראיתי ההרים והנה רעשים וכל הגבעות התקלקלו:

ראיתי והנה אין האדם וכל-עוף השמים נדדו:
ראיתי והנה הכרמל המדבר וכל-עריו נתצו:

No developed metrical theory is necessary to establish that either תהו or בהו is superfluous. Comparison of the rhythm and syllable count of the four cola commencing with ראיתי shows that v. 23 is overloaded. Clearly MT carries an interpolation inspired by Gen. i 2. Either תהו or בהו then, is the first element in a sustained image of devastation which depicts with bold hyperbole the onslaught of the foe and its consequences. The land is swept clean of its inhabitants, dust and smoke obscure the skies, the hills quake under the onset of a massive army. Afterwards the territory is denuded, man—and here beast too—is no longer in occupation, cities have been levelled, vegetation destroyed. There is, however, no chaos image here—whether as a confusion of the elements or as some universal cataclysm.[12] As Sutcliffe points out in the study referred to, the 'created world' is very much in place (mountains, hills, skies): he rightly rejects the statement that 'nothing is distinguished or defined'. 'Emptiness' is the theme of the imagery and this it is which gives rise to the vision of the land as תהו (or בהו). The text, in its association of תהו or בהו with ארץ (and the negative association of אור with שמים, despite its wholly different theme and context, may, together with the passages previously discussed, have influenced the choice of language in Gen. i 2.

At Is. xlix 4, לריק יגעתי לתהו והבל כחי כליתי the sense is clearly 'for nothing', that is, 'in vain'. Is. xlv 19 probably reflects the same usage, תהו בקשוני, 'seek me in vain', though the correction בתהו ('nowhere'?) has been conjectured.

In four occurrences the word is applied to 'false gods' or 'idols': I Sam. xii 21 bis, Is. xli 29 and xliv 9, here, strangely, of the makers of idols (the text may be doubted but the remedy of a verbal form $t\bar{a}h\hat{u}$, 'they have erred' is unlikely, the verb being hapax in the Old Testament and the post-biblical sense being 'wonder', 'doubt'). The idols, being impotent, are virtually 'no-things'.

According to the context of Is. xxix 21, 'the righteous is cheated by means of falsehood', ויטו בתהו צדיק, so תהו must be false evidence or a false accusation. The link between 'nothing' and 'false accusation' must, it seems, be a 'non-word' as a false god is a 'no-thing'. At lix 4 the evil rely upon such 'non-words', 'falsity', and 'tell lies'

בטוח על-תהו ודבר-שוא.

Whether the grounds for the rejection of the emendation ותהו in

ותהי יראתם אתי at Is xxix 13 are unassailable[13] seems uncertain. Were ותהו original the sense would be 'valueless', again, literally, 'nothing', 'vanity'.

Extra-biblical occurrences of תהו such as Sir. xli 10 and, in the Judaean Scrolls, 1QM 17, 4, 1QH 7, 2, imitate and echo Biblical phrases.

According to the arguments of the foregoing survey תהו, *a fortiori* תהו ובהו, can have nothing whatever to do with chaos in the sense of disorder, confusion or even formlessness. 'Desert' is not a primary reference, nor, in all probability, a secondary connotation, though the word may be used to describe deserts if another word for desert determines the context. The usual meaning is 'nothing': further significations are 'ineffectiveness', 'uselessness', or even 'falsity' (idols, false assertions). If an attempt be made to encapsulate the various meanings under one dominant heading (perhaps it should not) 'absence' might be appropriate: absolute absence of anything or absence of something which is alleged to be present. At any rate, a hierarchy of significations can be related to the cluster of root-morphemes noted in the foregoing section which are phonologically proximate to תהו and which signify 'erring', 'straying'. תהו then, may indicate, essentially, 'the state of being lost' hence helplessness, ineffectuality, impotence and thence, 'phenomenologically' non-being, nothing.

The evidence of the ancient versions is now considered, apart from Gen. i 2 itself. In general they reflect the basic perception of תהו propounded above. Septuagint renderings are varied but just over one half of the instances have 'nothing', 'vain'. Aquila has 'emptiness' ('nothing' for בהו). 'Nothing', 'empty', 'vain', are the Vulgate and Syriac preferences (Syriac, interestingly, 'in error' in three of de Lagarde's 'desert' passages—Job vi 18, xii 24, Ps. cvii 40). The targumic renderings are significant. In ten instances (there are nineteen occurrences of תהו apart from Gen. itself and the conjectured Is. xxix 13) we find למא 'nothing' (= לא מא), I Sam. xii 21 bis, Is. xl 23, xliv 9, xlix 4, lix 4, Job vi 18, xii 24, xxvi 7, Ps. cvii 40. At Jer. iv 23 תהו and בהו are translated in conformity with Gen. i 2 (but not at Is. xxxiv 11). In two instances למא is used to translate the parallel אין.[14] At Is. xlv 18 and 19 לריקנו is used. בשקר דין of Is. xxix 21 is an interpretation and Is. xxiv 10 eccentric. צחונא 'dryness' Dt. xxxii 10 is evidently influenced by the presence of מדבר and ישמן.

III

It will now be clear why this study rejects any notion of chaos (except the 'Hesiodic') in the phrase תהו ובהו in Gen. i 2. Neither the notion of disorder, nor even of a threatening vacuum inimical to man, 'anti-creational', is appropriate. The latter idea, perhaps even commoner in contemporary study, finds its expression most recently, for example, in B. Otzen's study.[15] With due acknowledgement to predecessors, notably J. Pedersen, Otzen states 'If the desert expands the cultivated world must give way and collapse. Thus the word תהו bears with it associations of danger which threatens human existence'. The previous discussion, it is believed, has shown that the 'desert factor' is marginal in the extreme and that it cannot be interpreted in this sense—even as a tool in the hand of the Creator. A state of תהו to which civilization may be reduced is the result of divine action, not the means by which that result is effected. The essential quality of תהו is that it is totally ineffective. It is employed in the Genesis account to mean precisely 'nothing'. בהו with its rhyming echo and semantic reference, 'emptiness', emphasises this sense and serves to create a rhetorical locution of immense power—the power which has enabled it, transformed in meaning, to take root in foreign languages far removed in place and time. Now it is not being suggested that we have, after all, an *ex nihilo* statement in the creation account: merely that the entire point of the phrase is to teach that the deity did not employ material in creating heaven and earth, specifically the body of תהום—Ti' amat.

The numerous and complicated problems of the terms and syntax of the first three verses of Genesis, on which so many have laboured so valiantly from antiquity to the present, and which have been so carefully surveyed by Westermann, cannot be treated in brief compass. It is, however, unnecessary to address most of them, I dare to believe, in order to make the point with which we are concerned. V.2 is quite different from the rest of the chapter but whatever its possible antecedents it is integral to the account which lies before us. It will not do to claim that it is traditional material which 'P' absorbed but could not fully assimilate (Gunkel) or that in the depiction of the created world an alternative and negative, threatening, possibility is deliberately held in equilibrium with that work—'God lifted the world out of the formless and over its own abyss he holds it unceasingly' (G. von Rad[16]). This accords ill with the entire thrust of Gen. i, encapsulated in the words וירא אלהים את-כל-אשר עשה והנה טוב מאד.[17] The key to the problem is polemic.[18] Within the framework of a 'true' account of creation the narrative attempts to obscure the central element of the most influential creation myth in the Israelite ambience. Many Old Testament passages indicate that Israelites, Judeans, knew the various versions of the Storm-god's battle with the Sea-god (*not* a 'chaoskampf'), a myth which permeated the ancient Near East, and that they associated it with creation (Psalms lxxiv, lxxxix) *pace* the numerous dissentient voices. During the exile they were especially exposed to the Babylonian version and this is of particular relevance to Gen.i, which most of us believe to be a product of that period. It is truly pointless to quibble over the divergent forms of *tehom* and Ti'amat (Proto-Semitic *tihām*, as in Arabic, with developed sense, and with the later Akkadian form *tāmtu*) or to argue for or against 'borrowing'. Who would not perceive that the sea-monster Ti'amat was the same being as תהום–תחת רבצת תהום? If תהום occurs in v. 2 that must be deliberate: one does not introduce gratuitously into the work designed to replace a world-view which one utterly rejects basic elements of that world-view. Clearly there is polemic here—but subtle, camouflaged polemic. The author does not deny that such an entity as Ti'amat-תהום ever existed. Such a strategy would have had scant success with those who knew the myths—still treated seriously (not 'poetic embellishments') shortly after the fall of the Judaean state, when the psalms referred to must have been composed. Rather, the author suggests that there was and is a תהום but this body of water was no opponent of the Creator which, after defeat, furnished materials for creation. After v. 2 תהום is not mentioned again but the Creator's organisation of the waters, מים, is fully described. Above all תהום is mentioned in the same breath as תהו, the 'nothingness', the totally impotent. This, it is maintained, is a pun. Subtly, it is suggested that the similar sound of תהו and תהום betoken a like nature—

ויקרא האדם את שם אשתו חוה כי היא היתה אם כל-חי.

It is proposed that we have here a sophisticated exploitation of the ancient Near Eastern belief that the name constitutes the being or is, at least, an immanent constituent of it. תהום then, is the designation of the waters as a non-personal, will-less, powerless entity, totally subject to the divine disposition. There was never really a battle between תהום and the creator, certainly it was no monster whose body was bisected to form heaven and earth. No material whatsoever was used by the Creator in bringing these elements into being. This, it is claimed, is the explanation of the phrase תהו ובהו, of its presence, meaning, and function in Gen. i.2.

The interpretation proposed may be checked by a comparison with v. 21. Why the mention of התנינים הגדלים? Gen. i uses nothing but the most general terms of all that is created:

רמש, בהמה, נפש חיה, עוף, שרץ, עצי פרי, עשב, דשא;

even sun and moon are called only מארת. Clearly the terrible תנין, the Ugaritic and Old Testament equivalent of Ti'amat, is here 'demythologized'. There is no single Tannīn who once offered battle to Yahweh: there are תנינים (note the plural) and they are great sea-creatures but they are simply a part of God's creation, no different in any significant sense from any other creature. As the Babylonian version of the myth is treated in a manner which attempts to neutralize its essential content so is the Canaanite version stripped of its salient features. Can the appearance of תנין and תהום as the sole 'individuals' mentioned in the creation account be a meaningless coincidence?

To return to v.2: there is probably a further element associated with the idea of תהו, though, in all probability, it did not determine the choice of the word itself. It has long been known that Philo of Byblus reported a 'Phoenician cosmogony' with elements reminiscent of Gen. i 2. Otto Eissfeldt[19] above all has maintained its authenticity, antiquity, and influence on Hesiod's Theogony. Whatever the history and development of this account before Philo it would appear to show that wind, darkness and an abyss ('chaos' in Greek) were the first existing elements in some cosmogony current in Phoenicia in OT times. Actually Hesiod's chaos seems a truer 'vacuum' than Philo's (Sanchuniaton's) 'murky abyss' and may reflect a more ancient 'Phoenician' version. It may well be that P's תהו ובהו (with חשך and רוח אלהים) derives from a familiar ancient concept.

A further word should be said on תהום, but first a glance at the ancient versions of Gen. i 2 itself. The Targumic צדיא וריקניא 'desolate and void' says nothing of confusion or deserts, no more 'inania et vacua' of the Vulgate. 'Invisible and unformed' of the Septuagint is inspired by the 'kind invisible and unshaped' of Plato's Timaeus 51 A; it was known to Philo of Alexandria and through the Vetus Latina to Augustine, hence his statement that the first matter was created 'confused and unformed... which I believe is called chaos by the Greeks',[19a] but here he is under influences to be noted in the next section. Symmachos, partially following the Septuagint, renders 'unformed and undistinguishable'. Interestingly, it is sometimes thought that תהום is the 'chaos word'. Eissfeldt, however, states that Hebrew has no word for chaos though he takes v. 2 to describe it—a 'formlose und sterile in Finsternis gehüllte und von Sturm gepeitschte flüssige oder schlammige Masse'. He takes the entire verse to refer, in fact, to the earth, that is, what was to be replaced by the earth.[20] Sutcliffe, in the work referred to, says that, besides תהו ובהו, Babylonian Ti'amat was identified with chaos and since תהום was identified with Ti'amat, it also was taken to be chaos. He then claims that in Genesis תהום is not chaos, it is a mere 'mass of waters' and he asserts the 'calm majesty' of the Genesis passage. But Ti'amat herself has nothing to do with chaos. Indeed she was a formidable opponent but there was nothing chaotic about her—or about Yam, Leviathan, Tannin, or any of the ancient villains of the Storm-Sea conflict. Sutcliffe himself notes that the influence of the chaos notion on the exegesis of Gen. i is a legacy from antiquity and he finds that it dominates 'all schools of thought' at least from 1877. Now that date precedes the publication of Gunkel's celebrated 'Schöpfung und Chaos' which first brought the recently discovered Ti'amat into prominence. In fact the view of Ti'amat as chaos was wholly inspired by the existing view of Gen. i 2! Perhaps we should have the courage to maintain that not only OT exegesis but many treatments of the Storm-Sea conflict, including whole sections, for example, of Paul Ricoeur's profound and challenging 'Symbolism of Evil', are flawed to the extent that they take chaos to lie at the root of the material which they strive to comprehend. There is no denial here of the reality which these studies engage. The subject belongs to the vast realm of man's perception of his predicament in an ambivalent cosmos and his mythological expression of that perception. Chaos, however, disorder and confusion, is not a symbol of that mythology. There is no word for chaos, in the sense discussed, in mythology[21]: that sense derives from the philosophers.

IV

The transformation of Hesiod's vacuum into a disorderly confusion of conflicting elements is noted in, for example, *Der Kleine Pauly* or the *Oxford Classical Dictionary*, though briefly. Anaxagoras of the fifth century appears to have set the process in motion with the concept of what Aristotle called the 'homoeomeries', expressed in the famous statement that originally 'all things were together'[22]. In the beginning there was a mixture of seeds of every qualitatively distinct natural substance, infinitely divisible into parts like each other and like the 'parent' seed. The seeds take their quality from the prevailing component but at every stage of division imperceptible portions of all other components remain within them. All things were unlimited, both in multitude and in smallness. We may pass over, for the most part, the long development of the seeds thus sown. Suffice it to note the speculations of the Stoics on the derivation of 'chaos' from *cheisthai* and *chusis* 'pouring', for they influenced Philo of Alexandria and following his interpretation of Genesis[23], apparently, Symmachos translates בהו by *sugchusis*, 'pouring together' or by the cognate verb in passages outside Genesis i 2, though at that verse he has 'unformed and indistinguishable' as already noted—but the ideas are close enough. Here is a sign of things to come. It is, however, Ovid, at the end of a long line of natural historical speculation, who, with the opening of his immensely influential *Metamorphoses,* bestowed upon European literature the concept that all began from chaos, where all seeds[24] of things were in a hopelessly confused strife, that 'rudis indigestaque moles'. Hence for example, *Paradise Lost* I 10 and the great chaos passage of Book II.

When, however, Symmachos apart, did Ovidian chaos begin to affect Biblical scholarship reliant mainly on the Vulgate, with the result that the phrase תהו ובהו, taken as 'chaos', 'utter confusion', became common on the lips of French and German speakers? The emergence of this locution seems to commence in the latter half of the sixteenth century.[25] Neither Luther nor Rabelais appear to know it: both may have contributed to its coinage.

Luther's various encounters with Gen. i, which cannot be adequately surveyed in brief compass, while rejecting certain philosophical notions ('Dimittenda hic est Platonis et Aristotelis opinio de Ideis et Atomis, stulta enim est et impia...)[26] show a growing tendency to borrow vocabulary originating in the chaos conception in connection with תהו ובהו. He makes use of the 'formless' rendering found in the Septuagint and in Symmachos. In his lectures on Genesis of 1535[27], he states that Augustine does not, as Ovid, call matter 'informe et rude illud chaos'. He then discusses the words תהו and בהו, transcribing them into Roman script. Though his interpretation is similar to that of ancient scholarship he does use such words as 'omnibus ... confusis quasi in rudem molem' which is Ovidian to the point of exact quotation. He compares Is. xxxiv 11 and states that all will be 'confusa et perturbata'. We conclude that there is not yet a German locution *tohu vavohu*, also that these texts from the pen of so great an authority may have helped to familiarize the words in educated European circles—in association with suggestions of formlessness and confusion, even explicit reminders of Ovid's chaos.

Moving to a somewhat different literary genre we find Rabelais in the *Quart Livre* of Pantagruel, ch. 17, narrating 'Ce mesme jour, passa Pantagruel les deux isles de Tohu et Bohu es quelles ne trouvasmes que frire ...'. 'Nothing to fry' means 'nothing to do' and Rabelais is well aware that Tohu and Bohu really mean 'nothing' or the like, for towards the end of the chapter he mentions that the fortress of Belima has been sacked—this is, of course, the word בלי-מה parallel to תהו in Job xxvi 7, which was regarded as so important a text for this discussion. Of course there was nothing to do, for in Tohu and Bohu there is nothing at all. Rabelais then takes up the idiom 'nothing to fry' and explains that a giant had consumed all the frying-pans. After developing this theme he returns to Bohu and Belima adding two more islands, Nargues and Zargues. 'Nargues' is *toulousain* for 'no!'. The reason for this apparently frivolous excursus is to note that Rabelais appears to know nothing of chaos in connection with Tohu and Bohu, though he is fully informed on that subject as his exposition of the Chaos of the Four

Elements in ch. 18 demonstrates. Nor does he seem to know anything of the later idiom *tohu-bohu*. Hebrew research apart, it might seem that Rabelais is telling us that this chapter is about nothing at all! Whether such a *jeu* might have deeper implications must be left to the Rabelaisants.

It is Voltaire, apparently, who determines the form and meaning of the locution for modern French: 'Tohu-Bohu signifie précisément chaos, désordre; c'est un de ces mots imitatifs qu'on trouve dans toutes les langues, comme sens dessus dessous ...'[28]

The earliest reference I have found is in Philippe de Marnix (Philips van Marnix) de Sainte-Aldegonde, the Flemish noble, theologian and statesman accredited with the composition of the words to the Wilhelmus Lied, the Dutch national anthem. An extract in E. Huguet[29] runs, 'pesle-mesler et confondre toute la machine de l'univers pour la reduire à son premier tohu vabohu.' The 'Oeuvres' of de Marnix appeared between 1579 and 1598.

For German the first references would appear to be in Goethe. There are no earlier quotations in D. Sander's dictionary which is furnished with 'belegen von Luther bis auf die Gegenwart'.[30]

It may be that despite consultation of many historical and etymological dictionaries[31] early references have been missed. The general situation, however, seems to be clear. *Tohu vavohu* meaning 'chaos' was first coined in the sixteenth century but becomes common in France and Germany only after the times of Voltaire and Goethe. Exegetes who learned the phrase in their mother-tongue in the nineteenth and twentieth centuries and who, moreover, were imbued with Ovid from their early years, probably formed their understanding of *tohu vavohu* before seeing a word of Hebrew.

It would appear then, that apart from the hints which stole into Biblical exegesis from Greek philosophy, the pervasiveness of classical learning together with the immense power of the popular locution—itself the child of the classical tradition, allied perhaps with exegesis such as Luther's—determined the understanding of תהו ובהו in Gen. i 2 as chaos. There is an amusing irony, therefore, in the words of the celebrated J. Burnet[32] 'chaos was not a formless mixture like the *tohu va vohu* of the first chapter of Genesis', or in those of W. Jaeger[33] in 1947 'The common idea of chaos as something in which all things are wildly confused is quite mistaken; and the antithesis between chaos and cosmos which rests on this incorrect view is a purely modern invention. Possibly the idea of *tohu va vohu* has inadvertently been read into the Greek conception from the biblical account of creation in Genesis.' Classicists today would not blame the transformation of chaos onto Gen. i 2. Jaeger's point about chaos and cosmos, however, was well made but since that time we have had, for example, books such as *Creation versus Chaos*[34], *Chaos to Cosmos*[35] and countless articles, Old Testament theologies, commentaries etc., which perpetuate this view of ancient thought.

Detail, of course, might be added, but the foregoing will serve, perhaps, as a summary account of how chaos entered Biblical exegesis.

NOTES

1. Primeval Chaos not Scriptural, *Miscellanea Biblica II*, Scripta P.I.B., pp. 203-215
2. *The Earth and the Waters in Genesis 1 and 2*, JSOT Sup 83, 1989.
3. Alan Jones of Oxford University, where this study was written, has kindly discussed this and associated matters with me at length. He regards the cardinal point concerning $tīh^{un}$ as a total lack of distinguishing features and consequent extreme difficulty of orientation.
4. *Etymologische Studien*, Leipzig, 1893, S. 14.
5. BzA III, 1898, S. 68.
6. Another translation: 'desire'. The matter involves complicated epigraphic questions and cannot be adequately discussed here.
7. Biblischer Kommentar, *Genesis*. There is far less emphasis on chaos, certainly with respect to 'confusion' in Westermann's commentary. While expressing reservation, however, with respect to several scholars who have suggested 'non-existence' as the sense of תהו, he endorses views which have emphasised the threatening, fearful nature of the expression as a whole ('grausam'), S. 142f.
8. *Orientalia*, 2, Göttingen, 1880, S. 60f.
9. G. Fohrer, Kommentar zum Alten Testament, *Hiob*, Gütersloh, 1963, interprets this passage in the light of standard ancient Near Eastern cosmology. It seems to me that we have a new conception, more in accord with Gen. i here. The point is not greatly affected but there would be truly 'nothing' beneath the earth (and possibly beneath the heavens also). S. 382-4.
10. There can be no more objection to this view of ארחות דרכם (a poetic hendiadys) than to דרך ארחתיך, Is. iii 12. Nor can I follow Fohrer, op. cit., S. 162, in translating יזרבו 'Wasserarmut' in the previous verse. In parallel with חם the reference is to heat (the alleged Akk. *zurrubu*, 'einengen' of Gesenius-Buhl, appears to be a ghost word).
11. The textual problem does not affect the issue (H. Wildberger, Biblischer Kommentar, *Jesaja*, ad loc.)
12. For a different view, with reference to the New Year Festival, W. McKane, I.C.C., *Jeremiah*, I, 1986, p. 106f.
13. HAL, תהו , following Wildberger, op. cit.
14. IQ Is. a and Pesh. אין for און, Is. xli 29.
15. *Myths in the Old Testament* (trans. from Danish), London, 1980, p. 33.
16. *Old Testament Theology* I (Eng. trans.) 1962, p. 144.
17. Cf. G. M. Landes, *Union Seminary Quarterly Review*, XXXII, 2, 1978, p. 81. While accepting primordial chaos Landes asserts that *tohu va-vohu* is 'not chaos'. His view of *tohu* is very close to that of this study (in fn. 14,

omitted in the reprint of this article in *Creation in the Old Testament*, ed. B.W. Anderson, Philadelphia and London, 1984).

18. The following view was expressed more fully in my study 'Differing Approaches to the Theomachy Myth in Old Testament Writing' (Hebrew) in *Studies in the Bible and Ancient Near East* for S. E. Loewenstamm, Jerusalem, 1978, ed. Y. Avishur and Y. Blau (Eng. summary vol. II, pp. 191-2).
19. FuF. 16, 1 (1940), S. 1 f.
19a. *De Genesi contra Manich.* I, 5, 9. PL 34 p. 178.
20. This view is similar to that of Augustine (e.g. *Conf.* XII, xxix 40) and Luther (e.g. *Vorlesungen über I Mose*, Luthers Werke, Weimar, 42. Band, S. 5-6, esp. the Latin version) with connections to Philo and LXX on the one hand and possibly Pseudo-Jon. צדיא מבני נש וריקניא מן כל בעיר on the other.
21. Eg. 'iz/sft', normally 'injustice', 'wrong-doing', contrasted in the texts with 'ma't' (maat), 'truth', 'justice' etc., is suspected of chaotic connections, H. Frankfort, *Ancient Egyptian Religion*, N.Y. 1948, pp. 49-58. For general orientation see J. Assmann, *Der König als Sonnenpriester*, Gluckstadt, 1970, esp. S. 58-61 with further references. I am grateful to John Baines for this title and for helpful discussion. The word chaos (not, apparently, as a specific translation equivalent of *izft*) is used liberally by Erik Hornung, *Conceptions of God in Ancient Egypt*, N.Y. 1982 (translation with additions etc. by John Baines of *Der Eine und die Vielen*, Darmstadt, 1971) in his attempt to describe and explain the 'non-existent', *iwtt*, a peculiarly Egyptian concept. It appears to 'exist' outside the world of man, is a threat to it but also regenerative of it; more cannot be said here, cf. *Conceptions* esp. pp. 158-165, 172-185, 195, 209, 212-216. The Egyptian concept is far less patient of analysis than *tohu* : it seems to me that the (modern) chaos concept has been at work here also.
22. M. Schofield, *An Essay on Anaxagoras*, Cambridge, 1980, p. 36 and p. 181 n. 1.
23. *De Op. Mundi* XI, 38; *De Aet. Mundi* 18.
24. Anaxagoras' seeds have become the four elements, cf. e.g. F. Bömer, *Metamorphosen*, Kommentar, Buch I-III, Heidelberg, 1969, S. 20.
25. 'Toroul boroul', the thirteenth century hapax, is probably a red herring though taken seriously in W.v. Wartburg, *Franz. Etym. Wtbch.* 20. Band, 1968, S. 286 ('ganz vereinzelt in afr.') and other dictionaries: see G. Raynaud, *Romania* t. XII, 1883, p. 266; Glossaire p. 229: 'Littré n'a pas d'exemple ancien'.
26. *Predigten*, 1527, Luthers Werke, Weimar, 24. Band, S. 24-26.
27. Ref. in n. 20.
28. *Dictionnaire philosophique*, Genèse, 1765, similarly *La Bible enfin expliquée*, Genèse, 1776.
29. *Dictionnaire de la langue française du seizième siècle*, 7, 1967.
30. *Wtbch. der deutschen Spr. mit belegen* etc., 1876.
31. Thanks are due to Jill Hughes of the Taylorian Library who most helpfully guided me to resources and dictionaries accessible and (almost) inaccessible, for advice on French matters to James Hiddleston of Exeter College, my *alma mater*, and for German to Christopher Wells, my guide to Luther. None of them is responsible for my sins of commission or omission.
32. *Early Greek Philosophy*, 1892, p. 7.
33. *The Theology of the Early Greek Philosophers*, pp. 13-14.
34. B.W. Anderson, N.Y. 1967, reprinted Philadelphia, 1987.

35. S. Niditch, Chico, Cal., 1985. A recent work heavily influenced by the chaos:cosmos notion is J. Levenson's *Creation and the Persistence of Evil*, San Francisco, 1988: that notion distorts the exposition of some, in my opinion, valuable observations.

GREEK LANGUAGE AND PHILOSOPHY IN THE EARLY RABBINIC ACADEMIES

A. Wasserstein

I feel honoured to have been allowed to take part in this tribute to David Patterson on his seventieth birthday. He has done much for the promotion of Hebrew studies in Britain. By singlehandedly founding and building up the Oxford Centre he has not only enriched Oxford but all students of Hebrew and other Jewish subjects throughout the world. We are all much indebted to him. This paper is gratefully offered by one who was among the first beneficiaries of the facilities provided by the Centre many years ago.

Semper crescat et floreat

Historical Judaism as we know it was shaped by its Hebrew inheritance and by the varied fortunes of the Jewish people throughout the ages. One of the most powerful forces that worked on the character of the religion and culture of Israel in the post-biblical period was the emergence of Hellenism as the dominant supra-national civilisation of the Near East. Israel had always been part of the wider civilisation of the area. There can be no doubt that the forefathers of the people of the Book had absorbed much from the oriental civilisations from which they had sprung; and it is clear that even in the hellenistic and Greco-Roman periods the Jews in Palestine and Mesopotamia were part of the other supra-national, Aramaic-speaking, civilisation of the Middle East that left its mark on the area even beyond the fall of Byzantine rule with the coming of Islam many centuries after the rise of Christianity. But a special historical significance of universal importance attaches to the Greek contribution to the mixture that was to become the full-blown religion of the Jews. The new form taken by Judaism in that period was to determine not only the religion of the Jews. Hellenism gave new dimensions to Judaism that were to survive Hellenism itself. The Hellenism that remained the dominant culture of the eastern part of the Roman empire made it possible for the universal aspirations of Hebrew prophecy to exert their power on western mankind through Christianity, that other Palestinian religion of Hebrew origin, the emergence of which is approximately contemporary with the flowering of rabbinic Judaism, historical Judaism *par excellence*. Christianity, precisely because it could build and grow on the hellenistic part of the inheritance of Judaism in language and thought, was prepared for offering its message to the world. The existence of a Greek translation of the Hebrew Scriptures[1] made it possible to preach the prophetic vision of the Kingdom of God directly in the language of the gentiles in the lands all around the Mediterranean world. The synagogues of Greek-speaking Jews in these lands were to be way-stations for the earliest Christians in their apostolic mission. The presence of Greek elements in rabbinic Judaism and the existence of hellenistic Jewry constituted a bridge between Palestine and the West. This was the real *praeparatio evangelica*, which made it possible for Christianity to shape the religious and moral, and thus the cultural, social and political, character of western mankind. Hellenistic influences on Judaism are therefore of more than merely Jewish historical interest.

In the last third of the fourth century B.C.E. Alexander had conquered and, for the first time in history, unified the whole of Greece; he extended his dominions to include Asia Minor, Mesopotamia, Syria, Palestine and Egypt; and, further east, Persia, Afghanistan and parts of India. The great oriental empires that had dominated these regions for many centuries were now replaced by a western power. The unity of Alexander's empire did not survive him; but the various successor states, especially, but not only, the Ptolemaic and Seleucid empires, were bearers and preservers of Greek civilisation. Hellenism now became an international, supra-national, civilisation that indelibly marked the life of the whole region. Though Aramaic remained for a long time one of the great international languages of the East, Greek became the language of administration and soon, for various reasons, such as the implantation of Greek settlers and the foundation of new Greek cities, acquired a status that, in matters of education and culture, while not displacing native languages, more than rivalled their importance and certainly influenced local culture and education. The oriental populations of the area were all in various degrees affected by these developments. Greek became the common,[2] even though often not the only, language of the educated classes of the hellenistic and Greco-Roman periods. Greek literature, philosophy and rhetoric now became available to people of non-Greek stock. The use of the Greek language, and the acquaintance with Greek ways of thinking could not but affect the cultures of the east. This at least partial hellenization of the Near East prepared the ground for the common culture of the world order that was to succeed the hellenistic states. Greek remained for many centuries the language of the Roman empire in the east.

The Jews were as susceptible to the lure and influence of Hellenism as their gentile neighbours. This is no less true of the Aramaic-speaking Jews in Palestine and Babylonia than of those of their co-religionists who, living in Asia Minor or in Egypt, or in Greek-speaking cities in Palestine and Syria,[3] had either adopted Greek speech or inherited it from their forebears. It is very likely that many of these were proselytes of gentile stock. It is important to remember the extent of the influence of the Greek language on the local vernaculars not only of the Jews.[4] It has been estimated that the number of Greek loan words or expressions in rabbinic Hebrew and Aramaic amounts to the astonishing total of well over 2000.[5] It must suffice here to mention in illustration only a few examples of well-known words in rabbinic literature that are of Greek origin:

ἀνδριάς	אנדרטא (See Payne Smith s.v. אנדריאנטא)
ἄσημον	אסימון (in Syr סאמא)
διαθήκη	דיתיקי
κατήγορος	קטגור (see Payne Smith s.v. קטרג; so also in Jewish Aramaic)
μητρόπολις	מטרופולין
νόμος	נימוס
πανδοκεῖον (πανδοχεῖον)	פונדק (6)
παράκλητος	פרקליט
παρρησία	פרהסיא
πεῖσαι (πείθω)	פייס
πίναξ	פנקס
πόλεμος	פולמוס (in Syriac פולהמוס)
στοά	אסטיו
στρατηγός	אסטרטיג
συνέδριον	סנהדרין (cf. Sanhedrin in English) (In Syriac without h)
συνήγορος	סנגור
φιλόσοφος	פלוספוס
Legio = λεγεών	לגיון
sandaliarius (from Gk root σάνδαλ–) =	סנדלר

It is significant and important, though not of immediate relevance, that, in one form or another, all these words occur also in Syriac, i.e. Christian, Aramaic.

Latin words would normally come into Hebrew and Aramaic via Greek; in the case of סנדלר, though the Latin *sandaliarius* is itself a derivative of a Greek word (σάνδαλον), the immediate Greek model (*σανδαλιάριος) for the Hebrew/Aramaic word does not seem to be documented in extant Greek literature, papyri or inscriptions, but is likely to have been 'borrowed back' by late Greek from Latin.[7] Readers will note the deformation apparent in the traditional rabbinic vocalisation of a number of these words, e.g. of סנהדרין, פולמוס, פונדק, פנקס, פרקליט *et mult. al.* (It would be hazardous to see in the appearance of the ה in the words סנהדרין and פרהסיה evidence for phonological conservatism exemplified by the retention of the internal breathing of the original Greek words parr*h*esia and sun*h*edrion. In Syriac the Greek *epsilon* is frequently represented by a ה and the appearance of that letter in the two examples above may be no more than an illustration of that phenomenon;[8] cf., e.g., the Syriac words derived from Greek beginning with πε on pp.3042 ff. of Payne Smith's *Thesaurus Syriacus*. (Indeed in the case of one of the Greek words noticed above, συνέδριον, the ה does not appear in the Syriac transcription though it appears in Jewish Aramaic.) The secondary development, by metathesis, of what had become in Hebrew and Aramaic a four-consonantal Semitic root קטגר to קטרג (so also in Syriac) testifies to the fact that Greek words incorporated into the Hebrew and/or Aramaic vocabulary soon developed a life of their own with the changes attendant upon all life.

Many of the Greek loan words found in rabbinic Hebrew and Aramaic may indeed not have been borrowed directly from Greek (or in some cases Latin) but from the Aramaic *koinē*.[9] It is evident that there exists a significantly large overlap between the collections of Greek loan words in Syriac (Christian) Aramaic and the corresponding part of the vocabulary of rabbinic Hebrew and Aramaic. The conclusion seems to impose itself that this points both to rabbinic receptivity for Greek and to the high degree of integration of rabbinic Judaism in the surrounding civilisation of Aramaic stamp. This rabbinic openness and receptivity to non-Jewish cultural influences is highlighted by the fact that the high frequency of loan words (directly or indirectly borrowed from Greek and to a minor extent from Latin) in the languages of the Rabbis is not paralleled in the sectarian literature represented in the Qumran scrolls. Kutscher has rightly noted[10] that the absence of Greek loan words there points to deliberate avoidance by the sectarians of speech habits that were commonplace in rabbinic literature.[11]

The fact that it is possible to point to deliberate avoidance of foreign loan words indirectly also shows that speakers of Aramaic (presumably both Jews and Gentiles) were aware of the foreign origin of the borrowed vocabulary. I have argued above that the presence of this vocabulary is an indication of receptivity, openness and integration. The same characteristics emerge even more strikingly in a related linguistic phenomenon, that of *calques*.[12] These 'translation-borrowings' are words or expressions of foreign origin that are formed in the ordinary ways of the host language from existing roots and in forms that are identical to those of other native words of similar function and are therefore not immediately recognizable as foreign imports; they borrow the sense of the model without taking the form of the original word; cf. Latin *individuum* from Greek ἄτομος (οὐσία), which, incidentally, was re-calqued in modern Greek, from Latin or some modern language, as ἄτομον = Engl. *individual*; Latin *qualitas, quantitas*, from Greek ποιότης, ποσότης; German *Fernsprecher* from Pseudo-Greek *telephone*; the inelegant modern Hebrew (Israeli) expression לא בא בחשבון may be regarded as an 'Abklatsch' (with some slight modification) of the equally inelegant German 'kommt nicht in Frage!'; and there are many other similar examples in all the languages of civilised nations. Such 'borrowings' are of especial interest to the student of cultures in contact, because it is unlikely that many, if any, speakers of the host language are aware of the foreign origin of the apparently native expressions they use. Hence they can be seen as indices of borrowing from the foreign language in situations where this borrowing may be unconscious: and thus as evidence of knowledge of the foreign language influencing the very thought of the native speaker.

Rabbinic Hebrew and Aramaic illustrate the same phenomenon: Here are some examples:

In the Hebrew Bible the setting of the sun is described by the verb בא ; but in rabbinic Hebrew the setting sun does not 'come'; instead the verb שקע and the derived noun שקיעה are used: they are calques of the Greek δῦναι and δύσις. The Bible does not know the expressions לתן את הדין, לתן דין וחשבון: but the Rabbis seem to have known the corresponding Greek expressions δίκην διδόναι, λόγον διδόναι and λόγον καί δίκην διδόναι (cf. the Syriac יהב פתגמא for λόγον διδόναι). The rabbinic Hebrew שולחני for 'banker' is a calque of the Greek τραπεζίτης (τράπεζα = table = שולחן).[13]

Of particular interest is the word בית in the sense of scientific or philosophical 'school' as in rabbinic Hebrew בית הלל and בית שמאי (see also in Syriac: בית אפיקורוס = the Epicurean School: בית אריוס the Arians; בית ארסטטלס = the Peripatetics; *et al.*). The Greek οἰκία (house) is used in the same sense: cf. Erotianus, *praefatio*; Galen, XII, 2, 145 K.

A similar linguistic imitation of a Greek locution can be observed at the very beginning of what may be described as the foundation legend of rabbinic Judaism. Aboth I, 1: משה קבל תורה מסיני ומסרה ליהושע. The historiographical pattern that informs this statement is precisely the same as that which characterizes the works of ancient Greek writers on the history of philosophy:

this history is described as one in which one thinker 'receives' his doctrines from his predecessor and 'hands them on' to his successor. The typical name for such histories of philosophy in Greek and hellenistic antiquity was "Διαδοχαί", and the appellation for the head of a philosophical school (e.g. the Academy, the Peripatos, the Stoa, the Epicurean School etc.) was διάδοχος.[14] The noun is derived from the verb διαδέχομαι = 'to receive and hand on' as in a relay race; hence it is also used of royal succession where one ruler succeeds his predecessor and in his turn is succeeded by his own successor. Here both the historiographical pattern of uninterrupted succession of the bearers of authority (as legitimating that authority) and the expression used to describe it are common both to rabbinic Hebrew and to Greek.

Both Greek and rabbinic historiography tend to see the chain of tradition as being divided into two schools of similar authority. For the Rabbis these are the Schools of Hillel and Shammai:

אלו ואלו דברי אלקים חיים הן (והלכה כבית הלל) (BT Eruvin 13 b).

For the Greeks see Diogenes Laertius, I 13-15: all Greek philosophers divided into two Schools, the Ionian (beginning with Thales and Anaximander) and the Italian (beginning with Pherekydes and Pythagoras).

These last two examples bring us into the field of philosophy. It is well known that hardly any Greek philosopher is ever mentioned by name in early rabbinic literature.[15] It is not to be expected that we should find evidence suggesting systematic study of Greek philosophy in the academies of the Rabbis.[16] Indeed there were times when the study of Greek wisdom (חכמת יונית) seems to have been frowned upon by the Rabbis. Thus, we read in the Talmud that it is forbidden to teach one's son Greek.[17] But it has long been recognised that far from the rabbinic attitude to the study of Greek being unanimously and at all times hostile there are many explicit indications in rabbinic literature of different attitudes prevailing at different times and in different circumstances. That R. Shim'on b. Gamliel could be quoted as saying[18] that in his father's house there had been five hundred students studying Torah and five hundred studying חכמת יונית clearly indicates a receptive attitude towards Greek among the Rabbis of the first century.[19] It must also be remembered that the Rabbis were acquainted with the Septuagint and that there were times when their attitude towards it was very favourable; see, e.g. Megilla 9 a-b; it has even been suggested that they were responsible for a Palestinian recension of that Greek translation in the middle of the first century, generations before Aquila.[20]

There is certainly evidence of some sort of rabbinic acquaintance and preoccupation with Greek philosophical problems, unsystematic, eclectic, syncretistic and often directed towards practical goals. Thus, some parts of ancient philosophical education, mathematics and astronomy, clearly were pursued in rabbinic circles for the practical purposes of calendaric determination of the feast days or for other halachic purposes connected with Sabbath observance (*eruv*) *vel sim*.[21] Another practical purpose of some philosophical study may have been the training that might be useful in disputations with heretics and infidels: thus R. Elazar b. Arakh requires דע מה שתשיב לאפיקורוס (Aboth II. 19; cf. Sanhedrin 38b).

That philosophical studies were often practised by means of mock disputations and school exercises is well known. It has been shown that some of the problems that were discussed during these exercises were also known and discussed in rabbinic circles.[22] A good deal of popular Greek philosophy was in any case in the air and will have pervaded the discourse of educated men even without systematic study or personal contact with pagan philosophers or their schools. There were the perennial problems of moral theology and philosophy; how to explain the suffering of the just and the prosperity of the wicked: צדיק ורע לו רשע וטוב לו (Berakhot 7a); the misfortunes and the helplessness of mankind and the consolations offered by beliefs in the resurrection of the dead, the immortality of the soul, and, not least, the hope of the coming of a saviour. Such questions would arouse a natural interest in philosophical discussion among Jews no less than among Gentiles.

The radical and paradoxical style of some Greek philosophical discourse, especially that of the Stoics,[23] finds its counterpart in that of the Rabbis:

Compare: πάντα τά ἁμαρτήματα ἴσα (e.g. Zeno: SVF I nos. 224-5) and R. Yohanan b. Zakkai in Hag. 5a: אוי לנו ששקל עלינו הכתוב קלות כחמורות (cf. also Aboth II.1).

The Stoic 'Only the wise man is free...' (SVF III nos 589-603) is paralleled by R. Yehosha b. Levi in *Pereq Qinyan Tora* (Aboth VI) אין לך בן חורין אלא מי שעוסק בתלמוד תורה.

One of the most interesting of these paradoxes (important because it addresses one of the central and fundamental problems of moral theology) is the following:

We read in Aboth III 15 a saying of R. Akiva: הכל צפוי והרשות נתונה, 'All is foreseen, but man has freedom of moral choice'.[24] On the face of it we have here an intolerable paradox. This is not the place to engage in a discussion of a problem that has occupied theologians of the Synagogue and of the Church for many centuries: how to reconcile the belief in providence with man's moral freedom and the attendant responsibility for human action. But it is worth noting that the problem was one shared and much discussed by hellenistic philosophers.[25] Thus, the Stoics expressed the combination of their belief in determinism combined with their assertion of freedom of moral choice and consequent human responsibility in a similarly paradoxical formulation: cf. for instance, Cleanthes ap. Epict. *Ench.* 53:[26]

ἄγου δέ μ', ὦ Ζεῦ, καὶ σύ γ', ἡ πεπρωμένη
ὅποι ποθ' ὑμῖν εἰμὶ διατεταγμένος
ὡς ἕψομαί γ' ἄοκνος ἢν δέ γε μὴ θέλω
κακὸς γενόμενος, οὐδὲν ἧττον ἕψομαι

In Seneca's Latin translation[27] the emphatic paradox is even more pointed:

duc, o parens celsique dominator poli,
quocumque placuit; nulla parendi mora est.
adsum impiger. fac nolle, comitabor gemens,
malusque patiar, quod pati licuit bono.
ducunt volentem fata, nolentem trahunt.

It is worth citing in this context also the parable ascribed to Zeno and to Chrysippus[28] in which a dog is bound to a carriage. What happens to the dog when the carriage starts moving? If it is a wise dog it will voluntarily run along with the carriage and all will be well. If it is a foolish dog it will resist, but its resistance will be of no avail; it will be dragged along and it will not fare so well as the other dog. The Stoics preach acceptance of what is in any case determined beforehand. In such submission to Fate, chosen voluntarily, the wise man, in the midst of the constraints of unalterable destiny, finds freedom.[29] Thus we also read in Aboth II, 4 (Rabban Gamliel, the son of R. Yehuda Ha-Nasi): עשה רצונו כרצונך כדי שיעשה רצונך כרצונו.

Sometimes in rabbinic and in Stoic (as in Christian) discourse the statement of a paradox takes the place of discursive or analytical treatment of a philosophical (or theological) problem.[30] It is not a matter for surprise that so much in rabbinic Judaism that is reminiscent of Greek philosophy comes from the hellenistic rather than from the classical period. There are, no doubt, chronological and even geographical reasons for this. From the very beginning of the hellenistic period there had been Greek philosophical Schools in Palestine and in the adjoining regions.[31] But it is clear that the influence of the Stoa was stronger than that of any other School. The hellenistic Schools, and especially the Stoa, were more fundamentally engaged in the ethical rather than in the logical or metaphysical or physical philosophies of, e.g., the Platonists or the Peripatetics; and the two Hebrew religions of Palestine, rabbinic Judaism and Christianity, shared the basic moral and cosmic optimism of stoic thought which, through its translation to the Roman empire, had become one of the formative influences on the character of Europe.

Notes

1. The Septuagint had been made to serve the needs of hellenistic Jews in Alexandria and elsewhere who had as early as the third century B.C.E. forgotten Hebrew or had never known it. The Pentateuch was the first to be translated and in the course of the next century and a half was followed by other books of the OT so that the whole, or practically the whole, translation was available by ca. 132 B.C.E. See the prologue of the Greek version of the Book of Jesus ben Sira, where the translator, the grandson of the author, writing in the thirty-eighth year of Ptolemy Euergetes refers to 'the Law and the Prophets and the other books' (prologus, lines 1-2; 8-10; 24-5; 27).
2. This is the reason why we use the appellation κοινή (=common) for the Greek language of the post-classical period.
3. See E. Schürer, *The History of the Jewish People in the Age of Jesus Christ*, vol. II (Edinburgh, 1979), pp. 85ff; V. Tcherikover, *Hellenistic Civilization and the Jews* (Philadelphia, 1959), pp. 90ff; A. H. M. Jones, *The Cities of the Eastern Roman Provinces* (Oxford, 1971), pp. 226-94 and index; F-M. Abel, *Géographie de la Palestine*, II (Paris, 1967), index; id., *Histoire de la Palestine depuis la conquête d'Alexandre jusqu' à l'invasion Arabe*, I-II (Paris, 1952), passim.
4. For borrowings from Greek in oriental languages see Eduard Schwyzer, *Griechische Grammatik*, (Handbuch der Altertumswissenschaft II i.1) I (Munich, 1953), pp. 145ff. esp. p. 154 (Hebrew and other Semitic languages); ibid., (Iranian); pp. 154ff. (Egyptian); p. 155 (Indian languages); p. 159 (Syriac); p. 160 (Coptic); p. 161 (Ethiopian); p. 163 (Armenian). See also W. C. Till, *Koptische Grammatik*, 2nd ed. (Leipzig, 1961), pp. 345ff; Anton Schall, *Studien über griechische Fremdwörter im Syrischen* (Darmstadt, 1960).
5. See S. Krauss, *Griechische und Lateinische Lehnwörter in Talmud, Midrasch und Targum* (Berlin, 1898/9). Krauss lists about 2400 Greek and ca. 240 Latin words. The shortcomings of this work have often been commented upon; cf. e.g. S. Fraenkel, ZDMG LII (1898) and LV (1901); S. Baron, *A Social and Religious History of the Jews*, 2nd ed. (Philadelphia, 1952), vol. III, p. 66; E. Schwyzer, op. cit., p. 32; G. Zuntz, 'Greek Words in Talmud', *JSS* I (1956), pp. 129-40; and see in particular the work of Krauss himself who on practically every page prints criticisms and corrections communicated to him by Immanuel Löw. But no error or doubt attaching to detailed identifications and interpretations can affect the overall impression created by the sheer quantity of the material. See also E. Y. Kutscher, *A History of the Hebrew Language* (Jerusalem, 1982), p. 137.
6. For an entertaining history of the wanderings of this word see E. Y. Kutscher, *Milim ve-toldotheihen* (Jerusalem, 1974), pp. 92-3 with the bibliography there cited.
7. This is a well-known process in the history of languages. Cf. modern Greek σινεμα from French *cinéma* from Classical Greek κίνημα ; and modern Greek σεναριο from French *scénario* from Italian scenario presumably from a postulated though nonexistent classical Greek *σκηνάριον . Cf. also modern Greek τηλέγραφος, τηλέφωνον and related terms, which in spite of their Greek appearance are clearly 'borrowed back' from modern European languages. Similarly Byzantine Greek φούνδαξ: this may have come into Byzantine Greek either directly from Arabic (which has taken it from the Syriac) or indirectly through some Romance language: see K. Vollers, in 'Beiträge zur Kenntnis der lebenden arabischen Sprache in Aegypten', ZDMG LI (1897), p. 300; and see E. A. Sophocles, *Greek Lexicon of the Roman and*

Byzantine Periods (Hildesheim, 1983) (reprint of edition Leipzig, 1914) s.v. φούνδαξ
8. See A. Schall, op. cit., p. 34.
9. See A. Wasserstein, 'Die Hellenisierung des Frühjudentums' in W. Schluchter (ed.), *Max Webers Sicht des antiken Christentums* (Frankfurt am Main, 1985), p. 288.
10. Op. cit., pp. 100-1.
11. The few exceptions in the so-called Copper Scroll are not relevant to our argument; see J. Allegro, *DJD V, Qumran Cave 4* (Oxford, 1968) p. 88f. That there may be a few calques to be found in Qumran literature (see Y. Yadin, *The Scroll of the War of the Sons of Light against the Sons of Darkness* (Oxford, 1962), p. 184; and Kutscher, op. cit., pp. 100-1) is equally irrelevant; for it is of the nature of *calques* that their users are often unaware of their true origin. See below.
12. For such 'Sprachabklatsche' see Schwyzer, op. cit., p. 32.
13. For more see Abba Bendavid, *Biblical Hebrew and Mishnaic Hebrew* (Hebrew) I, 1967, pp. 111 and 136ff.
14. It seems that Sotion (2nd cent. B.C.E.) was the first to write a work Διαδοχή (or Διαδοχαί) τῶν φιλοσόφων; in an informal way he had been preceded by Theophrastus and even by Aristotle. Others who used the title Διαδοχαί (vel sim.) for their histories of philosophy were Antisthenes of Rhodes (2nd cent. B.C.E.) Sosicrates (2nd cent. B.C.E.) and Alexander of Miletus (1st cent. B.C.E.). See H. Ritter and L. Preller, *Historia Philosophiae Graecae* (Gotha, 1898), pp. 3-4.
15. The name of Epicurus is mentioned, but only to typify the heretic; we hear (Mishna AZ 3, 4) of a philosopher called Proclus, of whom we know nothing or very little (see A. Wasserstein, 'Rabban Gamliel and Proclus the Philosopher', *Zion*, XLV (1980), pp. 257-67; and see ibid. note 6 for Epicurus); and Avnimos Ha-Gardi (or Ha-Gadri) who may be identical with the second century philosopher Oenomaus of Gadara (for whom see Wasserstein, 1980 note 7).
16. S. Lieberman (*Greek in Jewish Palestine*, New York, 1942, p. 1) cites the well-known statement of R. Shimon b. Gamliel (Sota 49b and parallels) that 'there were a thousand children (ילדים) in my father's house, five hundred studied Torah, and five hundred Greek wisdom (חכמת יונית)'; Lieberman, I fear, went rather too far in deducing from this that we have here 'first-hand evidence that an academy of Greek wisdom existed in [first century] Jewish Palestine under the auspices of the Patriarch'. R Shimon b. Gamliel's statement is not to be taken literally or in any other way that would entitle us to derive any conclusions at all about institutional arrangements (like 'academies of Greek wisdom under patriarchal auspices'). What we do learn from this interesting example of oriental hyperbole is something else: namely the speaker's favourable attitude to the study of Greek. See below.
17. Mishna Sota fin.; BT Sota 49b; cf. BQ 82; S. Lieberman, *Hellenism in Jewish Palestine* (New York, 1962) pp. 103-4.
18. See above; and see also BQ 83a; cf. Gittin 58a; PT Taanit IV.5; Echa Rabba III, 51 (Buber p. 131). Rabban Gamliel succeeded R. Yohanan b. Zakkai as president of the Academy at Yavne in ca. A.D. 80.
19. See on this and related issues Lieberman, op. cit., pp. 100 ff.
20. See Dominique Barthélemy, O. P., *Les Devanciers d'Aquila* (Leiden, 1963).
21. See A. Wasserstein, 'Astronomy and Geometry as Propaedeutic Studies in Rabbinic Literature' (Hebr.) *Tarbiz*, 1973/4, pp. 53-7 on Aboth III sub fin:
ר׳ אלעזר חסמא אומר קנין ופתחי נדה הן הן גופי הלכות תקופות וגמטריות פרפריות לחכמה

22. See BM 62a; *Sifra* to Lev 25, 36; Hekaton ap. Cic. *de off*. III, 15, 63, 23, 89f. W. Bacher, *Die Agada der Tannaiten* (2nd ed.) (Strassburg, 1903), p. 60 n. 1; and S. Lieberman, 'How Much Greek in Jewish Palestine?' in A. Altmann (ed.), *Biblical and other Studies* (Cambridge, Mass., 1963), pp. 123-41, esp. pp. 124 ff.
23. For stoic paradoxes see M. Pohlenz, *Die Stoa, Geschichte einer geistigen Bewegung* (4th ed.) I (Goettingen, 1970), p. 153.
24. It is worth reading the whole context, from the continuation of which I quote here only, from III 16, the following: ... ונפרעין מן האדם מדעתו ושלא מדעתו ...

    Cf. also AdRN A 39 and B44 where a similar saying of R. Eliezer b. Yosei ha-Galili is cited. It ought to be mentioned here that the interpretation I have presented above is supported by Maimonides and other medieval authorities and that it is shared by many modern commentators; but not by all: one of the most learned of modern writers, the late E. E. Urbach (*The Sages, Their Concepts and Beliefs*, Jerusalem, 1975, I, p. 257 and notes), believed that צפוי (translated above as = foreseen) should be understood as = 'seen, observed'; he argued that this verb in the sense of 'to foresee' is not documented before the third century (our text is quoted from the second century). I am not convinced by this argument. The linguistic material available to us is not well enough classifiable to allow of exact dating of individual word usages. Further, it seems to me that as interpreted by Urbach the saying would lose its very sophisticated stylistic pointedness, one that would not be expected to arise simply out of misunderstanding or misinterpretation, or out of the unconscious anticipation of a usage not yet known but about to emerge.
25. Epicurus constructed his whole physical doctrine in such a way as to be able to account for freedom of will in an otherwise rigidly determined universe: see A. Wasserstein, 'Epicurean Science', in *Hermes*, 106 (1976), pp. 484-94.
26. SVF I no. 527.
27. *Epist.* 107, 10. Cf. also St Augustine *de civ.dei*, V.8.
28. Hippolytus, *Philos.* 21 (DDG p. 571, 11 = SVF II no. 975).
29. See Pohlenz, op. cit., I, p. 155: '[Der stoische Weise] will nur was er kann, darum kann er auch, was er will.'
30. For more on this see Wasserstein, 1985, pp. 290ff.
31. See Martin Hengel, *Judentum und Hellenismus* (2nd ed.), Tübingen, 1973, p. 160.

'AGGADAH AND CHILDHOOD IMAGINATION IN THE WORKS OF MENDELE, BIALIK AND AGNON

David Aberbach

The creative use of *'aggadah* in descriptions of childhood is an outstanding and unprecedented feature of the works of the three most prominent Hebrew writers of the period 1881-1948: Mendele Mokher Sefarim (S.J. Abramowitz, 1835?-1917), Hayyim Nahman Bialik (1873-1934) and Samuel Joseph Agnon (1888?-1970). In particular, their biographical or semi-biographical works—Mendele's *Ba-yamim ha-hem* (Of Bygone Days, 1899, 1912–13, 1917 [Yiddish], 1903-17 [Hebrew]), Bialik's *Safiah* (Aftergrowth, 1903-23), and Agnon's story *Ha-mitpahat* (The Kerchief, 1932) show exceptional sensitivity and insight in depicting the effect of *'aggadah* on the child's inner world.[1] These works include some of their finest prose, and they clearly recognized the importance of *'aggadah* in the growth of their literary imagination, using it to explore both the collective Jewish consciousness as well as private obsessions which lie at the root of their creative drive.

To each of the three writers, the world of *'aggadah* seemed real and eternally present in childhood. Mendele, however, writing at a critical distance of over a half-century, conveys the reservations of a *maskil* who had devoted more time to his three-volume *Toldot ha-teva* (Natural History, 1862-1872)—the first work of its kind in Hebrew—than to any of his fictional works. Ignorance of and alienation from the natural world among the East European Jews, of which *'aggadah* and talmudic introspection generally was a symptom, were among Mendele's chief worries as a *maskil*. In the *Natural History*, he aimed to encourage the Jews to master this subject, though in fact the work's only lasting importance was that through it he became the first master of modern Hebrew prose. There is a gentle irony in the description of Shloyme in *Of Bygone Days*—the child that Mendele had been in Lithuania of the 1830s and 1840s—as being totally ignorant of the natural world, a mood reinforced by the mock-scientific catalogue of *'aggadic* creatures. For Shloyme's imagination was rooted, fascinatedly, in the Bible and Talmud. He had fixed in his mind, as did tens of thousands of Jewish children at the time, a whole array of animal, vegetable and mineral species which he had never seen—the only zoo he saw as a child was the human one around him—and some of which had existed only in the *'aggadah:*

> Of the natural world, with its variety of plants, animals and birds, Shloyme knew nothing. What did he care for the rye, the buck-wheat and potatoes, his daily fare? The harvest in the fields surrounding his village, the nearby forest and its trees, meant nothing to him. His imagination was full of other things: mandrakes, myrrh, onycha, galbanum, vines, dates, figs, pomegranates, olives, acacia-wood and gopher-wood. Of animal species he knew the he-goat from the time of Moses [*Numbers* 4:11]; the lion and leopard who taught might and valour to the Children of Israel [Mishnah *Avot* 5:20]; the hind, which taught them to run, like himself, in urgent haste [*ibid.*]; the wild ox crouching over a thousand hills [*Bava Batra* 75a]; the buffalo so huge—like Mount Tabor—that only its nose could fit into Noah's ark [*Bereshit Rabbah* 32]. Of creeping things he knew the viper and the *shamir*, created on Sabbath eve at twilight and used to cut stone for the Temple in Jerusalem [Mishnah *Avot* 5:6], and he knew of nits [*Shabbat* 107b]. Of birds he knew the turtle-dove, the wild cock which had brought the *shamir*; the *bar-yochna*, an egg of which had once fallen and drowned sixty cities and broken three hundred cedar trees [*Bekhorot* 57b]; and the *ziz-sadai*, that great bird whose wings block the sunlight [*Bava Batra* 73b, *Bereshit Rabbah* 22]. In short, Shloyme may have been born in the village, but he lived elsewhere... in time past, in a world that was no longer. He lived temporarily in this world, but his permanent residence was in that world. He visited his parents' house briefly, like a guest at an inn. He would eat and sleep and the next day would return to the other world... His way of life was that of thousands of other Shloymes—in memoriam, in memory of an ancestral way of life. As their ancestors had done,

so did they, to fulfil what is written and even what is not written: That is the way they lived in those days.[2]

Nevertheless, although Mendele appears to dismiss 'aggadah as a world of fantasy belonging to a bygone age (*Ba-yamim ha-hem*), he depicts the first stirrings of his artistic instinct through 'aggadic symbolism. He alludes several times in *Of Bygone Days* to the following 'aggadah, set after the destruction of the Second Temple in Jerusalem:

> Rabbi Yose said: Once while walking I entered one of the ruins in Jerusalem to pray. Elijah, of blessed memory, appeared and guarded the entrance until I had finished. Then he said: Peace upon you, rabbi! I replied: Peace upon you, my rabbi and teacher! He asked: Why did you come here? To pray, I replied. He said: You should have prayed on the road. I told him: I am afraid of being disturbed by wayfarers. He asked: My son, what sound did you hear in this ruin? I answered: I heard a heavenly voice moaning like a dove, saying: Oy that I have destroyed my house, burned down my sanctuary and exiled my sons among the nations! Elijah then said: My son, I swear by your life that the voice said this not just when you were praying but repeats it each day three times. What is more, each time the Jews in synagogues and houses of prayer say 'Amen, may the name of God be blessed...', the Holy One, blessed be He, shakes his head, as it were, and says: Happy the king praised so greatly in his house! What of the father who has exiled his sons! Woe to the sons exiled from their father's table!' (*Berakhot* 3b).

This 'aggadah first appears in *Of Bygone Days* in Mendele's description of his childhood friend, an eccentric named Hirzl who, among other talents, knew how to draw. One work of his stuck in the child's mind—a picture of Rabbi Yose and the dove, based on the talmudic legend. Again, the wonder of the child's experience is tempered by the gentle irony of the satirist:

> He drew 'Rabbi Yose' following the talmudic account, with Rabbi Yose (wrapped in *tallit* and crowned with *tefillin*, his face plaintive, his beard short, sharp and grey) praying in a Jerusalem ruin, hearing a heavenly voice moaning like a dove (a creature shaped somewhat like a dove, mouth agape) saying: Oy that I have destroyed my house, burned down my sanctuary and exiled my sons among the nations! This work astonished the village *mavens*: words they could find in praise of Rabbi Yose, but as

for the dove—their mouths hung ajar in speechless wonder—
Ribbono shel 'olam, what can we say at this marvel![3]

The picture and the *'aggadah* of Rabbi Yose struck a chord in the child's heart, for he determined to copy Hirzl's work. In this way, his later role as artist might be traced in part to this *'aggadah*:

> Shloyme wanted very much to imitate Hirzl and do work similar to his picture of Rabbi Yose and the heavenly voice moaning like a dove. However, it didn't turn out, and he excused himself, saying that he didn't have proper artist's materials. For carving he needed a sharp chisel, while the one he had, won in a raffle, was soft and notched; and as for painting, he needed all sorts of colours...[4]

The *'aggadah* takes on a deeper significance in the final chapters of *Of Bygone Days*, written shortly before Mendele's death, which give a brilliant and moving portrait of the author after his father's death when he was thirteen or fourteen. (In common with Bialik in the poem *Yatmut* [Orphanhood, 1928-33], Mendele seems to have waited a lifetime to write these chapters, which comprise one of the high points of his art.) Separated from his mother who could not support him, he lived in a village a few miles away. In his loneliness, memories of home came back to him, including Hirzl and his picture and the *'aggadah* of Rabbi Yose which, in this context, becomes virtually symbolic of the ruin of the author's family life:

> Hirzl the carpenter too—that old man childlike in his walk, his talk and his crazes—came to him with his violin and the picture he had done of Rabbi Yose, old, thin, wispy-bearded, wrapped in *tallit*, crowned with *tefillin*, praying in a Jerusalem ruin, above his head a dove moaning in misery, abandoned, dejected.[5]

Bialik, too, uses imagery of Jerusalem's ruin, especially in *Megillat ha-esh* (The Scroll of Fire, 1905), to convey a parallel disaster in his life: he had also lost his father and was separated from his mother, though at an earlier age than Mendele.[6] As a child, he had used *'aggadah* similarly, as an escape into a semi-idealized world of the past and, later, as a creative means of expressing and mastering the trauma and of unifying the fragmented parts of his life. In the first of three unsent drafts of his autobiographical letter to Joseph Klausner of 1903, Bialik confessed that his life 'consisted of nothing but broken tunes of various instruments, each one playing for itself and happening to be at the same place—and if they formed one partly whole tune, it's a miracle.'[7] In *Aftergrowth*, he writes of *'aggadah*, with its scintillating fragments which he attempted to unify into a whole, as a parallel to his own life:

> From the blurred letters of these dog-eared books—Humash, Rashi, Tanakh—which I studied in sporadic, disordered bits—rose in confused fragments long-forgotten generations and ages, peoples, lands and stories. I spoke with the ancients and took part in their lives and deeds. I did not need whole sections. I built myself their ruined world even out of verse fragments and shards of meaning...[8]

Owing to his years of labour with J.H. Ravnitzky on the *Sefer Ha-'aggadah* (The Book of *'aggadah*, first published 1908-10), Bialik knew *'aggadah* better than any writer before or since. His use of *'aggadah* reaches its artistic peak in *Aftergrowth*, particularly chapters 9-15, written at the start of the Russian Civil War in 1918-19. In these chapters, which give no sign of the turmoil surrounding him, Bialik creates a child's eye view of Judaism in which the imagination is free to roam and the child becomes virtually a part of the *'aggadic* world. In a Hebrew style of unique richness, beauty and charm, he describes the village of Radi, his birthplace in the Ukraine, as a mirror-image of this fantasy world, whose origin and guardian is God himself. All the people and objects surrounding him exist in relation to the Bible and Talmud: for example, a pit in a nearby field is none other than the pit where Joseph was cast by his brothers; the river Teterov is where Moses was hidden among the bulrushes; a sandy track is the wilderness crossed by the Israelites on their way to the Promised Land. *Aftergrowth* is by no means free of nightmare, isolation and depression, yet the reader may understand clearly here that for Jewish children in Eastern Europe, *'aggadah* could be a limitless source of entertainment and pleasure, an inner world with a language of its own: Hodu and Cush, the giants Ahiman, Sheshai and Talmai, the Zuzim, Nachbi ben Vafsi, the Gibeonites, Sambatyon, Og king of Bashan. *Aftergrowth* indirectly gives much insight into the capacity of the East European Jews to retain their distinctive religious identity, through imaginative empathy with the land of the Bible. The child in *Aftergrowth* does not just read about the Israelites in the desert—he becomes one:

> By day we crossed the desert, parched and thirsty, land of snake, viper and scorpion. The boys went beside their camels loaded with rolls upon rolls of powder, balsam and spices. The white-bearded elders, wrapped in turbans, rode ahead in glory and honour, on white she-asses, their dangling feet nearly scraping tracks in the sand. By night we rested in the forests. We lit

bonfires and slept round them barricaded by a gutter-like circle of stones, to protect against wild animals as Jacob had, according to Rashi [*Genesis* 28:11].[9]

Such fragments of *'aggadah* appear to link the author with a mythical world of wholeness and stability prior to the breakup of his family analogous to the state of the Jewish people prior to the destruction of the Temple and the exile.[10]

Agnon, in common with Mendele and Bialik, reconstructs in 'The Kerchief' a world of wholeness and innocent faith in which the child is certain of the historical truth of *'aggadah*, in this case the story of Rabbi Joshua ben Levi, Elijah and the Messiah:

> Rabbi Joshua ben Levi found Elijah standing by the cave of Rabbi Simeon bar Yochai. He asked: Will I enter the World to Come? Elijah replied: If this Master [God] wills it. Rabbi Joshua ben Levi said: There are two of us here, but I can hear three voices. When will the Messiah come? Elijah replied: Go, see for yourself. Where is he? asked Rabbi Joshua. Sitting by the gate of the city [of Rome], replied Elijah. How can I recognize him? asked Rabbi Joshua. Elijah replied: He sits among the diseased poor. Everyone else bandages and unbandages his wounds in a cluster. He bandages and unbandages each wound one by one, thinking, If I am wanted I must not be delayed (*Sanhedrin* 98a).

'The Kerchief', based upon Agnon's childhood memories of the town of Buczacz in Galicia at the end of the 19th century, tells of a child distressed by the absence of his father, a businessman whose work takes him each year to the great fair in Lashkowitz. The *'aggadah* of Rabbi Joshua ben Levi permeates the child's imagination, and his longing to bring his father home becomes entangled with the age-old Jewish yearning for messianic redemption:

> Throughout the time father was in Lashkowitz, I slept in his bed. Right after saying the *shema*, I would stretch myself out in the long bed and cover myself up to my ears as usual, so as to get up in case I heard the *shofar* of the Messiah. I loved thinking about the Messiah the King. I often contemplated and laughed heartily at the future astonishment in the world on the day when he would appear. Yesterday he was sitting binding and unbinding his wounds—and today he is king. Yesterday he sat unnoticed among the poor, some of whom treated him despicably, when the Holy One, blessed be He, suddenly recalled his oath to redeem Israel

Aggadah and childhood imagination

and gave him permission to appear in the world. Others might be angry with the poor for not treating the King Messiah with respect, but I felt love for them seeing as the King Messiah had chosen to sit among them. Others might feel disrespect for the poor, as they ate cheap black bread even on the Sabbath and wore filthy clothes, but I loved them as some of them had the merit of sitting with the Messiah.[11]

In a nightmarish dream, the child flies to Rome in search of the father-Messiah and finds him, as the *'aggadah* relates, sitting by the city gate binding and unbinding his wounds:

> ... as my eyes closed, I would take my *tzitzit* and count in its knots the number of days father would be in Lashkowitz. Green, white, black, red and blue lights whirled round, like those seen by wayfarers in the fields, forests, valleys and streams, and all sorts of treasures glittered and shone in them. I felt mischievous with joy at all that treasure hidden for us until the day the Messiah appeared, speedily in our time. Then a great bird came and pecked the light away. Once I took my *tzitzit*, tied myself to its wings and said: Bird, bird, take me to father. The bird spread its wings and brought me to a city called Rome. I looked down and saw a group of poor people by the city gates. One of them was sitting binding and unbinding his wounds. I looked away so as not to see his suffering, and a great mountain towered up full of thorns and briars, with wild animals grazing, unclean birds flying and repulsive crawling things. Suddenly a great wind came and tossed me onto the mountain. The mountain started to crumble and I was about to be crushed. I tried to scream but did not for fear that the unclean birds would peck at my tongue. Father came, wrapped me in his *tallit* and carried me to bed.[12]

The exceptional significance of 'The Kerchief' and its *'aggadic* source in Agnon's development as an artist is clear in his account of how, while still a child, he began to write. For his first poem was done in a state of longing for his father who, like the father in 'The Kerchief', was away at the Lashkowitz fair:

> When I was a child of six or seven, my father of blessed memory went to the fair in Lashkowitz. As I missed him very much I was sad all the time. One evening I came home from *heder* overcome with longing. I pressed my head against the wall and cried: Father, father, where are you, I have loved you deeply [in Hebrew

these lines rhyme]. I was amazed to have written this poem accidentally, my first Hebrew poem. After, I wrote many poems and stories but they seemed lightweight in comparison with those two lines which I had rhymed out of longing for my father.[13]

This longing was compounded by the mother's illness—she suffered from a heart ailment from which she eventually died—and her consequent difficulties in caring for Agnon, especially as he was the eldest of five children;[14] and in 'The Kerchief' both parents are distant from the child in contrast with the fantasy world of *'aggadah* which seems to offer him intimacy and the promise of salvation or release, if not through religious faith then through the power of the creative imagination and art. The 'action' of the story—the father's absence and, on his return, his gift of the kerchief to the mother, the mother's gift of the kerchief to the child on his *bar mitzvah* and, finally, the child's gift of the kerchief to the messiah-like beggar—might therefore be taken as symbolic of the forces underlying Agnon's creativity, and the potent blend of idealization and nightmare in his art.

To sum up: in each of the three writers, *'aggadah* appears to serve as a means of exploration and a screen of traumatic childhood experiences and relationships: the loss of the father and separation from the mother (Mendele and Bialik), and the absence of the father and a mother handicapped by illness and many children (Agnon). The *'aggadot* of the 'sons exiled from their father's table' (Mendele and Bialik), of the ruin of the Temple in Jerusalem and the wanderings through desert land (Bialik) and of Rabbi Joshua ben Levi and the wish to revive the impoverished Messiah and enable him to perform his role of deliverance (Agnon) have a dual function: they indirectly explore private childhood trauma and attempt to master it through art; and they return, as it were, to the 'childhood' of the Jewish people, to the *'aggadah* at which Bialik said he suckled as at his mother's breast, and the moment of greatest trauma—the destruction of the Temple—and attempt to overcome it as a prelude to the creation of a new national identity.

NOTES

1. English translations of these works appear in Ruth R. Wisse, ed., *A Shtetl and Other Yiddish Novellas*, New York: Behrman House, 1973; I.M. Lask, tr., *Aftergrowth and Other Stories*, Philadelphia: JPS, 1939; and Nahum Glatzer, ed., *S.Y. Agnon: Twenty-One Stories*, New York: Schocken Books, 1971. All translations in the present article are by David Aberbach.

2. *Kol Kitvei Mendele Mokher Sefarim* (Collected Works), 1 vol. edn., Tel Aviv: Dvir, 1947, p. 272.
3. *Ibid.*, pp. 282-3.
4. *Ibid.*, p. 287.
5. *Ibid.*, p. 295. The consequences of Mendele's experience of childhood bereavement, and its effect on his writings, are discussed by David Aberbach in *Realism, Caricature, and Bias: The Fiction of Mendele Mokher Sefarim*, London: The Littman Library, 1993. On loss as a precipitant of art, *see* David Aberbach, *Surviving Trauma: Loss, Literature and Psychoanalysis,* New Haven, Conn. Yale University Press, 1989.
6. See David Aberbach, *Bialik*, in Arthur Hertzberg, ed. *Jewish Thinkers.* London: Peter Halban and Weidenfeld & Nicolson. New York: Grove Press, 1988.
7. H.N. Bialik, *Ketavim genuzim* (Posthumous Works), Moshe Ungerfeld, ed., Tel Aviv: Dvir, 1971, p. 232.
8. *Kol kitvei Hayyim Nahman Bialik* (Collected Works), 19th edn., Tel Aviv: Dvir, 1958, p. 168.
9. *Ibid.*, p. 170.
10. On Bialik's sense of fragmentation as a spur to his work on *kinnus*, the ingathering of dispersed fragments of Jewish culture through the ages, see David Aberbach, *op. cit.*, p. 117.
11. *Kol sippurav shel Shmuel Yosef Agnon* (Collected Stories, 8 vols., 1953-62), Tel Aviv: Schocken, vol. 2, p. 257.
12. *Ibid.*, p. 258.
13. *Me-'atzmi el 'atzmi* (From Myself to Myself), Tel Aviv: Schocken, 1976, p. 26.
14. On the motif of the ill, dying and dead mother in Agnon's stories, see David Aberbach, *At the Handles of the Lock: Themes in the Fiction of S.J. Agnon.* London: The Littman Library, Oxford University Press, 1984, ch. 4.

JEWISH EDUCATION IN 19TH CENTURY RUSSIA IN THE EYES OF MENDELE MOKHER SEFARIM

Shmuel Werses

The broad spectrum of issues besetting Jewish education in 19th century Russia was a matter of great import to one of the outstanding figures of Yiddish and Hebrew literature, Shalom Jacob Abramowitz, best known by the pen-name Mendele Mokher Sefarim (1836-1914). That these educational issues were of deep concern to him is reflected in the polemical essays published at the outset of his career in Hebrew literature, as well as in some of his most representative work in both languages. Critical of the age-old Jewish methods of education, Mendele Mokher Sefarim (hereafter termed 'Mendele') also turned his attention to the Jewish schools established by the Russian authorities. The later polemical articles published in the contemporary Hebrew press did not limit themselves to words of reproof and criticism, but instead strove to offer constructive suggestions and proposals for the betterment of Jewish education.

Even the belletristic works published throughout Mendele's various periods of literary creativity are replete with realistic descriptions of contemporary educational institutions both traditional and modern, drafted in the critical spirit of his newspaper articles. Characteristics of this reciprocal relationship are at times discernible in his literary works, transforming them into a paradigm of general reality. Yet there are also instances in which Mendele diverges into realistic descriptions of the most minute detail even within the framework of his polemical essays.

Whereas Mendele's articles nearly always adhere closely to the actualities of the contemporary reality in which they were formed, the treatment of this subject within the framework of his literary creation had a twofold dimension. At times the closeness to reality and the striving for the normative are the forces which forge Mendele's words; such examples are generally contemporaneous with his newspaper articles examining various aspects of education. Yet at other times the perspective offered by the passage of time infuses a descriptive style of epic quality, or one that is personal and autobiographical. Such writing makes no ambitious claims for reform; it is content to bequeathe memories of a reality to a future generation unfamiliar with it.

Mendele himself not only experienced in his childhood and youth the traditional educational institutions that he describes from time to time with such acute perception and sensitivity, but also played an active role in the government-supported Jewish schools during his stay in the city of Kamenitz (1853-1856). Even during the period that witnessed his growing fame as a Yiddish and Hebrew novelist Mendele received acclaim as an educational figure. As director of a Talmud Torah school for boys from poor families in Odessa between 1870-1906, Mendele did much to alleviate the conditions of such establishments.[1]

Already in his first publication, printed in the Hebrew newspaper *Hamaggid* in 1857, Mendele brought up the subject of education, perhaps because of his didactic nature, perhaps because of its importance in the history of the Jewish people.[2] A young man barely twenty years old, Mendele expressed his views in *Letters About Education*, written in the form of a response to a friend and fellow teacher. Railing against his unruly pupils, the teacher hints darkly at harsh measures necessary for their education and general upbringing. Mendele, however, rejects such sentiments and instead advises his colleague in the ways of moderation and patience, and advocates methods which take into consideration youthful inclinations.[3]

As for the content of these studies, Mendele tended towards a fine balance of religious devotion and worldly wisdom—the rapprochement between Jewish learning and secular studies; the conciliation of the past with the actualities of the present. In order to bolster his argument and prove the wisdom of his advice, Mendele presented a streamlined survey of education as it developed amongst the Jewish people from biblical and talmudic times through the first generations following the exile of the Jews from their land. Following the custom of earlier writers of the Hebrew Enlightenment in Russia, Mendele cites chapter and verse testifying to the approval with which the talmudic sages regarded the acquisition of the language of the State and secular study. Winding up his 'letter', Mendele promises his friend a separate discussion of the educational issues so pertinent to Russian Jewry: an additional letter featuring practical suggestions for improving the present situation—a promise, however, that was never carried out.[4]

Characteristic of Mendele's views during the period which saw the publication of his *Letters About Education* is the comment printed in the margins. This comment reveals the transformation that he had experienced *vis-à-vis* secular studies, a transformation which he now takes the opportunity of disclosing to his readers:

> And I recall having once believed that any person who dabbled in worldly matters—or indeed any matter other than Gemara, Halakha, or Bible—was but an ignorant boor, an *'am ha-'aretz* with no claim to the wisdom of man. For, dear reader, I scorned and disdained any man who chose the way of *Haskalah* and Enlightenment. If I glimpsed a man writing in the tongue of a people not his own, or reading the highflown eloquence of a bygone age—such a man was a disgrace in my eyes; mine and my friends alike.

But now, Mendele goes on to say, profound changes had occurred: 'Yet because I would linger lovingly over God's Torah should I neglect the Torah of man? And for the sake of Torah scorn labour? For on the foundation of both does the world rest.'[5]

It is in the confident spirit of the Enlightenment and the objectives it proclaimed that the young Mendele in 1859 described a graduation ceremony at a local government-founded school for girls.[6] This report was sent in the form of a letter to *Ha-maggid* from the city of Berdichev in which Mendele was then residing. Impressed by the proficiency displayed by the pupils in Russian and German, in geography and mathematics, Mendele envisaged a glorious future: 'For upon seeing the people whose children will consecrate wisdom, whose sons will learn profundity and its daughters the ways of discernment—such a people shall also consecrate the remnant of Israel.' In the light of this experience Mendele anticipated a transformation of Jewish education: 'For they will unite Torah with wisdom; boys and girls will be sure to attend these schools.' Neither did he neglect to praise Czar Alexander II, 'the creator of light and maker of the Jewish Enlightenment'.

With the pasage of time Mendele was to become somewhat more apprehensive concerning the methods applied by the Russian government to the implementation of Jewish educational reform. Notwithstanding the standard high-flown expressions of loyalty and gratitude to the Russian government Mendele could not refrain from criticizing the methods adopted by the government in its efforts to overhaul Jewish education. In a series of articles published by *Ha-melitz* in 1865, and collected the following year into a single volume *The Eye of Justice* (*Ein mishpat*), Mendele describes the gloomy state of the government schools, pointing out mistakes and organizational failures. He lamented: 'Schools are in our midst—abject and lonely, with nary a student to flock to their portals; only in a trickle here and there from amongst the poor do they come.'[7]

While implicitly accepting the goals of such schools, 'to educate youth in the ways of religion and faith, and to teach them *derekh 'eretz*, the path of good breeding', Mendele believed that religious studies should be pursued in the Hebrew language. The practice of teaching Bible with the aid of a German translation was likewise brought into question; the author of *The Eye of Justice* suggests that the children, unused to the German tongue, might instead utilize the Russian language, the language of the State.[8] Mendele further advocated the employment of teachers well versed in Hebrew, capable of instilling the language in their young charges, and ended with a call for the publication of Hebrew textbooks to augment the various academic disciplines taught in these schools.[9]

The major thrust of Mendele's criticism in *The Eye of Justice* was directed at the organizational apparatus of the government-founded schools. He lamented the fact that the supervision of such schools was entrusted to Russian inspectors and administrators either unable or unwilling to recognize the special needs of Jewish teachers and pupils. Often lacking proper pedagogic training, these supervisors not only lorded it over their hapless pupils but over the teachers as well. They often displayed contempt for these Jewish teachers, thereby lowering morale, and causing many to abandon the profession. This was one of the reasons why the Jewish element was so sorely lacking in these schools. Mendele regarded these nominally Jewish schools as 'Christian schools', 'schools given over to gentile supervisors and inspectors'. It was surely no wonder, the author concluded, that the Jewish community held itself aloof and refrained from enrolling its children in such institutions.[10]

As a remedy for all these ills, Mendele proposed that the administration of these schools be entrusted to the Jews themselves. This conclusion held true for the Rabbinical seminaries similarly sponsored by the government. Mendele therefore appealed directly to the Russian authorities: 'Would it please [the government] to form a special committee of educated Jews—wise and learned, of true and noble demeanour—who will watch over the Hebrew schools, guiding them in the spirit of the people and installing teachers and curriculum as they see fit.'

It was only right, thought Mendele, that the direct supervision of such schools in every district be entrusted to Jews. Pending such change Mendele voiced the hope that they might regain the confidence of Jewish parents. The number of students would thereby increase; the level of studies in the Jewish spirit might possibly reach new heights.[11]

As for improvements in these government schools Mendele saw none, not even in articles written some ten years later.[12] In 1875 Mendele once again cited the deteriorating situation of these schools whose enrollment remained so low, changed by the reforms implemented in 1873. Even though administration of these schools was now solely in Jewish hands, Mendele did not perceive that the study of Jewish disciplines and the Hebrew language had significantly benefitted, inasmuch as Jewish studies now constituted but one third of the educational curriculum. The curriculum of these schools now resembled that of their Russian counterparts. Resignedly Mendele summarized matters:

> The fate of the new schools will not be favourable and will perhaps be worse than that of their predecessors, if due attention be not given to the sources of Jewish ills, and if the good and necessary medicines be not administered; those same ones which fostered the unfettered ideals of enlightenment of the spirit.

Mendele continued to monitor the network of schools sponsored by the Imperial government for the Jews of Russia. In 1878 he conducted a statistical survey of the number of students enrolled in these schools.[13] Once again he lamented the lack of participation by representatives of the Jewish public in the schools' administration, even though they were in essence funded from the candle-tax placed on the shoulders of the Jewish community. Mendele noted that the government 'had not submitted matters to the Jews themselves'. It should, therefore, come as no surprise that 'an awakened interest is quite lacking amongst them, and no sign of blessing can be glimpsed in any of the new amendments'.

Equipped now with detailed statistics, Mendele hoped to stimulate Jewish participation in the educational network that had in effect been established for Jewish use. He promised to persevere with the statistical surveys in the future.[14]

The traditional *heder*—that timeless and venerable institution of Jewish religious instruction—was a matter to which Mendele devoted special attention in his articles of the 1870s. In the article concerning the improvement of the Jewish situation in Russia, 'What Are We?' (Mah anu?), published in 1875,[15] Mendele took special pains to depict the world of the *heder* and the means of instruction employed there. In highflown and vigorous language Mendele described the tasks that fell to the lot of the erstwhile assistant (*Reish dukhna*) of the *heder* teacher, the proverbial *melamed*. Not least of his duties was the task of gathering his young pupils from their homes and leading them to the *heder*. Such a task was, in Mendele's eyes, rather akin to the shepherd who leads his flock to the slaughter. 'And on his shoulder the young children—the sons, our sons; the holy flock, our flock too.' And with final irony: 'Why then, may we ask, do the children weep?'[16]

In gloomy terms this article underlined that the very location of the *heder* was in the poorest and most squalid neighbourhoods. And as for the actual instruction, Mendele painted this dreary picture:

> One fellow seemingly fashioned as a human being, bare to his waist, was seated at a bench pulled up to a filthy table amongst the young children, screaming mightily along with them and lashing away with the strap in his hand. This is none other than the venerated *melamed* himself, the zealous instructor at his holy work; the beaten and tortured children are none other than his pupils![17]

A critical and emotional protrayal of *heder* life, incorporated within an article of polemic intent, represents Mendele's protest at the suffering of generations of Jewish children.

> Some are seated before their unyielding teacher, receiving hearty blows, slapped cheeks, yanked hair—sobbing and screaming in pain. Others have but just now managed to wriggle away from their terrible master who inflicts such furious blows. Their eyes are red from tears, their flesh will yet ache from the rod of his arrogance.[18]

The author of the article continues his comparison with the animal kingdom while describing the fate of the pupils, the victims who passively submit to a devouring beast of prey:

> And in their rush to line up before their harsh taskmaster they crowd together like terrified sheep who have caught the scent of a prowling wolf. And of those holy sheep whose moment for bending under the rod has not yet come, some of them wrap themselves up and plump themselves down like clods in the face of this imminent terror. Others bury their head in their arms like a sorrowing dove seeking the shelter of its wings while peering out with exhaustion; others roll around on the ground pecking away at the garbage.[19]

To this grim picture Mendele adds his ironic comment: 'How lovely are your tents, O Jacob, your tabernacles, O Israel' (Numbers 24:4). He cites the meagre achievements reaped by this method of *heder* education; a method that flings to the wayside those pupils who possess but a halting command of Hebrew, and that nips natural talent in the bud. The *heder* even causes the students' bodily strength to wither away. All in all, Mendele concludes with a grim and poignant echo from Genesis 4:10: '...the voice of the children's blood is crying out to you from these rooms of terror.'[20]

In this penetrating description of *heder* life the author of 'What Are We?' distinguishes between the various age groups taught within the *heder* walls. His criticism is not confined to the youngest pupils but also extends to the *heder* designed for more advanced students. Here his words of criticism are imbued with a certain disappointment: 'Your sons are not trained for the contingencies of reality, and they are not taught the requisites of human success and contentment.'[21] As for the feeble achievements that the *heder* has to offer, Mendele states sorrowfully: 'The boys possess no understanding of Bible, and their knowledge of the fine points of the holy books is weak indeed.' The teachers themselves are in principle neglectful and contemptuous of Bible instruction. Mendele does not fail to take such an attitude to task: 'For how is it possible to neglect Bible study, when it serves as the very foundation and core of the Jewish religion, and to abandon the study of the language in which are written all the laws and precepts that they study and teach?'

Even the instruction of Talmud, so central to the *heder* curriculum, does not emerge unscathed from Mendele's critical eye. Its method is faulty, the lessons steeped in the endless and hair-splitting harangues of *pilpul* and plunged into esoteric discussions far beyond the students' capabilities. On the other hand: 'Of the means and ways that prepare a man to make his way in the world, and the knowledge of crafts and decent behaviour—all of which have been forbidden by their teachers—they get not even a glimpse.'[22]

In view of the pitiful results yielded by *heder* education, the students who completed their studies found themselves totally unprepared to cope with the normal tasks of life. Into the mouths of such students Mendele placed words of bitter reproach towards the parents who had shirked their parental duties: 'Your woeful sons hereby testify against you, for not having prepared them with a good and fitting education and the means of making a living without shame. You have done ill, have prevented them from making a livelihood, and brought them to bitterness and sorrow.'[23]

The issue of *heder* instruction was treated once again in Mendele's article of 1878, 'Patriotism and Its History' (Ahava le'umit ve-toledoteiha).[24] In this article he continued to criticize the deplorable condition of the *melameds*: 'As for worldly knowledge and any kind of craft or trade they protest at any change in the educational *status quo*. They are apprehensive lest the proposed changes take place and they find themselves without the means of securing a living.' In Mendele's words:

> They use every stratagem to persuade the masses of the merits of the traditional educational methods. It is for this reason that they object to the instruction of general academic subjects and even prevent biblical study with its time-hallowed commentaries. And it is for this reason that, whenever some innovator awakens amongst us who would enlighten the people regarding the flaws of its education, and to entreat mercy for their sons—such a person will provoke nothing but grumbling and complaints. A clamour will arise in the Hebrew camp, as though the Evil One had arisen to deprive them of their Torah and to mock the people and desecrate the honour of the Israelite spirit.

The clash between traditional education and the government-sponsored schools is authentically delineated within the framework of Mendele's belletristic works, some of which are contemporaneous with his articles. Mendele's first Hebrew novel, *Fathers and Sons* (*Avot u-vanim*, 1868) illustrates this affinity of journalism and *belles-lettres* in its fictitious plot which takes place in the town of Kisalon ('Foolstown').[25] Generalized complaints concerning the alienation of the Jewish population from the government-sponsored schools are transformed into a specific and particular situation. Thus Mendele recounts the attempts to replace the local *heder* institutions with government-sponsored schools, attempts which wreak havoc amongst the Jews of Kisalon who retaliate with lamentations and a public fast. They dispatch messengers to the Hassidic Rebbe from the city of Kziv ('Fibtown'), entreating his prayers for the annulment of this harsh decree.[26] Unsuccessful though all these attempts are, the Jews nevertheless find various ways and means to circumvent the decree and avoid compliance with its demands. The *heders* continue to function while the new schools remain practically empty, successfully enrolling pupils only amongst poor families. The novel *Fathers and Sons* regales its readers with the ruses employed by the Jews of Kisalon upon the occasion of the Russian inspector's visit. Boys from the traditional *heders* are hustled into the government-sponsored school, filling the usually half-empty rooms to bursting point. The ploy is successful, and the inspector can find nothing but praise for the scene of humming activity right before his eyes. So successful in fact is this ruse that the regional authorities even contemplate opening an additional school to contain the overflow of students! The final touch of irony comes with the arrival of a medal of honour and letter of commendation to the Head of the Jewish Community—in reality one of the staunchest enemies of the government schools.[27]

The local Russian supervisor has his own part to play in this unfolding local drama. Well aware that most of the town's Jews have boycotted the government school, he nevertheless chooses not to reveal the true state of affairs to his inspector, having been suitably bribed by the local Jewish community. Yet it is not greed alone that motivates his actions, but also his total disinterest in the entire question of Jewish educational innovation. The narrator portrays the supervisor with these words: 'What's the point of racing around and showing any interest in a people for whom he cares nothing? It's all a shrug of the shoulders to him: teachers or *melameds*, *heder* or modern school. In his eyes, none of them is any good anyway!'[28]

Detailed descriptions of extreme realism also depict the *heder* in *Fathers and Sons*. The enlightened teacher, David, is appalled to hear 'a horrendous shriek and terrible shout' from the very *heder* he was intent upon visiting. Amidst the shouting came the sobbing of a young boy beaten for not having properly pronounced the weekly Bible portion. In the *heder*: 'Some ten young children were seated trembling and huddled together at a long table. Amongst the children stood a terrifying figure like a ravening wolf in a sheepfold.' The portrait of this *melamed* is painted in lurid colours: 'He is pug-nosed, of blotched complexion and spindly neck, wearing greasy pants and a *talit* dangling to his knees; a sweaty and soiled sash is wrapped around his middle. In his hand a cane, and on the table a sobbing boy with his breaches pulled down.'[29]

David's surprise visit to the *heder* at the moment of punishment is described in images of a man who wanders by chance into a cage full of chickens—only to find 'the cruel weasel crouching before the chick that is waiting to be devoured'. The surprised beast of prey is taken aback and attempts to flee. But the terrified chicks—the young children of the *heder*—regard the unannounced visitor as their saviour, and begin to breathe more easily. The reaction of the *melamed*, no less surprised than the children, is also portrayed with images from the animal kingdom: 'How the weasel glares at him and gnashes its teeth in confusion, peering furtively around for a chance to slither back into its hole!'[30]

Yet despite the overt hostility inherent in *Fathers and Sons*, Mendele displays a somewhat more lenient attitude towards the dispossessed *melameds* in his later writings of the *Hibbat Tziyyon* (Love of Zion) period towards the turn of the century. Sympathy for the main character, Leib Melamed, is evident in the story 'In the Days of Wrath', (Bi-yemei ha-ra'ash), published in 1889. The *melamed* of this story is induced by his poverty to emigrate to *Eretz Yisrael*, and his plight is narrated in a decidedly compassionate tone:

> Ah, poor *melamed*! Even in the midst of sorrows an evil eye is watching, the terror is great, slander grows apace, and a man will hound his brother into utter oblivion. It's not enough that Leib was deprived of his teaching, but was even forced to pay a fine, for they had denounced him for teaching without the permission of the authorities—such is the man Leib Melamed, a Jew both hungry and thirsty, who bears his suffering in silence, never emitting a sound, for the study of Mishnah does he ceaselessly ponder, and with the recital of Psalms bring contentment to his soul.[31]

The gloomy portrayal of *heder* life in *Fathers and Sons* is similarly depicted in the picaresque Yiddish story 'The Little Man' (Dos Klayne Menshele) of 1864, and most noticeably in the expanded version of 1879. It is with this publication that the author begins signing his belletristic Yiddish works 'Mendele', or 'Mendele Mokher Sefarim'.

Steeped in the spirit of Enlightenment, this satirical tale spins out the life story of Abraham-Yitzhak, the bullying community leader, and the details of his wretched youth. Composed in the manner of an autobiographical confession during his final days, Abraham-Yitzhak sums up his experience in the Talmud Torah school for poor children: 'A grave for burying the children of Israel, an educator of idlers and disturbed personalities.' The description of the corporal punishment of the young children, the woebegone pupils, is particularly eloquent.[32]

This description in 'The Little Man' allows a glimpse of the methods current for Bible instruction; a method which draws upon an antiquated form of Yiddish barely comprehensible to the students, or even to the teacher himself. Abraham-Yitzhak also recalls the visit of a Jewish supervisor who came from Petersburg in order to check up on the school's curriculum, incidentally examining the students' knowledge of Bible during the lessons. The narrator relates in a tragicomic style his utter failure when attempting to translate a passage from Genesis in his stumbling German. And he also describes how he was flogged by his teacher for having so embarrassed him in front of the distinguished visitor. In the end the young boy finds himself forced to leave the Talmud Torah, his capacity for enduring his teacher's physical punishments having failed him.

In the later stages of his desperate battle for existence, having failed miserably time and again in many an endeavour, the orphaned Abraham-Yitzhak also relates his bitter experiences as the assistant to a *melamed* in a private *heder* for young children. A dismal picture emerges as he enumerates his duties while serving the *melamed* and his family. He is given the usual task of gathering the pupils from their homes and tending to them in the *heder*. The description of the educational methods is openly critical. Leading the children back home, the assistant witnesses the children's gaiety as they prepare to leave the oppression of the *heder*.[33] All in all, the impression that emerges from 'The Little Man' is similar to the one the author evokes in his article 'What Are We', published during the same years.

Abraham-Yitzhak endures the bitterness of these experiences throughout his youth. He has developed into a man of substance and influence, and the will he leaves behind not only confesses his sins towards family and Jewish community, but also contains a special paragraph concerning the improvement of education for poor children. To carry out this goal he bequeathes a sum that will provide a Talmud Torah for the poor and a fund for its maintenance. Crafts and the language of the State are to be taught along with religious and Hebrew instruction, thereby preparing the boys to become craftsmen with a well-rounded education and enlightened spirit. The will appoints the godfearing rabbi of the community to execute this project, along with the *maskil* Gutman, whom Abraham-Yitzhak had formerly taken pleasure in harrassing. Yet now it is this same Gutman (and hence his eminently symbolic name) who is to oversee the carrying out of the educational project and the hiring of a capable teaching staff. Not content to introducing reforms only within the confines of his own community, Abraham-Yitzhak expresses the wish that his testament and confessions be printed and widely distributed for the sake of poor children's education throughout the Jewish communities of Russia.[34] It is noteworthy that the instigator of all these educational projects nevertheless does not aspire to eradicate the barriers of social class amongst the Jews. A special framework for the children of the poor is preserved even in this progressive expression of Enlightenment ideals.

Mendele's later belletristic writings evince a continuing interest in the education of Russian Jews during the second half of the 19th century. The realism that permeated his articles some forty years earlier can at times still be detected in his literary works of this later period. Thus Mendele's central novel, *In the Valley of Tears* (*Ba-'emek ha-bakha*), resumes the theme of government educational reforms and the reluctant Jewish community which resents these programmes. In some of the chapters first published in the pages of *Ha-shiloah* (1906), Mendele dwells on the past circumstances and mentions only in passing the changes wrought subsequently within the Jewish community. The growing linguistic assimilation of the Jews was at variance with the attitudes of the past, when the Jews had quite obstinately turned their backs on the government educational system. But now, Mendele notes ironically, these same Jews are doing everything in their power to penetrate Russian schools, blithely ignoring Jewish education. The author jeers at the parents who move heaven and earth in the attempt to enroll their sons in Russian schools: 'How these miserable creatures wriggle and squirm—how they try every ruse they can think of whether openly or in secret—until they are let in.' Even the most observant amongst them abandoned the traditional frameworks of Jewish education. The author turns his readers' attention to those early days when only the very few would turn to the government-sponsored Jewish schools: 'And those new schools established by the Imperial Government within the Pale of Settlement were like unto scabs in the eyes of Israel, for from their inception they had been created by outsiders—the pupils few and the teachers despicable.'[35]

From the perspective of the early 20th century Mendele sketches a gloomy portrait of the government Rabbinical Seminary in Zhitomir some forty years earlier. The old Rabbi Abraham of Kisalon, who functions within the context of this story as its narrator, is attempting to dissuade his former pupil Moshele from continuing his studies in this Seminary, and levels the harshest criticism at the students. Nominally groomed to serve as educated and enlightened Rabbis, the students in fact remain perfect boors, desecrators of the Torah and totally devoid of Jewish education. The old man's ranting reflects Mendele's views in his polemical articles of the 1870s. Now via his literary persona he states :

> These Jewish schools and Rabbinical Seminaries are held in scorn and contempt by our people, for from the very first they are not made by the Jews themselves, not by our sages and appointed leaders and not in their spirit. A grafted branch are they in Israel.[36]

The young man Moshele who is reporting this conversation now reveals in a letter to his father the conflicts and doubts that Rabbi Abraham's words have aroused. He asks himself about the purpose of studies in such an institution, for in the end he is most likely to find himself teaching in one of those regional government schools for Jews whose enrollment is so invariably low. No less daunting is the prospect of having to submit to the rule of a foreign Russian inspector. The young man's reflections on the lowly status that accompanies such a choice recalls from Mendele's articles of the 1860s and 1870s:

> The Jewish teacher must cringe before a non-Jewish appointee, who terrorizes him and does just as he pleases; just like this

gentile who runs the Rabbinical Seminary and rules our Jewish teachers with such highhanded arrogance and vulgarity. The teachers are diminished in the eyes of the pupils, and the honour of Torah and Hebrew studies sullied at one and the same time.[37]

In the light of such reflections Moshele resolves to pursue the study of medicine, though whether his intentions are indeed translated into deed in the Russia of those years is not narrated within the story's fictional framework.

The ways of Jewish education are also reflected in Mendele's autobiographical novel *In Those Days* (*Ba-yamim ha-hem*), composed at intermittent periods in his twilight years. The novel sprawls over a period of some fifteen years from 1840 to 1855; but a description of Jewish education of later years can nevertheless be discerned. In contrast to the sharply critical tone and Enlightenment views characterizing Mendele's articles and first stories of the 1860s and 1870s, the author of *In Those Days* is no longer seeking actively to influence the state of education. The writing is now from the vantage point of a man looking back to a bygone time, both in the historical sense and from the perspective of one who wishes to lay bare his past. A forgiving and serene tone now envelops the days of childhood, even when dwelling upon the flaws of traditional education. An elegiac nostalgia now pervades every detail of a childhood that no longer exists.

Within the autobiographical context of *In Those Days* are traces of the well known activities of Max Lilienthal, the ambitious Jewish educational reformer who had enlisted active cooperation from the Imperial government of Nicholas I.[38] The response to Lilienthal's crusade throughout Russia during the 1840s, in the attempt to drum up support form the Jewish religious leadership, is here narrated by Shlomo—none other than the childhood Mendele himself—who records a child's impressions of the hostile Jewish community's response to Lilienthal's entreaties and the government decrees. Mendele describes the public fast that the Jews proclaim and the prayers and pleas of a congregation desperate to abolish these secular government schools. It appears that no sector objected more strenuously to these plans than the *melameds*, who rightly feared being done out of their livelihood once the new system was introduced and other teachers installed. The autobiographical narrator also avails himself of the opportunity to report the hastily-engineered child marriages for the circumvention of the 'School Decree', and the discussions overheard in the city of his birth, Kapulia. But in the end the danger recedes, the *heders* are reinstated, and the apprehensions of the *melameds* dismissed. Mendele also sees fit to offer the familiar observation: 'Indeed some government Jewish schools actually were set up in a few cities, but the students were few, and all of them sons of the poorest families and the indigent of the people.'[40]

In contrast to the gloomy picture conjured up by *heder* life in the articles and early stories composed in the spirit of the Enlightenment, *In Those Days* now presents a moving portrait of Mendele's childhood education. He relates having had the good fortune to obtain a *melamed* whose understanding ways and artistic soul made a lasting and indelible impression upon the young boy. This is the figure of Lippa Ha-Reubeni: 'one of those inspired people of singular grace, blessed from the moment of their creation with good gifts: wisdom and talent and a compassionate heart, lacking in nothing but luck.'[41] A man who 'knew how to draw and could fashion all sorts of things out of wood, stone and copper'.

Mendele continues to emphasize the mutual affinity between the *melamed* who taught with such unconstrained good will and the pupil who so eagerly drank in his words. Even in his old age Mendele lavished praise on the manner adopted by Lippa Ha-Reubeni; the inspired and creative method of a teacher who taught this small group of boys for the sake of learning itself, not because of prosaic economic necessity. Even while engaged in teaching, the *melamed* would occupy himself with his artistic pastimes of painting and sculpture, yet never missing a single word of his pupils. 'At this time,' Mendele notes, 'he would be endowed with the loveliest of speech, explaining every subject thoroughly. His speech became a flowing stream drawing forth the uttermost pearls, his eyes aflame with the light of Torah.' Shlomo himself is swept up in a similar enthusiasm for his teacher: 'His soul longed for his rabbi's Torah, and drank his words in thirstily.'[42]

As an antithesis to the idyllic *heder* of Lippa Ha-Reubeni, Mendele mentions in passing the atmosphere that was typically the lot of most *heders*, an atmosphere of oppression and suffering:

> The teacher is determined to get the words of Torah into his pupil's heart, scolding at the top of his lungs with outstretched arm, and the chastized pupil becomes a dissembler by sheer necessity, pretending that his teacher's Torah has indeed found its mark—both of them sorrowful, neither one reaping any satisfaction from the other.[43]

Shlomo's sojourn in the presence of this admired figure lasted only till the age of twelve. For at this age Shlomo's father, the learned Rabbi Hayyim, took personal charge of his son's education, relinquishing his preoccupation with the worldly cares of commerce to teach the boy himself. Sketched out before us is an example of individual education that existed within the family, carried out in the tradition of ancient Judaism according to which a man must teach his sons. Rabbi Hayyim fulfilled this ideal with each of his sons, from the moment they completed their elementary study in the *heder* until the time that they stood beneath their wedding canopy. Mendele describes in great detail this individualized method of Talmudic instruction experienced by the narrator in the autobiographical *In Those Days*:

> Following the morning prayers his father would go over a chapter of Mishnah with him in the House of Study and Shlomo would then sit at home the whole day long learning Gemarah and the commentaries, reciting the lesson before his father—twice during the day and twice at night. And sometimes his father would awaken him before the dawn had yet broken, and walk with him to learn Torah in the House of Study.[44]

Even as he wrote these memoirs concerning the education of his distant youth, Mendele diverges at times from the purely descriptive and becomes caught up in the actuality of the period in which he had worked so tirelessly for Jewish educational improvement. His words return to the ideal educational tradition of the first generations, extolling its hierarchal qualities and modes of organization, citing: '...the obligation of the general public towards the young, [including] every single man whether rich or poor'.[45] On the other hand, Mendele laments in this autobiographical framework the deterioration of the present system which is grounded in social hierarchy:

> The wealthy who are set apart from their impoverished brethren have devised special schools of Talmud Torah, houses of refuge for the poor alone. But as for their own sons, they herd them off and give them into the hands of special *melameds* hired out of their own pocket. And the *melameds* who find themselves no longer in the public eye but instead left to their own devices— also herd themselves off on their own and make merchandise of their pupils. The obligation of a Jew to teach his son has now become a source of revenue.[46]

But it turns out that Shlomo, the main character of *In Those Days*, is fated not to study with his father until such time as he married, as had been the case with his brothers. For at the age of thirteen Shlomo lost his father and was shunted from *yeshivah* to *yeshivah* in various cities and towns. Amongst these towns were Timkevitz and Slutzk and, most importantly, the city of Vilna. He experiences the various teaching methods of eminent scholars. In his uncompleted autobiographical story Mendele depicts the world of *yeshivah* and the methods of teaching employed therein. The three-year period in which he studied in Slutzk is singled out for particular attention. The students of the *yeshivah* came from various far-flung places where they had acquired different branches of knowledge and learning methods; Mendele deplored the ensuing unevenness of attainment among these students :

> A mixed bag of pupils from various and sundry institutions of learning, not one of them knowing Bible, not to mention Mishnah or Gemarah. This leads to all kinds of unfortunate results: the patched together reasoning of *sevarah*, the extravagant nitpicking of *pilpul*, and the glib commentaries of utter confusion.[44]

The educational structure of the Slutzk *yeshivah* is portrayed in considerable detail. There are two levels of instruction: the upper class in which the Head of the *yeshivah* gives his Talmud lesson, and the second level which is taught by his assistant and reserved primarily for the newer students. And this is the method of instruction: 'Every morning after prayers this assistant teaches a page of Gemarah along with commentaries, according to its plain and simple meaning or *pshat*. He also questions the boys on this material to check whether they had studied the night before satisfactorily.'[45] But the head of the *yeshivah*, who occupies himself with the advanced students, 'teaches his lesson and then sharpens the boys on the words of the Sages using *pilpul* and *sevara*'. The rest of ths school day is likewise sketched out: 'The daily lesson over, the older students go off to study and prepare tomorrow's lessons where they choose, whereas most of the younger ones have to stay in class and prepare their lessons under the eye of their teacher.'[46]

Mendele also recounts experiences beyond those spent in studying; the adjustment to life in foreign surroundings and the difficulties of keeping body and soul together under the existing conditions. Particularly evocative is his description of the beginning of the academic year just after the festival of Sukkot:

> It is the time of the *yeshivah's* Great Fair and the 'Days'—that is, the days in which the citizens of the town provide the students with meals—are the primary merchandise. And while this business is going on the boys also do their commerce with the tables and benches. Concessions for sleeping on the benches at night are eagerly snatched up.[47]

It seems that the *yeshivah* experiences of *In Those Days* are given expression in another story, the semi-autobiographical 'The Calf of Tosafot Yom-Tov' (Eglato shel Tosafot Yom-Tov) published close to the time of the experiences described. Here, too, Mendele records the story of a boy bereft of home and family who studies in the *yeshivah* of another city while enduring a life of sorrow and deprivation: 'fulfilling the way of Torah by eating his "Days", by fitful sleeping, and a life of sorrow'. He even protests against these conditions and laments both for himself and his fellow students, calling out in anguish: 'Woe to us and, alas, our "Days"—days of shame, sorrow, and humiliation; suffering either the pangs of hunger or the bread of adversity—lazy and unearned bread in the house of others.' He summarizes the situation in words that carry more than a ring of despair and frustration: 'boot-lickers in our youth and good-for-nothings in our old age'.

The portraits of Jewish education in the writings of Mendele Mokher Sefarim are many faceted. The penetrating criticism and faithful depiction of personal experience reflect the deep and abiding preoccupation of a man of the Enlightenment, one who wished to contribute to the betterment of Jewish education in Russia. Yet the autobiographical descriptions written in the twilight of his life are imbued with a certain epic lyricism typical of the artist who is one of the major novelists of Hebrew and Yiddish literature.

Notes

1. See: J. Klausner, *The History of Modern Hebrew Literature* (Jerusalem,1950),Vol. VI, pp. 425-426.
2. See: S. J. Abramowitz, 'Letters About Education', *Ha-maggid* (1857) I:31, pp. 121-122. Also: *Mishpat shalom* (Vilno, 1860), pp. 47-86.
3. Ibid., pp. 48-55.
4. Ibid., p. 72.
5. Ibid., p. 73.
6. See: *Ha-maggid* (1859) III:44, p. 175.
7. See: S. J. Abramowitz, *The Eye of Justice* (Odessa, 1866), p. 28.
8. Ibid., p. 33.
9. Ibid., p. 31-32.
10. Ibid., p. 36.
11. Ibid., p. 39.
12. See: S. J. Abramowitz, 'O Shameless Nation', *Ha-maggid* (1875) XIX:23, pp. 198-199.
13. See: S. J. Abramowitz, 'An Assessment of Government Schools for the Sons of Israel in the Land of Russia', *Ha-melitz* (1878) IV:18, p. 348.
14. Ibid., XXIII:458.
15. See: S. J. Abramowitz, 'What Are We?', *Ha-shahar* (1875) no. VI, pp. 464-485; 526-534.
16. Ibid., p. 530.
17. Ibid., p. 531.
18. Ibid.
19. Ibid.

20. Ibid.
21. Ibid., p. 532.
22. Ibid., p. 533.
23. Ibid.
24. See: S. J. Abramowitz, 'Patriotism and Its History', *Ha-melitz* (1878) XIV:11, p. 220.
25. Concerning this novel see: D. Patterson, *The Hebrew Novel in Czarist Russia* (Edinburgh, 1964), pp. 5-7 (English). Also : S. Werses, *Story and Source* (Ramat-Gan, 1971), pp. 60-87. Also: D. Miron, *Between Vision and Truth* (Jerusalem, 1979), pp. 217-234.
26. See: S. J. Abramowitz, *Fathers and Sons* (Odessa, 1868), p. 74.
27. Ibid., p. 75.
28. Ibid., p. 76. For further information see: Z. Sharfstein, *The History of Jewish Education in Israel* (Jerusalem, 1962), Vol. III, pp. 297-299, 302-306. See also S. Zipperstein, 'Transforming the *Heder*: Maskilic Politics in Imperial Russia', *Jewish History. Essays in Honour of Chimen Abramsky* (London, 1988), pp. 87-109 (English).
29. Ibid., p. 102.
30. Ibid. For a comparison of the *heder* experience see the novels of Smolenskin and Broides. See Patterson, op. cit., pp. 168-171.
31. See, Mendele Mokher Sefarim: 'In the Days of Wrath', *Collected Writings...*(Tel Aviv, 1947), p. 106.
32. For a detailed account of this story see, S. Luria, Introduction to *Dos Klayne Menshele* (Haifa, 1984), pp. 11-45.
33. See Mendele Mokher Sefarim, 'Dos Klayne Menshele', *Complete Works...* (Yiddish) (Warsaw, 1928), pp. 14-15. Concerning harsh criticism of 'Talmud Torah', compare the letter of Yitzhak, *Fathers and Sons*, p. 83.
34. Ibid., pp. 15-16.
35. Ibid., pp. 24-25.
36. Ibid., pp. 148-149.
37. See, Mendele Mokher Sefarim, 'In the Valley of Tears', *Collected Writings...*, p. 237.
38. Ibid., p. 246.
39. Ibid.
40. See, Mendele Mokher Sefarim: 'In Those Days', *Collected Writings...*' pp. 275-276. Concerning the projects of Max Lilienthal see: R. Mahler: *History of the Jewish People in Modern Times* (Merhavia, 1970), Vol. II, Section 1, pp. 96-104.
41. See, 'In Those Days', p. 268.
42. Ibid., pp. 267-268.
43. Ibid., p. 268.
44. Ibid., p. 277.
45. Ibid., p. 303.
46. Ibid., p. 301.
47. Ibid.
48. Ibid., pp. 300-301.
49. Ibid., p. 301.
50. See, Mendele Mokher Sefarim, 'The Calf of Tosafot Yom Tov', *Collected Writings...*, pp. 359-360.

THE ROLE OF HIGHER EDUCATION IN ZIONIST SOCIETY

S. Ilan Troen

Israeli universities are widely appreciated as an intellectual reservoir which are expected to contribute to the solution of social and political problems, to the development of the country's economy, and to the strengthening of its physical defence.[1] As is the case with many developing countries throughout the world, the objectives of Israeli higher education are largely derived from the western experience over the past century. That a system based on these values and expectations should have emerged in Israel is not in itself remarkable since the concept of the social utility of the university is widely adopted. There are nevertheless some unique aspects to the development of the Israeli system in terms of the social expectations placed on it, the ethos of practicality which energizes it, and an anomolous structure of governance and finance which make it dependent on sources outside the State. An historical analysis of the origins and development of Israel's universities can illuminate these characteristics of the Israeli variation of a universal phenomenon.[2]

Origins

More than 20 years before the establishment of the State of Israel in 1948, the Zionist settlement in Palestine had organized two complementary institutions: the Technion in Haifa (opened 1924) and the Hebrew University in Jerusalem (opened 1925). The Technion was devoted to training engineers and technical workers while the Hebrew University developed the humanities, social sciences, natural sciences and medicine. Together, these institutions afforded a fairly comprehensive range of research and teaching for the country's population. Despite their different orientations, both institutions stem from common origins, values and expectations which have continued to influence their development to the present.

The sustained movement to establish a Jewish university dates from the beginning of the twentieth century when, at the Zionist Congress of 1901, it was suggested that such a university must become part of the Zionist colonization programme in Palestine. In July 1902 this proposal was published in a detailed pamphlet, *Eine Jüdische Hochschule*. It called for the creation of a Jewish university that would advance the cultural and technological development of a Jewish community in Palestine as a necessary complement to the political preparations for a state. The authors were three men in their twenties: Martin Buber, a philosopher from Vienna, Chaim Weizmann, a chemist from Geneva University and Berthold Feiwel, a journalist from Berlin. Their pamphlet has come to be viewed as the founding document of the Hebrew University as well as of the Technion.[3]

Considering that the Jewish population of Palestine at the time was under 50,000, the proposal for a university was visionary. Recognizing this, the authors invested their document with as many statistics as possible in an attempt to demonstrate the practicality of their programme. One extensive section justified a Jewish university as a response to the frustrations and sufferings of large numbers of Jewish youth who were growing up 'half-educated' as a consequence of the exclusionary quotas of European universities. A second set of numbers gave detailed estimates demonstrating the viability of their proposal. Although they made reference to the need for Jewish studies in contributing to a national revival, their emphasis was on the technological and scientific nature of the proposed institution. They viewed the university primarily in practical terms and in response to immediate problems.

In imagining these institutions, the authors derived much from the German university culture in which they were socialized academically and in which Buber and Weizmann established themselves professionally. Scholars investigating the sources of Israeli higher education have universally noted the importance of the German model for the internal organization and academic culture of the Israeli university. Thus, it has been widely appreciated that Israeli universities have benefited from the transfer of the Germanic commitment to the freedom to teach and the freedom to learn (*lehrfreiheit* and *lernfreiheit*). The German influence was no less significant for the social function that was conceived for these institutions, especially the appreciation that successful colonization depended on scientific research.[4]

The activities of Otto Warburg (1859-1938), who was active in establishing both the Technion and the Hebrew University, illuminate what Zion's colonizers expected from science in the settlement process. Independently wealthy and related to the famous banking family of Warburg, he received a Ph.D. in botany in 1883 and spent the best part of the next two decades advancing German imperial interests as a scientist. Among his accomplishments was the founding of a journal that dealt with the selection and development of suitable plants for exploitation (*Der Tropenflanzer*) and involvement with colonization work especially in the Cameroons, Togoland and the Ottoman Empire. Thus, his personal experience was firmly grounded in active participation in a colonization effort that emphasized scientific research for development.

Authorized by the Zionist Congress of 1903 to establish a Palestine Commission, which he administered until 1907, Warburg assumed increasing responsibility, becoming a member of the Restricted Executive Committee (1905-1911), and then its chairman and, in effect, the President of the Zionist Organization from 1911 to 1920, when Weizmann replaced him. During these two decades, Warburg was a leading exponent of 'practical' Zionism or that branch which argued for constructive activity within *Eretz Yisrael* rather than merely relying on diplomatic efforts to secure the homeland. In these efforts, he drew on knowledge which derived from personal experience with the German Imperial system in its Asian and African colonies.[5]

Key features of the German system were the experimental station which systematically attempted to improve local crops as items for international trade; training farms for preparing unskilled natives in the latest methods of agricultural production; and microbiological laboratories for the control of tropical diseases. Warburg was a witness and a participant in the exportation of German science to Africa and the Middle East where it was expected to stimulate economic development and improve public health and living conditions. If the experience Warburg brought with him to the Zionist movement was unique, the knowledge of the system in which he worked was widespread. As one of Warburg's associates in the Zionist movement noted:

> Germany is a land from which we can learn much. If the Germans spread out so energetically today throughout the entire globe, if their agricultural settlements as well as their commercial and industrial undertakings meet with success in all lands and climes, so do the Germans owe this to the fact that they sent out their economists, their professors as pioneers. As in war, so too in the economic struggle, do the Germans win because of their teachers.[6]

With these precedents in mind, Warburg and his colleagues successfully urged the Zionist Organization in 1903 to establish a commission for the planning of Palestine. Its function was to gather data, to explore Palestine and neighbouring countries, to set up stations for agricultural experimentation, to engage in research on local diseases, and to provide information on the acquisition of real estate. It was through this instrument that social scientists, natural scientists and medical personnel were to make their way to Palestine under the auspices of the Zionist Organization.

The Zionist Organization was not the first to import into Palestine a European and utilitarian approach to knowledge. In the second half of the nineteenth century, British, French and German philanthropic organizations were engaged in making the Jewish population of Palestine more productive through the creation of educational institutions.[7] However, the activities of the Zionist Organization represent a quantum leap forward. They were designed to pave the way for the transformation of a barren and backward country into a modern, prosperous and healthy society that would be able to receive the anticipated legions of pioneers. The conception of scholarly institutions as spearheads of an advancing frontier represented a significant advance in the use of universities as a stimulus to social or economic development. Aside from the German colonial model, only the American land-grant university operated on such an ambitious perception of the value and utility of science. From the universities of Michigan and Wisconsin to Berkeley, Americans in the last part of the nineteenth century viewed scientific institutions as instruments for developing new regions.[8]

From the beginning, proponents of higher education in Israel have emphasized the social and economic value of applying scientific research to local problems. The plans drawn up for the Hebrew University in the early 1920s under the guidance of an international academic committee that included the English zoologist, Lord Rothschild, and the German botanist, Otto Warburg, called for three institutes: one in the Humanities that would include Jewish Studies and Oriental Studies, and institutes for Chemistry, Microbiology and Tropical Diseases that would lead to Faculties of Science and of Medicine. In the initial stages, there was considerable debate over the balance between research and teaching. The French Rothschilds were insistent on research—indeed they had previously made clear that they would not participate in funding a teaching university. Only Weizmann's considerable diplomatic skills succeeded in obtaining their crucial support by assuring them of a research emphasis despite the possibility of some teaching. In fact, the Hebrew University offered only graduate degrees until after the creation of the State. The development of higher education, then, has been consistently marked by an emphasis on research, not only among the professoriate but among the lay leadership and financial supporters of Zionist settlement.[9]

This expectation that university research would be directed towards solving problems related to settling the country has been a distinguishing characteristic of Israeli higher education. This message continues to echo in the literature universities create about themselves. For example, the Weizmann Institute presents itself 'as a unique experiment in scientific pioneering'. It was intended from its founding in 1934 'not only to pursue science for its own sake but also to play an active role in developing the land and its economy'. Ben-Gurion University proclaims that it is 'charged with a mandate—to spearhead the development of the Negev'. The Technion proudly maintains that 'over the years, more than 25,000 graduates have made indispensable contributions to Israel's agricultural and industrial development, economic growth and national security'. The Hebrew University declares that it is 'a living symbol of the cultural rebirth of the Jewish nation in its ancestral homeland' and that its mission is 'to serve the State of Israel by training its scientific, educational and professional manpower'.[10]

Despite occasional protests to the contrary from within the professoriate, Israeli universities were never designed to be ivory towers. They have always been and continue to be directly engaged in the process of nation-building and of maintaining and strengthening the State. This may not be unusual in instances where higher education is a product of a governmental decision and controlled by state authorities. It is remarkable in the Israeli case since Israel's universities long preceded the establishment of the State and have remained significantly dependent on external resources for governance and finances.

Science and Colonization

It is essential to remember that in the early years of settlement, Palestine was virtually 'terra incognita'. The literature of the Zionist movement is replete with amateur attempts to catalogue the country's resources and offer potential colonizers practical information on how to settle the land. It is revealing that perhaps the most successful work of this genre was written ten years after its authors actually immigrated to Palestine. David Ben-Gurion and Yitzhak Ben-Zvi, Zionist leaders and future founders of the State, came to realize after living in the country how little Zion's pioneers knew of the land they intended to colonize. When forced into exile by the Ottoman authorities during the First World War, they utilized the opportunity to research the literature on Palestine at the New York Public Library and collaborated on a two-volume guide to settling the country. Although it engendered popular excitement as to the possibilities of transforming a barren and neglected land into a modern and prosperous country their effort did not prove significant as an adequate guide. Serious and systematic colonization required more substantial and original research than this or any other survey based on available knowledge could provide.[11]

The search for water was one essential way in which scientists contributed to reclaiming the land. Although written in the area of Jewish Studies, it is noteworthy that the first doctoral dissertation produced in an Israeli university focused on a problem central to a people re-establishing itself in an arid country. The research was entitled: *De Aqua—Research into the studies of the Land of Israel and its folklore during the period of the Bible and the Mishna.*[12]

On a more practical and systematic basis, the Hebrew University's Geology Department became a leading force in the search for underground water in areas that had become arid and barren over the centuries. In the 25 years before the State, research under the leadership of Professor L. Picard resulted in the discovery of water at places like Nahalal, Mishmar Haemek, Ginegar, the Carmel near Yagur, the Ephraim Mountains near Gal Ed, and in the corridor between Tel Aviv and Jerusalem. Each find made possible the founding of a new settlement or the expansion of an older one thereby adding to the numbers of settlers the country could absorb.[13]

There were serious deficiencies in other areas of knowledge. Settlers knew little or nothing about the plants and animals with which they had to work and live. They lacked knowledge of how soil conditions and climate affected the growth of the plants they selected for cultivation. As a consequence botany and zoology developed into major fields. During the 25 years before the State, Hebrew University scientists surveyed most of the country and diffused their findings in professional and popular literature. This research had actually been initiated prior to the First World War by such scientist-pioneers as Aaron Aaronsohn and Israel Aharoni. Such work became intensified at university laboratories from the mid-1920s so that after two more decades of systematic and intensive investigation there was a more or less complete inventory of the flora and fauna of the country.

The work was carefully planned and executed. The first priority was to establish what was living in the Land of Israel. The second was to explore the ecology of the country—how did these organisms exist and what was the relationship between them and their surroundings. This research was supported by the Jewish colonizing agencies responsible for solving the practical problems related to settlement. For example, university botanists worked together with the Jewish National Fund in superintending the development of forests throughout the country. They established a Desert Botanical Laboratory at Beersheva which was designed to explore the possibilities of settling the southern desert. In addition, there were projects for the classification of plants in terms of candidates for afforestation, for decorative purposes, for medicinal value, for industrial use and for pasturage. Still other projects involved the collaboration of biologists and entomologists on problems of insect and weed control and on diagnosing and eradicating diseases of fish ponds.[14]

University chemists also made a crucial contribution to reclaiming the land, providing analysis of soils with a view to agricultural applications. Indeed, it was for this objective that chemistry was proposed as one of the original institutes to be established at the Hebrew University. Due to scarcities caused by the Second World War, university chemistry laboratories expanded their work to produce insecticides, agricultural fumigants and preventives of citrus decay in addition to products and scientific instruments for military use.[15]

University-based natural scientists also produced significant if less tangible consequences by disseminating the new knowledge through extension programmes. Aimed primarily at educators and youth, they fostered a knowledge and an intimacy with the new land and with rural life and, in this way, they attempted to engender affection and loyalty to the new homeland.

Science and National Revival

Although the 1902 document emphasized applied sciences and technology, it also discussed the need for Jewish Studies, viewing them as a means for achieving the national revival of the Jewish people. Even as Jewish youth could not find places in many European universities, so too had the study of the culture and history of the Jewish people been excluded from the curriculum or at best relegated to a minor position within a department of theology or religion. It was therefore argued that only an institution under the control of Jews could give proper treatment to their culture. Although such an institution could be established in Europe or elsewhere, it would be most likely to flourish in a Jewish country. The establishment of a university in the homeland was a proper and necessary concern of Zionists who were dedicated to the 'normalization' of the Jewish people. Jews would be rehabilitated as a nation not only by returning to their own land but by re-establishing a culture that was authentically theirs.

It was generally accepted that normalization required placing Jewish Studies in a secular framework. Bialik, the national poet, framed this well in his address at the inauguration of the Hebrew University on Mount Scopus in 1925. He argued that the creation of a national secular university was essential for replacing the traditional religious-educational frameworks of the *heder*, *beit hamidrash* or *yeshivah*—the traditional settings for Jewish schooling and scholarship. In a secular university, Jewish culture could be approached scientifically and thereby without the bias and filter of religion. Moreover, sensing that traditional Jewish culture in Europe was on the verge of disintegration, Bialik claimed the builders of a new culture in Zion must hasten their work 'before the last light is extinguished in other countries. This we hope to do in the institution on Mount Scopus whose doors have today been opened.'[16] The insight was unfortunately prophetic. The drive to analyze and transmit Jewish culture and history through universities became an urgent and common concern after the Holocaust. That responsibility, modestly undertaken in 1925, is now energetically conducted in schools, departments and university-anchored research institutes throughout the country.

Conflicts over the naming of universities and determining the language of instruction became important landmarks in defining the new culture. It was ultimately decided that the university in Jerusalem would not be called the 'Jewish' university because of concern with the term's associations with religion. In the ears of the founders, 'Hebrew' had a more secular and nationalistic sound since 'Hebrews', like 'Israelites', suggested a people while Jews were associated with a religion.

The problem of determining the language of academic discourse was especially bitter, taking on the form of a *kulturkampf* that aggravated the Jewish communities in Palestine and the Diaspora. A German-Jewish philanthropic organization, the Hilfsverein der deutschen Jüden, took much of the responsibility for the initial organization of the institution and demanded German be the language of instruction for the sciences.[17] Like parallel French or English educational societies they intended that Jewish topics be taught in Hebrew but secular ones would be offered in the language of the sponsoring society. In this manner they expected Jewish youth in Palestine to acquire a valuable tool that would provide access to a major European society. Opposing this position was a coalition of Zionists from all parts of the political spectrum who insisted that then the exclusive sacredness and therefore the remoteness of Hebrew would be diminished. Hebrew would become a living language for a living people.

A similar debate erupted over Yiddish. Shortly after the opening of the Hebrew University, a substantial donation was received from America for the study of Yiddish. So vigorous was the opposition both within the University and among key supporters, that it was not for another quarter of a century, indeed after Independence and after the millions who spoke Yiddish as their mother tongue had lost their lives in the Holocaust, that Yiddish instruction entered the curriculum and became a topic for scholarly research. At the earlier period, the desire to break with what were viewed as the corruptions of life in the lands of exile and to assert cultural independence was overwhelming.[18]

The impact of the new, Zionist-oriented Jewish Studies extended far beyond the academy. They became part of the politics of achieving national revival. The most manifest and dramatic illustration is found in the uses to which historical research, particularly archaeological, was put. One of the original complement of topics included in Jewish Studies in the early days of the Hebrew University, archaeology became crucial for advancing Zionist claims in the international struggle over the rights and extent of Jewish settlement in Palestine. Indeed, historical scholarship continues to play an important role in public debates over conflicting claims to the Holy Land.[19]

One crucial battle during the pre-Independence period that still has implications for the pattern of settlement was over the economic absorptive capacity of the country. On the basis of this formula, the British regulated Jewish immigration and thereby affected the demographic composition of the country. On the basis of historical evidence, opposing sides generated two conflicting interpretations: Zionism's supporters blamed people, particularly the Arabs, for the failure to maintain the fertility of the Holy Land; defenders of Arab claims argued that changes in the climate rather than human enterprise were responsible for the country's prosperity or poverty. From this debate a fierce moral-political argument emerged. Zionists claimed that, unlike the Arabs who had abused the country's resources, Jews had shown that they could make the land prosper. Archaeological evidence supported the view that Palestine's absorptive capacity could be expanded by conservation, reforestation and modern farming methods.

Thus, in the generation before Independence, Zionists came to rely heavily on a discipline that blended philology, linguistics, critical textual analysis, the study of material culture and whatever else was available into an instrument of great analytic power. They believed that the archaeological revelations of the social and economic history of the area would support the Zionist position. The picture that emerged from this research was of a Palestine in which there were dense populations in some areas as early as the Iron Age. In the Roman-Byzantine period, there was a peak of four or more millions—three times as many inhabitants as were present in Palestine during the inter-war period. It appeared that historic Palestine enjoyed a flourishing agriculture, considerable international trade, large towns throughout the country, even in the Negev desert, and large cities on the coast. Evidence of past prosperity and high population densities supported the claim that this could happen again in the present, particularly with the modern technology employed by Zionist pioneers.

The findings of that generation's archaeological research were succinctly summarized at an international conference sponsored by the Research Council of Israel shortly after the establishment of the State. Although the battle for a state was over and Israel could now decide for itself at what rate it should take in immigrants, the old themes persisted. As A. Reifenberg, a Hebrew University archaeologist, claimed: 'The Israel we see today is but the ruin of a once flourishing country... It is human mismanagement which has brought about a continuing deterioration in the natural conditions.' Placing Palestine in an international context, other scholars from Western Europe, the United States and North Africa concurred that in Palestine as well as in other desert areas in the world, it was people and their culture rather than climate that was the major factor in what was termed the struggle between the 'Desert and the Sown'. Organization and social values were held to be the key to national development.[20]

Science and Security

The return of Jews to Zion was more than a question of refashioning national culture and reclaiming the land. Given the advantage in numbers and the power of the forces arrayed against Zionist settlement, it was essential that scientists from nearly every part of the university play a role in the effort to achieve national objectives and to defend and maintain the Jewish presence. While it is common for university-based science to contribute to the defense of modern societies, in the Israeli case connections between military leaders and politicians with academics are very close and enjoy widespread understanding and support. Since the closer one comes to the contemporary period the more difficult and sensitive it becomes to document the interaction between universities and the military, several historically-oriented illustrations may be employed to demonstrate the depth and range of the connection.

Probably the greatest impetus to university involvement with defence problems was stimulated by the needs of the British army during the Second World War. In December 1940 the British, at the Eastern Group Supply Conference held in New Delhi, designated Palestine as the main resource for the British Army's war effort in the Middle East. This decision was of great importance for it stimulated the development of Zionist industrial and manufacturing capabilities. The British could initially draw upon an indigenous textile industry, a steel foundry, a fabrication plants, machine tool enterprises, and substantial chemical and pharmaceutical industries. The list of industrial products Jewish Palestine was capable of producing was extensive and provided the base for further rapid development. This capacity was soon expanded and transformed in order to build minesweepers and repair warships at the port of Haifa, manufacture spare parts for tanks and other vehicles and produce explosives. For example, practically all of the land mines planted by the British in the North African desert were produced in Palestine as were many replacement parts for RAF planes. Moreover, an extensive range of components of products vital for communications and weapons were manufactured often directly in university laboratories. This effort depended on the presence of highly-trained personnel in engineering and the applied sciences as well as further stimulating an appreciation for their significance.[21]

This war-time experience was also a valuable prelude to the struggle for Independence. By 1946 a committee of leading scientists, many of whom had worked on behalf of the war effort, had begun a fruitful cooperation with the Haganah. The effort was discreetly carried out in a host of locations including universities which became sites for research and development as well as the training in and the storage of arms. By the time the war commenced, university researchers were meeting a wide variety of needs—from making mortar shells, armoured glass and communications equipment to providing intelligence. The intimacy between the academy and the military was also manifest in the ease with which scholars and students made the transition to fighting units, and was strikingly illustrated by the appointment of an archaeologist as Chief of the General Staff.

This connection has been considerably strengthened in the years since independence as Israel has had to compensate for numerical inferiority with qualitative superiority. Academic planners have tended to direct the development of their institutions in ways that would assist the national defence effort. The effort which produced the most spectacular results was the decision at the Technion during the War of Independence to recruit leading scientists in aeronautics from England and the United States. Beginning in 1950 a faculty was organized which became the academic base for Israel's single largest manufacturer and major export-earner, the Israeli Aircraft Industries. In aeronautics as in a host of other hi-technology areas, far less could have been achieved without the active involvement of the country's universities.[22]

The earliest connection between the military and university scientists was probably in a field very distant from research laboratories and illustrates the variety of ways in which a university can become involved in crucial matters of defence. In the aftermath of Arab attacks on the Jewish community in 1929, the Haganah asked Yohanan Ratner, an architect at the Technion who later became Dean of the Faculty of Architecture and a senior member of Haganah and IDF General Staff, to advise on means for improving the defence systems of isolated agricultural settlements. This led directly to the development of a defence-oriented design expertise including techniques for the design of buildings, the location of settlements and provisions for their defence that has literally shaped the Israeli landscape. In the pre-State period, perhaps the best known example is found in the design of pre-fabricated settlements, termed Stockade and Tower (*Homa u-migdal*). Fifty-four of these were established between 1936 and 1939 and became a major factor in establishing and defending the borders of what became the State of Israel.[23]

The collaboration continued and deepened in the post-Independence period as social scientists as well as architects were engaged in the development and execution of a national plan that called for the assimilation of hundreds of thousands of settlers and new immigrants in hundreds of newly-constructed communities throughout the country. Two examples, both involving the Hebrew University, are interesting illustrations of how university campuses, as frontier settlements, have been used for strategic purposes.

When the Hebrew University authorities began searching for an alternative site in Jerusalem, after the Mount Scopus campus had been left isolated beyond the 1949 armistice lines, they approached the Government for assistance. It was Ben-Gurion, serving as both Defence Minister and Prime Minister, who decided on the basis of military considerations that a new location relatively distant from the city should be chosen. The armistice lines which left Israel in control of the western portion of Jerusalem had also left that section surrounded on three sides by hostile, Jordanian territory. This meant that the city could only be reached by a vulnerable and attenuated land corridor. In order to fill in that corridor with settlements to reduce vulnerability, he advocated locating the Hebrew University and a new Hadassah Hospital in the area around Ein Karem. In justification, he cited the example of Russian railroad stations which were placed outside cities in order to draw out the population in the desired direction. Although the main campus was built closer in to the city than he wanted, the hospital and medical school were built at the selected site and have fulfilled their intended purpose.[24]

A variation on this theme occurred after the 1967 war when the Israeli Government decided to extend its control over East Jerusalem which had been under Jordanian rule. The major instrument for accomplishing this was re-establishing a massive, fortress-like campus on Mount Scopus and then linking it in a continuous, concrete wall of new neighbourhoods to Jewish, West Jerusalem. Political considerations determined that dormitories were among the first buildings constructed in order to establish in the area a living Jewish presence—or 'facts' as it has come to be termed. The new Mount Scopus campus, which has been one of the largest and most expensive construction projects supported by the Government, has been designed to extend Israeli control both by location and through design features. It is appropriate that it has been largely Ratner's students who were in charge of the project.[25]

It was entirely characteristic of the relationship between the country's academic and political leadership that a university campus should be so directly employed on behalf of objectives defined by military planners. In the university Senate debate on the issue, few voices were raised against the move on political grounds. Much of the debate centred on questions of economy, practicality and efficiency. Ultimately, appeals to nostalgia for returning to the old campus, claims of the national status of the university and the willingness to fulfill the role assigned by the government in establishing Jewish control over Greater Jerusalem, tipped the scales in favour of the invitation to relocate on Mount Scopus.[26]

Political dissension on campuses has not deterred universities from undertaking security responsibilities as defined by the political leadership. During the Second World War, for example, both the Technion and the Hebrew University made military service mandatory. At Jerusalem, all unmarried students between 20 and 30 were required to register for the British army. This requirement was criticized by the university's President, Judah Magnes. As a pacifist, he vigorously maintained that the right of conscience in university communities must not be violated.[27]

Although Magnes's protest failed on that occasion, he left an important legacy. During his service as the head of the Hebrew University, he superintended an institution that had on its faculty representatives of every shading of political opinion from the historian Joseph Klausner, a right-wing Revisionist, to the philosopher Martin Buber, a leading member of *Brit Shalom* which urged accommodation with the Arabs. Magnes himself died while on a mission to the United States in 1948 to lobby against the establishment of a Jewish state. In Magnes's terms he successfully transplanted from his native America a tradition of academic freedom which prized tolerance on the campus. As this tradition has worked itself out, Israeli universities have remained remarkably quiescent. Despite even severe criticism by many members of the academic community, universities have continued to participate actively and extensively in carrying out the State's security policies without the disruptions that have beset campuses elsewhere.[28]

Continuities of Structure

The period of enormous growth following Independence did not alter the research-orientation and applied character of the pre-State universities. The major changes were in the greatly expanding student population and the incorporation of additional areas of study through new departments, schools and faculties. Local demands for higher education led to the establishment of 'new universities' which were founded on the same principles of organization and purpose as the older institutions. Throughout the expanded system, responding to the country's needs remained the primary goal.

Independence created demand for civil servants, economists, administrators, and other experts. Teachers and social service professionals were needed as the country nearly tripled in its first three years through mass immigration. The Hebrew University organized rapidly for research and instruction in the social sciences, social work and education as relevant government offices such as the Ministry of Education and the Ministry of Social Welfare made grants to the university and supported students. The surge in immigration created needs and opportunities in health care leading to the development of a Faculty of Medicine while the process of establishing a modern State required a Faculty of Law to prepare lawyers to write laws and regulations and to administer and interpret them. In effect, the manpower requirements of the new State shaped higher education.[29]

This powerful service-orientation also contributed to the failure of a major innovation in education reform. A trio of leading figures with Anglo-American academic experience—President Magnes, Rector Leo Roth, and Professor Dushkin of the School of Education—sought to introduce a B.A. in General Studies. Personally influenced by English and American concepts of liberal arts, they also shared the postwar enthusiasm for university reform as manifest in the new departures at Harvard and Columbia. Roth, while Rector during 1941-3, had already begun urging a new structure of learning which would incorporate an American-type liberal arts programme for the first degree and specialization at higher levels. Moreover, he wanted all students to have a general as well as a Jewish education. A version of this concept was introduced in 1950 under Dushkin's guidance but soon disappeared. The established academic culture as expressed in research and professionally-oriented departments worked against an educational concept which elevated individual development to a major educational objective. The 19th century Oxford ideal that the fruit of learning is 'not a book, but a man' was apparently out of place in the Israeli context.[30]

Although the Planning and Grants Committee has recently encouraged interest in a General Studies B.A., it has been far more active in advancing new programmes indicated by its manpower studies—accounting, computer sciences, biotechnology, and health service professions. Areas defined as a national priority, such as computer sciences, even benefit through significant financial incentives. In more general terms, engineering and natural sciences receive about three-quarters of governmental allocations while the social sciences, humanities and arts share the remainder. The ethos of practicality and demonstrable utility has continued to dominate.

The institutionalization of these values has been universal. Unlike the postwar European experience where the opening of new universities provided opportunities for educational innovation and the creation of alternatives, Israeli institutional development followed the path of imitation. Typically, local leaders in Haifa, Tel Aviv and Beersheva sought to transplant that which existed at the Hebrew University or the Technion. Imitation was abetted by the fact that the older institutions generally superintended the early development of the new ones. This process was possible or perhaps inevitable because the system of higher education developed in Israel without the benefit of a coherent national education policy and a central authority responsible for implementing it.[31]

Diaspora Jewry also continues to contribute to the maintenance of a utilitarian ethos. They not only established higher education and have continued to finance it, they participate in its governance. Up to a third of the members of Board of Governors of Israeli universities and their executive committees are drawn from foreign supporters. Moreover, it is common that the Chairman of the Board of Governors is a prominent Jew from the Diaspora. It is even expected that he will have sufficient stature to be able to intervene effectively in a time of financial crisis with the government on behalf of his university.

The impact of this continuing involvement of world Jewry was noted by Professor Selig Brodetsky, President of the Hebrew University just after Independence. A recent immigrant from England, Brodetsky observed that this unusual system of funding reflects a pattern of governance and control that is unique. He found that the university was of and for the Jewish people, 'a people's university', he claimed:

> As far as the Hebrew University is concerned, it is essentially a people's university. Although it receives a small measure of

State aid today, the Government plays no part in the shaping of its policy, and even if that aid should be multiplied many times over the University would still remain firm in it determination to maintain its intellectual freedom and its liberty to appraise and to criticise.

Independence from intervention and direction remain a fair description of the relationship between Israeli universities and the government.[32]

It is reasonable to expect that where higher education has been a product of a governmental decision and controlled by state authorities, its objectives are defined in terms of satisfying the needs of the state. In the Israeli case the same result has been achieved, even though universities long preceded the establishment of the State - and despite the fact that governance and finances significantly depend on external sources. Indeed, the active participation of world Jewry has probably mitigated any thought of imposing a national system characterized by institutional specialization. It has also reinforced the commitment of all universities to well-established patterns of service since it is the opportunity to participate in nation-building that continues to excite the imagination and define the responsibility of the Diaspora. As Buber, Weizmann and Feiwel advocated at the beginning of the century, Israeli higher education has developed through a unique and fruitful partnership between the Jewish people in the Diaspora and in their homeland. This partnership is likely to ensure that Israeli universities continue to be instruments for national development.

Notes

1. Such claims are to be found most clearly and authoritatively expressed in the Annual Reports of the Council of Higher Education. See, for example, Council for Higher Educational, The Planning and Grants Committee, *Annual Report No. 8; Academic Year 1980/81*, pp. 8-9.
2. For a background on Israeli universities see Joseph Ben-David, 'Universities in Israel: dilemmas of growth, diversification and administration', *Studies in Higher Education*, 11, no. 2 (1986), pp. 105-30; Yaacov Iram, 'Higher Education in Transition—the Case of Israel—A Comparative Study', *Higher Education*, 9 (1980), pp. 81-95.
3. Martin Buber, Berthold Feiwel and Chaim Weizmann, *Eine Jüdische Hochschule* (Berlin, 1902) [Hebrew translation, Jerusalem, 1958]. See, too, David Biale, 'The Idea of a Jewish University', *Like All the Nations? The Life and Legacy of Judah L. Magnes*, ed. by W. Brinner and M. Rischin (New York, 1987), pp. 127-8.
4. For a useful essay on German higher education see Eric Ashby, 'The Future of the Nineteenth Century Idea of the University', *Minerva*, 6 (1967), pp. 3-17. For the influence of the German colonization experience on Zionism see Derek Penslar, 'Engineering Utopia: The World Zionist Organization and the Settlement of Palestine, 1897-1914', unpublished PhD dissertation, University of California at Berkeley, 1987.
5. Penslar, pp. 79-96.
6. Penslar, pp. 99-100.
7. Kurt Grunwald, 'Jewish Schools under Foreign Flags in Ottoman Palestine', *Studies of Palestine during the Ottoman Period*, ed. by Moshe Ma'oz (Jerusalem, 1975); Norman Bentwich, *Jewish Schools in Palestine* (New York, 1912). For a fuller discussion see S. Ilan Troen and Walter Ackerman, 'The History of Childhood in Israel', *Children in Comparative and Historical Perspective: An International Handbook*, ed. by R. Hiner and D. Hawes (Westport, 1991).
8. Frederick Rudolf, *The American College and University: A History* (New York, 1965), ch. 12 and Lawrence Veysey, *The Emergence of the American University* (Chicago, 1965), pp. 131ff.
9. *The Hebrew University of Jerusalem: Its History and Development* (Jerusalem, 1942), pp. 1-6; *Hebrew University of Jerusalem: Its History and Development* (Jerusalem, 1939), pp. 4-7.
10. Such statements are to be found throughout the publicity material produced by the institutions. See, for example, Weizmann Institute of Science, *Rehovot*, vol. 10 (1989), no. 4.
11. Ben-Gurion, David and Ben-Zvi, Itzhak, *Eretz Israel in the Past and in the Present*, [Hebrew] (Jerusalem, 1979). For an elaboration of the topic see Troen, S. Ilan , 'Calculating the "Economic Absorptive Capacity" of Palestine; A Study of the Political Uses of Scientific Research', *Contemporary Jewry*, vol. 10 (1989), no. 2, pp. 19-38.
12. *The Hebrew University of Jerusalem 1925-1950* (Jerusalem, 1950), pp. 84-5.
13. *The Hebrew University of Jerusalem 1925-1950*, pp. 128-9.
14. *The Hebrew University of Jerusalem 1925-1950*, pp. 130ff.

15. *The Hebrew University of Jerusalem 1925-1950*, pp. 124-7.
16. *Inauguration of the Hebrew University of Jerusalem* (Jerusalem, 1925), pp. 36-41; see, too, Bialik, Chaim [Hayyim] N., *Bialik's Speeches on the Hebrew University* (Jerusalem, 1937) [Hebrew].
17. Rinott, Moshe, *Hilfsverein der deutschen Jüden—Creation and Struggle*, [Hebrew] (Jerusalem, 1971) and Alpert, Carl, *Technion: The Story off Israel's Institute of Technology* (New York, 1982), pp. 36-75.
18. Klausner, Joseph, *Menachem Ussishkin* (London, 1940), pp. 55-6; Biale, p. 136.
19. Troen, 'Calculating the "Economic Absorptive Capacity" of Palestine'.
20. Reifenberg, A., 'The struggle between the "Desert and the Sown"', in *Desert Research: Proceedings. International Symposium Held in Jerusalem, May 7-14, 1952. Sponsored by the Research Council of Israel and UNESCO, Jerusalem: 1953*, pp. 378-391. This position was probably most popularly advocated by Lowdermilk, Walter C., *Palestine: Land of Promise* (London, 1944).
21. Alpert, pp. 115ff and 202-16.
22. Sherman, Arnold and Paul Hirschhorn, *Handbook of Israeli High Technology* (Jerusalem, 1986), pp. 110-122; Alpert, pp. 236ff.
23. Ratner, Yochanan, *My Life and Myself* (Tel Aviv, 1979) [Hebrew], pp. 217 ff; Orren, Elchanan, *Settlement in the Years of Struggle; Settlement Strategy before the State, 1936-1947* (Jerusalem, 1978) [Hebrew].
24. Wigoder, Geoffrey, *The Crown of Wisdom: Sixty Years of the Hebrew University*, typescript, Jerusalem, Hebrew University, April 1985, pp. 173-4.
25. Kroyanker, David, *Jerusalem: Planning and Development 1982-1985*, New Trends (Jerusalem, 1985); Hashimshoni, A, Schweid, Y and Z. Hashimshoni, *Jerusalem Master Plan 1968* (Jerusalem, 1972) [Hebrew]; Wigoder, pp. 197-211.
26. Wigoder, pp. 194-212.
27. Wigoder, pp. 115-19.
28. Goren, Arthur A., ed., *Dissenter in Zion: From the Writings of Judah L. Magnes* (Cambridge, 1982), ch. 4; and Band, A., 'Gown and Town' in *Like All the Nations? The Life and Legacy of Judah L. Magnes*, pp. 155-63.
29. *The Hebrew University of Jerusalem 1925-1950*, pp.120-4.
30. Council of Higher Education, Planning and Grants Committee, *Studies for the 'Bachelor's' Degree in the Basic Sciences in Israel*, ed. by J. Ben-David and Y. Nevo (Jerusalem, 1980) [Hebrew].
31. For background on the founding of the Planning and Grants Committee see Aranne, Lydia, *Government Policy Toward Higher Education in Israel* (Jerusalem, 1970); Iram, Yaacov, 'Quality and Control in Higher Education in Israel', *European Journal of Education*, 22, no. 2 (1987), pp. 145-59.
32. *The Hebrew University of Jerusalem 1925-1950*, pp. 161-5.

SMOLENSKIN, BEN-YEHUDA, AND THE JEWISH EDUCATION OF THE FUTURE

George Mandel

In the years 1879-81 an important debate took place in the Hebrew press between Peretz Smolenskin, who was one of the leading figures in the Hebrew *Haskalah*, and Eliezer Ben-Yehuda, who made his debut in public life with the article that initiated the debate.[1] One of the things about which they disagreed was the nature of the education that was desirable for Jewish children in the modern world. I shall argue in this article that their views on this subject may well reflect differences between their own educational experiences. Ben-Yehuda's contributions to the debate and, even more, his account (in his autobiography) of his own schooldays in Russia in the mid-1870s suggest that his experiences at school played an important part in the formation of his Zionist views and the formulation of his reasons for opposing the programme for the Jewish future that Smolenskin had been putting forward since the beginning of the decade.[2]

Smolenskin believed that Jewry was in danger of extinction through total assimilation into the Gentile majority. The source of the danger, in his view, was the doctrine that he used to refer to as the '*Haskalah* of Berlin' (after the city in which Moses Mendelssohn had lived and worked) because Smolenskin believed that the doctrine had originated with Mendelssohn and his disciples. According to this doctrine Jewishness was purely a matter of religion and no longer had any national connotation; by nationality, Jews were French or German or whatever, according to the country in which they lived and whose citizenship they held.

Smolenskin's way of combating this—in his eyes—false doctrine was to put forward an alternative, 'true', doctrine: that the Jews were indeed a nation, though of a unique kind. They were 'a people of the spirit', whose nationality was wholly cultural, with no political or territorial aspects.

Ben-Yehuda, too, believed that the Jewish people was in danger of extinction through assimilation (though he was more inclined than Smolenskin to believe that Jews could survive in the Diaspora as a purely religious group[3]). In particular, he agreed with Smolenskin that the Hebrew language was in danger of dying out as an active force in Jewish life. However, Ben-Yehuda argued that the only way to prevent this was for the Jews to re-settle Palestine in large numbers and make Hebrew their everyday spoken language there. The Jews who did this would be safe from assimilation because of the concentration of so many of them in one place, and because the various communities in Syria (a geographical term that then included Palestine) lived separately in such a way as to prevent assimilation.[4]

Ben-Yehuda thus agreed with Smolenskin that the main danger facing the Jewish people was that of assimilation, but he disagreed about the best way to meet that danger. This disagreement stemmed from a difference in the way the two men understood the nature of the threat. According to Ben-Yehuda it was not the *Haskalah* of Berlin, or any other ideology, that was the chief cause of assimilation; it was the conditions of modern life themselves that were the cause. Now that the Jews had emerged from the ghetto they were bound to be influenced strongly by the non-Jewish environment:

> Is the Berlin Enlightenment alone the cause bringing all this evil down upon us? Actually, even in countries where the Jews have never heard of the name Moses Mendelssohn or of his teachings, Jewish youth is repeating the pattern of the Jews in Germany by turning away from its people and from the language of its forefathers. The *Maskilim* of Berlin wrote many books and created elaborate theories to prove that we are not a people; the Jews of all other countries, in every land where the sun of enlightenment has shone upon them, are thinking the same way, with only the difference that they do not find it necessary to waste many words in justifying themselves.[5]

This disagreement between Smolenskin and Ben-Yehuda is reflected in their views on education. Given their shared wish to combat assimilation, it is hardly surprising that both writers were concerned with the question of how best to educate Jewish children in such a way that they would remain faithful to the Jewish people when they grew up. Smolenskin's recommendations may be found in his essay 'Et la'asot' ('A time to act') which appeared in 1872-3.[6] Granted, he wrote, that under existing circumstances it was not possible to impart to all Jews a thorough knowledge of Hebrew and Jewish law, yet one thing *was* possible: to teach all Jewish children enough Hebrew to make them able to read the Hebrew Scriptures. During the hour every schoolday that Gentile children spent on religious education, Jewish children should study the Bible, and if they did this for three or four years under skilled teachers they would be able to understand it in the original language.[7] This would be enough to make them faithful to their people even in later life.[8]

We do not know whether Ben-Yehuda ever read 'Et la'asot', with its specific proposals for the way in which the teaching of the Hebrew Bible was to be accomplished within the framework of a modern general education, but the idea that Jewish children should be taught the Scriptures in Hebrew is found elsewhere in Smolenskin's writings and was well-known to be an important part of his programme. In particular, it is found in the last section of his later essay 'Et lata'at' ('A time to plant').[9] We know from references in Ben-Yehuda's works that he was familiar with this essay;[10] indeed, we shall see later that he wrote an explicit reply to a proposal made in the last section of it.

Unlike Smolenskin, Ben-Yehuda had no faith in the power of schoolteachers to instil a knowledge of Hebrew into Jewish children:

> Our national-minded authors cry 'Teach your children Hebrew': excellent advice, but we are powerless to follow it, because children do not do everything that their parents want them to. The young will not obey our command to learn Hebrew, just as we disobeyed our parents' instructions not to follow the prophets of the *Haskalah*. Time and place rule a man and determine his direction. In our days, and in the lands where we dwell, no amount of effort to teach our children Hebrew will succeed. It's a dead language for the new generation, no better than Greek or Latin, and just as pupils abandon these languages when they leave school, so Jewish children will abandon Hebrew...
>
> Let those who have tried to teach their children Hebrew stand up and say whether I am not right! Which of our *maskilim* and learned men have children who know Hebrew and care about it?[11]

Although Smolenskin is not mentioned here by name, Ben-Yehuda surely had him in mind when he wrote of the 'national-minded authors [who] cry: "Teach your children Hebrew"'.

Smolenskin also proposed setting up seminaries to train rabbis and teachers, in which the pupils would study both Torah and general (*i.e.*, non-Jewish) subjects.[12] 'On this great and weighty step', he wrote in the last section of 'Et Lat'at', 'depends the existence of Israel, its Torah, its learning, its honour, its unity, and its strength in the days to come'.[13] This provoked an explicit attack from Ben-Yehuda, who wrote that few parents would send their children to these seminaries, and asked rhetorically whether those children who did attend them would not forget whatever Hebrew they had learned as soon as they left them, just as was happening with Latin and Greek.[14] 'Won't the child regard [Hebrew] as a heavy burden placed on it by its parents and teachers....?'[15] Ben-Yehuda usually referred to Smolenskin with respect even when disagreeing with him. Here, for the only time, he was provoked to sarcasm at Smolenskin's expense:

> [Smolenskin wants] to strengthen our declining national consciousness... to unite all Jews in feeling... to plant the hope of redemption in all our hearts... and therefore he proposes ... rabbinical seminaries!
>
> Rabbinical seminaries will perform all these miracles. They will infuse a different spirit into the whole people, they will bring about a change of heart....[16]

It seems clear today that Ben-Yehuda was right and that Smolenskin did not understand the strength of the impersonal social forces operating to whittle away knowledge of Hebrew among the Jews. Ben-Yehuda was perhaps the first person who did grasp what was happening — the first, at any rate, to explain it in print. This difference in perception may well have some of its roots in the differences between the educations that they themselves had received. In their early years, both received the traditional Jewish education of the *heder* and the *yeshivah,* and both were eventually attracted by the *Haskalah*. Ben-Yehuda, however, who was born some seventeen years later than Smolenskin, in the relatively liberal reign of Tsar Alexander II, then went to a Russian state school (in Dünaburg), something Smolenskin never did. In his autobiography Ben-Yehuda described how the influence of his fellow-pupils turned him into a supporter of the Russian revolutionary movement:

> Not many days passed before I became a nihilist in all respects, like most of my school friends, particularly the Jewish ones. Without much hesitation I, too, vowed to dedicate my whole life to the people—that is to say, the *Russian* people!...
>
> There is no need to say that the more nihilism captivated my soul, the further I drifted away from the Jews and from all the concerns of the Jewish community, which seemed to me so

> small and insignificant in comparison with the great Russian people! Slowly, all the threads that connect each individual Jew to the Jewish people snapped within me, one after the other. Nothing in Jewish life interested me any more, and I felt myself—or at least it seemed to me that I felt myself — to be completely Russian.[17]

In spite of this Ben-Yehuda did not leave the Jewish fold for good, and in his last year at school he became a Jewish nationalist, largely because of the influence on him of the Bulgarian national movement. However, he was far from typical in this respect. The great majority of his Jewish school-fellows rejected his new beliefs and remained aloof from Jewish concerns. It seems unlikely that attempts to instil a love of Hebrew or feelings of Jewish loyalty into the Jewish pupils at Dünaburg, even if made by good teachers, would have stood much chance of success. It is therefore not hard to understand why Ben-Yehuda found Smolenskin's arguments unconvincing.

It is also not hard to guess at a connection between Smolenskin's views and his own education. He and his fellow-*maskilim* had succeeded in learning European languages, which they had had to teach themselves or, at least, study at their own initiative outside any organized educational framework. Why, then, should not Jewish children of a later generation be able to master Hebrew, particularly if it were to be taught to them at school? Ben-Yehuda's reply is that Smolenskin is neglecting the question of motivation, including what today would be called peer-group pressure. The *maskilim* had felt a strong desire to learn European languages; Jewish children feel no such desire to learn Hebrew. In an open letter to Smolenskin, Ben-Yehuda wrote that 'our youth are abandoning our language—and why? Because in their eyes it is a dead and useless tongue.'[18] Earlier in the letter he compared Hebrew with Latin and Greek,[19] a comparison that we have found twice before in his writings. Clearly, it was one that appealed to him.

Even before criticizing Smolenskin's ideas concerning Jewish education, Ben-Yehuda had put forward proposals of his own. Not long after he first advocated the resettlement of Palestine by Jews he wrote two articles about education in that country.[20] The most important proposal in them was that Hebrew be made the language of instruction in the Jewish schools, so that the children would get used to speaking it 'always, even for personal and intimate matters'.[21] What we have here is a glimpse of the idea for which Ben-Yehuda later became famous, viz., the revival of spoken Hebrew. He had come to believe that even in a Jewish Palestine Hebrew could not survive as a mainly literary language, used side-by-side with other, spoken languages. In the event, making Hebrew the language of the classroom did indeed prove to be the single most effective step in bringing about its revival as a spoken tongue.[22] It is perhaps more than mere chance that the idea of the revival should have made its first appearance in an article by Ben-Yehuda whose subject was Jewish education.

Notes

1. On this debate, see G. Alkas, 'Ha-pulmus ha-'ideologi bein Smolenskin u-Ben-Yehuda', *Ha-'olam* (2 January 1941), pp. 203-4; A. Hertzberg, *The Zionist Idea* (New York, 1959), pp. 142-65; G. Mandel, 'The Debate between Peretz Smolenskin and Eliezer Ben-Yehuda', to be published in the proceedings of the International Inter-Disciplinary Conference on Peretz Smolenskin held in Oxford in 1991.
2. For a fuller discussion of the reasons for Ben-Yehuda's conversion to 'Zionism' before the invention of the word), see G. Mandel, 'Why did Ben-Yehuda suggest the revival of spoken Hebrew?' in L. Glinert (ed.), *Hebrew in Ashkenaz* (New York, 1993), pp. 193-207.
3. P. Smolenskin, *Ma'amarim*, vol. II (Jerusalem, 1925), p. 30 (English version in Hertzberg, *The Zionist Idea*, p. 146); *Kol kitvei Eliezer Ben-Yehuda*, vol. I (Jerusalem-Talpioth, 1941), p. 32 (Arabic pagination) (Hertzberg, p. 165). All subsequent references to *Kol kitvei* in these notes are likewise to volume I (the only one that appeared) and, unless otherwise stated, to the section paginated with Arabic numerals.
4. *Kol kitvei*, pp. 54-5, from Ben-Yehuda's article "Al devar ha-hinnukh' which first appeared in *Havatzelet*, X (Jerusalem, 1879-80), issues 13 and 14.
5. Hertzberg, *The Zionist Idea*, p. 163. The passage is from 'Mikhtav le-Ven-Yehudah'(*Kol kitvei*, pp. 27-33 or *Ha-shahar*, X, pp. 241-5) which was written in December, 1880.
6. *Ha-shahar*, IV (Vienna, 1872-3), pp. 1-8, 65-72, 129-44; reprinted in P. Smolenskin, *Ma'amarim*, vol. I (Jerusalem, 1925), pp. 164-205.
7. *Ma'amarim*, vol. I, p. 176.
8. Ibid., p. 177. On this page, Smolenskin speaks of the children studying the Hebrew Bible 'for four or five years' rather than 'for three or four years' as on the preceding page.
9. *Ma'amarim*, vol. II, p. 285. 'Et lata'at' was first published in *Ha-shahar*, vols. VI (1874-5), VIII (1876-7) and IX (1877-9).
10. *Kol kitvei*, pp. 8 (Hebrew pagination), 59.
11. *Kol kitvei*, pp. 75-6. The quotation is from Ben-Yehuda's essay 'Degel hale'umiyyut' which appeared in *Ha-maggid* (Lyck), XXIV, 1880, issues 35-7.
12. *Ma'amarim*, vol. II, pp. 286-90 (from 'Et lata'at').
13. Ibid., p. 286.
14. *Kol kitvei*, pp. 60-1, from 'Self maskileinu' *Havatzelet*, X, issues 28 and 29.
15. Ibid., p. 61.
16. Ibid., p. 60.

17. *Kol kitvei*, pp. 6-7 (Hebrew pagination), from Chapter Two of Ben-Yehuda's autobiography, *Ha-halom ve-shivro*. English translation by T. Muraoka: *A Dream Come True* (Boulder, etc., 1993).
18. *Kol kitvei*, p. 30; English translation from Hertzberg, p. 163 (with slight emendations).
19. *Kol kitvei*, p. 29; Hertzberg, p. 161.
20. 'She'elat hahinnukh' and 'Al devar hahinnukh', *Kol kitvei*, pp. 43-56. The articles first appeared in *Havatzelet* in November 1879 and January 1880.
21. *Kol kitvei*, p. 53.
22. C. Rabin, A short history of the Hebrew language (Jerusalem n.d. [1973]), pp. 70-3; J. Fellman, The revival of a classical tongue. Eliezer Ben-Yehuda and the modern Hebrew language (The Hague, 1973), pp. 48-55, 94-111, 117-8.

PURPOSE AND LANGUAGE IN TWO SEVENTEENTH CENTURY PADUAN HEBREW CHRONICLES*

Alan David Crown

The Jewish community of Padua suffered two major calamities in the seventeenth century. These were the outbreak of the plague in 1631-2 which decimated the ghetto, and the riot in August 1684 when the citizens of Padua attacked the ghetto and blood was shed on both sides. Both of these events are well documented.[1] One of the Rabbis of Padua, Abraham Catalano,[2] chronicled the events of 1632 in his moving and vivid diary of the plague, *Olam hafukh*.[3] The second event is recorded by Solomon Eliezer Ghirondi in his work *Sefer ma'aseh nisim*[4] which was written in Padua in the year of the events recorded therein. Both works are couched in substantially different styles though they have common grammatical elements and the difference between their styles is instructive for the history of the language in the period. The purpose of this study is to consider the contribution of these chronicles to our knowledge of the Hebrew of the period.

In the several histories of Hebrew that have now been written,[5] there is a uniform tendency towards a commitment to the thesis that development and change in Hebrew is diachronically based. Thus, the conclusion is unavoidable from all these sources that the formative influences on the style and language in which a text is written are most likely to be primarily the period and secondarily the place in which it is composed. In any event there

---

* This article is written in acknowledgement of David Patterson's special contribution to our knowledge of the development and enrichment of the Hebrew language in the last two centuries.

is a marked tendency in our current histories of the language to gloss over the Hebrew of the seventeenth century and Italy gets short shrift indeed.

Despite this consensus a comparison of the texts before us suggests that some modification is needed to the emphasis placed on chronology in evaluating the writing of Hebrew in seventeenth century Italy, for despite the common language elements there are substantial differences in style which seem to be related to the purpose for which these texts were written and it appears that purpose in writing is a factor which needs to be taken into consideration. Let us first consider the purpose for which the later text was written and its contribution to our knowledge of the Hebrew of the period.

In 1684, during the siege of Buda by the armies of Venice, Austria and Poland the rumour was put about that the Jews of Buda had assisted the Turks in their defence of the city against the besiegers.[6] One result of this allegation was the outbreak of anti-Jewish riots in Italy, not the least of which was in Padua. On Sunday 20 August 1684, the citizens of Padua attacked the ghetto, and though the onslaught was frustrated by the civic authorities of Padua, with the assistance of the Venetian rulers, some blood was shed on both sides and considerable anxiety was felt by the Jews who feared that the incident would develop into a wholesale massacre.

Contemporary Jewish writers spoke of the escape as a miracle. Until the second world war destabilized the Paduan community, the 10th of Ellul (the day before the riot began according to Ghirondi) was observed by the Paduan Jewish community—under the terms of the Talmudic injunction to give thanks after escape from danger— as a special Purim known as the Purim of Buda.

Several descriptions of this incident have been published, as well as a number of Italian documents which relate to these events.[7] While *Sefer ma'aseh nisim* presents a concise summary of events in and around the Padua ghetto, it becomes clear from comparison with other accounts of the same events that a number of details are lacking, though they do not detract from the historical value of the document both as a specific source of information about the events described and in general, for details of the ghetto of Padua. But before the document can be mined as a source of historical data its style should be noted carefully. The work is one of that *genre* of Hebrew chronicles, well known from a slightly earlier period, which draws extensively on mutant Old Testament terminology and phrasing, sometimes utilizing single clauses and at other times incorporating whole sentences either intact or with slight changes of tense or with the addition of a few original words. Ghirondi seems to have utilized the quotation device to an extreme degree. Thus, the historian must approach Ghirondi's text with some degree of caution, for it is difficult to determine how appropriate and how

Purpose and language in 17th Century chronicles

accurate each quotation is for the event it was trying to describe and how much of the text is literary frill and embellishment for stylistic (recitative) purposes. Two examples illustrate the problem. While one may hesitate to accept as a literal description of the type of spoil to be found in the ghetto the quotation from Judges 5:30 'spoil of many colours and needlework' the description may be the literal truth, for the ghetto was a centre of the staple industry of Padua, the cloth industry. On the other hand, it may well be that the description of the gates of the ghetto as 'gates of brass' (Isaiah 45:2) may be rather more wide of the mark though the gates may well have been strengthened by metal bars.

It is also very probable that the list of occupations of the people involved in the riot (see below) should not be taken at face value but should be considered as a literary exercise with the objective of heightening the drama of the situation. The Italian Hebrew writing of the period contained many elements of such artifice and often included elaborate puns based on homophones in Hebrew and Italian.

When we make even a brief comparison with the text of Catalano's *Olam hafukh* we see that it was quite possible for a chronicler of this period and location to write in an intelligent mix of Hebrew and Italian. Ghirondi, clearly, was at considerable pains to avoid the use of Italian words or idioms even when it would have been comparatively easy to include them or when such a usage would have conveyed the meaning of his text more clearly than the Hebrew he employed. Ghirondi did transcribe proper names into Hebrew letters for there was no way of avoiding this and, strangely, the names of two different types of troops, cuirassiers and bombardiers, were also given in transcription. This exception to his rule supports the argument (see below) that there may have been an ulterior motive for this. By and large, however, Ghirondi avoided transliterating Italian words into Hebrew even though he may have been forced to rely on somewhat less specific Hebrew equivalents for Italian words which would have conveyed his meaning with greater precision. The effect on our understanding of his chronicle becomes especially clear when we examine his adaptation of Biblical Hebrew terms of rank to the Paduan nobility and officialdom. Thus the rank of *Podesta* is given the less precise equivalent of *sar* and there are a number of other Paduan officials whose precise ranking is lost because of the loose translation פחות וחורים. Whereas Catalano used the transliterated form of גיטו 'ghetto', Ghirondi employed the less precise חצר for both the ghetto and the yard of the synagogue (in which a cesspit was located) with the result that the narrative is not always clear.

By the exercise of the ingenuity which is one of the hallmarks of the 'quotation' genre Ghirondi was able to find Hebrew equivalents, whether from the Bible or from the Mishna, for almost all the words he needed, though on occasion he was forced to resort to Aramaic, resulting in a mixed phrasing. Thus we note שמא ירגום. On other occasions he drew phrasing from the Aramaic of Daniel under the influence of the association of ideas—he associated the word decree, טעם, which occurs several times in that work, with the decrees of the rulers of Padua and Venice. It is evident that some of the Hebrew equivalents he produced must rank as neologisms either because of their extension of the basic and accepted meaning to something for which there had hitherto been no equivalent, or because of his extension of a form to create a new form. Moreover, he vocalized some of his Hebrew to ensure that the correct form was read. Thus he vocalized סָפָרִים presumably to avoid confusion with the reading סְפָרִים.

Ghirondi seems to have a reasonable mastery of Hebrew. While one might consider that he copied some of his quotations directly from the written pages of the Bible—in such a manner, one supposes, he reproduced the *ketiv* reading from Jeremiah 6:25 תצאי (fol. 4 line 11 of the manuscript) rather than the *keri*, תצא —he appears in the main, to have relied upon his memory. A very clear indicator of the use of memory is the way in which the negative *al* in the source text is often presented as *lo* in the chronicle. The loose mode in which the article is employed in both Ghirondi's and Catalano's work is probably a reflex in Hebrew of the Italian usage in which the definite article is required before a noun used in the general or abstract sense. In Ghirondi the article is regularly used after the preposition ל and in Catalano it is used with the first word in the construct. However, its manifestation in the middle of Biblical quotations would suggest that Ghirondi was relying on his memory rather than copying directly from a text. The interchange of homophones in the quotation from 1 Sam. 22:2 נושה v. נושא (fol. 1 line 5) would seem to indicate an aural or memory dependence rather than a graphic dependence. In other words Ghirondi had an excellent knowlege of the Bible though he could not reproduce it accurately. Even with such a knowledge the technique of stringing together quotations and adapting them to the relevant time, gender and number must have been a chore. Likewise his invention of Hebrew neologisms for tradespeople by extending existing terms might have given the author pleasure but not the freedom to express himself. It might well have been easier for him to follow the example of Catalano and write some words in transcription from Italian. One can only suggest that Ghirondi had some purpose in mind in establishing this style other than that of presenting readers with a plain chronicle of events, despite the author's claim[8] that he was recording the incident for the sake of history.

We do not know the exact date of composition of this piece but the retrospective reference to Marco Antonio Justinian as Doge of Venice would appear to place it in the period after his Dogeship ended, that is, after 1688. By this time the escape of the Paduan community had come to be celebrated as a miraculous deliverance and was observed as a local Purim. We may suspect that Ghirondi was writing a text that would read well as a liturgy, employing phrases that had a known import, and where there was a careful series of word plays that could be played upon in the ceremonial reading. The opening phrases of the chronicle certainly seem to imitate the opening phrases of Esther, substituting the Doge's name, date and rank for the royal names and attributes in Esther. Thus, 'In the days of Marco Antonio Justinian, he being His Excellency the exalted Doge of Venice...." His pun on the name of the *bombardieri* (*bombere* may mean rogue or villain) the soldiers who changed their role in the incident, leads one to suspect that this word, which was scattered throughout the account,[9] was the occasion for merriment in the recital as when one reads the name Haman in the *Megillat Esther*.

The long prayer with which the chronicle concludes (fol. 9: line 19 to the end of the chronicle) seems to have liturgical overtones and enhances the suspicion that Ghirondi was writing a *megillah* for use in the local Purim.

Ghirondi's need was not for precision in the Hebrew language or in conveying his meaning to his listeners but for an easily read text, which was mellifluous and tripped lightly from the tongue, despite its solemn message. Thus he took liberties with words and extended their meaning. Unfortunately, there was no Hebrew revival in his day and no Ben-Yehuda to record his usage, so that his contributions to Hebrew were lost. The majority, but not all, of his contributions came in his description of the rioters, which, it might be suggested was not a real description but which was intended to be read in the local *megillah* as one reads the list of Haman's sons slain in addition to the five hundred dead of Shushan. The list is complex—it appears to rely both on the sources from which phrases were drawn and on associated ideas. Sometimes the meaning becomes clear from the association of ideas or sounds and at other times one has to rely on imagination. There are places where no association is visible whether it be in Hebrew or Italian, phone or graph. In the following translation sources are marked and the quoted words indicated by asterisks. The list reads, '...itinerant merchants of wool and linen, *of silverware, gold, garments, myrrh and spices,* (1 Kings 10:25) *all who play the lyre and the pipe*, (Genesis 4:21) knife grinders and vendors, hairdressers and scribes, vendors of wine, oil and all manner of drinks, cooks and vendors of fruit, legumes, vegetables and herbs, donkey drivers, sailors, saddlers, fishermen, hunters, wood-carvers, sculptors and embroiderers, horse and mule dealers, waggoners, coachmen and litter bearers, dyers and all who work in wool, weavers, spinners and bleachers, bakers, tailors, milliners, vendors of eggs both of domestic and wild fowl, spirit vendors, tanners, potters, vendors of cheese and of fresh and salt fish, farm labourers, vintners and husbandmen'.

Of this list we may offer the following extensions of meaning.

1) בעלי ריחיים—coachmen. In the parts of the list where this term occurs there is an association of persons working with horses, mules or driving carts. The extent of this part of the list is defined by the term ba'alei. The normal meaning of 'millstones' for reihayim does not fit the context and one looks for an alternative meaning that suits the context more closely. Ben-Yehuda[10] was aware of a meaning associated with 'someone who works with horses' a meaning which seems to derive from a Biblical context (Deuteronomy 24:6). This may well be the association here. Rabin[11] has suggested that the phrase refers to some sort of carriage with large wheels like millstones. If the following words ba'alei tzavim be read as meaning litter-bearers[12] a suitable association of ideas with some differentiation in meaning would lead us to translate this phrase as 'coachmen' with perhaps a pun on some local name for a coach with an oversized wheel.

2. חורים. The sense of 'noblemen' is hardly appropriate in the position in which the word appears in the list. It appears among a list of those who work in the manufacture of cloth, a Paduan staple industry in the seventeenth century both for the Jewish and the non-Jewish community. In this context one may assume that the word has some connection with the industry. A suitable sense is derived from the Aramaic pa'el form חוור which is well attested in Hebrew in the sense of growing pale, to whiten, and in חור, a form of white cloth. In the context of the list of occupations in the manuscript a suitable sense might be one who bleaches cloth. Such a meaning would account for the inexplicable sequence of the list which puts bakers in juxtaposition with tailors and clothiers. Unless there is some unknown meaning of 'ofim which would connect it with the cloth industry[13] the thought of bleaching or whitening cloth (and the bleacher's clothes would have been white or white in patches) clearly reminded the author of someone who was often white, from flour in this case, namely the baker, who had not yet appeared elsewhere in this artistically contrived list.

3. מושחים. In this context it is not easy to see any special meaning for this word and it might be better to consider it to be a spelling error for מושחזים. It occurs either as the last word in a list of musical performers (but the quotation from Genesis would indicate that it does not belong in this list) or else as the first word in a list of knife users and artificers. It might apply to

those who whet knives and perhaps oil them in the process, but the word *mushhazim* would serve conveniently for this.

Outside the list of occupations one notes the word מרמה (folio 3 line 11) which would seem to be inadequate in the context in the normal meaning of 'deceit'. In the context *mirmah* is used in apposition to עכבה 'delay' and should be seen as connected to that word in some appropriate way. The impression given in the text is that the leader of the cuirassiers in Padua was instructed to carry out his orders to rescue the Jews of the city from the rioters without delay and without any pretexts for not carrying out his orders. *Mirmah* would thus seem to mean 'excuse' in the context and the verse in which it appears should be read as 'without any delay and without any excuse'. Thus we see the meaning extended from 'trickery' to pretext or excuse.

Catalano's *Olam hafukh* was clearly written as a record of events in the plague of 1631-1632. The author, a young Rabbi and physician, a graduate of the medical school of the university of Padua and of the equally famous rabbinical academy of that city wrote his plague diary as a chronicle to serve as a memorial for the dead, including his own wife and children, as a detailed account of the community's inner organization to fight the plague and as a medical text to guide future generations in the use of sovereign remedies. The writer was concerned to be precise in his Hebrew and rarely resorted to direct quotations from the Bible. Instead, he wrote in a Hebrew that is a mixture of the Biblical narrative style with some of its characteristics such as the *vav* consecutive, and forms which are more akin to the spoken and literary Hebrew used today. Thus, while Catalano's Hebrew drew heavily on the Bible as an indirect source, it incorporated the Hebrew resources available to him from the Mishnah and the liturgy. Some Aramaisms occur but in the main the Hebrew is remarkably pure and intelligible. Where there was no precise equivalent to a Hebrew form the author did exactly the opposite of Ghirondi—instead of attempting to extend the limited semantic range of Biblical terms he used Italian words which he transliterated into Hebrew. Italian words were overlined to ensure that there was no danger of misunderstanding. Sometimes, usually on the first occasion an Italian word was used in transcription, he added vocalization to these words to avoid any possibility of ambiguity.[14] Subsequent usages were of the consonantal text only if the word were a proper name.

The author adapted Italian words to Hebrew usage. The most common example was the supplying of Hebrew inseparable prepositions to Italian words as if by transcription to Hebrew characters they could be treated as Hebrew forms. The only preposition not found so treated is ב. There are several instances where a Hebrew pronominal suffix was added to an Italian noun. One instance is the use of the form מאנדראט׳ in a context where it obviously means 'my commission' instead of the expected form *mandatto mia*. We may suspect that the same has happened to *quartièro,* in a context where the meaning 'his quarter' is expected. In other words the Italian *quartière* appears to have been treated as a Hebrew form and the third person singular pronominal suffix o/v has displaced the final letter in Italian. We cannot be too dogmatic about this as the word *quartièro* is also a word which regularly appears in Italian. On one occasion Catalano converted a Hebrew root, פלט to an Italian form, *palto,* overlining the word to show that it was to be understood as Italian, where it developed the meaning of 'freely'.

There is a tension between orthography and phonology in some of Catalano's transcriptions. Evidently he had problems in transcribing Italian sounds into Hebrew characters and experimented, producing different forms of the same word. The transcription of the word *petécchia,* 'typhus spots', is an obvious example. Catalano was clearly uncertain as to how to transcribe the cluster *eccia* (=ekia) and produced the forms פיטיג׳י and פיטצ׳י. He was clearly dissatisfied with his first attempt (perhaps because d also served to transcribe the nasal ñ as in *montagna*) and used the second transcription thereafter. Despite the obvious intention of giving a degree of precision to the narrative by using Italian words, the tension between phonology and orthography means that sometimes words are not as easily translated as the author would have liked. One example is in the still unsolved problem of the form מוזי. The word which best fits the context is the Italian *mucchio,* 'wagon load' (of corn), but the transcription system in the manuscript does not allow us to see such a word in the Hebrew characters. On the one hand we may suggest that Catalano's uncertainty of the proper transcription of the 'k' phone led him to present the form found or, alternatively, in the Paduan dialect of the period the word *mucchio* was softened to *muschi* in pronunciation. An equally difficult example is the word אינויסטיתי which, according to Freedman's principles of transcription should be read as *investi di* but the word makes better sense if it is read as a passive participle 'investiti'—invested in.

Several characteristics of Catalano's Hebrew would appear to be Italian rather than Hebrew. Some of these are echoed in the work of Ghirondi. The parallel usages between Ghirondi and Catalano reminds us that we cannot entirely set aside the location or the chronological factor. Despite a general shortage of pronouns which is not always compensated for by pronominal suffixes on the verbs (a reflex of Italian practice?) the chronicle begins with a strangely placed first person singular pronoun, אני viz. ראיתי אני עני that is, I myself have seen ....In this case אני = the Italian *mi*. To some extent the Hebrew imperfect takes on an omni-temporal form. While this may well be, according to Hebrew theorists, where the imperfect in biblical Hebrew originated, its use in this document is no prescient archaizing but combines both the future of Hebrew and the Italian conditional which, in expressing uncertainty, doubt, hypothesis, uses the form of the future.

Of the fifteen paragraphs beginning with ויהי the word is used as a semi-auxilliary with a following infinitive construct in a least seven instances. In each instance the following clause focuses on a continuing situation or a conditional or subjunctive idea. The underlying grammatical structure is Italianate and not Hebrew. In the remaining cases *vayehi* is followed by a preposition with telic force and a verb in the perfect to continue the narrative.

Another form of narrative consecution tends to be achieved with the sequence אז usually, but not always, followed by an imperfect followed by a *vav* consecutive or by the structure אחר הדברים האלה followed by a perfect.

Both Catalano and Ghirondi employ some abbreviations כמהר. הקק. הנל. Both of them use the indicator of the object את rather sparingly.

The negative in both Ghirondi and Catalano reflects an Italian and not a Hebrew usage, viz. לא פשע ולא חטאת = non...nè.

In both texts passive forms of the verb appear both in *niph'al* and *pu'al*, with a preference for the *pu'al*, for example, מעומד ומוטבע בצואה. The *nitpa'el* form is quite frequent in Catalano but not in Ghirondi.

It is clear from the comparison of these texts that the differences between them do not simply reflect a chronological stage through which Hebrew passed but reflect the purposes for which the texts were written. Catalano's purpose was to convey information precisely and scientifically for readers, not just in Italy but wherever Jews were to be found. It is easy enough to criticise the style of Catalano on the grounds that it is replete with 'incorrect grammar and sytax, unidiomatic expressions and confusion of Hebrew and Talmudic Aramaic'[15]. We cannot deny, of course, that the style is heavily influenced by Italian—clearly the place in which the text is written has a major influence on the vocabulary and syntax of the text—but Catalano's account is heavily shaped by the need to convey information in terms which the reader would understand, so that he felt free to add Italian words where Hebrew was inadequate. By contrast, Ghirondi's purpose appears to have been to create a more elegant, or at least, pseudo-biblical, piece that would take its place in the local liturgy. In itself it is by no means a work of quality and cannot match the prose and poetry of the Golden Age in Spain. It is a pastiche from the Old Testament, mixed with Aramaisms, ungrammatical with but a few flashes of an inventive mind. It too contains Italian traces in that it uses the local names in transcription and has grammatical forms, clearly influenced by contemporary vernacular usage, in common with those of Catalano. Nevertheless, the text is a valuable caution to us that every diaspora writing of the period should be considered not solely in terms of locality or chronology and integration into a diachronic picture developed by the historians of Hebrew but in terms of the purpose of its author. Rabin's sympathetic judgement of the Hebrew of this age[16] does not go far enough. It is not just the age that mattered, nor even its locale—it is the objective for which a Hebrew text was written which ultimately governed its form.

Notes

1. See C. Roth, *Il Purim di Buda* (1934) and idem, *A History of the Jews in Italy* (Philadelphia, 1946), pp. 388-9; and G. Gabrielli, *Italia Judaica* (Roma, 1924). See also R. Calimani, *The Ghetto of Venice* (Milano, 1988), p. 151.
2. On Catalano and his affairs see the index in Edwardo Morpurgo, *Notizie sulle Famiglie Ebree Esistite a Padova nel XVI Secolo* (Udine, 1909), p. 5. Strangely enough Ghirondi is not included in this listing.
3. The text is known to us in at least two manuscripts. The first of these is preserved in the British Library, BL Or 27047 where the same manuscript contains some additional poems on the subject by Moses Catalano and the second is Catalano's autograph copy in the Montefiore collection.
4. Not to be confused with a work of the same name by Jacob Cohen which describes events in the Ancona Purim of 1796. The text is known to us from a manuscript in the Montefiore collection.
5. See the long article in the *Encyclopaedia Judaica*, and E. Y. Kutscher, *A History of the Hebrew Language* (Jerusalem and Leiden, 1982) and Chaim Rabin, *A Short History of the Hebrew Language* (Jerusalem, 1973). These and other works tend to follow the same theme, that Hebrew responds to both the place and the time in which it is written. While the writer has no disagreement with this it is clear that a third factor, often neglected, is the purpose for which a text was written.
6. See Roth, *A History of the Jews in Italy*, pp. 388-9.
7. Cf. A. Büchler, 'Buda, Purim of' in *Jewish Encyclopaedia* (New York, 1902). Büchler claimed that the Buda Purim was partly in honour of the Jews of Buda in the belief that they were, in fact involved in the defence of the city. However, Ghirondi denies this in his account. He would appear to be supported by Fr Marco d'Aviano in a letter of 1 October 1684. See A. Ciscato, *Gli Ebrei in Padova* (Padova, 1901) document XXX and G. Gabrielli, Italia Judaica (Rome, 1924), pp. 38-9, 64 and Büchler, loc. cit. for bibliography.
8. The author says 'write this for the sake of the next generation in order that you can recount it to your children'.
9. A quotation from Ps. 115:6 'and they had mouths and they spoke not and ears and they heard not' attaches to the name *bombardieri* and leaves one with the impression that this is an oblique anti-Christian polemic. Such an interpretation would support the idea that the name *bombardieri* was greeted with a burst of noise.

10. See E. Ben-Yehuda, *A Dictionary Thesaurus of the Hebrew Language* (New York, 1960 edn.) p. 6531, n. 4.
11. In a private communication in which a number of words in this passage were discussed.
12. See Jacob Moreira, *Kehillat Ya'akov* (London, 1772), p. 96.
13. It is not impossible that the author has needed to find some word to describe the weavers of the fine organza mesh produced by the newly flourishing silk industry and worked from a hypothetical root 'thick web' to describe the fine weave of this web-like material which became a Padua staple. See Jastrow, *Dictionary of the Targumim*, p. 107.
14. See the work of Alan Freedman, *Italian Texts in Hebrew Characters*, Mainzer Romanische Arbeiten, Bd. viii (Wiesbaden, 1972), who demonstrates that the transcription of Hebrew words in Italian was done according to reasonably fixed principles to avoid ambiguity.
15. See Chaim Rabin, *A Short History of the Hebrew Language* (1st edn., Jerusalem, 1973), p. 60.
16. Ibid., p. 60, 'it would be better to take it [Hebrew of the seventeenth century] as an expression of a period of upheaval and ferment in which the urge for decorativeness and clever tricks brought about a 'breaking of the vessels' in language.

MOSES MENDELSSOHN AS POLITICAL EDUCATOR

Lionel Kochan

Mendelssohn, as Jewish thinker, has always been the object of controversy and this is almost as true of the contemporary world as of the past.[1] This in itself testifies not only to the importance of his thought but also to its continuing relevance. As I hope to show, despite the momentous and tragic events which have transformed the optimism of the late eighteenth century into the uncertainty and pessimism of the late twentieth, it is Mendelssohn who first staked out the framework within which organized Jewish life could be acceptable to the modern world. It might indeed be argued that he taught the Jews how to live in the modern world.

This is all the more surprising given that the bulk of Mendelssohn's philosophical and other works does not concern itself with Jewish matters at all. Nevertheless, it is as an exponent of precisely such matters that the memory of Mendelssohn survives and flourishes. His participation in the German and European Enlightenment is all but eclipsed by his contribution to the Jewish cause—in particular by his work as educationalist.

The translation and interpretation of the Pentateuch (the *Biur*), produced under Mendelssohn's aegis and with his co-operation is one significant testimony to this endeavour. This work would serve both to facilitate the linguistic assimilation of German Jewry to its environment and also to stem its growing lack of familiarity with Hebrew. Influential contemporary rabbis such as Rabbi Ezekiel Landau, the Chief Rabbi of Prague, did not welcome Mendelssohn's work, fearing that it would achieve the former objective at the expense of the latter.[2] But later generations took a more favourable view and the *Biur* and translation won broad acceptance in rabbinical circles as an invaluable pedagogic tool.[3]

If the *Biur* can be seen in the light of Mendelssohn's activity as religio-cultural educator, then his treatise *Jerusalem or On Religious Power and Judaism*, stands out as his contribution to the political education of the Jews. There is a strong and undeniable element of paradox here, for the treatise is addressed primarily to the Christian world.[4] For all that, the resonance of the work, and its relevance, was to be felt particularly in Jewish circles, particularly in respect of Jewish self-perception, at a crucial epoch in its evolution towards the modern world.

This is not immediately obvious. Mendelssohn presents *Jerusalem* as an exercise in political theory, supposedly dissociated from contemporary concerns. He is, by his own admission, engaged in the quest for an answer to the familiar question: 'Which form of government is the best?'[5] The frame of reference is the relationship of church and state. This is ostensibly a wholly abstract enquiry to which Mendelssohn gives a wholly abstract response: 'Under all circumstances and conditions, I consider the infallible measure of the excellence of a form of government to lie in the degree to which it achieves its purposes by morals and convictions; in the degree, therefore, to which government is by education itself.'[6] As for the relationship of church and state, this must be neither discordant nor agreed; only the disunion of the two bodies will enable liberty of conscience to flourish.[7]

In keeping with this approach, the first part of *Jerusalem* contains scarcely any specific reference to existing states or churches or political institutions. This apparent abstraction and pose of detachment from contemporary concerns does not correspond to Mendelssohn's objective. To some extent this has been acknowledged, even by those historians—such as Alexander Altmann—who prefer to understand *Jerusalem* as an exercise in political theory. It is true that Altmann speaks of Mendelssohn's hope that his work 'would reinforce the cause of Jewish civil admission'; that his was 'an ultimately Jewish concern aiming...at the removal of oppressive laws that deny the Jew civil equality'; that Mendelssohn's 'plea for liberty of conscience and civic equality, which is at the heart of the work as a whole, was meant to secure for the Jewish people a fair share in the modern world which was about to dawn'.[8] But this is valuable rather as exposition of Mendelssohn's real agenda than as an indication of the particular circumstances to which *Jerusalem* was a response. Far from being a search to determine 'which form of government is the best', Mendelssohn's search has the narrower aim of determining which form is 'best' for the Jews—though there is no conflict between the particular and the general in this context. What is 'good for the Jews' is no less good for everyone else.

Mendelssohn epitomises this in terms of a government that rules 'by morals and convictions';[9] and this in terms of contemporary Jewish life is translated into a demand for the disbandment of the contemporary *kehillah*, the dissolution of its institutions and the abrogation of rabbinical authority, particularly the authority to issue writs of excommunication (*herem*) against recalcitrants and lawbreakers. This is the only way in which the *kehillah*, the Jewish counterpart of the union of church and state, can be converted into an instrument that is compatible with establishment of liberty of conscience. 'Both [state and church] must teach, instruct, encourage, motivate,' Mendelssohn writes. 'But neither may reward or punish, compel or bribe....The right to our own convictions is inalienable, and cannot pass from person to person; for it neither gives nor takes away any claim to property, goods or liberty.'[10] 'Neither state nor church,' he continues, 'is authorised to judge in religious matters; for the members of society could not have granted that right to them by any contract whatsoever.'[11]

Much of what Mendelssohn writes is paralleled in the celebrated quasi-contemporary pamphlet of Zalkind Hourwitz, *Apologie des Juifs* (1789). This was originally composed as a submission to the competition organised in 1785 by the Société Royale des Arts et des Sciences of Metz on the topic: 'Est-il des moyens de rendre les Juifs plus heureux et plus utiles en France?' Hourwitz reached much the same conclusion as did Mendelssohn: that if the Jews were to become happy and useful to the state then they must be admitted to citizenship; that rabbis and lay elders ('syndics') must cease forthwith to enjoy any authority over fellow Jews outside the synagogue; that the *Juiverie* (that is, the *kehillah*) must be destroyed, and its synagogues, hospitals, cemeteries etc. become voluntary institutions.[12]

This parallelism in the terms of political education reflects a parallel origin in the circumstances of Jewish communal life. It was only possible for Mendelssohn, and also Hourwitz, to call for the dissolution of Jewish communal organization, the abrogation of rabbinical authority, the transformation of compulsory membership into voluntary adhesion and support because such profound changes were in fact already well developed. The growing distinction between rich and poor, the increasing curb by the Christian authorities on rabbinical use of the *herem*, the assimilation in culture, dress and language of sections of both the richest and poorest elements in Jewish society, the reluctance of elected honorary officials to assume office—all these negative aspects pointed to the demise of the traditional *kehillah*.[13] In truth, Jewish society was in very much the same degree of crisis as was the *ancien régime* in general. By the same token, these very symptoms of crisis also justify and validate Mendelssohn's plea for the removal of the coercive power of the state and its relegation to an impartial educational agency, as enunciated and argued in Part I of *Jerusalem*.

II

Does this mean that Mendelssohn's role as educator of his people was no more than pushing at an open door? Is he but 'the owl of Minerva', able to do no more than discern the contemporary twilight of a traditional institution? In fact, Mendelssohn was also able to anticipate and propound a future Judaism reconstructed on the ruins of the past. Writing in the early 1780s he could yet envisage a pattern that would hold good for the nineteenth and twentieth centuries, in terms both of doctrine and practice. In this sense he determined a pattern of self-awareness that profoundly modified Jewish self-consciousness in the modern world. He opened the eyes of his fellow Jews to the political possibilities inherent in modernity. Mendelssohn, it seems, writing in the heyday of the European Enlightenment, could envisage an imminent future in which the state would become a wholly secular institution on the lines adumbrated in Part of *Jerusalem*. It is true, of course, that he also viewed with suspicion and doubt the Patents of Toleration issued by the Habsburg Emperor, Joseph II, in 1781-2. Their purpose, he feared, was to assimilate the Jews to the point of loss of identity.[14] But this blemish, serious though it was, could not obscure the general movement towards *raison d'état* as the governing motive of contemporary rulers and the rejection of the state as a religious institution with all the consequences thereby entailed for those who did not adhere to the dominant religion. Even if, in contemporary Prussia—as Frederick the Great's highly restrictive 'Juden Reglement' of 1750 made flagrantly clear, the secular state could be no less intolerant than its religious predecessor, this again could not, over a period, obscure or deny the general trend.[15] Put differently, the ideal system of government sketched out in Part One of *Jerusalem* was approaching realization. Mendelssohn could now anticipate the separation between what might well be called the 'state' and 'civil society'. In such a situation—to adopt the well-known phrase from J. L. Gordon's poem—a Jew was 'a man' abroad and at home 'a Jew'.[16]

Mendelssohn could look forward to this separation with all the more alacrity because 'Judaism', at least in the terms of his definition, was already ideally constituted to enter the new world of burgeoning secularization. The definition had two main thrusts, each of which had momentous consequences and is calculated to emphasise Mendelssohn's role as educator of his people: first, Judaism lacked any binding articles of faith, nor had it ever known any such constraints on thought or conscience or behaviour. Those articles of belief that it did contain were identical with the religion of reason and of natural religion accessible to universal human understanding.[17] Thus, when Maimonides 'conceive[d] of the idea of reducing the religion of his fathers to a certain number of principles', this was, according to Mendelssohn, 'a merely accidental idea', which did, moreover, become a matter for debate amongst Hasdai, Albo, Abrabanel and the Kabbalists so that, 'although the thirteen articles of Maimonides have been accepted by the greater part of the nation, no one, as far as I know, has ever branded Albo a heretic because he wanted to reduce their number and lead them back to far more universal propositions of reason.'[18] In other words, whether Judaism comprehends matters of belief going beyond those yielded by universal reason, and, if so, what they precisely are, remains as uncertain as ever.

The second thrust in Mendelssohn's redefinition of Judaism is far more debatable, if not controversial, and concerns his denial to Judaism of any political aspirations. The denial in fact was a necessity if the Jews were to qualify for to the equality of civil rights that the new ideal state, in the process of formation, promised to bestow. For all its limited role, it could not tolerate the existence of competing jurisdictions. It alone would enjoy the monopoly of power.

To be sure, Mendelssohn arrived at his position of denial through the pursuit of an historical evolution. The situation of original Judaism, what he calls the 'Mosaic constitution', was quite other in that 'state and religion were not conjoined but *one*; not connected but identical. Man's relation to society and his relation to God coincided and could never come into conflict'. The oneness of God 'is such as not to admit the least division or plurality in either the political or the metaphysical sense....Hence, in this nation, civil matters acquired a sacred and religious aspect, and every civil service was at the same time a true service of God....everything down to the last police measure was part of the *divine service.*'[19]

But this 'Mosaic constitution' with its coincidence of obligations came to an end with the destruction of the Temple. This dissolved 'the civil bands of the nation...religious offenses were no longer crimes against the state; and the religion, as religion, knows of no punishment, no other penalty than the one the remorseful sinner voluntarily imposes on himself.'[20] Hourwitz took an identical view: '*quant aux loix politiques, les Juifs, depuis leur dispersion, n'ont et ne peuvent point avoir des loix politiques. Celles de Moyse sont bien connues et n'ont aucune influence sur leur conduite actuelle.*'[21]

For both thinkers this was a truly providential development. It fitted the modern Jews to enjoy their due status of equality within the modern state and, in civil society, to remain Jews. This is the point of Mendelssohn's closing appeal to the Christian readers of *Jerusalem*: 'Let everyone be permitted to speak as he thinks, to invoke God after his own manner or that of his fathers, and to see eternal salvation where he thinks he may find it, as long as he does not disturb public felicity, and acts honestly towards the civil laws, towards you and his fellow-citizens.'[22]

This would enable man to fulfil his dual duty to God and Caesar—through civil society to the former, through the state to the latter. The message to the Jewish world is precisely the same, though here naturally the medium of duty to God is through Judaism and not Christianity. In an appropriately modified terminology, Mendelssohn counsels 'the House of Jacob [to] adapt yourselves to the morals and the constitution of the land to which you have been removed, but hold fast to the religion of your fathers too.'[23]

III

In this way Mendelssohn pioneered a religio-political version of Judaism that could accept the terms of emancipation as proposed by the French Revolution within a few years of his own death in 1786 and serve later as a model for the different paths that emancipation took in the western world. It was also, as Gordon's poem attests, not without parallels in Eastern Europe.[24]

But this was not achieved without doing a certain amount of violence to earlier Jewish history and thought: this applied most crucially, of course, in relation to Mendelssohn's central thesis of the separation between the political and the religious. In effect, he made of Judaism a continued adherence to the Covenant and an exercise of the 'personal commandments'.[25] This may well be the effect of *force majeure* on the loss of sovereignty. But there is certainly an important distinction to be made between the acceptance of *force majeure* and actually building its consequences into the cornerstone of Judaism. This is to neglect the constant aspiration towards sovereignty. This is not only a refrain of the liturgy but took specific form in the unending (though varying) effort to delimit through the maxim—'the law of the land is the law'—an area of jurisdiction where Jewish law, that is sovereignty, would prevail.[26]

Mendelssohn's reading of Jewish history, however, eliminates this theme entirely. Subsequent to the destruction of the Temple, his reading of Judaism is, as it were, 'stateless'.

But this is not the end of the matter. Continuity and survival do not at all go by default. Mendelssohn transferred the burden from a political institution, however varyingly conceived in the circumstances of the Dispersion, to the indirect operation of the 'personal commandments', the *mitzvot*. This is not made explicit, admittedly, and in fact it would appear that his theory of signs and symbols actually denigrates the *mitzvot*; for example, he makes an important distinction between 'actions which are demanded as actions and those that merely signify convictions'. Circumcision is addressed as an example of the former: 'a foreskin is cut off: the circumcizer may think and believe whatever he pleases of the practice itself, just as a creditor who obtained satisfaction through the courts is repaid, no matter what the debtor may think of his obligation to pay.'[27] But can a ceremony and practice which initiates the new-born into the Covenant and a life of good deeds, and prepares him for marriage be presented in such quasi-mechanical and formalistic terms? There is no suggestion that the *mitzvot* might fulfil a pedagogic and educational task, as Jewish tradition had always maintained.

So much for the negative side. But Mendelssohn also saw the *mitzvot*, the 'personal commandments', in ideal terms, in terms of a way of life: 'In everything a youth saw being done, in all public as well as private dealings, at all gates and at all doorposts, in whatever he turned his eyes or ears to, he found occasion for inquiring and reflecting....teaching and life, wisdom and activity, speculation and sociability were most intimately connected.'[28]

If such is the content of the personal commandments, then their political relevance is to constitute that area where Jew serves God. Mendelssohn adapted the God-Caesar dichotomy to his own purposes, that is, in return for the Jews' acceptance of the rule of Caesar, they should be permitted to worship God in their own way, unimpeded by any attempt to impose the dictates of a dominant religion.[29] In other words, this division corresponds to that between politics and civil society. It formed the common ground on which Jew and Christian could contract a 'civil union'.[30] But Mendelssohn also emphasised that if the Christian world would not 'unite with us as citizens,' for example would not accept that Jews could not intermarry with Christians, nor eat with them, etc., then 'civil union could not take place.'[31]

This fear proved unfounded. The terms of the contract as envisaged by Mendelssohn at the end of the eighteenth century, were realised—fitfully, it is true—throughout Western and much of Central Europe and served as a lasting political lesson in self-perception to his fellow-Jews.

Notes

1. For a short summary of conflicting assessments see A. Shohet, *Im hilufei tekufot* (Jerusalem, 1960), pp. 242-246; also I. Barzilay, 'Smolenskin's polemic against Moses Mendelssohn in historical perspective', *Proceedings of the American Academy for Jewish Research*, LIII, 1986, pp. 11-48.

2. Cf. A. Altmann, *Moses Mendelssohn—A Biographical Study* (London, 1973), pp. 381 ff.
3. M. Hildesheimer, 'Moses Mendelssohn in rabbinical literature', *Proceedings of the American Academy for Jewish Research*, LV, 1988, pp. 79-133.
4. I have used the translation by Allan Arkush, Hanover/London, 1983. (Referred to below as *Jerualem*.)
5. *Jerusalem*, p. 42.
6. Ibid.
7. Ibid., p. 33.
8. See Altmann's introduction to *Jerusalem*, pp. 4, 14, 28.
9. See note 6 above.
10. *Jerusalem*, p. 61.
11. Ibid., p. 62.
12. Hourwitz, op. cit., pp. 35, 38, 84.
13. See Shohet, op. cit., passim; also C. Abramsky, 'The Crisis of Authority within European Jewry in the 18th Century' in S. Stein and R. Loewe (eds.) *Studies in Jewish Religious and Intellectual History* (London, 1979), pp. 13-28.
14. M. Mendelssohn, *Gesammelte Schriften* (Leipzig, 1844) V, pp. 671, 677.
15. See J. Israel, *European Jewry in the Age of Mercantilism, 1550-1750* (Oxford, 1985), passim.
16. See the translation of 'Awake my People', in P. Mendes-Flohr and J. Reinharz (eds.), *The Jew in the Modern World* (Oxford, 1980), pp. 312-313.
17. *Jerusalem*, pp. 89, ff.
18. Ibid., pp. 100-101; see also M. Kellner, *Dogma in Medieval Jewish Thought* (Oxford, 1986).
19. *Jerusalem*, p. 128 (italics in original).
20. Ibid., p. 130.
21. *Apologie*, p. 65.
22. *Jerusalem*, p. 139.
23. Ibid., p. 133.
24. See n. 16 above.
25. *Jerusalem*, p. 134.
26. See S. Shilo, *Dina de Malchuta dina* (Jerusalem, 1974).
27. *Jerusalem*, p. 83.
28. Ibid., pp. 119-120.
29. Ibid., pp. 132, 139.
30. Ibid., p. 135.
31. Ibid.

DAVID PATTERSON
A Bibliography
compiled by R. May

Books

The Foundations of Modern Hebrew Literature (London, 1961).
Abraham Mapu: The Creator of the Modern Hebrew Novel (London, 1964; Ithaca, NY, 1968). [Hebrew version of ch. 6 in *Moznayim*, xx (1965), pp. 395-400, and of ch. 9, ibid., (1967), pp. 417-22]
The Hebrew Novel in Czarist Russia (Edinburgh, 1964).
A Phoenix in Fetters: Studies in Nineteenth and Early Twentieth Century Hebrew Fiction (Savage, Maryland, 1988 [really 1990]).

Translations

The King of Flesh and Blood [*Melekh basar va-dam*, by Moshe Shamir] (London, 1958; New York, 1958).
Children's Machzor for the New Year and Day of Atonement, with a new translation (London, 1966).
Children's Siddur for Sabbaths and Festivals, with a new translation (London, 1975)
Out of the Depths [*Min ha-metsar*, by Joseph Hayyim Brenner] (Boulder, Colorado, 1993).

Articles, Papers, Lectures

'The Hebrew Historical Novel', *Sifrut*, i (1955), pp. 51-7.
'Saul Tchernichovsky', ibid., ii (1956), pp. 14-28.
also in *Jewish Writing Today* (London, 1973), pp. 63-71.
'The Use of Songs in the Novels of Abraham Mapu', *Journal of Semitic Studies*, i (1956), pp. 382-8.
'The Poetry of Yehudah Halevy, *Jewish Quarterly*, iv, no. 3 (1956-7), pp. 4-8.
also in *Caravan: A Jewish Quarterly Omnibus* (London and New York, 1962), pp. 257-67.
'Moses Mendelssohn's Concept of Tolerance', in A. Altmann, ed., *Between East and West: Essays Dedicated to the Memory of Bella Horovitz* (London, 1958), pp. 149-63.
also in D. Cohn-Sherbok, ed., *A Traditional Quest: Essays in Honour of Louis Jacobs* (Sheffield, 1991), pp. 180-93.
Hebrew Literature: The Art of the Translator (London, 1958).
also in Jewish Book Annual, xvi (1958), pp. 68-80, and in P. Goodman, ed., Essays on Jewish booklore (New York, 1972), pp. 261-73.
'Israel Weisbrem: A Forgotten Hebrew Novelist of the Nineteenth Century', *Journal of Semitic Studies*, iv (1959), pp. 37-58.
'The Portrait of Hasidism in the Nineteenth-Century Hebrew Novel', ibid., v (1960), pp. 359-77.
'Some Religious Attitudes Reflected in the Hebrew Novels of the Period of Enlightenment', *Bulletin of the John Rylands Library*, xlii (1960), pp. 395-411.
'The First Fifty Years of Collective Settlement in Israel', *Jewish Journal of Sociology*, ii (1960), pp. 42-55.
'Brenner',*Work*, x, no. 29 (1960), pp. 26-7.
'Hebrew Drama', *Bulletin of the John Rylands Library*, xliii (1961), pp. 88-108.
'Some Literary Trends', *Jewish Chronicle* (21 April 1961), Supplement, pp. xii-xiii.
'Some Linguistic Aspects of the Nineteenth-Century Hebrew Novel', *Journal of Semitic Studies*, vii (1962), pp. 309-24.
'Philosophers of Emancipation', in R. Goldwater, ed., *Jewish Philosophy and Philosophers* (London, 1962), pp. 124-48.

'Zionist Philosophers', ibid., pp. 149-74.

'The Portrait of the "Saddik" in the Nineteenth-Century Hebrew Novel', *Journal of Semitic Studies*, viii (1963), pp. 170-88.

'Sickness and Death in the Hebrew Novel of the Haskalah', *Jewish Journal of Sociology*, v (1963), pp. 84-93.

'Epistolary Elements in the Novels of Abraham Mapu', *Annual of Leeds University Oriental Society*, iv (1964), pp. 132-49.

'The Writer and the Legend' [on S. J. Agnon], *Ariel*, xi (1965), pp. 22-5.

also in *Adam*, xxxi, nos. 307-9 (1966), pp. 9-12.

'Epistolary Elements in the Hebrew Novels of the Enlightenment', *Annual of Leeds University Oriental Society*, v (1966), pp. 86-99.

'The Preservation of Enlightenment', *Jewish Heritage*, x, no. 2 (1967), pp. 34-9.

'Ha-yesodot ha-epistolariyim ba-roman ha-'ivri shel tekufat ha-haskalah', *Fourth World Congress of Jewish Studies, Papers*, ii (Jerusalem, 1968), Hebrew section, pp. 59-64.

Six entries in *Encyclopaedia Britannica* (Chicago, etc., 1970).

Four entries in *Encyclopaedia Judaica* (Jerusalem, 1971-2).

'The Emergence of Modern Hebrew Literature', in D. Daiches and A. Thorlby, eds., *Literature and Western Civilization*, [v] (London, 1972), pp. 363-86.

'From Mapu to Mendele', *Proceedings of the Fifth World Congress of Jewish Studies*, iii (Jerusalem, 1972), European-language section, pp. 37-50.

'Yosef Haim Brenner', *Ariel*, xxxiii-xxxiv (1973), pp. 107-14.

'Ancient Hebrew Law in Modern Hebrew Literature', *Journal of Jewish Studies*, xxv (1974), pp. 169-80.

also in B. S. Jackson, ed., *Studies in Jewish Legal History in Honour of David Daube* (London, 1974), pp. 169-80.

'Jewish Studies: A Major Rescue Operation', *Times Literary Supplement* (16 April 1976), p. 470.

Hebraica in Helsinki', ibid., (29 October 1976), p. 1372.

'Ha-makhon le-limmudei 'ivrit mitkaddemim be-Oxford', *Proceedings of the World Union of Hebrew Studies* (1976)

'Modern Hebrew Literature Goes on *Aliyah*', *Journal of Jewish Studies*, xxix (1978), pp. 75-84.

'Meir at Oxford', in A. H. Friedlander and F. S. Worms, eds., *Meir Gertner: An Anthology* (London, 1978), pp. 27-32.

'Holocaust and Renaissance', *Jewish Quarterly*, xxvii, no. 1 (1979), pp. 61-10.

'Meir Wallenstein', in C. Rabin et al., eds., *Studies in the Bible and the Hebrew Language Offered to Meir Wallenstein on the Occasion of His Seventy-Fifth Birthday* (Jerusalem, 1979), pp. 1-4.

'Some Aspects of the Transference of Hebrew Literature from Eastern Europe to Eretz Yisrael', ibid., pp. 45-66.

'Conversational Uses of the Root Dabhar in Neo-Biblical Hebrew', in A. I. Katsh and L. Nemoy, eds., *Essays on the Occasion of the Seventieth Anniversary of the Dropsie University 1909-1979* (Philadelphia, 1979), pp. 365-70.

'Yosef Hayyim Brenner on the Centenary of his Birth', *Jewish Book Annual*, xxxviii (1980-1), pp. 117-26.

'A Weighty Question, by Eliezer Ben-Yehuda', in E. Silberschlag, ed., *Eliezer Ben-Yehuda: A Symposium in Oxford* (Oxford, 1981), pp. 1-12.

'Revival of Literature and Revival of Language', ibid., pp. 13-24.

'The Influence of Hebrew Literature on the Growth of Jewish Nationalism in the Nineteenth Century', *Hebrew Studies*, xxii (1981), pp. 103-12.

also, with minor amendments, in R. Sussex and J. C. Eade, eds., *Culture and Nationalism in Nineteenth-Century Eastern Europe* (Columbus, Ohio, 1985), pp. 84-95.

'The Oxford Centre for Postgraduate Hebrew Studies', *Midstream*, xxviii, no. 1 (1982), pp. 18-20.

'A Growing Awareness of Self: Some Reflections on the Role of Nineteenth Century Hebrew Fiction', *Modern Judaism*, iii (1983), pp. 23-37.

'Changing Approaches to Society in Nineteenth Century Hebrew Literature', in *Inauguration of the Jacob and Shoshana Schreiber Fellowship in the History of Contemporary Judaism* (Israel, 1983), pp. 9-25.

'Ahad Ha-Am and Smolenskin', in J. Kornberg, ed., *At the Crossroads: Essays on Ahad Ha-Am* (Albany, 1983), pp. 36-45.

'Moving Centers in Modern Hebrew Literature' in G. Abramson and T. Parfitt, eds., *The Great Transition: The Recovery of the Lost Centers of Modern Hebrew Literature* (New Jersey, 1985), pp. 3-10.

'The Portrait of Jewish Participation in the Polish Revolt of 1961-64 Reflected in Two Stories by Perez Smolenskin', *Hebrew Studies*, xxvi (1985), pp. 307-18.

'Hebrew Studies', in T. H. Aston, Gen. ed., *History of the University of Oxford*, v (Oxford, 1986), pp. 535-50.

'University Teaching of Modern Hebrew Literature in Translation: Parameters and Limitations', in L. I. Yudkin, ed., *Modern Hebrew Literature in English Translation* (New York, 1987), pp. 7-26.

A Darkling Plain: Jews and Arabs in Modern Hebrew Literature. The 1988 Maurice A. Stiller Lecture (Oxford, 1988).

'Mapu', *Nineteenth-Century Literature Criticism*, xviii (1988), pp. 292- 303.

Out of Bondage: Two Centuries of Modern Hebrew Literature. The Fifteenth Sacks Lecture (Oxford, 1989).

Five entries in G. Abramson, ed., *The Blackwell Companion to Jewish Culture* (Oxford, 1989).

'Moshe Shamir: *The King of Flesh and Blood* - Literary Source and Creative Imagiration' in L.I. Yudkin (ed.): *Israeli Writers Consider the Outsider.* (Cranberry, New Jersey: Fairleigh Dickenson University Press, 1993), pp. 100-111.

'A Legend in His Time' in *Tradition and Trauma*. Studies in the Fiction of S. J. Agnon. (Boulder, San Francisco, Oxford, Westview Press, 1994), pp. 1-8.

Selected Reviews

The Autobiography of Solomon Maimon, Sifrut, i (1955), pp. 71-3.

R. Mahler, *History of the Jewish People in Modern Times.* Vol. 1, *Journal of Semitic Studies*, i (1956), pp. 297-8.

S. D. Goitein, *Shete Massoth 'al Sepher Yirmeyahu*, ibid., iii (1958), pp. 89-90.

S. D. Goitein, *'Omanut ha-Sippur ba-Mikra'*, ibid., pp. 90-3.

S. J. Kahn, ed., *A Whole Loaf: Stories from Israel, Jewish Chronicle* (23 January 1959), p. 23.

H. J. Zimmels, *Ashkenazim and Sephardim, Journal of Theological Studies*, N. S. xi (1960), pp. 211-12.

M. Ribalow, *The Flowering of Modern Hebrew Literature, Jewish Chronicle* (19 February 1960), p. 21.

H. G. Richardson, *The English Jewry under Angevin Kings, Tarbut* (1962), pp.

M. Haran, ed., *Yehezkel Kaufmann Jubilee Volume, Bibliotheca Orientalis*, xxi (1964), pp. 78-9.

J. Gould and S. Esh, eds., *Jewish Life in Modern Britain, Jewish Observer and Middle East Review* (9 October 1964), pp.

J. Parkes, A History of the Jewish People, ibid., (13 November 1964), pp.

J. Katz, *Exclusiveness and Tolerance, Journal of Theological Studies*, N. S. xvi (1965), pp. 568-70.

A. Steinberg, ed., *Simon Dubnow: The Man and His Work, English Historical Review*, lxxx (1965), pp. 878-9.

S. Y. Penueli and A. Ukhmani, eds., *Hebrew Short Stories, Jerusalem Post*. Weekly Overseas Edn. (1 January 1968), pp.

A. J. Band, *Nostalgia and Nightmare: A Study in the Fiction of S. Y. Agnon, Jewish Chronicle* (24 May 1968), Supplement, p. viii.

E. Silberschlag, *Saul Tschernichowsky: Poet of Revolt, Western Humanities Review*, xxiii (1969), pp. 264-5.

'On Translating the Bible' [review of the *New English Bible*], *Jewish Heritage*, xiv, no. 3 (1972), pp. 46-50.

B. Halpern, *The Idea of the Jewish State*. 2nd edn., *Jewish Journal of Sociology*, xiv (1972), pp. 254-6.

Gates of Repentance: Services for the High Holy Days, Journal of Jewish Studies, xxv (1974), pp. 465-6.

L. Weinberger, *Jewish Prince in Moslem Spain: Selected Poems of Samuel Ibn Nagrela*, ibid., p. 465.

Editorial

Sifrut, iii (1957) [with C. Rabin].

Studies in Modern Hebrew Literature. Four volumes (1964-73).

The B'nai B'rith Jewish Heritage Classics [with L. Edelman]. Fourteen volumes (1970-8).

Studies in the Bible and the Hebrew Language Offered to Meir Wallenstein on the Occasion of His Seventy-Fifth Birthday (Jerusalem, 1979), [with C. Rabin et al.].

Jewish Studies Microfiche Project.

Reprint of rare Hebrew works dating from last quarter of eighteenth century, undertaken by AMS Press, New York, Fifteen volumes (1967-9).

with G. Abramson: *Tradition and Trauma, Studies in the Fiction of S.J. Agnon.* (Boulder, San Francisco, Oxford: Westview Press, 1994)

Index of Names

Aaron b. Shmuel of Hergershausen 80
Aaronsohn, Aaron 266
Abrabanel, Isaac b. Judah 303
Abraham 27
Academy, The 22
Adam 27
Agnon, S.J. 65, 233, 238-240
Ahad Ha-'am (Asher Ginsberg) 39, 44, 47, 48, 50, 51, 53, 54, 65, 132, 133, 164
Aharoni, Israel 266
Ahiasaf 41
Akiva, Rabbi 148, 154, 227
Al-Ghazali 'Abu Hamid 41
Albeck, Chanoch 197
Albo, Isaac 303
Alcimus 171
Aleichem 40, 48
Alfred, Laws of 103
Alexander of Macedon 222
Alexander Balas 171
Alexander II (Czar) 245, 282
Alliance Israelite Universelle 157
Allon, Gedalya 197
Altmann, Alexander 300
American Israelite, The 38, 40
Anaxagoras 215
Anaximander 226
Antiochus IV 170
Antiochus V 171
Apion 171
Aquila 211, 226
Aranne, Zalman 10
Aristobulus I 169
Aristotle 215, 216
Arnold, Matthew 19
Artapanus 170

Asch, Sholem 48
Augustine, St 214, 216

Baeck, Leo 196, 199, 200, 201
Baer, Yitzhak 200
Bamberg, Fritz 200
Band, Arnold 129, 132
Baneth, E 197, 200
Baneth, D.H. 197, 200
Bar-Ilan University 11-23
Baron, Samuel 48
Barth, J 205
Ben Azzai 148
Ben Yohai, R. Simeon 147, 153
Ben Zoma 148
Ben-Avigdor [Shalkovich, A.L.] 40
Ben-Gurion University of the Negev 265
Ben-Gurion, David 9, 11, 12, 160, 265, 272
Ben-Rafael, E 165
Ben-Yehuda, Eliezer 40, 279-285, 291, 292
Ben-Zvi, Yitzhak 265
Benjamin of Tudela 117, 121
Berdiczewski, M.J. 40, 65, 132, 133
Bergen-Belsen 15
Berger, Peter 17
Berlin, University of 14, 51, 199
Berlin, Meir 40
Berlin, Saul 132, 138-139
Bernfeld, S. 44
Bershadski, Joshua 40
Bialik, Hayyim Nahman 41, 42, 44, 48, 65, 132, 233, 236-238, 240, 268-269
Bik, Yankev Shmuel [Jacob Samuel] 84
Bilgray, Albert 51
Borokhov, Ber 86
Blank, Sheldon 48

INDEX OF NAMES

Boston, University of 94
Bologna, University of 94
Borodianski, Chaim 200
Brainin, Reuben 44, 51
Brandeis, University 16
Brandon, S.G.F. 189
Branstätter, M.D. 63
Brattslaver, N. 87
Braudes, Reuben Asher 63
Brenner, J.H. 131
Breslau Seminary 196, 198, 199
Brigham Young University 16
Brit Shalom 273
Brodetsky, Selig 275
Brody, Hayyim 48
Brunschvig, Robert 98
Buber, Martin 262, 273, 276
Buechler, Adolph 196
Burnet, J 217
Buttenweiser, Moses 42

Cairo Genizah 77, 117-119, 120-121
Cambridge Codex 77
Canaanite Movement 161
Cassel, David 196
Catalano, Abraham 287, 290, 294-298
Cato the Censor 168
Centre de Droit Hebraïque (Sorbonne) 94
Chicago, University of 184
Childs, B.S. 32
Chmielnitzki, Bogdan 80
Choniates, N. 115
Chrysippus 228
Churgin, Pinkhos 12, 18, 19
Cleanthes 228
Cohen, Boaz 98
Cohn, Haim 101
Cohon, Samuel S 51, 53
Collegio Rabbinico (Florence) 198
Columbia University 274
Columbus, Christopher 85

Daube, David 30, 96
David 26
de Marnix, Philippe 217
de Lagarde, P 206, 211
de Haas, Jacob 40
Dead Sea Scrolls 169

Delepierre, Octave 150
Denning, Lord 102
Deutsch, Gotthard 39, 40, 41, 43, 48
Dilthey, Wilhelm 199
Dinah 24ff
Dinur, Ben Zion 9
Diogenes Laertius 226
Dolitsky, Menachem 44
Don-Yehiya, Eliezer 165
Donne, John 17
Dorff, E 108
Douglas, Mary 105
Dropsie College 198
Druyanov, Alter 48
Dushkin, A.M. 274
Dworkin, Ronald 106, 107

École Rabbinique 195
Ehrenpreis, Mordecai 41
Eichorn, Max 44, 48
Eisenstein, J.D. 40
Eissfeldt, Otto 214
Elazar b. Arakh 227
Elazar, Daniel 21, 165
Elbogen, Ismar 197-198, 200, 201
Elia, son of Caleb 115
Elijah 238
Elijah b. Solomon Zalman [Vilna Gaon] 85
Elisha b. Avuyah 143-156
Elon, Menachem 96-97, 108
Enelow, H.G. 48
Englander, Henry 53
Ephraim 27
Epicurean School 225, 226
Epolemus 170
Epshteyn, Yekhiel-Mikhl [Epstein, Jehiel Michal b. Avraham Halevi] 80
Epstein, J.N. 197, 201
Epstein, I 196
Erotianus 225
Erter, Isaac 42
Esau 29
Euchel, Isaac 132, 139
Eustathius, Archbishop 118
Eve 27
Even-Zohar, Ittamar 67
Ezekiel the Tragedian 168
Ezra 168

INDEX OF NAMES

Feder, Tuvia 84
Feierberg M.Z. 48, 66
Feiwel, Berthold 262, 276
Feldman, Ephraim 42
Felsenthal, Bernard 43, 53
Fineschriber, William H 42
Fish, Stanley 62
Fishman, A 165
Fox, M. 21
Fränkel, S 205
Franklin, Benjamin 84
Frederick the Great 302
Freud, Sigmund 84
Fried, Abraham 25, 48
Friedland H.A. 51
Friedman, Menahem 165
Friesel, Eviatar 44
Frischmann, David 132, 133
Frug, Simeon 48

Galen 225
Gamliel Rabban 226, 228
Geiger, Abraham 38, 196, 201
Geneva, University of 262
Glueck, Nelson 51
Ghirondi, Solomon Eliezer 287-291, 294, 295
Ginzburg, Mordechai Aharon 63
Goethe, Johann Wolfgang von 217
Goldziher, I 196
Gordon, Nathan 42
Gordon, J.L. 43, 44, 48, 63, 66-67, 143, 144, 302, 304
Gordon, Jacob 48
Gotlober, Abraham Baer 63
Gottheil, Richard 40, 43
Graetz, Heinrich 4, 196, 199
Greenberg, Irving 183
Greenberg, Moshe 106
Grossman, Louis 42, 43
Gunkel, Hermann 212, 215
Guttmann, Julius 200, 201
Guttmann, Jacob 196, 200

Ha-emet 144
Ha-kohen, Adam 68, 69
Ha-Me'assef 43, 131, 135
Ha-magid 66, 244, 245
Ha-melitz 246
Ha-shahar 2, 3, 4, 6, 7, 253

Ha-shiloah 52, 254
Hadassah Hospital 272
Haganah, The 271
Hailsham, Lord 104
Halevi, Judah 148
Halkin, Simon 131, 136
Ham-Canaan 24
Haman 291
Hamor 24, 26
Hananel, Rabbenu 71
Harburg, I. 48
Harkavy, Alexander 86
Harris, Roy 75
Harvard University 94
Hebraica 145
Hebrew University, The 198, 261, 262, 264, 266-270, 272, 273, 274, 275, 276, 277
Hebrew Union College viii, 37-58, 198
Heidegger, Martin 15
Heidelberg, University of 183
Heinemann, Yitzhak 196
Heller, James 47, 48
Heller, Max 47
Herzl, Theodor 158
Herzog, Isaac 98
Hesiod 214, 215
Hilfsverein der deutschen Jüden 268
Hillel, Rabbi 226
Hochschule für die Wissenschaft des Judentums 195ff
Holtz, Avraham 129
Homer 168, 173
Hopkins, Simon 201
Hopkins, Gerard Manley 17
Hourwitz, Zalkind 301, 303
HUC Monthly, The 47-48
HUC Journal, The 39, 42, 43, 48, 53
Huguet, E 217
Humboldt, W. 14

Ibn-Ezra, Avraham 71, 120, 207, 208
Idelsohn, Abraham 51
Institute of Advanced Legal Studies, The 93
Ionian School, The 226
Isaac 27
Isaacs, Nathan 48
Ishmael 27
Ishmael, R 147

INDEX OF NAMES

Israel (Jacob) 25
Israeli Aircraft Industries 273
Israelitisch-Theologische Lehranstalt 195
Isserlin, Yisroel b. Pesakhye [Israel b. Petahiah] 78
Istituto [Collegio] Rabbinico 195
Italian School, The 226

Jacob 24ff
Jacobs, Louis 98, 106
Jaeger, W 217
Jauss, Hans Robert 132
Jefferson, Thomas 201
Jesselson, Ludwig 16
Jesus 101, 102, 172, 180, 183, 188, 189, 190
Jewish Agency, The 52
Jewish Institute of Religion 198
Jewish Law Annual, The 93
Jewish Law Association, The 93
Jewish National Fund 267
Jewish Theological Seminary (USA) 198
Jews' College 196
Jezebel 30
Joseph 27
Joseph II 302
Josephus Flavius 170, 172, 173
Joshua 26
Joshua b. Levi, R 238, 240
Jost, I.M. 66
Judaen Scrolls 211
Judah Ha-nassi, [The Prince] R 13
Judah of Regensberg 79
Judas Maccabee 169
Jüdisch-Theologisches Seminar 196
Justinian 116

Kalisher, Rabbi 158
Kallen, Horace 47
Kant, Immanuel 200
Karo, Joseph 87
Katz, Jacob 130
Kennedy, J.F. 201
Khotsh, Tsvi-Hirsh 80
Kimmerling, B 165
Kirschenbaum, A 106, 111
Klausner, Joseph 129, 130, 131, 152, 236, 275
Klein, Penina 12
Kohler, Kaufman 42ff, 51, 52

Kook, Rabbi Zvi Yehuda 10, 158
Krister, Stendahl 184
Kurzweil, Barukh 130, 131, 132, 138
Kutscher, E.Y. 224

Laban 27, 28
Laemmel School 157
Lahover, Y.F. 129, 130
Lamm, N 106
Landau, Ezekiel 299
Lauterbach, Jacob 47
Leah 29
Lebensohn, Micah Josef 40
Lee, Laurie 31
Lefin, Mendl (Satanover) 84
Lehman-Wilzig, S.N. 165
Leibowitz, Y. 165
Levi 25, 26, 28, 32, 33
Levias, Caspar 39, 41, 42, 43, 44
Levine, Shmaryahu 40, 46
Levinsohn, Isaac Baer 84
Levush, The (Mordechai Yafe) 78
Libenblum, Moses Leib 48, 63
Liberman, Aharon Shmuel 144, 150
Liebman, Charles 165
Lifshitz, Yehoyshue-Mordkhe 85, 86
Lilienthal, Max 255
Lilienblum, M.L. 63, 143-156
Lokstein, Joseph H 10
Loew, Israel 196
Lot 27
Lovitch, Meyer 42
Luncz, A.M. 40
Luther, Martin 81, 216, 217
Luz, E 165
Luzzatto, S.D. 195
Luzzatto, Moshe Hayyim 131, 132

Maccabaean Revolt 168
Maccoby, Hyam 189
Magnes, Judah 40, 42, 46, 49, 51, 273, 274
Maharil, The [Yaakov b. Moshe Molin] 77, 79
Maimon, Solomon 63, 133
Maimonides 71, 77, 103, 305, 303
Maimonides, Code of 107
Malchus Cleodemus 170
Malter, Henry 41, 46
Manasseh 27

INDEX OF NAMES

Mane, M.Z. 43
Mannheimer, Sigmund 42
Mansch, Philip 86
Mapu, Abraham 40, 44, 48, 63, 68, 69
Marco Antonio Justinian 291
Marcus, J. 48, 49
Margolis, Max 46, 47
Marx, Karl 177
Masliansky, Z.H. 40
Maybaum, S 197
Mendele Mokher Sefarim (S.J. Abramowitz) 40, 48, 85, 233, 236, 238, 240, 243-261
Mendelsohn, S. Felix 48
Mendelssohn, Moses 84, 279, 280, 299-306
Meyer, Jacob 48
Meyer, Michael 42, 45, 46
Michigan, University of 264
Mielziner, Moses 39
Mieses, Matisyohu 86
Mill, John Stuart 67
Mises, Judah Leib 144
Mizrah u-ma'arav 51
Moberly, Walter H 19
Montefiore, Claude 49
Morgenstern, Julian 47, 48
Moses 10, 27, 28, 29, 30, 99, 105, 170, 237
Mount Holyoke College viii
Müller, D.H. 196

National Christian Leadership Conference for Israel (NCLCI) 182
National Council of Churches 182
Ner Ma'aravi 38, 39
Neumark, David 46, 47, 50, 51, 53, 55
New York University 94
Newman, Cardinal 12
Nicholas I (Czar) 255
Niebuhr, Reinhold 186
Nietzsche, Friedrich 51
Niketas Choniates 115
Noah 24, 27
Noahide Laws 107, 168
Novak, David 107
Novalchovich, J.L. 48

O'Neill, Ernest 180
Oriental Insitute [University of Oxford] vii

Otzar ha-yahadut 41
Otzen, B 212
Ovid 215, 216, 217
Oxford Centre for Postgraduate Hebrew Studies vii, 93, 175
Oxford, University of 13, 21

Palestine Liberation Organisation (PLO) 182
Pompaditha 15
Pannenberg, Wolfhart 187, 188
Papirna, A.J. 65
Parkes, James 181, 188
Passamaneck, Stephen 95
Patterson, David vii, 23, 76, 93, 157, 167, 175, 190, 203, 221, 287
Patterson, José vii
Paul 102
Pedersen, J 212
Peli, Pinchas 176
Peretz, J.L. 40
Peripatetics 225, 229
Peripatos, The 226
Perl, Joseph 42, 144
Pfisterer, Rudolf 184
Pherekydes 226
Philipson, David 42
Philo of Alexandria 31, 168, 214
Philo of Byblus 214
Picard, L 266
Pinski, David 48
Plato 214, 216
Platonists, The 228
Popper, Karl 17
Potiphar 27
Pythagoras 226

Qirisani, Jacob 41
Qumran Scrolls 224

Rabbinerseminar (Berlin) 196
Rabelais, François 216-217
Rabin, Chaim 292, 296
Rachel 29
Raisin, Jacob 44
Raisin, Max 43, 44, 48, 53
Rakover, N 108
Rama [Rami] b. Hama 148
Ramban (Rabbi Moshe b. Nahman) 71
Rapoport S.J. 44

Rashi   65, 70, 71, 120, 237, 238
Ratner, Yohanan   272
Ravitsky, A   165
Ravnitsky, J.H.   237
Rebecca   27
Rebetsin, S.   88
Reifenberg, A   270
Rentdorff, Rolf   183-184
Reuben   27
Rhine, A.   43
Richmond, Harry   48
Ricoeur, Paul   215
Rosenzweig, Gerson   40
Rosett, A   108
Roth, Cecil   10, 11, 14
Roth, Leo   274
Rothschild, Lord [Lionel Walter]   264
Rubinstein, S   7
Ruether, Rosemary   188
Rylaarsdam, J Coert   184

Sadan, Dov   133
Saltman, Avrom   11
Saltykov-Shchedrin, Mikhail   150
Samet, M.   165
Samuel b. Judah Ha-Bavli   115, 116
Samuel the Nagid   115
Sander, D   217
Satanow, Isaac Ha-Levi   44, 132, 137, 138, 140
Schacht, Joseph   99
Schechem   24, 29, 30, 31, 32
Schechter, Solomon   77
Scheinkin, Menachem   40
Schloessinger, Max   46
Scholem, Gershom   200-201
Schonberg, David   108
School of Law, Boston University   94
'Shoresh'   7
Schreiber, Aaron   108
Schulman, Kalman   40
Schürer, Emil   24
Schwartzberg, S.B.   38
Schweid, E   165
Seligsohn, David   51
Seneca   228
Septuagint, The   226
Sforno Ovadiah ben Ya'akov   71
Sha'anan, Avraham   129, 153

Shalom Aleichem [Shalom Rabinowitz]   40, 48
Shammai, Rabbi   226
Shapira, H.N.   129, 131
Shapira, Moshe Haim   10
Sharot, S   165
Shavit, Uzi   129, 131
Shechem   24, 25, 29, 30, 31, 32
Shim'on b. Gamliel   226
Shohet, Azriel   130
Shulhan Arukh, The   64, 71, 87
Silver, Abba Hillel   47
Silver, Mendel   44
Simeon   25, 26, 28, 32
Simon (Hasmonaean)   171
Smith, Payne   224
Smolenskin, Peretz   63, 279-285
Sofer, Moses [Hatam Sofer, Khsam Soyfer]   87
Sokolow, Nahum   40
Solomon   24, 84
Solomon, N.   97
Sombart, Werner   200
Sorbonne, The   94
Stanford University   94
Steinberg, Jacob   40
Steinschneider, Moritz   41
Steinthal, H.H.   196
Stendhal, K.   184
Stoa, The   226, 228
Stöcker, Adolf   196
Stoics, The   215, 227, 228
Sun Myung Moon   179
Sura   13
Susannah   103
Sutcliffe, E.F.   204, 210, 214
Symmachos   214, 215, 216
Syrkin, Nahman   40

Tacitus   171
Tal, Uriel   165
Tarphon   154
Taviov, M.   39
Taxay, Marshall   48
Tchernichowsky, S.   48, 132
Technion, The (Haifa)   261, 262, 265, 273, 275, 276
Thales   226
Thon, Isaiah   41
Torczyner, H (Tur-Sinai)   199-200, 201

INDEX OF NAMES

Tschernichowsky, Saul 48, 132
Tsumura, D.T. 204, 206

Urbach, Ephraim 108

Vatican II 101
Voltaire [François Marie Arouet] 217
Von Rad, G 212
Vulgate, The 211, 216

Wacholder, Ben Zion 106
Warburg, Otto 263-264
Wegner, Judith Romney 106
Weiler, Moses C 51
Weiler, G 165
Weinryb, Bernard (Dov) 130
Weinstein, Jacob 50
Weisbard, P.H. 108
Weizmann, Chaim 262, 263, 276
Weizmann Institute 265
Wesleyan University 16
Wessel, Harry E 49

Wessely, N.H. 68, 69, 82-83, 84, 130, 133, 136, 137
Westermann 206, 212
Wiener, Max 201
'Wilhelmus Lied', The 217
Wisconsin, University of 264
Wise, Isaac Meyer 38, 42, 43
Wise, Stephen 40
Wolfssohn, Aharon 144
World Zionist Organisation 264

Yafe, Mordechai [The Levush] 78-79
Yahuda, A.S. 197
Yehoshua b. Levi, R 154, 227
Yehuda ha-Nasi, R 228
Yellin, David 51
Yeshiva University 16
Yohanan bar Zakkai, R 227

Zalmen of St Goar 77
Zederbaum, Alexander 85
Zeno 228
Zionist Congress (1903) 265
Zunz, Leopold 196

For Product Safety Concerns and Information please contact our EU
representative GPSR@taylorandfrancis.com
Taylor & Francis Verlag GmbH, Kaufingerstraße 24, 80331 München, Germany

www.ingramcontent.com/pod-product-compliance
Lightning Source LLC
Chambersburg PA
CBHW071153300426
44113CB00009B/1190